(RE)CONSIDERING WHAT WE KNOW

(RE)CONSIDERING
WHAT WE KNOW

Learning Thresholds in Writing, Composition, Rhetoric, and Literacy

EDITED BY
LINDA ADLER-KASSNER
ELIZABETH WARDLE

UTAH STATE UNIVERSITY PRESS
Logan

© 2019 by University Press of Colorado

Published by Utah State University Press
An imprint of University Press of Colorado
245 Century Circle, Suite 202
Louisville, Colorado 80027

All rights reserved

The University Press of Colorado is a proud member of the Association of University Presses.

The University Press of Colorado is a cooperative publishing enterprise supported, in part, by Adams State University, Colorado State University, Fort Lewis College, Metropolitan State University of Denver, Regis University, University of Colorado, University of Northern Colorado, University of Wyoming, Utah State University, and Western Colorado University.

ISBN: 978-1-60732-931-2 (paperback)
ISBN: 978-1-60732-932-9 (ebook)
https://doi.org/10.7330/9781607329329

Library of Congress Cataloging-in-Publication Data

Names: Adler-Kassner, Linda, editor. | Wardle, Elizabeth (Elizabeth Ann), editor.
Title: (Re)considering what we know : learning thresholds in writing, composition, rhetoric, and literacy / Linda Adler-Kassner, Elizabeth Wardle.
Description: Logan : Utah State University Press, an imprint of University Press of Colorado, 2019. | Includes bibliographical references and index.
Identifiers: LCCN 2019032316 (print) | LCCN 2019032317 (ebook) | ISBN 9781607329312 (paperback) | ISBN 9781607329329 (ebook)
Subjects: LCSH: Composition (Language arts)—Study and teaching. | Literacy—Study and teaching.
Classification: LCC LB1575.8 .R4 2019 (print) | LCC LB1575.8 (ebook) | DDC 372.62/3—dc23
LC record available at https://lccn.loc.gov/2019032316
LC ebook record available at https://lccn.loc.gov/2019032317

Cover photograph by Nkosi Shanga.

To all the writing students, teachers, and researchers who work to change conceptions of writing every day

and

to Michael Spooner, who changed conceptions of writing through the many cutting-edge book projects he signed during his tenure at Utah State University Press.

CONTENTS

Acknowledgments   xi

Editors' Introduction: Threshold Concepts, *Naming What We Know*, and Reconsidering our Shared Conceptions
  Linda Adler-Kassner and Elizabeth Wardle   3

PART 1: CHALLENGES, CRITIQUES, AND NEW CONCEPTIONS

1 Recognizing the Limits of Threshold Concept Theory
    Elizabeth Wardle, Linda Adler-Kassner, Jonathan Alexander, Norbert Elliot, J.W. Hammond, Mya Poe, Jacqueline Rhodes, and Anne-Marie Womack   15

2 Literacy Is a Sociohistoric Phenomenon with the Potential to Liberate and Oppress
    Kate Vieira, Lauren Heap, Sandra Descourtis, Jonathan Isaac, Samitha Senanayake, Brenna Swift, Chris Castillo, Ann Meejung Kim, Kassia Krzus-Shaw, Maggie Black, Ọlá Ọládipọ̀, Xiaopei Yang, Patricia Ratanapraphart, Nikhil M. Tiwari, Lisa Velarde, and Gordon Blaine West   36

3 Thinking like a Writer: Threshold Concepts and First-Year Writers in Open-Admissions Classrooms
    Cassandra Phillips, Holly Hassel, Jennifer Heinert, Joanne Baird Giordano, and Katie Kalish   56

4 Writing as Practiced and Studied beyond "Writing Studies"
    Doug Hesse and Peggy O'Neill   76

5 Rhetoric as Persistently "Troublesome Knowledge": Implications for Disciplinarity
    Jennifer Helene Maher   94

6 The World Confronts Us with Uncertainty: Deep Reading as a Threshold Concept
    Patrick Sullivan   113

7   Expanding the Inquiry: What Everyday Writing with Drawing Helps Us Understand about Writing and about Writing-Based Threshold Concepts
    Kathleen Blake Yancey   135

PART 2: USING THRESHOLD CONCEPTS TO ENGAGE WITH WRITING TEACHERS AND STUDENTS

8   Doors between Disciplines: Threshold Concepts and the Community College Writing Program
    Mark Blaauw-Hara, Carrie Strand Tebeau, Dominic Borowiak, Jami Blaauw-Hara   161

9   Extending What We Know: Reflections on the Transformational Value of Threshold Concepts for Writing Studies Contingent Faculty
    Lisa Tremain, Marianne Ahokas, Sarah Ben-Zvi, and Kerry Marsden   175

10 Threshold Concepts and Curriculum Redesign in First-Year Writing
    Heidi Estrem, Dawn Shepherd, and Susan E. Shadle   194

11 Framing Graduate Teaching Assistant Preparation around Threshold Concepts of Writing Studies
    Aimee C. Mapes and Susan Miller-Cochran   208

12 Threshold Concepts and the Phenomenal Forms
    Deborah Mutnick   227

13 Grappling with Threshold Concepts over Time: A Perspective from Tutor Education
    Rebecca Nowacek, Aishah Mahmood, Katherine Stein, Madylan Yarc, Saul Lopez, and Matt Thul   244

14 "I Can't Go On, I'll Go On": Liminality in Undergraduate Writing
    Matthew Fogarty, Páraic Kerrigan, Sarah O'Brien, and Alison Farrell   261

PART 3: THRESHOLD CONCEPTS AND WRITING: BEYOND THE DISCIPLINE

15 Rethinking Epistemologically Inclusive Teaching
    Linda Adler-Kassner   281

16   Using a Threshold Concepts Framework to Facilitate an
     Expertise-Based WAC Model for Faculty Development
     Elizabeth Wardle   297

17   Talking about Writing: A Study of Key Writing Terms Used
     Instructionally across the Curriculum
     Chris M. Anson, Chen Chen, and Ian G. Anson   313

     Editors' Conclusion: Expanding and Examining What
     We (Think We) Know
     Linda Adler-Kassner and Elizabeth Wardle   328

     About the Authors   333

ACKNOWLEDGMENTS

We'd like to thank the contributors to this collection. Their generosity and willingness to think with us and with one another will, we hope, move forward the discussion about threshold concepts in/and our discipline.

Thanks to Rachael Levay and colleagues at Utah State University Press and University Press of Colorado.

We also would like to thank the contributors to *Naming What We Know*, without whom the discussions in this book couldn't have occurred.

Thanks to Nkosi Shanga for the cover photo, which serves as yet another beautiful visual metaphor for our thinking.

And we are grateful to Angela Glotfelter for her outstanding organizational and formatting efforts.

(RE)CONSIDERING WHAT WE KNOW

Editors' Introduction

THRESHOLD CONCEPTS, NAMING WHAT WE KNOW, AND RECONSIDERING OUR SHARED CONCEPTIONS

Linda Adler-Kassner and Elizabeth Wardle

When we organized the thought experiment that became *Naming What We Know* (*NWWK*) in 2013, we had in mind producing a collection whose primary audience would be students, teachers, and researchers within the discipline but that might be used for those audiences for purposes beyond the discipline. When we identified this goal, we were cognizant of the extent to which virtually everyone who writes—which is to say virtually everyone—considers writing to be "their business" and of the agency experience affords people to generate everything from opinions to policy about writing (Adler-Kassner 2017; Adler-Kassner and Wardle 2015). While we had long engaged in extensive collaborations with stakeholders and interested others from a variety of contexts, we hoped that building on efforts to define and compile key ideas from the discipline, as Paul Heilker and Peter Vandenberg (1994) did in *Keywords in Composition Studies* and Iris Ruíz and Raúl Sanchéz did later in *Decolonizing Rhetoric and Composition Studies: New Latinx Keywords for Theory and Pedagogy* (2016), could prove productive for writing professionals as we engage in those discussions. In our case, we found threshold concepts a useful starting point for these considerations.

The idea of threshold concepts was created by Jan H. F. Meyer and Ray Land (2006), faculty members in mathematics (Meyer) and literature (Land). They were conducting research into characteristics associated with good learning at the University of Durham, where they both worked at the time; they created the term based on their extensive interviews with faculty members from across disciplines. Threshold concepts are concepts crucial for epistemological participation in disciplines, the lenses learners must see through and see with to be successful.[1] When we discuss threshold concepts (e.g., Adler-Kassner and Wardle 2015;

DOI: 10.7330/9781607329329.c000

Adler-Kassner and Wardle 2016), we tend to use the term "community of practice" (Wenger 1998) rather than *discipline* since disciplines can be understood as communities of practice, and threshold concepts are also operative in sites well beyond academic disciplines.

Meyer and Land (2006) identified characteristics associated with learners' encounters with threshold concepts. The presence of these characteristics in learners' experiences also can be helpful for identifying what makes something a threshold concept. The first, useful for consideration of the community of practice, is that threshold concepts are bounded; that is, they are *not* threshold concepts in *all* communities of practice but are associated with specific communities of practice (or, possibly, specific intersections among distinct communities of practice), as well as with the values and ideologies of these communities. We discuss this subject in greater detail, along with several collaborators, in chapter 1 of this collection. Encounters with threshold concepts—that is, learners' initial experiences with them and their journeys to and (when it occurs) through them—occur within a liminal space. Learners spend time in this space moving, often in nonlinear ways, to (and hopefully through) the concept. In presentations and workshops we often describe this as a two-steps-forward-one-step-back process.

The nonlinear movement is occasioned by another characteristic of threshold concepts identified by Meyer and Land (2006) and developed in greater detail in its initial introduction by educational psychologist David Perkins (2006): troublesomeness. As ways of being associated with epistemes often new to learners (especially at introductory levels but also at advancing levels of participation), threshold concepts can butt up against different types of preexisting knowledge: ritual or inert knowledge (37); conceptually difficult, foreign, or alien knowledge (38–39); or tacit knowledge (40). Including this last kind of troublesome knowledge, we have found, is especially useful as we engage with faculty as they think about threshold concepts (and/in writing) in their own teaching, as it provides an important bridge to the literature on novice-expert practices (e.g., Bransford, Brown, and Cocking 1999): the more expert one is, the more the constituent elements of that expertise become tacit and seem to be common sense. But as Etienne Wenger (1998) explains, "Common sense is commonsensical because it is sense held in common" (47); the realization among faculty that "my discipline is not the universe" (Adler-Kassner and Majewski 2015, 190) can be a powerful threshold concept that prompts reconsideration of teaching practices.

A third characteristic of threshold concepts is that they are integrative. That is, once learners see them, it becomes possible to identify them in multiple sites. They also are often irreversible, a fourth characteristic. Once one sees through and sees with a threshold concept—one example we invoke in chapter 1 is *writing is social and rhetorical*, a threshold concept described by Kevin Roozen (2015) in *NWWK*—it is very difficult to go back. That is, it is unlikely a person would say that while they *once* believed writing is social and rhetorical, a change of heart has led to the belief that writing is produced independently, in isolation, without any input from others, or that writing is only ever about what is happening cognitively. This experience of integration and irreversibility leads to a shift in one's discursive practices, a "reformulation of the learner's meaning frame and an accompanying shift in the learner's ontology or subjectivity" (Land, Rattray, and Vivian 2014, 199). This shift is a significant sign that one is passing through the portal of a threshold concept, moving from a liminal stage of movement into a different stage that signals full participation.

Our own journey to this framework and its usefulness came through other research. Linda was involved in a study with a historian colleague exploring characteristics associated with "good learning" in writing and history; Elizabeth became acquainted through Linda's work. Both of us also participated in the Elon University seminar Writing and the Question of Transfer from 2011 to 2013, where we were collaborating with colleagues from around the world to think about questions concerning how knowledge circulates. As the idea of threshold concepts was explored during this period, we both realized it describes a level of learning we had been trying to name but could not quite reach. For example, Elizabeth and Doug Downs had for several years been working on identifying content of the field appropriate and necessary for first-year college student writers; the threshold concepts framework brought that content into sharper view, as is now evident in several editions of *Writing about Writing* framed around threshold concepts of writing.

On the heels of our independent research and the Elon seminar, we embarked on the collaboration that became *Naming What We Know*. As we explain in the introduction to that earlier collection and in chapter 1 of this book, we asked a number of teacher-researchers in our field to be part of a thought experiment: could we, through extended discussion via a wiki, begin to articulate some threshold concepts of our discipline? Over a period of several months, twenty-nine of the original forty-five we contacted participated in this effort, which ultimately became the first part of *NWWK*. The threshold concepts described there are outlined at the end of this chapter as appendix 0.1.

In the intervening several years, we have continued our own work related to threshold concepts, some of which is represented in independently authored chapters in this collection. At the same time, we have collaborated with and heard from many writing colleagues around the country about their experiences with threshold concepts and/or the threshold concepts framework. Some have explained how they have found these useful or important; some have explained they have found them to be problematic in any number of ways. While the two of us have continued to engage with threshold concepts as a useful theoretical framework for our own research, teaching, and professional-development work, we have done so as reflective and critical practitioners: we interrogate our own practices and the practices of others in and through the idea of threshold concepts not from the perspective of "true believers" but as inquisitive and critical researchers who see theories as lenses that may be more or less useful, depending on the needs and goals for which they are being used.

It is from this latter perspective—of reflective and critical practice—that we embarked on this second collection. For it, we wondered, how have threshold concepts of/in our discipline been taken up, challenged, found useful or highly problematic? When we circulated a call for proposals for this collection, we received far more proposals than we could possibly accept, an initial indication suggesting the idea of threshold concepts as described in *NWWK*, or as described in the literally hundreds of other articles, book chapters, and books about threshold concepts in other disciplines by researchers from around the world, was resonating with disciplinary colleagues. This collection, then, provides insight from those colleagues into themes we hope provide insight and opportunities for additional inquiry, a subject to which we return in the conclusion to the collection.

WHAT THIS BOOK DOES

One theme of this book concerns reconsideration of questions associated with a word in the title of our first collection, *naming*. The chapters in part 1 of the collection both raise questions about the ideas of certainty and consensus associated with naming threshold concepts of a discipline and seek to expand these concepts. Chapter 1, coauthored by the two of us and several collaborators, outlines some of the challenges inherent in the very idea of threshold concepts. Our coauthors—Jonathan Alexander, Norbert Elliot, J. W. Hammond, Mya Poe, Jacqueline Rhodes, and Anne-Marie Womack—also propose "aspirational" threshold concepts they contend are central to the practices of many in the field. Next, Kate Vieira, Lauren Heap, Sandra Descourtis, Jonathan Isaac,

Samitha Senanayake, Brenna Swift, Chris Castillo, Ann Meejung Kim, Kassia Krzus-Shaw, Maggie Black, Ọlá Ọládipọ̀, Xiaopei Yang, Patricia Ratanapraphart, Nikhil Tiwari, Lisa Velarde, and Gordon Blaine West describe and define a number of new threshold concepts they believe are central to the field's history, theory, and practice. All are associated with literate practices under the auspices of their title, "Literacy Is a Sociohistoric Phenomenon with the Potential to Liberate and Oppress." Following their contribution, Cassandra Phillips, Holly Hassel, Jennifer Heinert, Joanne Baird Giordano, and Katie Kalish, all faculty members at University of Wisconsin two-year colleges at the time their chapter was written, extend the idea of threshold concepts by proposing a thoughtful and scaffolded threshold concept pedagogy that takes into account needs of underprepared students at two- and four-year colleges who have had many negative writing experiences. Doug Hesse and Peggy O'Neill, in the following chapter, discuss possible limitations of currently articulated threshold concepts about writing. They posit that a field named "writing studies" must also include creative writing and journalism and, in this case, new and revised concepts must be articulated. Jennifer Maher also takes issue with the name "writing studies" and argues that rhetoric is central to the field and is, itself, a threshold concept. Patrick Sullivan focuses attention on the concept of deep reading, offering definition, examination of troublesomeness, and applications of the concept within and beyond education. Part 1 concludes with Kathleen Blake Yancey's chapter, which takes up important concepts associated with everyday writing, especially drawing. Collectively, then, the chapters in part 1 acknowledge the contingency of knowing and naming, recognize the capaciousness of our field, and attest to the importance of being aware that any name for our field must be both inclusive of and connected to the varied work in which we all engage.

Chapters included in part 2 of the collection focus on threshold concepts in action and practice, demonstrating the innovative ways they have been used in writing courses and programs.

The first four chapters in part 2 focus on the ways programs have used work around threshold concepts to shape the focus of writing programs and faculty. In chapters 8 and 9 respectively, Mark Blaauw-Hara, Carrie Strand Tebeau, Dominic Borowiak, and Jami Blaauw-Hara, who are at Northern Michigan College, and Lisa Tremain, Marianne Ahokas, Sarah Ben-Zvi, and Kerry Marsden, who are at Humboldt State University, describe the ways faculty who teach writing but are not necessarily trained in rhetoric and composition or writing studies were able to productively share ideas across difference as a result of a threshold concepts framework. Notably, these chapters are coauthored by the faculty who are the subjects of the analysis; their first-person reflections provide insight into two instances in which a threshold concepts framework, along with threshold concepts of the discipline, are used by instructors who bring a variety of backgrounds, expertise, and insights to these discussions. As such, they offer models for how threshold concepts might serve as a productive framework for conversation across what might appear to be incommensurable disciplinary divides—being careful not to use the framework to provide checklists, prescriptions, or mandates. In chapter 10, Heidi Estrem, Susan Shadle, and Dawn Shepherd outline how they have used this framework as they have revised their first-year writing program's curricula, engaging in simultaneous collaborative faculty-development work. Aimee Mapes and Susan Miller-Cochran, in chapter 11, also direct their attention to threshold concepts and pedagogical education, focusing on graduate students.

The final three chapters in part 2 examine students' relationships to writing and threshold concepts through coursework and practice. Deborah Mutnick examines the important intersections among threshold concepts, troublesome knowledge, and Marx's conception of phenomenal forms. Her chapter challenges readers to consider the relationship between troublesomeness and trauma, expanding the idea of troublesome knowledge. Chapters 12 and 13 center on students' experiences of learning threshold concepts of writing. In chapter 12, Rebecca Nowacek, Aishah Mahmood, Katherine Stein, Madylan Yarc, Saul Lopez, and Matt Thul focus on how writing tutors learn threshold concepts about writing that impact their tutoring practices across time—or don't. As Nowacek et al note in their introduction, there are few such studies of how students learn threshold concepts across time, so this chapter is an important beginning to the empirical conversation we hope to see in the near future. In chapter 13, Matthew Fogarty, Páraic Kerrigan, Sarah O'Brien, and Alison Farrell, who are affiliated with Ireland's Maynooth University writing center, discuss the experiences of students themselves with learning threshold concepts about writing in an institution with no writing infrastructure. The chapters in part 2 of this collection, then, offer a variety of perspectives from which readers can observe threshold concepts in process and in action, considering how and whether a threshold concepts framework and/or particular concepts might (or might not) productively contribute to ongoing activities.

In part 3, contributors take up questions about how the threshold concepts framework can help us engage in conversations beyond writing studies. In individually authored chapters, each of us describe professional-development programs we facilitate on our respective campuses, in which the notion of threshold concepts has provided a useful framework for helping faculty see what they already know and do in new ways they can then share more productively with students. Chris Anson, Chen Chen, and Ian Anson round out the section, describing constraints faculty and students face when there is no shared language around writing—a vocabulary problem that can often be traced back to disciplinary concepts of what writing is and how it works.

While we return to takeaways from this collective consideration in the conclusion, we want to reinforce a few points in this framing introduction. First, as we noted in *Naming What We Know*, threshold concepts are contingent, contextual, and threshold-for-now. They are not intended to be a checklist, and it is not possible to take the ideas in these chapters—nor in any description of threshold concepts—and reduce them to easily accessible, ready-to-digest ideas that can be packaged into a quick and easy curriculum. There are always more concepts to be named, additional exploration of the boundaries surrounding the realms where these concepts are operative, and discussions to be had about the relevance of the concepts named. We hope all of these will be taken up in future work.

Second, a point central to this collection. The threshold concepts framework itself creates certain boundaries that include and exclude particular ideas—and this, too, is a fruitful subject for exploration. While we think it is important to name the rules of the game or ways of thinking and practicing in a discipline so newcomers can get a clearer sense of the landscape, we should at no time use those mapping and naming exercises to suggest there is one coherent narrative of our (or any) discipline—or that what are named as common ways of thinking and practicing are the only important ideas in a given discipline. While this book is not primarily about aspirational or emerging areas of consensus that might become threshold concepts, we thought it was important to lay out explicitly some of the cutting-edge work of the field that would not typically be named when the threshold concepts framework is the lens being used. As with *Naming What We Know*, readers of this book are invariably going to be our colleagues, some of the thousands of professionals who work with writers and writing in classrooms, centers, programs, and other sites of activity around the world. To be sure, important questions are raised through this collection and our shared work that we should continue to discuss at conferences, in books like this one, in articles and chapters, in blogs, and in wikis. In many ways, they cycle back to a point made by the chapters in part 1:

naming matters. Naming the discipline, naming threshold concepts, and naming activities that stem from those concepts have consequences for those we consider to be at the center of all of this work: our students, instructors in our programs and centers, colleagues in our institutions. We hope *(Re)Considering What We Know* raises new questions and ideas that can help advance this discussion in productive and fruitful ways.

APPENDIX 0.1

Threshold Concepts articulated in Naming What We Know
(*Utah State University Press, 2015*)

Metaconcept: Writing is an activity and a subject of study
  Concept 1: Writing is a social and rhetorical activity
    1.1 Writing is a knowledge-making activity
    1.2 Writing addresses, invokes, and/or creates audiences
    1.3 Writing expresses and shares meaning to be reconstructed by the reader
    1.4 Words get their meaning from other words
    1.5 Writing mediates activity
    1.6 Writing is not natural
    1.7 Assessing writing shapes contexts and instruction
    1.8 Writing involves making ethical choices

  Concept 2: Writing speaks to situations through recognizable forms
    2.1 Writing represents the world, events, ideas, and feelings
    2.2 Genres are enacted by writers and readers
    2.3 Writing is a way of enacting disciplinarity
    2.4 All writing is multimodal
    2.5 Writing is performative
    2.6 Texts get their meaning from other texts

  Concept 3: Writing enacts and creates identities and ideologies
    3.1 Writing is linked to identity
    3.2 Writers' histories, processes, and identities vary
    3.3 Writing is informed by prior experience
    3.4 Disciplinary and professional identities are constructed through writing
    3.5 Writing provides a representation of ideologies and identities

Concept 4: All writers have more to learn

    4.1 Text is an object outside of oneself that can be improved and developed

    4.2 Failure can be an important part of writing development

    4.3 Learning to write effectively requires different kinds of practice, time, and effort

    4.4 Revision is central to developing writing

    4.5 Assessment is an essential component of learning to write

    4.6 Writing involves the negotiation of language differences

Concept 5: Writing is (also always) a cognitive activity

    5.1 Writing is an expression of embodied cognition

    5.2 Metacognition is not cognition

    5.3 Habituated practice can lead to entrenchment

    5.4 Reflection is critical for writers' development

NOTE

1. Engineering faculty member Mick Flanagan maintains a comprehensive site on threshold concepts at https://www.ee.ucl.ac.uk/~mflanaga/thresholds.html; for a brief discussion on threshold concepts and their usefulness for writing faculty see Adler-Kassner and Wardle (2016).

REFERENCES

Adler-Kassner, Linda. 2017. "Because Writing Is Never Just Writing: CCCC Chair's Address." *College Composition and Communication* 69 (2): 317–40.

Adler-Kassner, Linda, and John Majewski. 2015. "Extending the Invitation." In *Naming What We Know: Threshold Concepts of Writing Studies*, edited by Linda Adler-Kassner and Elizabeth Wardle, 186–202. Logan: Utah State University Press.

Adler-Kassner, Linda, and Elizabeth Wardle. 2015. *Naming What We Know: Threshold Concepts of Writing Studies.* Logan: Utah State University Press.

Adler-Kassner, Linda, and Elizabeth Wardle. 2016. "What Are Threshold Concepts?" In *A Rhetoric for Writing Program Administrators*, edited by Rita Malenczyk, 64–75. Anderson, SC: Parlor.

Bransford, John, Ann Brown, and Rodney Cocking, eds. 1999. *How People Learn: Brain, Mind, Society.* Washington, DC: National Academies Press.

Flanagan, Mick. N.d. Threshold Concepts: Undergraduate Teaching, Postgraduate Training, Professional Development, and School Education. Last modified March 17, 2019. https://www.ee.ucl.ac.uk/~mflanaga/thresholds.html.

Heilker, Paul, and Peter Vandenberg. 1994. *Keywords in Composition Studies.* Portsmouth, NH: Heinemann.

Land, Ray, and Julie Rattray, and Peter Vivian. 2014. "Learning in the Liminal Space: A Semiotic Approach to Threshold Concepts." *Higher Education* 67 (2): 199–217.

Meyer, Jan H. F., and Ray Land, eds. 2006. *Overcoming Barriers to Student Understanding: Threshold Concepts and Troublesome Knowledge.* London: Routledge.

Perkins, David. 2006. "Constructivism and Troublesome Knowledge." In *Overcoming Barriers to Understanding: Threshold Concepts and Troublesome Knowledge*, edited by Jan H. F. Meyer and Ray Land, 32–47. London: Routledge.

Roozen, Kevin. 2015. "Writing Is a Social and Rhetorical Activity." In *Naming What We Know: Threshold Concepts of Writing Studies*, edited by Linda Adler-Kassner and Elizabeth Wardle, 21–23. Logan: Utah State University Press.

Ruiz, Iris D., and Sanchéz, Raúl. 2016. *Decolonizing Rhetoric and Composition Studies: New Latinx Keywords for Theory and Pedagogy*. Logan: Utah State University Press.

Wardle, Elizabeth, and Doug Downs. 2020. *Writing about Writing*. 4th ed. Boston: Bedford/St. Martins.

Wearn, Andy, Anne O'Callaghan, and Mark Barrow. 2016. "Becoming a Different Doctor: Identifying Threshold Concepts: When Doctors in Training Spend Six Months with a Hospital Palliative Care Team." In *Threshold Concepts in Practice*, edited by Ray Land, Jan H. F. Meyer, and Michael T. Flanagan, 223–238. Rotterdam/Boston/Taipei: Sense Publishers.

Wenger, Etienne. 1998. *Communities of Practice*. Cambridge: Cambridge University Press.

PART 1

Challenges, Critiques, and New Conceptions

1
RECOGNIZING THE LIMITS OF THRESHOLD CONCEPT THEORY

Elizabeth Wardle, Linda Adler-Kassner,
Jonathan Alexander, Norbert Elliot, J.W. Hammond,
Mya Poe, Jacqueline Rhodes, and Anne-Marie Womack

Editors' note: Unless otherwise indicated, the we in this chapter refers to Linda and Elizabeth. Other coauthors' contributions are noted in the text.

THRESHOLD CONCEPTS: BACKGROUND AND PURPOSES

In "Threshold Concepts and Troublesome Knowledge," Jan Meyer and Ray Land (2006) explain that "interviews and wider discussions with practitioners in a range of disciplines and institutions" (6) led them to identify the characteristics associated with threshold concepts that have become familiar to researchers who have adopted or adapted this framework for thinking about learning and teaching. That is, threshold concepts are transformative, probably irreversible, integrative, potentially troublesome, and bounded. It's this latter idea that is significant for this chapter. Specifically, as Meyer and Land explain, threshold concepts are "possibly often (though not necessarily always) *bounded* in that any conceptual space will have terminal frontiers, bordering with thresholds into new conceptual areas. It might be that such boundedness in certain instances serves to constitute the demarcation between disciplinary areas, to define academic territories" (6). They follow this with two illustrations: one from a faculty member in cultural studies and one from veterinary sciences, both of whom explain the consequences for students of seeing through or seeing with threshold concepts from other disciplines, or of invoking ways of thinking and practicing (Hounsell and Anderson 2009) associated with operationalization of threshold concepts inconsistent with the threshold concepts of the discipline.

The idea that threshold concepts serve as portals into disciplinary participation has become an important one for teachers, learners, and researchers working with the idea. A number of researchers describe how faculty have incorporated threshold concepts into teaching (e.g., Baillie and Johnson 2008; Berg, Erichsen, and Hokstad 2016; Martindale et al. 2016; McGowan 2016; Sibbett and Thompson 2008) or considered learners' movements around these concepts (e.g., Cousin 2006; Rattray 2016; Timmermans 2016), or how individuals and groups have attempted to explore and describe the threshold concepts of their disciplines (e.g., Reimann and Jackson 2006; Taylor 2006; Wearn, O'Callaghan, and Barrow 2016). Underscoring these uses of threshold concepts is the idea that making them more explicit enables learners greater access to elements associated with knowledge-making practices and ways of seeing *in* a discipline through expertise. *Naming What We Know* (Adler-Kassner and Wardle 2015) is one illustration of how threshold concepts within a discipline can be identified, as twenty-nine teacher-researchers in writing studies attempted to name and define some of the threshold concepts of writing studies. In doing so, this group—which we facilitated, and to which we also contributed—was attempting to look back at the research and practice of those within writing studies and affiliated disciplines like English education, sociolinguistics, and educational psychology and to articulate some of the ideas that were (1) threshold to writing studies as an academic discipline; (2) threshold to writing in/and learning; and/or (3) threshold to teaching writing.

Since its publication, *Naming What We Know* and this attempt to describe some of the threshold concepts of writing studies has taken on a life of its own, as texts are wont to do. It has become widely used in classrooms, which was somewhat surprising as the book was not written as a textbook per se (though now it can be purchased in a classroom edition that only includes the threshold concepts section, at the request of readers). It has generated numerous conference panels and informed other studies, including theses and dissertations. Critiques have also been leveled or implied, and concerns have been voiced (e.g., Alexander 2017). While the two of us have generatively expanded our work with threshold concepts in professional development (primarily working with faculty from other disciplines, as we discuss in chapters 15 and 16), we have also had some time to consider the limitations of the threshold concepts framework.

Drawing on these developments, in this chapter we first consider several critiques of and complications related to threshold concepts theory. Then, our chapter coauthors look at some ideas that do not get named and included when threshold concepts are the organizing principle.

THRESHOLD CONCEPTS: CRITIQUES, CONCERNS, AND LIMITATIONS

Here we outline four critiques, concerns, and limitations of the threshold concepts framework and discuss how those critiques apply to the *Naming What We Know* project in rhetoric and composition.

Critique 1: Threshold Concept Theory Focuses on Boundedness between Disciplines Rather Than Connections and Interdisciplinarity.

One of the characteristics of threshold concepts, according to Meyer and Land (2006), is their boundedness: "Any conceptual space will have terminal frontiers, bordering with thresholds into new conceptual areas" (6). Thus, it is easy to critique a threshold concepts framework for potentially sustaining disciplinary divisions rather than helping foster interdisciplinary connections: "Sharing a way of thinking with others allows access to communities, but it may also reduce acceptance or capacity to participate in another community" (Meyer, Land, and Davies 2008, 67). As we discuss further below, naming threshold concepts can easily reify them and contribute to a sense that boundaries between disciplines are rigid and impermeable.

At the same time, naming threshold concepts can be useful precisely because they help shed light on boundaries that are often invisible, or at least difficult to see. Threshold concepts "stand in distinct relationship to each other. . . . They may complement each other, forming a web of interrelated threshold concepts . . . , [or] define distinct contrasting schools of thought" (Meyer, Land and Davies 2008, 67). Making these concepts explicit, say Meyer, Land and Jason Davies, "opens up new sources of variation that do not come into view until the concept of learning is seen as a relationship between the individual, the phenomenon, and others," sources of variation within and among threshold concepts and their disciplinary boundaries (67).

The relevance of the threshold concepts framework for interdisciplinary work has also been taken up by a number of scholars. For example, Aminul Huq, Marcia D. Nichols, and Bijaya Aryal (2016) have examined correlations among threshold concepts in various disciplines. Jason Davies (2016) has argued that careful consideration of threshold concepts and their similarities and differences across disciplines might actually assist learners and scholars attempting to engage in interdisciplinary work. Davies points out that the incommensurability so common to interdisciplinary endeavors can not only be explained but "emphatically predicted by threshold concepts . . . given their 'transformative,' 'irreversible,' 'integrative,' 'bounded,' and 'troublesome' nature" (122). Members of an interdisciplinary group, he says, can "approach the same task and materials very differently" (123). If the underlying differences are not understood and examined, "much time can pass with a truce rather than genuine engagement" (124). This observation helps explain the difficulty students can often face when their faculty are "literally arguing from different premises, with the implication that meaning-making construction and intellectual reference points are as different as the physical buildings" (121). Threshold concepts offer "a way to begin the task of understanding why disciplinary differences can run so deep" (121). At the same time, Davies says, making these disagreements explicit can stop threshold concepts "from becom[ing] 'threshold guardians,'" defenders of walls surrounding disciplines (125). The process of identifying threshold concepts, then, can become a starting point and help offer vocabulary to interdisciplinary groups: what all members of an interdisciplinary team "have in common is that . . . they all operate with threshold concepts . . . [these concepts] are thus potentially a great leveler, and their articulation at some point . . . is usually a necessary part of collaboration" (131).

Given the concerns about the ways threshold concepts could impede interdisciplinary efforts, the *Naming What We Know* (*NWWK*) project could be understood as solidifying disciplinary boundaries. Certainly, as we note above, discipline-specific knowledge has in some ways been defined to be *exclusive* in order to distinguish one field from *other* fields (Bender 1993). While fields like writing studies have been informed by a number of other disciplines, there are beliefs, orientations, and research findings from our field that set it apart from other fields. Not recognizing this expertise, as we argue in *NWWK*, has many implications. Some of these are associated with institutional decisions. For instance, funding for faculty lines in many institutions is associated, at least in part, with the disciplines to which faculty belong. Other implications can be associated with writers, writing instructors, and/or the ways writing is taught and learned. As we and others have noted elsewhere, many feel free to define "good writing," create definitions of "good writers," and create assessments to sort writers and writing. The threshold concepts of our discipline can help inform these discussions—*if they are named* and if the *project* of naming continues to take into consideration the changing nature of the field's knowledge and understandings. Too, as both of us have experienced in work with faculty across disciplines on defining and describing threshold concepts, the differences experts often point to in conjunction with inter- or cross-disciplinary work are associated with learning by those well beyond novice status—that is, advanced undergraduates or graduate students. At the novice level, which is to say the level of introductory coursework, recognizing the existence of disciplinary boundaries via threshold concepts can itself be a threshold concept. It is our hope, then, that given Davies's (2016) argument as outlined above, explicitly naming what we understand about writing can actually foster cross-disciplinary work with stakeholders from other communities of practice.

Critique 2: Threshold Concepts Imposes a Particular Kind of Order That Shapes Epistemic Contexts (Whether We Name Them or Not)

Threshold concepts are, by definition, retrospective. They represent snapshots of disciplinary communities, descriptions of what is taken as established within a discipline at a particular moment. There is, then, a critique to be leveled regarding the method by which those of us involved in the initial process of *NWWK* went about our work: it could be seen as attempting to impose a particular kind of stability and order that privileges the past. To complicate this possibility even more, it could be said that naming threshold concepts may also suggest an objective social reality at odds with constructivist perspectives that view reality as constantly *in* production and created by practices and beliefs. These perspectives, in fact, are foundational to many of the threshold concepts named in *NWWK*.

Literature from feminist, decolonial, and poststructuralist methodologies highlights these concerns. Underscoring them is an essential tension between positivist and constructivist assumptions about what knowledge is and about how it is created. A positivist perspective "[assumes] an objective external reality and [emphasizes] the need for inquirers to be objective in accessing that reality, and focuses on generalization and cause-effect linkages" (Baxter Magolda 2004, 32). Sociologist John Law (2004), critiquing positivist methods of social science research, argues that this perspective stabilizes existing processes and practices. This stabilization begins from questions designed to explore what is extant and extends through the "framing assumption" of methodologies: "that there are definite processes out there waiting to be discovered." Law goes on to say, "Arguments and debates about the character of social reality then take place *within* this arena" (6).

In a constructivist perspective, however, methods and the process of exploration look quite different: "Realities are multiple, context-bound, and mutually shaped by interaction of the knower and known" (Baxter Magolda 2004, 35). From this perspective, Law (2004) argues, "the argument is no longer that methods *discover* and depict realities. Instead, it is that they participate in the *enactment* of those realities" (45). As Annemarie Mol explains, "Realities are not explained by practices and beliefs but are instead produced in them" (quoted in Law 2004, 59). Thus, Law argues, "if we are interested in multiplicity then we also need to *attend to the craftwork implied in practice,*" including the practice that simultaneously constructs and reifies realities (59). Ultimately, then, Law says Mol is issuing a methodological warning. "If we want to understand practice and the objects generated in practice, then we need to make sure we don't get caught up in that reversal. . . . Realities are not explained by practices and beliefs but are instead produced in them" (59).

From our perspective, then, this creates a bind. While we concur with Law and Mol's perspective that practice reifies and creates realities, we also recognize that the realities that can be created through writing-associated practices can be quite harmful for our students, colleagues, and institutions. We also recognize that historically, the reality created through the practice of teaching writing has been normative. For example, James Berlin's histories of the field (1984, 1987), Peter Elbow's notions of voice (e.g., 1973), and even the practice of portfolio assessment (e.g., Yancey 1992) have led to realities in the field—that is, common wisdom—about who, what, and how "we" are.

Threshold concepts are ideas that have been constructed as they have been enacted across time by groups of people—people, to be sure, with the power to be heard (which we say more about in the critiques below). Threshold concepts were not created by the participants in the *NWWK* project; those participants were trying to name and explain the enactments of shared ideas as they had witnessed and participated in them across time. However, naming those ideas and publishing them in the form of a static book continues to enact and construct them, and thus to produce and reproduce particular kinds of realities, and may make it difficult to interrogate norms or imagine a different kind of future.

Jonathan Alexander and Jacqueline Rhodes contribute to this thinking. Writing with and to us, they have drawn on queer theory to complicate further the idea of normalization we see as an undercurrent through our discipline.

Jonathan and Jacqueline:

> Queer theoretical perspectives should lead scholars to question both the sedimentation of ways of thinking into norms and how such sedimentation forecloses on the power of writing itself to act as a form of inquiry (which, ironically, works against the threshold concept that "writing

enacts and creates identities and ideologies"). Our work as queer theorists in the aftermath of the social turn has motivated our skepticism about threshold concepts and our concern that they might become normative ways of thinking about writing. The queer theoretical project is one invested in interrogating norms and questioning normalizing assumptions, specifically around sex, sexuality, and gender, but also in terms of other embodied human experiences, such as ability, age, class, race, and ethnicity.

While we value such a project of queer critique, particularly in questioning how threshold concepts might become norms and thus normalizing moves in standardizing writing instruction, we also want to forward a more utopian queerness. In *Cruising Utopia,* José Esteban Muñoz (2009) asks us to undertake the "work of not settling for the present" and of "asking and looking beyond the here and now" (28). Muñoz recovers a sense of openness and possibility for the future that is not foreclosed upon by the "no-future" queer time Lee Edelman, Jack Halberstam, and others have famously put forward (Ruti 2017, 5). Instead, Muñoz wants us to consider how our hopes for the future constitute an aspirational thinking and feeling that critiques the present and its inadequacies while also attempting to envision a better world. Such utopian thinking and feeling are hardly prescriptive; he neither offers nor encourages "blueprints" for the future. Rather, such thoughts and feeling bring to the fore the utopian sensibility Muñoz believes lies always latent within queerness—a drawing toward and desire for alternative paths that deviate from the straight and narrow and that, in their deviation, suggest possibilities for more just, equitable, capacious, and open futures. Some queer theorists link such utopian gestures directly to writing as a technology. For instance, in their introduction to *Queer Times, Queer Becomings,* E. L. McCallum and Mikko Tuhkanen (2011) assert that "reading and writing, narrating, or analysis . . . have a power to open up innovative forms of intimacy that betoken not only new modes of becoming, but new ways of affiliation with others and alternative modes of transmission" (13). We forward such "new modes of becoming" as the promise of queer critique.

We ask: Does the very idea of threshold concepts preclude this perspective? We might argue that threshold concepts can foreclose too quickly on how our understanding of writing may change and develop over time. Imagining the future in ways threshold concepts may preclude, then, may be one of our most creative ways to revise the present. Such revision is only possible if we remember writing often functions as a powerful technology of interrogating the present and imagining future possibilities. A refusal to name fully what we know—that is, to name threshold concepts of a discipline or a context so as to be open to the future—acknowledges that present circumstances, and the concepts that currently exist, need not determine a future. That future remains queerly open for composing. In the process of refusal, we hold on to the ongoing work of critique offered by queer theory while also honoring the openness and possibility afforded by a turn to utopian horizons and any desire we might cultivate to imagine the future differently.

Critique 3: Any Set of Ideas Stable Enough to Be Named Will Inevitably Reflect and Privilege Particular Viewpoints and Leave Out Others

If realities are constructed, it follows that when there is consensus around those constructions, consensus invariably reflect the values and ideologies of a dominant culture. Other ideologies and values are not recognized as valid or perhaps even acknowledged at all within dominant frameworks. Threshold concepts of a discipline, whether articulated explicitly or not, are ideas that have been reified by a dominant cultural group—*some* members of the discipline and not necessarily others—those with the power to be heard. Those ideas are reinforced through disciplinary practices that inherently maintain stability and propagate particular values and points of view—classes, curricula, graduate programs, hiring practices, peer review, scholarship, and so on. Meyer and Land (2006) explain that a "non-trivial" issue with threshold concepts is the possibility that "they might become part of a 'totalising' or 'colonising' view of the curriculum," exerting a "normalizing function in a Foulcaldian sense" (17). As Glynis Cousin (2006) cautions, "A threshold concept can be a form of disciplinary property and as such, its presentation in a curriculum may carry an inherent tendency to invite congealed understandings. . . . An essentialist reading of threshold concepts is best resisted by sustaining a sense of their provisional explanatory capacity" (4).

In the larger threshold concepts literature, there is not as yet an agreed-upon methodology for explicitly identifying threshold concepts of a discipline. For this reason, when we conceived the *NWWK* project, our first instinct was to ensure a lot of people were involved. The two of us alone certainly had no authority to name concepts for an entire field—and a complicated, interdisciplinary one at that. We gathered a group of teachers and researchers, trying to make that group as representative as possible—but it inevitably represented our own networks, connections, views, and biases. We invited many others beyond those who participated, but inevitably those who chose to participate were more likely people who knew us and had some confidence that working with us and others would be a productive experience. This, of course, illustrates the earlier point: ideas, ideologies, and structures produce and reproduce themselves. Thus, though a group of people articulated some of what we described as threshold concepts of writing studies, rather than one or two individuals, a larger critique still holds: *Who says* the concepts in *NWWK* are threshold concepts? Why do these people get to name ideas that stand as thresholds representing an entire field? What's been left out, and what would it look like if an entirely different group of people identified threshold concepts? These questions would be appropriate and important for any group of people in any field attempting to identify central ideas with which learners struggle.

While we considered these concerns during the process of compositing *NWWK*, our own goals, values, priorities, and ideologies suggested the potential benefits outweighed the risks. Our primary concern was that precisely because there are many normative ideas about what "good writing" is, means, and looks like that circulate among different groups of people, students can suffer when stakeholders who don't study writing misunderstand how writing works. At the same time, when those with some expertise about these things—expertise, to be sure, that has been validated through dominant cultural practices associated with the credentialing systems of graduate school and employment, especially within the academy—argue with one another about what else we could say and how differently we should say it, nothing changes: assessments, gatekeeping literacy devices, placements, high-stakes writing instruction, and testing all continue when students, parents, teachers, policy makers, and others act from misconceptions about writing.

Yet this possibility does not negate the fact that there is more that needs to be said. Other groups of people must name what they know, too, and challenge ideas that have been named by others. We can always ask what is not being named, as well as emphasize the reasons naming can be important in (though is not always sufficient for) changing material conditions.

Critique 4: Threshold Concepts by Their Nature Are Not Revolutionary or Cutting Edge to Those in the Field (Though They May Still Be Deeply Problematic, Troublesome, or Revolutionary to People Outside That Field)

By definition, threshold concepts are articulations of established and widely agreed-upon knowledge/ideas/orientations in bounded spaces—concepts participants in the spaces have come to accept as foundational. They are central ideas most people working in the field would not question or perhaps even think about consciously. In fact, they may seem so obvious to long-time practitioners as to seem too obvious to talk about. Consider a threshold concept in *NWWK*: *writing is social and rhetorical.* Consider the opposite statement: writing is not social or rhetorical. Do any practitioners associated with rhetoric, composition, or writing studies believe this latter statement? Does any current scholarship in our field proceed from the belief that writers are lone workers who write in absolute isolation, unhindered by social interactions, prior knowledge, other texts, and so on? This view seems unlikely right now (though the view that writing is social and rhetorical was not always such a prominent and widely accepted idea). There are many complications to what is meant by social and rhetorical, of course, but if a scholar were to submit an article to any journal in the field based on the opposite assumption, it seems highly unlikely it would be accepted. Yet many people who do not study writing and rhetoric for a living commonly assume such things about writing because of popular misconceptions about writing. (And other fields who may not actively disagree with the claim that writing is social may have different understandings of what social means and forefront different assumption about language. Some linguists, for example, might be more likely to forefront the idea that language is cognitive.)

Here then, is a paradox of threshold concept theory and of any process of attempting to articulate threshold concepts: threshold concepts are, by definition, conservative in the sense that they are the most frequently agreed-upon knowledge of a field at a particular moment in time. At the same time, when they are named (and sometimes they are only implied or assumed), they identify widely agreed-upon ideas and methodologies rather than pushing forward revolutionary thinking. Thus there are many important ideas in any discipline that are not (perhaps yet, perhaps ever) threshold concepts. The most revolutionary or difficult ideas in any area at a given time will not, by definition, meet the criteria for threshold concepts as laid out by Meyer and Land—nor will ideas and ideologies shared by those without disciplinary power and authority to speak or be heard. These ideas may become threshold concepts as paradigms shift or more research is conducted, but during that time of research, theorizing, and enacting, they are something other than threshold concepts.

It is important to recognize, then, that not all important ideas in a discipline are threshold concepts; in fact, according to this way of imagining the terrain, it's possible that *the most important* ideas *for* and *in* a discipline at a given time might not be threshold concepts because most people in the field don't (yet) understand them or can't recognize them. Meyer, Land, and Baillie allude to this point by referencing Thomas Kuhn, who said:

> The practices of both development and discovery in science are community-based activities. To discover and analyze them, one must first unravel the changing community structure of the [discipline] over time. During periods of development, periods of discovery, a shifted paradigm is forged by the concentrated collective intention of a group of practitioners. Any study of paradigm-directed . . . or paradigm-shattering . . . research must begin by locating the responsible group or groups . . . The pre-paradigm

period, in particular, is regularly marked by frequent and deep debates over legitimate methods, problems, and standards of solution, though these serve rather to define schools than to produce agreement. (quoted in Meyer, Land, and Baillie 2010, 27–28)

This latter point seems particularly important: at times there may be "schools" of thought or specialized areas in a larger field, including our own, in which particular ideas are commonly accepted, but they may not be understood or even recognized by other schools within the broader field.

At the same time, the agreed-upon and at time obvious and conservative threshold concepts of a discipline are troublesome and perhaps revolutionary for *those outside the discipline*. Non-economists rarely understand opportunity cost and start seeing transactions and opportunities in new ways when—or if—they do. The ideas that writing is social and not solitary, that good writers are not just "born that way," and that what counts as "good writing" depends on context can all feel revolutionary to students who've been led to believe they are "bad writers" and who are "sorted" into basic writing classes because they need feedback from others or don't "get it right" the first time or don't write using dominant and privileged forms of English. Meyer and Land (2006) first formulated the threshold concept framework because they noticed, when interviewing colleagues about learning, that students in all disciplines have particular spots where they tend to get tripped up and struggle to move forward—yet learners must move through those "stuck places" or "learning thresholds" if they want to do work in those fields.

In other words, these troublesome learning thresholds can be hard and even feel revolutionary to those coming to them and to the field for the first time. But they are *not* where the cutting edge of the field's internal work is happening. They are ideas necessary for engaging in work of the field, but that engagement is only the beginning. And, of course, newcomers who engage with the ideas of the field change the work and ideas of the field. That is why threshold concepts are only ever stable for now. Maintaining this tension is central to being able to do work while also being able to critique that work and move past it innovatively.

LOOKING BEYOND THRESHOLD CONCEPTS

Next, we turn our attention to some of the ideas circulating in rhetoric and composition that are currently not so commonly understood and agreed upon as to be broadly named *threshold concepts.* Given the critiques described above, it seems useful to turn our attention in this chapter, if only briefly, to what is ignored or missed if we only name the dominant and most widely accepted ideas.

Within our field at this moment, there are a number of sites where boundary-pushing work is happening that is not acknowledged in a discussion of the broad threshold concepts recognized by the broad discipline—and it is important to remember this particular limitation when we engage *with* threshold concepts. Here, Anne-Marie Womack, J. W. Hammond, Mya Poe, and Norbert Elliot, and Jonathan Alexander and Jacqueline Rhodes outline three ideas they consider to be threshold concepts because within particular scholarly communities within the discipline they are commonly accepted and understood; at the same time, they are not widely represented as taken for granted throughout the entirety of the research literature in the field, ideas that *must* be participated in or seen through and seen with for disciplinary participation. They may thus be working more toward *changing* accepted and enacted social realities. They are evidence of a point we seek to press: threshold concepts are where our work *begins* for learners, not where it *ends.* Any work seen as truly innovative, cutting edge in the best of senses, in any discipline, is work that *pushes* on paradigms, that works from the inside to *broaden* boundaries, not to reify them.

Writing Only Occurs within Accessible Conditions
ANNE-MARIE WOMACK

Writers need accessible tools and environments because *writing is not natural* (Dryer 2015), and *writing depends on technology* (Brooke and Grabill 2015), and *writing is an expression of embodied cognition* (Bazerman and Tinberg 2015, p. 74)—three threshold concepts identified in *NWWK.* These concepts, however, do not fully account for problematic perceptions of the body, which separate body and mind and define them in normative, exclusionary ways. In contrast, disability studies promotes an integrated view of the person, often using the compound term *bodymind.* The field emphasizes differences in bodyminds and fosters inclusion through accessible flexible conditions.

Disability and rhetoric inform one another. Writing is not a static independent activity but rather an interaction shaped by social contexts and communities. In the same way, disability is not a static individual condition but rather an evolving interaction among people, environments, and tools. For example, if a video lacks closed captioning, deaf students are excluded from analyzing it. In classrooms with laptop bans, disabled students could be left without a way to communicate. For timed writing assignments, learning disabled students may need extended time. Writing conditions (spaces, modes, tools, time) privilege certain abilities over others, often disabling writers different from an imagined norm. Integrating disability, though, is generative, revealing diverse ways of sensing, being, doing, and writing. In this sense of the word, *disabling* our norms has "transformative potential in rhetoric and composition" (Brewer 2016), changing practices for disabled and nondisabled students alike.

When nondisabled students read a video transcript in a quiet library, for instance, they demonstrate one of the key principles of *universal design*: inclusive design is better design for all. Following this ideal requires that instructors build disability into the framework of systems.

To promote access, composition instructors must both plan for difference (Dolmage 2003) and accommodate immediate needs (Kerschbaum 2015). Disability scholars recommend flexible conditions and redundant, multimodal texts that enable users to engage through multiple senses. That means that equivalent information appears in each modality, not that different information is conveyed in complementary text and image (Yergeau et al. 2013). Though accommodations may seem like special circumstances, they are far from out of the ordinary.

Instead, accommodation is the norm (Davis 2013). Teachers always change information and adapt processes, often with the goal of making knowledge accessible to students (Womack 2017). That's not a justification for low standards, a popular misconception about disability; that's a call for accessible conditions that allow students to meet rigorous standards, as well as an interrogation of which standards are truly essential.

This kind of revisionary threshold concept, as Hammond, Poe, and Elliot argue next, suggests where our focus should be rather than where it historically has been. Our field's threshold concepts are limited (and limiting) insofar as they focus on dominant groups and ways of writing. Paradoxically, too, while disability and accessibility have not been fully accounted for in current threshold concepts, accessibility is already a central function of threshold concepts themselves, which make specialized, seemingly counterintuitive concepts understandable to novices. Any framework that strives to increase access needs disability. Amidst discussions of threshold concepts, we as compositionists must examine the many ways disability and writing intersect, challenge, and transform one another because ultimately writing demands access(ibility).

Writing Assessment Must Be Ethical

J. W. HAMMOND, MYA POE, AND NORBERT ELLIOT

In assessing writing, writing studies researchers attend to the social construction of language with respect to the effects of assessment on students in specific contexts (Scott and Inoue 2015). In doing so, we recognize writing assessment is deeply connected to identity (Roozen 2015), including shifts in migration and demographic patterns (Hussar and Bailey 2018; International Organization for Migration 2017; Teixeira, Frey, and Griffin 2015) and individual students' histories and body-mind differences (Yancey 2015; Womack, above). For these reasons, the design of contemporary writing assessment always involves making ethical choices (see Duffy 2015).

Philosophically, the ethics of writing assessment demand we support student learning (O'Neill 2015; Scott and Inoue 2015) while creating opportunity structures (Moss et al. 2008) and advancing social justice (see Rawls 2001). By creating opportunity structures through assessment, we make it possible for all students to succeed through educational access, advancement, and attainment (Elliot 2016). By advancing social justice, we acknowledge writing assessment carries ideological significance and can be used to confront injustice (Green 2016; Inoue 2015; Poe and Inoue 2016; Poe, Inoue, and Elliot 2018).

Methodologically, to create opportunity structures and advance social justice, the first principle of ethical writing assessment design is *fairness* (American Educational Research Association, American Psychological Association, and National Council on Measurement in Education 2014; Elliot 2016; National Council of Teachers of English 2017). As an evidential category integrating validity and reliability, fairness may be usefully defined as "the identification of opportunity structures created through maximum construct representation. Constraint of the writing construct is to be tolerated only to the extent to which benefits are realized for the least advantaged" (Elliot 2016). Innovations in fairness methodologies have included attention to design (Inoue 2015; Mislevy et al. 2013), impact (Poe et al. 2014), and consequence (Slomp, Corrigan, and Sugimoto 2014). Also, empirical techniques examining differential validity and differential prediction should be used to ensure that competency-based writing assessments (such as end-of-course or rising junior examinations) have equal meaning and predictive power for all groups (Berry 2015; Elliot et al. 2016).

Employing techniques like these before scores are used provides stakeholders necessary evidence to document that neither intentional nor unintentional discriminatory practices are being used to disenfranchise students from their own education.

A social justice stance applied to writing assessment extends beyond threshold concept theory in significant ways, naming less what assessment *has been* than what it can and *should be* (Hammond 2019; Poe and Elliot 2019). First, this stance creates a restorative milestone in the history of writing assessment by placing evidence of fairness at the center of assessment. It moves practitioners beyond validity and reliability, the evidential categories dominant groups have privileged. Second, while this stance is enriched by retrospective historical analysis, its analytic aim is forward looking and constitutive. It leverages knowledge about past assessments to help us advance opportunity to learn. It thus makes history actionable, a means of charting ethical paths for intervention. Third, this stance is theoretically and methodologically inclusive, troubling the boundedness often characteristic of threshold concepts. Benefitting from measurement research on fairness *and* theoretical scholarship on social justice, this stance invites integration of and enrichment through a diversity of critical perspectives, including feminist, poststructuralist, and critical race theories. Fourth, this stance privileges multidisciplinarity and connectedness. It enables a wide variety of educational stakeholders to collaborate in designing assessments that advance opportunity to learn. And finally, fifth, this stance is intentionally revolutionary and cutting edge: it demands inclusion of diverse learners—learners too often relegated to the margins within dominant assessment frameworks or made hypervisible by them.

Writing Is World-Building
JONATHAN ALEXANDER AND JACQUELINE RHODES

NWWK identifies, rightly we think, the threshold concept *writing enacts and creates identities and ideologies* (48). We would like to pivot this formulation a bit and claim a new aspirational threshold concept: *writing is world building*. Writing is never simply communicating what's already known, but, in the very process of writing, composing, inquiring, discovering—we create what we know. In many ways, writing studies scholars and practitioners already know this; theorists and pedagogues of the social turn and beyond have brought us rich ways of thinking about writing as not only refraction and dissemination but also as a shaping force in how we understand ourselves, both subjectively and more collectively as cultural and political actors in ecologies of meaning.

Indeed, writing helps us explore our sense of self and our relations with others, often in ways that use difference productively to foster better understanding, confront (and celebrate) incommensurabilities, and—at best—collectively build the future. Such an understanding rarely situates writing as easy or lacking in contention, but it's precisely the function of writing as (frequently difficult) inquiry that prompts us to conceive writing as world building, as a working through differences to co-inhabit the world.

As we've suggested in the portion we've contributed earlier in this chapter, we are somewhat skeptical of the very idea of threshold concepts. As we seek to extend the theory, then, we simultaneously remain resistant in some ways to it. At the same time, our work as queer scholars has motivated our development of this aspirational threshold concept, for queer theory's different manifestations are deeply invested in forms of critical inquiry and "worlding." This paradox is reflected in our understanding of writing itself as a technology of confronting what we know, as well as what we could know. Writing is, for us, most significantly an act of invention, and it's one that opens us to probing and generating thoughts, feelings, and even ways of being we might not have yet imagined. Writing is thus queer in the sense of enabling critique but also opening us up to possible futures.

CONCLUSION: THE LIMINAL SPACE

In "Threshold Concepts and Issues of Liminality," Meyer and Land (2006) repeat a story about an encounter between Albert Einstein and Gregorio Ricci-Curbastro, "inventor of . . . tensor calculus" (25). As the story goes, they say, "Einstein, in a somewhat anxious state, was complaining to Ricci . . . about the fact that he was *stuck*. Ricci explained to him what tensor calculus could do, and Einstein immediately saw it as a solution for his problems" (25). Prior to this encounter, Meyer and Land speculate, "Einstein may well have been in a liminal state, temporarily suspended" because he lacked components of a framework "to express and progress his thinking. . . . Having reached the stage of development that he had . . . he could not go backward . . . but he could not go forwards either without acquiring the language of tensor calculus" (25). While we certainly make no claims to understanding either relativity or tensor calculus, this possibly apocryphal story is important for the case we lay out here. Without the language (and signifying properties) of tensor calculus, according to the story, the pieces of Einstein's theory of relativity simply *weren't*. With that language, the pieces came together into something that *was*.

As all the authors of this chapter have outlined, there are important critiques to be made of the threshold concepts framework and of the project of attempting to articulate these concepts for an entire field. The aspirational threshold concepts here remind us that simply naming accepted and conventional concepts might be important for learners; at the same time, it is both never enough and an endeavor whose very undertaking is in some ways vexed. Both discussions seem essential for the work of a healthy and productive field; that is, continuing to consider, in an ongoing and ever-evolving way, what might be our threshold concepts. At the same time, we must also consider the ideological and material implications of such an effort. Each project, individually and in dialogue with the others, represents attempts to enact inclusive practice. If we want learners and stakeholders to join us in our work, we must be able to clearly and explicitly explain what it is we are doing and what basic assumptions we make that are different from those made in other communities of practice. For those with whom threshold concepts resonate, these concepts can be a way to identify the constituent elements of expertise. In this sense, they provide one way of helping newcomers and nonexperts understand explicitly the values and methodologies and generally agreed-upon findings of a particular field. Without explicitly identifying our threshold concepts, it is too easy for us to serve as gatekeepers or for newcomers to feel confounded by unstated assumptions and values. For our field in particular, not identifying clearly what we know about how writing and language work can leave us powerless to make change in the broader world of policy, testing, legislation, and so forth. Threshold concepts are *one* way to articulate elements of a framework through which we understand the worlds created in and through writing and through which we might bring others into that way of seeing. Doing this work with others is an inclusive practice. But it is not *solely* an inclusive practice.

We must also consider the effects of identifying threshold concepts so the effort itself is as expansive as possible and so threshold concepts are never understood as the only ideas around which we work. There are utilitarian and pragmatic purposes of threshold concept theory—and there are distinct limits to what this kind of theory can offer. Threshold concepts thus are not by any means *the only ideas* we should be discussing with one another and with learners. Naming and exploring threshold concepts for the purposes of welcoming learners and positively influencing policy and legislation around language can be useful and sometimes even necessary—but they are never entirely sufficient for the work of world building and changing making our field has long committed to do.

REFERENCES

Adler-Kassner, Linda, and Elizabeth Wardle, eds. 2015. *Naming What We Know: Threshold Concepts of Writing Studies*. Logan: Utah State University Press.

Alexander, Jonathan. 2017. "Queering What We Know about Writing." *WPA: Writing Program Administration* 41 (1): 137–49.

Alexander, Jonathan, and Michelle Gibson. 2004. "Queer Composition(s): Queer Theory in the Writing Classroom." *JAC* 24 (1): 1–21.

Alexander, Jonathan, and Jacqueline Rhodes. 2011. "Queer: An Impossible Subject for Composition." *JAC* 31 (1–2): 177–206.

Alexander, Jonathan, and Jacqueline Rhodes. 2012. "Queer Rhetoric and the Pleasures of the Archive." *Enculturation* 13. http://enculturation.net/queer-rhetoric-and-the-pleasures-of-the-archive.

Alexander, Jonathan, and David Wallace. 2009. "The Queer Turn in Composition Studies: Reviewing and Assessing an Emerging Scholarship." *College Composition and Communication* 61 (1): W300–W320.

American Educational Research Association, American Psychological Association, and National Council on Measurement in Education. 2014. *Standards for Educational and Psychological Testing*. Washington, DC: American Educational Research Association.

Baillie, Caroline, and Anne Johnson. 2008. "A Threshold Model for Attitudes in First Year Engineering Students." In *Threshold Concepts within the Disciplines*, edited by Ray Land, Jan H. F. Meyer, and Jan Smith, 129–42. Rotterdam: Sense Publishers.

Baxter Magolda, Marcia. 2004. "Evolution of a Constructivist Conceptualization of Epistemological Reflection." *Educational Psychologist* 39 (1): 31–42.

Bazerman, Charles, and Howard Tinberg. 2015. "Text Is an Object Outside of Oneself That Can Be Improved and Developed." In *Naming What We Know: Threshold Concepts of Writing Studies*, edited by Linda Adler-Kassner and Elizabeth Wardle, 61–62. Logan: Utah State University Press.

Bender, Thomas. 1993. *Intellect and Public Life: Essays on the Social History of Academic Intellectuals in the United States*. Baltimore: Johns Hopkins University Press.

Berg, Terje, Morten Erichsen, and Leif M. Hokstad. 2016. "Stuck at the Threshold: Which Strategies Do Students Choose When Facing Liminality within Certain Disciplines at a Business School?" In *Threshold Concepts in Practice*, edited by Ray Land, Jan H. F. Meyer, and Michael T. Flanagan, 107–18. Rotterdam/Boston/Taipei: Sense Publishers.

Berlin, James. 1984. *Writing Instruction in Nineteenth-Century American Colleges*. Carbondale: Southern Illinois University Press.

Berlin, James. 1987. *Rhetoric and Reality: Writing Instruction in American Colleges, 1900–1985*. Carbondale: Southern Illinois University Press.

Berry, Christopher M. 2015. "Differential Validity and Differential Prediction of Cognitive Ability Tests: Understanding Test Bias in the Employment Context." *Annual Review of Organizational Psychology and Organizational Behavior* 2: 435–63.

Brewer, Elizabeth. 2016. "Temporarily Able-Disciplined: Enabling, Disabling, and Cripping Rhetoric and Composition." Presentation at the Conference of the Council of Writing Program Administrators, Raleigh, NC, July 16.

Brooke, Colin, and Jeffrey Grabill. 2015. "Writing Is a Technology through Which Writers Create and Recreate Meaning." In *Naming What We Know: Threshold Concepts of Writing Studies*, edited by Linda Adler-Kassner and Elizabeth Wardle, 32–34. Logan: Utah State University Press.

Cousin, Glynis. 2006. "An Introduction to Threshold Concepts." *Planet* 17 (1). https://www.tandfonline.com/doi/abs/10.11120/plan.2006.00170004.

Davis, Lennard. 2013. "The End of Identity Politics: On Disability as an Unstable Category." In *The Disability Studies Reader*. 4th ed. Edited by Lennard Davis, 263–77. New York: Routledge.

Davies, Jason. 2016. "Threshold Guardians: Threshold Concepts as Guardians of the Discipline." In *Threshold Concepts in Practice*, edited by Ray Land, Jan H. F. Meyer, and Michael T. Flanagan, 121–34. Rotterdam: Sense.

Dolmage, Jay. 2003. "Mapping Composition: Inviting Disability in the Front Door." In *Disability and the Teaching of Writing: A Critical Sourcebook*, edited by Cynthia Lewiecki-Wilson and Brenda Jo Brueggemann, 14–27. Boston: Bedford/St. Martin's.

Dryer, Dylan. 2015. "Writing Is Not Natural." In *Naming What We Know: Threshold Concepts of Writing Studies*, edited by Linda Adler-Kassner and Elizabeth Wardle, 27–28. Logan: Utah State University Press.

Duffy, John. 2015. "Writing Involves Making Ethical Choices." In *Naming What We Know: Threshold Concepts of Writing Studies*, edited by Linda Adler-Kassner and Elizabeth Wardle, 31–32. Logan: Utah State University Press.

Elbow, Peter. 1973. *Writing without Teachers*. Oxford: Oxford University Press.

Elliot, Norbert. 2016. "A Theory of Ethics for Writing Assessment." *Journal of Writing Assessment* 9 (1). http://journalofwritingassessment.org/article.php?article=98.

Elliot, Norbert, Alex Rudniy, Perry Deess, Andrew Klobucar, Regina Collins, and Sharla Sava. 2016. "ePortfolios: Foundational Measurement Issues." *Journal of Writing Assessment* 9 (2). http://journalofwritingassessment.org/article.php?article=110.

Green, David F. Jr. 2016. "Expanding the Dialogue on Writing Assessment at HBCUs: Foundational Assessment Concepts and Legacies of Historically Black Colleges and Universities." *College English* 79 (2): 152–73.

Hammond, J. W. n.d. "Making Our Invisible Racial Agendas Visible: Race Talk in Assessing Writing (1994–2018)." *Assessing Writing* 42 (forthcoming).

Hounsell, Dai, and Charles Anderson. 2009. "Ways of Thinking and Practicing in Biology and History: Disciplinary Aspects of Teaching and Learning Environments." In *The University and Its Disciplines: Teaching and Learning within and beyond Disciplinary Boundaries*, edited by Carolin Kreber, 71–83. New York: Routledge.

Hussar, William J., and Tabitha M. Bailey. 2018. *Projections of Education Statistics to 2026* (NCES 2018-019). US Department of Education, National Center for Education Statistics. Washington, DC: US Government Printing Office. https://nces.ed.gov/pubs2018/2018019.pdf.

Huq, Aminul, Marcia D. Nichols, and Bijaya Aryal. 2016. "Building Blocks: Threshold Concepts and Interdisciplinary Structures of Learning." In *Threshold Concepts in Practice*, edited by Ray Land, Jan H. F. Meyer, and Michael T. Flanagan, 135–51. Rotterdam: Sense.

Inoue, Asao B. 2015. *Antiracist Writing Assessment Ecologies: Teaching and Assessing Writing for a Socially Just Future*. Fort Collins, CO: WAC Clearinghouse and Parlor. https://wac.colostate.edu/books/perspectives/inoue/.

International Organization for Migration. 2017. *World Migration Report 2018*. Geneva: International Organization for Migration. http://publications.iom.int/system/files/pdf/wmr_2018_en.pdf.

Kerschbaum, Stephanie. 2015. "Anecdotal Relations: On Orienting to Disability in the Composition Classroom." *Composition Forum* 32. http://compositionforum.com/issue/32/anecdotal-relations.php.

Law, John. 2004. *After Method: Mess in Social Science Research*. New York: Routledge.

Martindale, Linda, Ray Land, Julie Rattray, and Lorraine Anderson. 2016. "Exploring Sources of Trouble in Research Learning for Undergraduate Nurses." In *Threshold Concepts in Practice*, edited by Ray Land, Jan H. F. Meyer, and Michael T. Flanagan, 239–51. Rotterdam/Boston/Taipei: Sense Publishers.

McCallum, E. L., and Mikko Tuhkanen, eds. 2011. Queer Times, Queer Becomings. Albany: SUNY Press.

McGowan, Susannah. 2016. "The Career of Threshold Concepts in a Large–Lecture History Course: An Examination of Uptake of Disciplinary Actions." In *Threshold Concepts in Practice*, edited by Ray Land, Jan H. F. Meyer, and Michael T. Flanagan, 39–52. Rotterdam/Boston/Taipei: Sense Publishers.

Meyer, Jan H. F., and Ray Land. 2006. Overcoming Barriers to Student Understanding: Threshold Concepts and Troublesome Knowledge. London: Routledge.

Meyer, Jan H. F., Ray Land, and Caroline Baillie, eds. 2010. *Threshold Concepts and Transformational Learning*. Boston: Sense.

Meyer, Jan H. F., Ray Land, and P. Davies. 2008. "Threshold Concepts and Troublesome Knowledge (4): Issues of Variation and Variability." In *Threshold Concepts in Practice*, edited by Ray Land, Jan H. F. Meyer, and Michael T. Flanagan, 59–74. Rotterdam/Boston/Taipei: Sense Publishers.

Mislevy, Robert J., Geneva Haertel, Britte H. Cheng, Liliana Ructtinger, Angela DeBarger, Elizabeth Murray, David Rose, Jenna Gravel, Alexis M. Colker, Daisy Rutsein, and Terry Vendlinski. 2013. "A 'Conditional' Sense of Fairness in Assessment." Educational Research and Evaluation: An International Journal on Theory and Practice 19 (2–3): 121–40.

Monson, Connie, and Jacqueline Rhodes. 2004. "Risking Queer: Pedagogy, Performativity, and Desire in Writing Classrooms." JAC 24 (1): 79–91.

Moss, Pamela A., Diana C. Pullin, James Paul Gee, Edward H. Haertel, and Lauren Jones Young, eds. 2008. Assessment, Equity, and Opportunity to Learn. Cambridge: Cambridge University Press.

Muñoz, José Esteban. 2009. Cruising Utopia: The Then and There of Queer Futurity. New York: New York University Press.

National Council of Teachers of English. 2017. "NCTE Vision Statement." NCTE.org. http://www.ncte.org/mission/vision.

O'Neill, Peggy. 2015. "Assessment Is an Essential Component of Learning to Write." In *Naming What We Know: Threshold Concepts of Writing Studies*, edited by Linda Adler-Kassner and Elizabeth Wardle, 67–68. Logan: Utah State University Press.

Poe, Mya, and Norbert Elliot. N.d. "Evidence of Fairness." *Assessing Writing* 42 (forthcoming)

Poe, Mya, Norbert Elliot, John Aloysius Cogan Jr., and Tito G. Nurudeen Jr. 2014. "The Legal and the Local: Using Disparate Impact Analysis to Understand the Consequences of Writing Assessment." *College Composition and Communication* 65 (4): 588–611.

Poe, Mya, and Asao B. Inoue. 2016. "Toward Writing Assessment as Social Justice: An Idea Whose Time Has Come." *College English* 79 (2): 119–26.

Poe, Mya, Asao B. Inoue, and Norbert Elliot, eds. 2018. *Writing Assessment, Social Justice, and the Advancement of Opportunity*. Fort Collins, CO: WAC Clearinghouse.

Rattray, Julie. 2016. "Affective Dimensions of Liminality." In *Threshold Concepts in Practice*, edited by Ray Land, Jan H. F. Meyer, and Michael T. Flanagan, 67–76. Rotterdam/Boston/Taipei: Sense Publishers.

Reimann, Nicola, and Ian Jackson. 2006. "Threshold Concepts in Economics: A Case Study." In *Overcoming Barriers to Student Understanding: Threshold Concepts and Troublesome Knowledge*, edited by Jan H. F. Meyer and Ray Land, 115–13. London and New York: Routledge/Taylor & Francis Group. Rawls, John. 2001. *Justice as Fairness: A Restatement*. Edited by Erin Kelly. Cambridge, MA: Harvard University Press.

Roozen, Kevin. 2015. "Writing Is Linked to Identity." In *Naming What We Know: Threshold Concepts of Writing Studies*, edited by Linda Adler-Kassner and Elizabeth Wardle, 50–52. Logan: Utah State University Press.

Ruti, Mari. 2017. *The Ethics of Opting Out: Queer Theory's Defiant Subjects*. New York: Columbia University Press.

Scott, Tony, and Asao B. Inoue. 2015. "Assessing Writing Shapes Contexts and Instruction." In Naming What We Know: Threshold Concepts of Writing Studies, edited by Linda Adler-Kassner and Elizabeth Wardle, 29–31. Logan: Utah State University Press.

Sibbett, Caryl, and William Thompson. 2008. "Nettlesome Knowledge, Liminality and Taboo in Cancer and Art Therapy Experiences." In *Threshold Concepts in Practice*, edited by Ray Land, Jan H. F. Meyer, and Michael T. Flanagan, 227–42. Rotterdam/Boston/Taipei: Sense Publishers.

Slomp, David H., Julie A. Corrigan, and Tamiko Sugimoto. 2014. "A Framework for Using Consequential Validity Evidence in Evaluating Large-Scale Writing Assessments: A Canadian Study." Research in the Teaching of English 48 (3): 276–302.

Taylor, Charlotte E. 2006. "Threshold Concepts in Biology: Do They Fit the Definition?" In *Overcoming Barriers to Student Understanding: Threshold Concepts and Troublesome Knowledge*, edited by Jan H. F. Meyer and Ray Land, 87–99. London and New York: Routledge/Taylor & Francis Group.

Teixeira, Ruy, William H. Frey, and Robert Griffin. 2015. States of Change: The Demographic Evolution of the American Electorate, 1974–2060. Washington, DC: Center for American Progress, American Enterprise Institute, and Brookings Institution. https://cdn.americanprogress.org/wp-content/uploads/2015/02/SOC-report1.pdf.

Timmermans, Julie A. 2006. "Changing Our Minds: The Developmental Potential of Threshold Concepts." In *Threshold Concepts in Practice*, edited by Ray Land, Jan H. F. Meyer, and Michael T. Flanagan, 3–20. Rotterdam/Boston/Taipei: Sense Publishers.

Wearn, Andy, Anne O'Callaghan, and Mark Barrow. 2016. "Becoming a Different Doctor: Identifying Threshold Concepts: When Doctors in Training Spend Six Months with a Hospital Palliative Care Team." In *Threshold Concepts in Practice*, edited by Ray Land, Jan H. F. Meyer, and Michael T. Flanagan, 223–238. Rotterdam/Boston/Taipei: Sense Publishers.

Womack, Anne-Marie. 2017. "Teaching Is Accommodation: Universally Designing Composition Classrooms and Syllabi." *College Composition and Communication* 68 (3): 494–525.

Yancey, Kathleen Blake, ed. 1992. *Portfolios in the Writing Classroom: An Introduction*. Urbana, IL: NCTE.

Yancey, Kathleen Blake. 2015. "Writers' Histories, Processes, and Identities Vary." In *Naming What We Know: Threshold Concepts of Writing Studies*, edited by Linda Adler-Kassner and Elizabeth Wardle, 52–54. Logan: Utah State University Press.

Yergeau, Melani, Elizabeth Brewer, Stephanie Kerschbaum, Sushil Oswal, Margaret Price, Cynthia Selfe, Michael J. Salvo, and Franny Howes. 2013. "Multimodality in Motion: Disability and Kairotic Spaces" *Kairos* 18 (1). racti.technorhetoric.net/18.1/coverweb/yergeau-et-al/.

2
LITERACY IS A SOCIOHISTORIC PHENOMENON WITH THE POTENTIAL TO LIBERATE AND OPPRESS

Kate Vieira, Lauren Heap, Sandra Descourtis, Jonathan Isaac, Samitha Senanayake, Brenna Swift, Chris Castillo, Ann Meejung Kim, Kassia Krzus-Shaw, Maggie Black, Ọlá Ọládipọ̀, Xiaopei Yang, Patricia Ratanapraphart, Nikhil M. Tiwari, Lisa Velarde, and Gordon Blaine West

Literacy is sociohistoric phenomenon that has spread widely through the circulation of people, practices, and texts.[1] Understanding the contours of this sociohistoric trend we call *literacy* is essential for effective literacy instruction: whether we are cognizant of it or not, when we intervene in people's literacy development as educators, administrators, researchers, and writers, we are also intervening in history, aligning ourselves with particular ideologies of literacy and distancing ourselves from others. In other words, the social history of literacy profoundly matters for our work in the present.

While literacy is commonly understood as a set of skills, and while skills play a role in how it is experienced, current literacy research takes a wider view to understand literacy as a set of sociohistorically situated practices. Defining literacy in this way means *what we know* about literacy primarily derives from studies of how it has been used, defined, and experienced in particular settings. For example, some influential studies have examined literacy's use: among segregated working-class communities in the South (Heath 1983), multiliterate communities in Liberia (Scribner and Cole 1981), religious communities in Iran (Street 1984), African American churchgoers (Moss 2002), college students (Brandt 1990), inner-city residents (Cushman 1998), biliterate Mexican labor migrants (Kalmar 2001), Tuvalu islanders (Besnier 1995), and the list goes on. One of the conceptual problems arising from studying literacy in particular contexts is that there appears to be no easy way to

DOI: 10.7330/9781607329329.c002

generalize about literacy's consequences. Subsequently, we can't really say what literacy *does* to a people or a society.

But what we can talk about—and talk about in theoretically rich and grounded ways, ways that have consequences for teaching and research—is what literacy *can* do under certain social conditions. And grounded studies of literacy practices in particular settings, like the ones we cite above, provide an important guide. The trick to understanding literacy, they reveal, is that it is almost never *on its own.* It is always tied up in complex agendas, personal histories, technological changes, shifting winds of power, individual bodies. For this reason, it is incumbent upon educators and researchers to understand the conditions under which literacy can liberate, and the conditions under which it can oppress.

In this chapter, we first describe the broad contours of some ways literacy has been used to oppress and liberate. Then, each subsequent section explains how particular aspects of literacy—its connection to identity, its status as a racialized social process, its embodiment, its materiality, its economic purchase—participate in oppression and liberation. This treatment of *what we know* about literacy is not exhaustive. (After all, it also begs the question of who exactly "we" are.) But our hope is that this synthesis of some widely understood ways literacy can act in contexts of inequality will serve as an invitation to readers to see literacy in their lives, classrooms, and communities in critical ways, perhaps adding their own analyses of literacy's consequences to *what we know*. To aid readers in this project, we end with implications of what literacy's embeddedness in a sociohistorical context means for socially just literacy education. In this way, this chapter extends concepts outlined in the original *Naming What We Know* (Adler-Kassner and Wardle 2015) in order to more fully account for the sociohistorical influences that continue to shape ideologies of literacy and literacy events. We push here for an active and critical stance towards literacy, one that calls for using what we know in the service of more equitable and just educational practices.[2]

LITERACY CAN BOTH OPPRESS AND LIBERATE
LAUREN HEAP AND KATE VIEIRA

Literacy is so often touted as an unconditional good that its use as a political tool to oppress people often gets erased. But in order to responsibly use and teach literacy, researchers, educators, and everyday writers and readers should be aware of its problematic history.

People and institutions have taken up literacy to colonize the Americas (Mignolo 2003); to promote the interests of corporations above those of ordinary readers and writers (Brandt 2001; Graff 1991); to racially engineer social groups (Prendergast 2004); to reinforce global educational inequities (Stornaiuolo and LeBlanc 2016); to regulate the movement of people of color across borders through immigration papers (Vieira 2016) and otherwise perpetuate immigrants' "legal, economic, and cultural exclusion" (Wan 2014, 35); as a stand-in for anti–African American racism, thereby promoting white supremacy (Young 2009); and as a punishable offense, particularly for enslaved African Americans who learned to write (Cornelius 1991). This list is necessarily incomplete, and clearly some ways literacy has been used to oppress are more nefarious than others. Nonetheless, this accumulation of historical instances points to how literacy's ideologies and technologies can be mobilized to enact violence (Stuckey 1991).

At the same time, because liberation and oppression exist in a dichotomy housed within hegemony, literacy can also be liberatory. For example, that writing among people of color has been considered dangerous to white supremacy in the example above highlights its liberatory potential. How to best use literacy for liberatory purposes has been a subject of much research. For example, liberatory pedagogue Paulo Freire (1970), in his work with Brazilian peasants pre-military dictatorship, argued for literacy as a way to dismantle oppressive structures. As Freire put it, reading the word and reading (and rewriting) the world is a dynamic process. Others have emphasized the power of critical and expressive discourse to help writers and readers develop empowered identities, social visions, and social change. To offer another necessarily incomplete list of examples, methods of critical and expressive discourse have been taken up in urban classrooms (Camangian 2015; Weinstein 2009), in programs for formerly incarcerated girls (Winn 2011), among Cherokee Indians developing and using their own syllabary (Cushman 2011), to develop syncretic historic and embodied narratives in a university migrant leadership program (Gutiérrez 2008), and in using feminista/chicana educational approaches among high-school girls whose lives have been impacted by violence in Juárez, Mexico (Cervantes-Soon 2017).

These examples of liberatory literacy pedagogy teach that literacy has the potential to be transformative: as we practice our literacies, we in turn change through that practice (Delpit 1993; Prior and Shipka 2003; Rosenblatt 1994), and as we make our writing public, our words can change the world (Lorde 1984). Literacy, as Freire theorized, involves action. Such change can be geared towards liberatory ends, giving literacy the potential to reform rather than conform to systems of hegemony.

As a result, educators have the power to shape literacy's consequences for students. There is a popular idea that education and teachers should be neutral, not pushing political agendas or religious beliefs, but literacy, as a sociohistoric phenomenon that resonates with the power dynamics with which it comes into contact, can never be neutral. Literacy's legacy lingers in contemporary practices. For example, morality has historically been tied up in the spread of many Western literacies with concerns for the souls of receivers of literacy instruction, and morality remains an integral aspect of many literacy pedagogies and ideologies. These ideologies and others reverberate through everyday literacy practices, with the result that educators, readers, and writers are influenced in ways they may not fully realize. A critical awareness of literacy's potential to both liberate and oppress, then, is crucial for socially just writing and writing pedagogy. The rest of this chapter highlights particular areas on which readers may focus such awareness and, finally, how such awareness may be enacted in classrooms.

LITERACY AND IDENTITY ARE COCONSTITUTIVE

SANDRA DESCOURTIS, JONATHAN ISAAC,
SAMITHA SENANAYAKE, AND BRENNA SWIFT

In the first edition of *Naming What We Know*, Kevin Roozen writes about the threshold concept *writing is linked to identity* (Roozen 2016, 50). We want to build on that notion here: *literacy* (including but not limited to writing) and identity are *coconstitutive*, by which we mean they are mutually informing and reinforcing. Our identities—corresponding to class, race, gender, sexual orientation, ability, citizenship status, and other identity markers—are entirely imbricated in how literacy is enacted, constrained, and operationalized.

Scholars (Baxter 2003; Brandt 1998; Cornelius 1991; Kalmar 2001) have long pointed out that powerful interests actively suppress or extend literacy access to marginalized people who inhabit nondominant identities—identities such as immigrant, queer, poor, disabled, Black, trans, and others. Deborah Brandt (1998) reminds us that acquiring literacy skills (reading and writing but also nonalphabetic literacy) and engaging in literate practices comes with a financial, political, or ideological cost often shaped by the economic and material needs of powerful institutions—needs that tend to exploit those already at the margins of society. Failing to see literacy and its acquisition through the prism of identity and power has *real* consequences—it cuts off an understanding of literacy acquisition as a political project and prevents a more nuanced understanding of how we can work to enact more just literacy practices and pedagogy.

If we recognize literacy and identity as coconstitutive, then, we can see literacies, including nonacademic and nonalphabetic literacies, as enacting "identity kits," the complex discourses and sets of practices associated with particular social roles (Gee 2015). In this way, literacy becomes something people *do*, not something they simply possess (Kynard 2013).

Seeing literacy as something one *does* moves beyond the focus on discrete skills acquired in classroom settings to emphasize a more complete set of "social and cultural practices" surrounding identity and representation (Kynard 2013, 32). In particular, the research programs of Brandt and Kate Vieira have highlighted literacy as self-representation—the (re)definition of identity—and collective action (Miller 2016). Their work allows us to recognize the myriad expressions of identity that can disrupt systems of oppression—expressions that can include poetry (Ife 2016) and rap (which University of Virginia hip-hop professor A. D. Carson famously used to deliver his dissertation). Fully acknowledging the recursive connections among literacy, identity, and self-representation will help us move past simplistic constructions of literacy that further the role of literacy instruction in perpetuating oppression. Recognizing that literacy and identity are coconstitutive might instead support literacy's role as a tool of resistance for people from marginalized groups, who have historically used both academic and nonacademic literacies to intervene in dominant ideologies. In this way, it may also contribute to context-sensitive understandings of threshold concepts themselves (Blaauw-Hara et al., this volume).

WRITING IS RACIALIZED

CHRIS CASTILLO AND ANN MEEJUNG KIM

While writing may seem to be a skill or means of communication that has nothing to do with race, every act of writing is racialized. In this section, we explain how. But before we get started, a quick refrain. We are international scholars of color. We diverge at points in this section from standard academic English, what linguists have called the *language of wider communication* (LWC), as a direct result of our awareness of the legacy of LWC as a construct associated with whiteness (Smitherman 2006). Our desire to incorporate aspects of African American vernacular English here derives from our continued study of people of color's language practices and from our desire to acknowledge and validate those practices—especially as those language practices serve as knowledge bases and influenced our own written and speech patterns and styles. But we ain't code switchers. We code breakers. We take the patterns and styles in the LWC and break them, play with them, and rebuild them for our own purposes and projects. We are one from Korea and one from the Chi, and our language "sprang out of the need to identify ourselves as a distinct people" (Anzaldúa 1987, 55). In a country where English is the standard, we can identify neither with the standard language nor with the language we speak at home, in the streets, or at work. So we created our own. We bring this linguistic invention into this section to exemplify our central point: that writing is racialized.

First, race ain't an inherent quality of writing. Rather, race is attached to writing over time and on multiple levels. It occurs simultaneously in a specific time and space and also across time and space; it occurs at home and in institutions; it occurs online and on paper; it occurs with family and with colleagues. The racialization of writing is so central to the infrastructure of North American life—so normalized—that the process is nearly invisible.[3]

Second, as a result of writing's racialization, literacy education is also a raced and racializing process. Ever since literacy scholar Shirley Brice Heath uncovered the profound ways working-class White and working-class African American children develop language skills differently, scholars have called for the need to focus their attention more explicitly on how racial differences in literacy education are socially, materially, politically, and historically produced. Such scholars have shown how literacy is (unjustly) treated as a "white property" (Ladson-Billings 2003) and a "white property right" (Prendergast 2004), belonging to Whites and systematically withheld from racially marginalized Others, perpetuating racial educational inequality.

Third, such racial inequities can inhere in the scholarly, aesthetic, and pedagogical values ascribed to academic writing. In institutions of higher education, for example, the first-year writing course often acts as a as a checkpoint of assimilation. As most first-year writing courses dedicate themselves to instructing their students on the conventions of academic writing, and most institutions of higher education require students to complete a first-year writing course, the success of students in higher education can hinge on their ability to "write white" "in order to compete with 'White Americans'" (Fordham quoted in Young 2009, 129). But, when some students try to give alphabetic form to their oral configurations of language, certain instructors do not take into account the "oral language paradigms and practices that shape the writing of some ESD students [English as a second dialect students]" (Coleman 2017, 487). As a result, instructors who adhere to traditional notions of academic writing often tell students *ain't* is an antiquated word no longer used in wider circulation. They often tell students to remove contractions in their writing, to spell *can't* as *cannot*. They often tell students to add a *g* at the end of the suffix *ing* and to include an *a* in the conjunction *and*.[4] In other words, such instructors can hear and see the linguistic variations in student's speech patterns and writing but assume there is something wrong or incomplete in their use of language.

Schools often reinforce such ideologies by measuring student writing "based on the kinds of scholarship that have traditionally been published" (Stanford 2011, 118). These assessment practices can "reproduce social outcomes that arrange groups of people along ostensibly racial lines" (Inoue 2012, 6). In this view, academic writin' is white writin', nd academic writin' is good writin' (Flores and Rosa 2015). Such associations can also adhere to racially marked multilingual writers, as there is a tendency in first-language composition to categorize such writers into an ESL, EFL, ELL, L2 "division of labor" (Matsuda 2006). Thus, through the circulation and recirculation of academic writin' in schools, journals, and books, good writin' can come to be associated with whiteness.

Writing's association with whiteness in institutions of higher education, however, ain't left unchallenged in North America. Beginning with the recognition that people develop particular dialects based on specific sociohistorical context (NCTE's Students' Right to their Own Language), and following with the notion that people learn to crystallize those dialects with the aid of others in particular sociocultural settings (Moll, Sáez, and Dworin 2001), writing teachers have transitioned towards leveraging dialects "as a resource for producing meaning in writing, speaking, reading, and listening" (Horner et al. 2011, 303). In the first-year writing classroom, they have included pedagogical practices such as "self-directed writing" (Lovejoy 2014), "expressivist writing" (Palmeri 2012), "multigenre research papers" (Welford 2011), and debate activities that emphasize the use of one's own language in writing and speech (Graff 1991). All these pedagogical practices leverage student voices in order to ensure students not only learn to speak and write in their own dialect but also become exposed to other dialects they can combine with their own unique mode of talking and writing. Students, then, can agentively intervene in the racialization of writing through their own writing processes.

LITERACY IS EMBODIED
Kassia Krzus-Shaw

In the original *Naming What We Know*, the threshold concept *writing is (also always) a cognitive activity* recognizes how psychoanalytic and physiological conditions factor into embodied writing practices. This section builds on this foundation to describe how literacy is rooted in socially and spatially situated bodily experiences—and how such embodiment matters (Canagarajah 2018; Prior and Shipka 2003).

Writing is rooted in bodily expression, whether due to our sensorium response to the material world, a visceral gut response, emotional distribution through literacy's materials, or the body's situatedness in its environment (Ahmed 2010; Fleckenstein 2003; Hawhee 2015; Merleau-Ponty 1962; Perl 2004). Regardless of how literacy is expressed within its socially contextual limitations, when the body enacts literacy, it carries the shape of its material surroundings (Squier 2004). This relationship is simultaneously empowering and limiting, especially when the boundaries between body and text, inside and outside, blur and accentuate power and social hierarchies (Crowley and Selzer 1999; Mackenzie 2009; Pennebaker and Evans 2014). Scholars such as Cherríe Moraga and Gloria Anzaldúa (2002), Jacqueline Rhodes and Jonathan Alexander (2015), Malea Powell (2012), Elaine Richardson (2006), and others have worked to show how this connection effectively shapes literacy responses of resistance to oppressive power structures. In these situations, literacy moves through, by, and beyond the body to create recursive relationships with one's cultural, social, and material environment (Crowley and Selzer 1999).

Bodies also act as an "epistemological site" for literacy (Crowley and Selzer 1999; Owens and Van Ittersum 2013), meaning bodies are marked with social and cultural labels. Sharon Crowley and Jack Selzer describe such labels as "sexed, raced, gendered, abled or disabled, whole or fragmented, aged or young, fat, thin, or anorexic" (361). When bodies "inhabit" spaces through these labels, they become a "site" of meaning-making. For example, bodies marked as "illiterate" may experience obstacles for accessing the material conditions of literacy, furthering reifying power structures.

Such bodily labels shape—but do not determine—the performance of individual literacy practices. Someone marked as "illiterate" may circumvent the traditional space of literacy (by choosing a community commons instead of a classroom) to deliver a powerful message of resistance. They might do so by altering the expected genres of literacy (musical lyrics instead of a written document), by using unexpected tools of literacy (spray paint instead of a pen), challenging norms of authorship (community collaboration versus individual work), or creating new terms of literacy altogether. These practices and performances extend from the body in response to social labels through cultural and material processes with distributed social consequences (Haas and Witte 2001).

Literacy is likewise always practiced by individuals with diverse bodily contexts, including a range of abilities. For example, we know bodies can change and adapt in response to the social contexts of literacy (Miller 2016; Walters 2014). Drawing on the insights of disability studies, Elisabeth Miller's study of the writing practices of people with aphasia has pointed out that the body is a "technology of literacy." The body as a literacy technology is often enacted through performance and play to create new spaces that directly challenge normative literacy practices, thereby creating new literacy frameworks (Kerschbaum 2014). Though many of these practices and frameworks are often unacknowledged by dominant and normative social contexts, understanding literacy as embodied provides opportunities to recognize bodily agency and performance possibilities as critical literacies (Crowley and Selzer 1999; Hawhee 2004; Knoblauch 2012). In other words, as Anne-Marie Womack describes in this volume, recognizing literacy as rooted in the bodily experience can afford opportunities to push back against the established social and material boundaries of literacy in creative new ways.

LITERACY IS MATERIAL

MAGGIE BLACK, QLÁ QLÁDIPỌ̀, KASSIA KRZUS-SHAW, AND XIAOPEI YANG

Literacy is not just something we do, it is also something that is. It lives in the pen, the spray paint (Cintrón 1997), the printing press (Eisenstein 2005), the post office (Vincent 2000), the internet (Vee 2013). In other words, literacy is a "thing . . . , still there after the people around it are gone" (Brandt and Clinton 2002, 348). Because literacy is popularly thought of as a skill—decoding words on a page, for example—its material aspect is often overlooked. But its status as a "thing" matters for the issues of equity that animate this chapter.

The materiality of literacy interacts with its social contexts, which can imbue those materials with power. For example, immigration papers can resonate with state authority (Vieira 2016), diplomas can resonate with educational prestige, and laptops gifted to family members can resonate with love (Vieira 2019). Put differently, "Literacies are materialized in things," or objects that give them meaning and power (Burnett et al. 2014, 12). Our interactions with and around those objects shape our literacy practices, making literacy simultaneously something one does (see "Literacy and Identity" above) and some *thing*.

Literacy's "thingness" also means it can travel (Brandt 2001) and become recontextualized in new spaces (Kell 2009). Let us, for example, consider this aspect of writing in the context of transnational migration. When people make the decision to migrate, they take their literacies with them. But, they may have to adapt those literacies to suit the social and economic realities of their destination. It is also a common practice for migrants to stay connected to those they left back home through texts, emails, and calls. In this context, the thingness of literacy is exemplified in how it is transferred across borders between migrants and their family members in their homeland. Email exchanges, video calls, and the gift of devices that aid communication serve not only as markers of love but also as avenues for family members to acquire new forms of literacies—such as digital literacy and composition skills (Vieira 2018). Understanding the inherent power of literacy to travel across time and space is essential for two reasons. First, it highlights the often-ignored and nontraditional spaces where literacy acquisition takes place (Delgado Bernal, Burciaga, and Flores Carmona 2012). Second, such knowledge also casts a broader light on the power of literacy to connect people in an age of neoliberal globalization.

Literacy's materiality is also a crucial piece of its meaning-making ability, making attention to multimodality a powerful site for learning (Rowsell 2012; Shipka 2011; Vasudevan 2014) and communication (Madianou and Miller 2012). Multimodality helps individuals move beyond the confinement of texts and imagine new ways of meaning-making. For instance, a study of the link between multimodality and belonging has shown how diverse groups of young people make "meaning in the everyday moments of intercultural communication and narrative encounters" (Vasudevan 2014, 64).

Literacy's sociomateriality (Vieira 2016) means such technological changes interact with sociohistorical changes. Every literacy has a lifespan because literacy is context based and forms a part of larger material human and nonhuman systems. Its incarnations, and the value of these incarnations, thus differ across generations, making it an "an unstable currency," volatile and always evolving in relation to social norms, economic shifts, and technological innovation (Brandt 2001, 9). These changes often give rise to new forms of literacies, devalue or lower the status of old literacies, or sometimes add values to them. Thus, the values and expectations of literacy, the conditions under which literacy is produced, circulated, and acquired, are always taking on new material forms—forms that merit our attention for the social power they embody and confer.

LITERACY IS AN ECONOMIC RESOURCE
Kate Vieira

We often think of literacy as having more to do with expression and meaning-making than with money and finances, yet literacy is deeply imbricated in economic transactions, making economics (along with religion and government) one of the central "domains" of literacy (Goody 1986). Understanding literacy's often hidden relationship to money is key to understanding its potential to both liberate and oppress.

First, literacy fuels economic growth in many societies. For example, in ancient Mesopotamia, one of the birthplaces of writing, a complex inscription system involving clay tablets was developed to document who did and did not pay taxes. This writing-based bureaucratic structure allowed the temple economy to manage agricultural production and thus grow (Schmandt-Besserat 1980). This is one of the ways literacy can become, as Annette Vee (2013) has pointed out, "infrastructural" to a society.

Second, just as literacy can contribute to economic growth, so too does literacy require economic investment. Writing in particular requires raw materials, specialized human labor, and the technological development to make that writing happen. For example, the rise of literacy in medieval England depended on wax to seal envelopes (materials), scribes (labor), and quills (technology) (Clanchy 2013).

Third, as an economic resource, literacy's financial value is often dictated by laws of supply and demand. In the example of medieval England above, for example, where wax or ink was in short supply, fewer people could be trained to be scribes, making the work of writing, crucial to the king's increasingly bureaucratic reign, more valuable (Clanchy 2013). Likewise, in the wake of state investment in public education in modern

Europe, literacy was less remunerable as an individual skill because there was a surplus of it (Vincent 2000).

The result is that the value of peoples' literacies often shifts—many times unexpectedly and inequitably—in concert with larger political and economic trends. This volatile valuation of literacy is perhaps uniquely visible in transnational environments. In sites as diverse as postcommunist Slovakia (Prendergast 2008), the Mexico-United States border (Hernández-Zamora 2010), Central Africa (Blommaert 2008), and the Philippines (Lagman 2015), the economic consequences of global neoliberalism often curtail peoples' abilities to trade their literacy training for fair compensation. As literacy is carried across unequally positioned national borders, the value of migrants' literacy often depreciates (Lorimer Leonard 2013).

If the example above reveals how literacy is inequitably valued across geographic space, literacy research has also shown how literacy can be inequitably valued across historical time, especially as literacy standards change. Put simply, a high-school diploma is not worth as much today as it was fifty years ago. As literacy standards change, some people are economically lifted (think computer coders), and others are left behind (think typists). Keeping up with changing literacy standards requires investment—investment that depending on age, gender, race, social class, and other positions—is not equally accessible. Based on a study of oral histories of literacy collected in Wisconsin, representing lives across the twentieth century, literacy scholar Brandt (1998) called this uneven process of literacy's spread "sponsorship," whereby corporations and other distant agents invest in the literacy practices of particular people in order to extract that literacy and thereby gain by it. Dependent on the vagaries of capitalist production imperatives in the knowledge economy, systems of sponsorship can entrench inequitable access to literacy and therefore access to its economic benefits.

Just as larger economic forces—the temple economy, global neoliberalism, colonization, oligarchy—can shape what writers earn from their writing, so too can savvy and strategic writers leverage their literacy skills to make money. Consider a few selective examples of how ordinary people have leveraged writing for economic gain: indigenous communities in Peru used Khippu, a native meaning-making system involving knotting, to counter the power of the Spanish alphabet (Saloman and Niño-Murcia 2011). In another quite different context, a 2011 study of online poker players revealed how expert authors leveraged both their reputations and internet savvy for maximum cash for selling high-priced poker strategy manuals (Laquintano 2010). And in contemporary computer-coding bootcamps, low-income adults of color are learning computer coding in the hopes of entering into well-remunerated careers (albeit with uneven results) (Byrd 2020). Under certain historical conditions, writing can be a financially advantageous undertaking for those who can adapt—and keep adapting—to markets, technologies, institutions, and conventions (Watkins 2015).

In sum, literacy is deeply imbricated in the economic realm. It is never free. As literacy scholar Allan Luke (1996) notes, the value of literacy often depends on its market value and on individuals' access to institutions that can interpret or convert these literacy resources into material resources. An awareness of its cost and its tendency to exploitation by powerful financial interests entails a responsibility on the part of scholars, educators, and writers committed to equity: to be aware of the inequitable distribution of literacy; to commit to broad access to it; to promote socially just economic policies; and to cultivate, value, and invest in public writing.

CONCLUSION: SOCIALLY JUST LITERACY PEDAGOGY ADDRESSES POWER, CONTEXT, AND HISTORY

PATRICIA RATANAPRAPHART, NIKHIL M. TIWARI, LISA VELARDE, AND GORDON BLAINE WEST

The previous sections have delineated how literacy's imbrication in identity, race, the body, materiality, and economics can contribute to its potential to liberate or oppress. But what does "what we know" about literacy in these respects mean for how we teach it? Here we suggest that precisely because literacy has been used to oppress, subjugate, and dehumanize, pedagogically it must be used to directly counter oppressive uses of literacy. As we describe below, to enact liberatory literacy pedagogy within an increasingly globalized world requires a recognition of not only how literacy practices are embedded within specific contexts but also of how these practices are networked across space and time and utilize a number of materials and modalities (Canagarajah 2018; Hawkins 2018).

How literacy is taken up and operationalized is related to how it is understood. On one hand, it is often used as a tool to reproduce normative practices. On the other hand, it can be seen and taught as a social practice situated within contexts, housed within ideologies, and embodied within the mind, the body, and the material. What teachers believe to be the purpose of literacy is therefore undergirded by what they understand to be the consequences of it in the lives of their students. When mobilized for liberatory purposes, it tends to space and historicity, as well as the conflicts and tensions of individuals' lived experiences (Freire 1970; Gutiérrez 2008; Winn 2011). Socially just literacy pedagogy may, therefore, foster opportunities for rich discussions and action around the ideologies that are transmitted and resisted in the act of be(come)ing literate in a particular space and time.[5]

Liberation, however, is a tricky concept. In looking at literacy as a contextually situated practice, the act of becoming literate involves taking on values and beliefs and ways of being. Some have argued that when literacy is seen in this way, not everyone has access to or can gain access to those literacies (Gee 2015). Others, however, argue that people, especially nondominant groups, can master, and should master, secondary, dominant discourses. They claim doing so will also empower individuals to shape those discourses in more equitable ways, since literacies and discourses are fluid and dynamic (Delpit 1993). Recent work in the field has made the case that for literacy to be truly liberatory, its conceptualization must be defined by marginalized groups to serve the needs they feel will best benefit their own liberation (Cervantes-Soon 2017; Kalmar 2001; Winn 2011).

To confront power, literacy pedagogy often draws on and privileges individual experiences and narratives to help learners establish authorship of their own stories in opposition to the stories that have been imposed on them. One example of this type of pedagogy is *testimonio*, "a genre that exposes brutality, disrupts silencing, and builds solidarity," especially as it has been developed by Chicana feminists (Delgado Bernal, Burciaga, and Flores Carmona 2012, 363). *Testimonio* takes different forms, from formal written pieces, to performance pieces, to informal conversations among peers. The learning of literacy in this way allows for new literacy users to author their own stories in opposition to the stories of self and identity that have been imposed on them (Gutiérrez 2008). It might also promote the kind of open-minded "deep reading" Patrick Sullivan describes as a way to engage with *testimonio*, to hear the experiences of others (this volume).

In other contexts, under different forms of oppression, this power of authorship affords different possibilities. Developing literacy and pedagogies take shape in response to the needs of communities in these different contexts. Often, grassroots efforts emerge in response to injustices and are formed by individual and collective efforts to speak back to power and write paths to liberation. For example, Kalmar describes how a migrant worker community in the United States used biliteracy in ways that crossed and rewrote the social and linguistic borders that continue to violently perpetuate injustices. (Kalmar 2001). And in this volume, Anne-Marie Womack uses a disability studies lens to describe the liberatory potential of writing under accessible conditions. Thus, literacy pedagogy may act as a medium through which possibilities are both imagined and enacted.

Playfulness and creativity are also key in developing subversive literacy pedagogies, particularly as they emerge from both individual and collective needs. As shown in Tomás Mario Kalmar's (2001) examples of learning *liricamente*, Spanish speakers learned English from other community members through the creative and coconstructed development of dictionaries that drew from Spanish language and literacy practices. Maisha T. Winn (2011) shares a different example of the importance of play in developing subversive literacies for liberation. In her work, young women in a prison-industrial complex worked collectively to both write and perform their own stories. Similarly, Anne Haas Dyson's (1997) work with young learners brought to light the transformative power of creativity. By engaging popular culture in both writing and play, young children investigated different identities, negotiated understandings of their world, and authored storylines that ran counter to official school curricula. Thus, playfulness allows for a space in which dominant literacies and power can be reimagined. Play, in fact, might be a pedagogically productive way to mediate the "unsettling shifts in perspective" the process of learning about threshold concepts themselves can provoke (Mutnick, this volume). In this space, the authoring of stories is often the first step in acting differently in the world to gain degrees of liberation.

In thinking about the pedagogical implications for teaching literacy, teachers should begin with three questions in mind: How does literacy function as an oppressive force in the lives of students? How might varied embodied and performed literacy practices serve as means to interrogate and challenge inequities? And finally, what are the possibilities literacy pedagogy can afford in creating a more socially just world?

NOTES

1. When we discuss literacy as a social trend, we use *literacy* in the singular for conceptual clarity around its implications, which coalesce around certain axes, what we have identified here as *liberation* and *oppression*. In other moments, we use *literacies* in the plural to emphasize the vibrant diversity and multiplicity of practices, perspectives, and contexts.
2. We build in particular from concept three in the original *Naming What We Know*.
3. This process of attaching "racial meaning to a previously racially unclassified . . . social practice" over time is precisely the process that racializes writing (Omi and Winant 2015, 64).

4. The phonetic variation of the word *and* as *nd* can be heard in the hook (that is, chorus) of Dr. Dre's and Snoop Dogg's song "Nutin' But a 'G' Thang" and in many other hip-hop lyrics that both inform and build from AAVE.
5. The act of becoming literate also includes ethical assessment, to which a social justice orientation can contribute (Hammond, Poe, and Elliot, ch. 1 in this volume).

REFERENCES

Adler-Kassner, Linda, and Elizabeth Wardle, eds. 2015. *Naming What We Know: Threshold Concepts of Writing Studies*. Logan: Utah State University Press.

Ahmed, Sara. 2010. *The Promise of Happiness*. Durham, NC: Duke University Press.

Anzaldúa, Gloria. 1987. *Borderlands/La Frontera*. San Francisco: Aunt Lute.

Baxter, Judith. 2003. *Positioning Gender in Discourse: A Feminist Methodology*. London: Palgrave.

Besnier, Niko. 1995. *Literacy, Emotion and Authority: Reading and Writing on a Polynesian Atoll*. New York: Cambridge University Press.

Blommaert, Jan. 2008. *Grassroots Literacies: Identity and Voice in South Central Africa*. New York: Routledge.

Brandt, Deborah. 1990. *Literacy as Involvement: The Acts of Writers, Readers, and Texts*. Carbondale: Southern Illinois University Press.

Brandt, Deborah. 1998. "Sponsors of Literacy." *College Composition and Communication* 49 (2): 165–85.

Brandt, Deborah. 2001. *Literacy in American Lives*. New York: Cambridge University Press.

Brandt, Deborah, and Katie Clinton. 2002. "Limits of the Local: Expanding Perspectives on Literacy as a Social Practice." *Journal of Literacy Research* 34 (3): 337–56.

Burnett, Cathy, Guy Merchant, Kate Pahl, and Jennifer Rowsell. 2014. "The (Im)Materiality of Literacy: The Significance of Subjectivity to New Literacies Research." *Discourse: Studies in the Cultural Politics of Education* 35 (1): 90–103.

Byrd, Antonio. 2020. "'Like Coming Home': African American Adults Tinkering and Playing Toward a Code Bootcamp." *College Composition and Communication*.

Camangian, Patrick Roz. 2015. "Teach Like Lives Depend on It: Agitate, Arouse, and Inspire." *Urban Education* 50 (4): 424–53.

Canagarajah, Suresh. 2018. "Translingual Practice as Spatial Repertoires: Expanding the Paradigm beyond Structuralist Orientations." *Applied Linguistics* 39 (1): 31–54.

Cervantes-Soon, Claudia G. 2017. *Juárez Girls Rising: Transformative Education in Times of Dystopia*. Minneapolis: University of Minnesota Press.

Cintrón, Ralph. 1997. *Angels' Town: Chero Ways, Gang Life, and the Rhetoric of the Everyday*. Boston: Beacon Press.

Clanchy, T. Michael. 2013. *From Memory to Written Record: Europe 1066–1307*. Malden, MA: Wiley-Blackwell.

Coleman, Charles F. 2017. "Our Students Write with Accents: Oral Paradigms for ESD Students." *College Composition and Communication* 48 (4): 486–500.

Cornelius, Janet Duitsman. 1991. *"When I Can Read My Title Clear": Literacy, Slavery, and Religion in the Antebellum South*. Columbia: University of South Carolina Press.

Crowley, Sharon, and Jack Selzer, eds. 1999. *Rhetorical Bodies*. Madison: University of Wisconsin Press.

Cushman, Ellen. 1998. *The Struggle and the Tools: Oral and Literate Strategies in an Inner City Community*. Albany: SUNY Press.

Cushman, Ellen. 2011. *The Cherokee Syllabary: Writing the People's Perseverance*. Norman: University of Oklahoma Press.

Delgado Bernal, Dolores, Rebeca Burciaga, and Judith Flores Carmona. 2012. "Chicana/Latina Testimonios: Mapping the Methodological, Pedagogical, and Political." *Equity & Excellence in Education* 45 (3): 363–72.

Delpit, Lisa. 1993. "The Politics of Teaching Literate Discourse." In *Freedom's Plough: Teaching in the Multicultural Classroom*, edited by Theresa Perry and James W. Fraser, 285–95. New York: Routledge.

Dyson, Anne Haas. 1997. *Writing Superheroes: Contemporary Childhood, Popular Culture, and Classroom Literacy*. New York: Teachers College Press.

Eisenstein, Elizabeth L. 2005. *The Printing Revolution in Early Modern Europe*. New York: Cambridge University Press.

Fleckenstein, Kristie S. 2003. *Embodied Literacies: Imageword and a Poetics of Teaching*. Carbondale: Southern Illinois University Press.

Flores, Nelson, and Jonathan Rosa. 2015. "Undoing Appropriateness: Raciolinguistic Ideologies and Language Diversity in Education." *Harvard Educational Review* 85 (2): 149–71.

Freire, Paulo. 1970. *Pedagogy of the Oppressed*. New York: Seabury.

Gee, James Paul. 2015. *Social Linguistics and Literacies: Ideology in Discourses*. 5th ed. New York: Routledge.

Goody, Jack. 1986. *The Logic of Writing and the Organization of Society*. Cambridge: Cambridge University Press.

Graff, Harvey J. 1991. *The Literacy Myth: Cultural Integration and Social Structure in the Nineteenth Century*. New Brunswick, NJ: Transaction Publishers.

Gutiérrez, Kris D. 2008. "Developing a Sociocritical Literacy in the Third Space." *Reading Research Quarterly* 43 (2): 148–64.

Haas, Christina, and Stephen Witte. 2001. "Writing as an Embodied Practice: The Case of Engineering Standards." *Journal of Business and Technical Communication* 15 (4): 413–57.

Hawhee, Debra. 2004. *Bodily Arts: Rhetoric and Athletics in Ancient Greece*. Austin: University of Texas Press.

Hawhee, Debra. 2015. "Rhetoric's Sensorium." *Quarterly Journal of Speech* 101 (1): 2–17.

Hawkins, Margaret R. 2018. "Transmodalities and Transnational Encounters: Fostering Critical Cosmopolitan Relations." *Applied Linguistics* 39 (1): 55–77.

Heath, Shirley Brice. 1983. *Ways with Words: Language, Life and Work in Communities and Classrooms*. New York: Cambridge University Press.

Hernández-Zamora, Gregorio. 2010. *Decolonizing Literacy: Mexican Lives in an Era of Global Capitalism*. Bristol: Multilingual Matters.

Horner, Bruce, Min-Zhan Lu, Jacqueline Jones Royster, and John Trimbur. 2011. "Language Difference in Writing: Toward a Translingual Approach." *College English* 73 (3): 303–21.

Ife, Fahima. 2016. "Maktivist Literacies: Black Women's Making, Activism, and Writing in DIY Spaces." PhD diss., University of Wisconsin–Madison.

Inoue, Asao B. 2012. "Grading Contracts: Assessing Their Effectiveness on Different Racial Formations." In *Race and Writing Assessment*, edited by Asao B. Inoue and Mya Poe, 79–94 New York: Peter Lang.

Kalmar, Tomás Mario. 2001. *Illegal Alphabets and Adult Biliteracy: Latino Migrants Crossing the Linguistic Border*. New York: Routledge.

Kell, Catherine. 2009. "Placing Practices: Literacy and Meaning-Making across Space and Time." In *The Future of Literacy Studies*, edited by Mike Baynham and Mastin Prinsloo, 75–99. London: Palgrave.

Kerschbaum, Stephanie. 2014. *Toward a New Rhetoric of Difference*. Urbana, IL: NCTE.

Knoblauch, A. Abby. 2012. "Bodies of Knowledge: Definitions, Delineations, and Implications of Embodied Writing in the Academy." *Composition Studies* 40 (2): 50–65.

Kynard, Carmen. 2013. *Vernacular Insurrections: Race, Black Protest, and the New Century in Composition-Literacies Studies*. Albany: SUNY Press.

Ladson-Billings, Gloria. 2003. Foreword to *Making Race Visible: Literacy Research for Cultural Understanding*, edited by Stuart Greene and Dawn Abt-Perkins, vii–xi. New York: Teachers College Press.

Lagman, Eileen. 2015. "Moving Labor: Transnational Migrant Workers and Affective Literacies of Care." *Literacy in Composition Studies* 3 (5): 1–24.

Laquintano, Timothy. 2010. "Sustained Authorship: Ebooks, Value, and Participatory Culture." *Written Communication* 27 (4): 469–93.

Lorde, Audre. 1984. "Poetry Is Not a Luxury." In *Sister Outsider*, 36–39. Trumansburg, NY: The Crossing.

Lorimer Leonard, Rebecca. 2013. "Traveling Literacies: Multilingual Writing on the Move." *Research in the Teaching of English* 48 (1): 13–39.

Lovejoy, Kim. 2014. "Code-Meshing through Self-Directed Writing." In *Other People's English: Code-Meshing, Code-Switching, and African American Literacy*, edited by Vershawn Ashanti Young, Rusty Barrett, Y'Shanda Young-Rivera, and Kim Brian Lovejoy, 130–40. New York: Teachers College Press.

Luke, Allan. 1996. "Genres of Power? Literacy Education and the Production of Capital." In *Literacy in Society: Genres of Power*, edited by Rugalya Hasan and Geoffrey Williams, 308–38. New York: Longman.

Mackenzie, Catriona. 2009. "Personal Identity, Narrative Integration, and Embodiment." In *Embodiment and Agency*, edited by Sue Campbell, Letitia Meynell, and Susan Sherwin, 100–125. Philadelphia: Penn State University Press.

Madianou, Mirca, and Daniel Miller. 2012. *Migration and New Media: Transnational Families and Polymedia*. New York: Routledge.

Matsuda, Paul Kei. 2006. "The Myth of Linguistic Homogeneity in U.S. College Composition." *College English* 68 (6): 637–51.

Merleau-Ponty, Maurice. 1962. *Phenomenology of Perception*. Translated by Colin Smith. London: Routledge and Kegan Paul Ltd.

Mignolo, Walter. 2003. *The Darker Side of the Renaissance: Literacy, Territoriality, and Colonization*. Ann Arbor: University of Michigan Press.

Miller, Elisabeth L. 2016. "Literate Misfitting: Disability Theory and a Sociomaterial Approach to Literacy." *College English* 79 (1): 34.

Moll, Luis C., Ruth Sáez, and Joel Dworin. 2001. "Exploring Biliteracy: Two Student Case Examples of Writing as a Social Practice." *Elementary School Journal* 101 (4): 435–49.

Moraga, Cherríe, and Gloria Anzaldúa, eds. 2002. *This Bridge Called My Back: Writings by Radical Women of Color*. Berkeley, CA: Third Woman.

Moss, Beverly J. 2002. *A Community Text Arises: A Literate Text and a Literacy Tradition in African-American Churches*. Cresskill, NJ: Hampton Press.

Omi, Michael, and Howard Winant. 2015. *Racial Formation in the United States*. New York: Routledge.

Owens, Kim Hensley, and Derek Van Ittersum. 2013. "Writing With(out) Pain: Computing Injuries and the Role of the Body in Writing Activity." *Computers and Composition* 30 (2): 87–100.

Palmeri, Jason. 2012. *Remixing Composition: A History of Multimodal Writing Pedagogy*. Carbondale: Southern Illinois University Press.

Pennebaker, James W., and John F. Evans. 2014. *Expressive Writing: Words that Heal*. Enumclaw, WA: Idyll Arbor.

Perl, Sondra. 2004. *Felt Sense: Writing with the Body*. Portsmouth, NH: Heinemann.

Powell, Malea, et al. 2012. "Stories Take Place: A Performance in One Act" (chair's address). *College Composition and Communication* 64 (2): 383–406.

Prendergast, Catherine. 2004. *Literacy and Racial Justice: The Politics of Learning after Brown v. Board of Education*. Carbondale: Southern Illinois University Press.

Prendergast, Catherine. 2008. *Buying into English: Language and Investment in the New Capitalist World*. Pittsburgh: University of Pittsburgh Press.

Prior, Paul, and Jody Shipka. 2003. "Chronotopic Lamination: Tracing the Contours of Literate Activity." In *Writing Selves, Writing Societies*, edited by Charles Bazerman and

David R. Russell, 180–238. Fort Collins, CO: WAC Clearinghouse and Mind, Culture, and Activity.

Rhodes, Jacqueline, and Jonathan Alexander. 2015. *Techne: Queer Meditations on Writing the Self.* Logan: Utah State University Press. https://ccdigitalpress.org/book/techne/.

Richardson, Elaine. 2006. *Hiphop Literacies.* New York: Routledge.

Roozen, Kevin. 2016. "Writing Is Linked to Identity." In *Naming What We Know: Threshold Concepts of Writing Studies,* edited by Linda Adler Kassner and Elizabeth Wardle, 50–51. Boulder: University Press of Colorado.

Rosenblatt, Louise M. 1994. "The Transactional Theory of Reading and Writing." In *Theoretical Models and Processes of Reading.* 4th ed. Edited by Robert B. Ruddell, Martha Rapp Ruddell, and Harry Singer, 1057–92. Newark, DE: International Reading Association.

Rowsell, Jennifer. 2012. "Artifactual English." In *Language, Ethnography, and Education: Bridging New Literacy Studies and Bourdieu,* edited by Michael Grenfell, David Bloome, Cheryl Hardy, Kate Pahl, Jennifer Rowsell, and Brian V. Street, 190–31. New York: Routledge.

Salomon, Frank, and Mercedes Niño-Murcia. 2011. *The Lettered Mountain: A Peruvian Village's Ways with Writing.* Durham, NC: Duke University Press.

Schmandt-Besserat, Denise. 1980. "The Envelopes That Bear the First Writing." *Technology and Culture* 21 (3): 357–85.

Scribner, Sylvia, and Michael Cole. 1981. *The Psychology of Literacy.* Cambridge, MA: Harvard University Press.

Shipka, Jody. 2011. *Toward a Composition Made Whole.* Pittsburgh: University of Pittsburgh Press.

Smitherman, Geneva. 2006. *Word from the Mother: Language and African Americans.* New York: Routledge.

Squier, Susan Merrill. 2004. *Liminal Lives: Imagining the Human at the Frontiers of Biomedicine.* Durham, NC: Duke University Press.

Stanford, Nichole E. 2011. "Publishing in the Contact Zone: Strategies from the Cajun Canaille." In *Code-Meshing as World English: Pedagogy, Policy, Performance,* edited by Vershawn Ashanti Young and Aja Y. Martinez, 114–42. Urbana, IL: NCTE.

Stornaiuolo, Amy, and Robert Jean LeBlanc. 2016. "Scaling as a Literacy Activity: Mobility and Educational Inequality in an Age of Global Connectivity." *Research in the Teaching of English* 50 (3): 263–87.

Street, Brian V. 1984. *Literacy in Theory and Practice.* New York: Cambridge University Press.

Stuckey, J. Elspeth. 1991. *The Violence of Literacy.* Portsmouth, NH: Boynton Cook Publishers.

Vasudevan, Lalitha M. 2014. "Multimodal Cosmopolitanism: Cultivating Belonging in Everyday Moments with Youth." *Curriculum Inquiry* 44 (1): 45–67.

Vee, Annette. 2013. "Understanding Computer Programming as a Literacy." *Literacy in Composition Studies* 1 (2): 42–64.

Vieira, Kate. 2016. *American by Paper: How Documents Matter in Immigrant Literacy.* Minneapolis: University of Minnesota Press.

Vieira, Kate. 2018. "Shifting Global Literacy Networks: How Emigration Promotes Informal Literacy Learning in Latvia." *Anthropology & Education Quarterly* 49 (2): 165–82.

Vieira, Kate. 2019. *Writing for Love and Money: How Migration Drives Literacy Learning in Transnational Families.* New York: Oxford University Press.

Vincent, David. 2000. *The Rise of Mass Literacy: Reading and Writing in Modern Europe.* Malden, MA: Blackwell.

Walters, Shannon. 2014. *Rhetorical Touch: Disability, Identification, Haptics.* Columbia: University of South Carolina Press.

Wan, Amy J. 2014. *Producing Good Citizens: Literacy Training in Anxious Times.* Pittsburgh: University of Pittsburgh Press.

Watkins, Evan. 2015. *Literacy Work in the Reign of Human Capital.* New York: Fordham University Press.

Weinstein, Susan. 2009. *Feel These Words: Writing in the Lives of Urban Youth.* Albany: SUNY Press.

Welford, Theresa Malphrus. 2011. "Code-Meshing and Creative Assignments: How Students Can Stop Worrying and Learn to Write Like da Bomb." In *Code-Meshing as World English: Pedagogy, Policy, Performance,* edited by Vershawn Ashanti Young and Aja Y. Martinez, 21–54. Urbana, IL: NCTE.

Winn, Maisha T. 2011. *Girl Time: Literacy, Justice, and the School-to-Prison Pipeline.* New York: Teachers College Press.

Young, Vershawn Ashanti. 2009. "'Nah, We Straight': An Argument against Code Switching." *JAC* 29 (1/2): 49–76.

3
THINKING LIKE A WRITER
Threshold Concepts and First-Year Writers in Open-Admissions Classrooms

Cassandra Phillips, Holly Hassel, Jennifer Heinert, Joanne Baird Giordano, and Katie Kalish

> *First Year Writing matters because it touches more students than any other college-level course—whether these students complete college or not. We can never underestimate the power of the classroom to create changes for students, the community, and the world.*
>
> —Carolyn Calhoon-Dillahunt

The 2015 volume *Naming What We Know* (*NWWK*) (Adler-Kassner and Wardle), launched as a collaborative endeavor by scholars in the field who spelled out five metaconcepts reflecting disciplinary knowledge, initiated a scholarly conversation about threshold concepts in writing studies. This disciplinary work grew out of many iterations of threshold-concept research that traces its origins to the study of undergraduate teaching and learning improvement (Cousin 2006). Ray Land, Glynis Cousin, Jan Meyer, and Peter Davies (2005) explored "why certain students 'get stuck' at particular points in the curriculum whilst others grasp concepts with comparative ease" (53). They postulated that disciplinary ways of knowing and thinking may account for these differences and may provide teachers with a framework to reconsider the design and teaching of their courses to improve student learning (53). In addition to reflecting disciplinary experts' ways of knowing, threshold concepts can serve as a tool for unpacking the core concepts disciplinary experts have internalized by identifying what barriers, learning roadblocks, and misconceptions new learners of a discipline face.

Within this definitional context, then, we are interested in first-year writing as the earliest and most widespread circumstance in which most new college learners begin to engage with writing studies concepts at the college level. In her chair's address at the 2018 Conference on

DOI: 10.7330/9781607329329.c003

College Communication and Composition, Carolyn Calhoon-Dillahunt (2018) advocated for the recentering of first-year writing in the field of writing studies, in fact identifying it as the site where scholars have the "greatest ability to influence—policy, pedagogy, professionalization, students—through our teaching and scholarship and where there is the greatest exigence" for this work. First-year writing, Calhoon-Dillahunt noted, is "the space where we can best exercise our power through disciplinarity." However, she observed, "despite the significant space that First Year Writing occupies in our field, our scholarship fails to account for the 'teaching majority' or the spaces in which they work." Shelley Rodrigo and Susan Miller-Cochran (2018) note that these spaces are often in two-year colleges; open-access institutions (which includes two-year colleges but also some four-year colleges and universities) are also included. Writing about two-year institutions, Rodrigo and Miller-Cochran say that attending to these spaces is "an essential part of our disciplinary dialogue"; the same holds true for other open-access campuses (58).

Disciplinary knowledge will be strengthened by fully accounting for two-year and open-access institutions for several reasons. First, they *are* sites of access, and providing that access is a social justice issue. Second, those institutions—especially two-year colleges—are where the majority of students take first-year writing, including those who graduate four-year institutions: as reported in *Inside Higher Ed*, "46 percent of all students who completed a 4-year degree had been enrolled at a 2-year institution at some point in the past 10 years" (Smith 2015). Additionally, as more and more students (and parents and legislators) press for students to have completed college credits prior to graduating high school, these numbers will likely increase, in part because dual-enrollment courses are most commonly found at two-year colleges.[1] Data demonstrate that students at two-year institutions are not a small subset of college students; rather, they represent the majority of students in higher education. In fact, students who are returning adults, multilingual speakers, students of color, and low-income and first-generation college students are all more likely to attend a two-year college and therefore more likely to fit a "nontraditional" profile than are those students at a selective or residential college. They are what Elaine Maimon calls "the new majority" (quoted in Brown 2018).

With these realities in mind, we hope to accomplish several goals in this chapter. First, we look at the ways students in a first-year writing class in an open-access two-year college encounter a curriculum based on documents that are said to provide guidance about what students in first-year writing should know (including but not limited to the *Framework for Success in Postsecondary Writing* and the *WPA Outcomes Statement for First-Year Composition*), analyzing portfolios in a representative section of English 101: College Writing and Critical Reading. Through our analysis of portfolios from a representative section of this English 101 course, we distill and remodel threshold concepts proposed in *NWWK* for first-year writing in open-access institutions. This analysis brings the voices of students whose experiences often are not reflected in writing studies scholarship, voices of students whose pathways to college and to postsecondary writing differ from those who start at four-year residential campuses, to the discussion. As we show, students like those in our small study are the kinds of writers who benefit most from having clear, transparent, and explicit disciplinary knowledge available to them.

As in other fields, introductory writing courses do not reflect the sum total of knowledge about the discipline; however, first-year writing courses provide a foundation for students' future work as writers in college. For students at open-access campuses, first-year writing is often the first exposure to and primary experience with academic writing and typical college genres. Building on what students say about their experiences—many of them through multiple iterations of one or more of the courses in the sequence—we offer a snapshot of the misconceptions students brought with them to first-year writing, of the learning roadblocks they encountered and sometimes overcame in the course of the class, and how they spoke about their learning process as writers (past, present, and future). Through this analysis, we also draw some conclusions not only about what threshold concepts in first-year writing look like in nonselective institutions' writing contexts but also about why this population of first-year writers must be an important consideration for identifying threshold concepts, given that they are the largest group of US college students by institution type (Snyder and Dillow 2013, 356).

Next, based on this analysis, we propose some revised threshold concepts for first-year writing that seem especially germane for students in open-access institutions. While our focus is on students in a two-year college classroom, our analysis and suggestions are likely relevant for students in two- and four-year open-access institutions. Threshold concepts have often been defined as learning how to "think like" or to know and see like professionals and experts in a specific field. Building on this language in the context of first-year composition, Kathleen Blake Yancey, Liane Robertson, and Kara Taczak (2014) suggest, "When applied to FYC, we began to consider how we might help students think like writers" (4). What we hope to capture is the first opportunity many students have with a call to "think like a writer."

In undertaking this effort to flesh out threshold concepts for first-year writing from this perspective, we advance earlier work done by Doug Downs and Liane Robertson (2015) and by Elizabeth Wardle and Downs in their textbook *Writing about Writing* (2017). Downs and Robertson (2015) aim to "examine first-year composition with an eye toward teaching threshold concepts of and about writing" (105) and focus on human interaction (rhetoric), textuality, epistemology, and writing process. They show how these concepts are effective for framing first-year writing courses in order to address "misconceptions in students' writing knowledge and of teaching for learning transfer to later, different writing situations" (106) through their connections to pedagogical examples. *Writing about Writing*—the only first-year writing textbook that explicitly uses threshold concepts as part of its pedagogical framework—similarly presents threshold concepts for first-year writers.

Our approach to threshold concepts complements these forays in several ways. First, the framework we offer is deductively crafted—in other words, it is drawn from our decades of experience as teacher-scholars in basic writing, first-year writing, writing studio, and intermediate composition courses, as well as from the student work we collected as part of a larger grant-funded professional-development project.[2] In our study, the curriculum for the course was structured on a foundation of experts' disciplinary knowledge about writing and writers and used pedagogical approaches that reflected this knowledge—just as the threshold concepts in *NWWK* do. However, the participants in our study were not learning directly about threshold concepts, as the course in which they were enrolled was taught before *NWWK* was published (and was part of a curricular-reform and faculty-development project). That being said, examining student learning through threshold concepts, then, is one way to centralize disciplinary values within these varied contexts.

DISCIPLINARY KNOWLEDGE, CURRICULUM DESIGN, AND THE NEEDS OF FIRST-YEAR WRITERS

For students in open-access institutions (and others, as well), learning to think like writers is a journey made more challenging but ultimately more impactful through a threshold concept lens. This is not to say students in open-access two-year (or four-year) institutions "stand in" for all first-year writers but rather to say the learning needs of these students should receive greater attention in shaping the field of writing studies. The foundational body of knowledge about students in college composition is largely drawn from research undertaken at four-year institutions. If we build the knowledge of first-year writing on that foundation, we underrepresent what we know about writing and writers, specifically within academic contexts (see Lovas 2002).[3] The majority of articles published in major journals in writing studies do not address two-year writing students, who tend to be from marginalized groups; situate in only a limited way the student populations who are the subjects of the research study; and erase differences among students and student populations in ways that then mean two-year college students' writing experiences are unrepresented in the scholarship on writing (Hassel and Phillips, under review). The students in our study illustrate the often circuitous pathway open-admissions writers (in our specific case, two-year college students) take through the first-year writing sequence.[4]

As table 3.1 demonstrates, the students in our study had mixed success. To consider how these students interacted with a curriculum designed around disciplinary standards that helps them think like writers, our analysis focuses on a section of English 101 taught by Rachel, a faculty member who reflects the teaching majority in first-year writing: she works off the tenure track, is master's credentialed, and has a decade of teaching experience working across our writing sequence of nondegree credit and first-year writing. As Mark Blaauw-Hara, Carolyn Tebeau, Dominic Borowiak, and Jami Blaauw-Hara and Lisa Tremain, Marianne Ahokas, Sarah Ben-Zvi, and Kerry Marsden note in their chapters in this volume, writing instructors come from a wide range of academic backgrounds within English, including literature, technical writing, creative writing, and others, and sometimes the disciplinary knowledge of writing studies is reflected neither in curriculum nor in pedagogy. Blaauw-Hara et al. discuss this in greater detail in their chapter, noting that "adopting threshold concepts as a departmental framework is difficult in that it invites an identity dissonance, as it asks instructors from varied backgrounds to coalesce under a singular composition-centered focus" (173). In this instance, the program in which Rachel taught was noted as excellent, having won the CCCC Writing Program Certificate of Excellence in 2017 (Conference on College Composition and Communication 2017). As a part of this group, Rachel used the components of the disciplinary-based department curriculum and used accepted pedagogical practices in support of disciplinary first-year outcomes. As Downs and Robertson (2015) note, a department curriculum, while not explicitly designed with threshold concepts mind, can be implicitly guided by them through its focus on disciplinary outcomes (105). We could not analyze these experiences with threshold concepts

Table 3.1. Overview of student success and progress through the first-year writing sequence by placement into the first-year writing sequence, repetition of courses, and academic standing at the end of their enrollment with the campus

Writing program coursework	Students
Placed into developmental writing (English 098)	4/14 (28%)
Repeated developmental writing (English 098)	1/14 (7%)
Repeated English 101	8/14 (57%)
Completed English 101 at some point	8/14 (57%)
Completed second-semester course (English 102) at some point	7/14 (50%)
Students on probation or suspension (eventually) who started in English 101	7/14 (50%)

if the course were not tied directly and comprehensively to disciplinary outcomes for first-year writing.

In drawing our conclusions, we examined the writing students completed over the course of a semester: a self-assessment paper, a position paper, a rhetorical analysis, an argumentative research paper, and a final reflective essay. We also examined the course syllabus and assignment instructions. The instructor also assessed students' academic and nonacademic experiences in the course by responding to the following questions:

1. What is your overall assessment of the student's progress toward achieving course learning outcomes and core writing-requirement completion?
2. What specific barriers (if any) made it difficult for the student to achieve the learning outcomes for the course and make progress toward completing the core writing requirement?

We incorporated Rachel's responses into our assessment of individual students' progress. Ultimately, Rachel's reflections and our analysis of students' efforts revealed patterns of student struggles and successes with disciplinary knowledge. These struggles and successes led us to define new threshold concepts for first-year writers in open-access institutions. Table 3.2 lists these concepts and their relationships to earlier concepts included in *Naming What We Know*.

FIRST-YEAR WRITING THRESHOLD CONCEPT 1: WRITING CAN BE TAUGHT AND LEARNED.

For first-year writers in open-admission institutions, our study suggests that a first-year writing threshold concept focused on writing processes

Table 3.2. Relationship between threshold concepts for first-year writing and threshold concepts in *Naming What We Know*

New/revised threshold concepts for first-year writing	Relationship to *Naming What We Know* (metaconcepts and subconcepts)
Writing can be taught and learned	All writers have more to learn; Writing is (also always) a cognitive activity
Writers write for different purposes and audiences, and often in genres with predictable conventions	Writing is a social and rhetorical activity; Writing speaks to situations through recognizable forms
Reading and writing are interconnected activities	Not directly reflected in NWWK
Writing processes are individualized, require readers, and require revision	Revision is central to developing writing; Reflection is critical for writers' development

and metacognition is best expressed as *writing can be taught and learned*. Because so many students in open-admissions classrooms have had challenging prior reading and writing experiences, this threshold concept is transformative because it challenges students' prior perspectives. For example, the ability to write effectively is not something inherent, intrinsic, or fixed but rather something that improves through experience and practice. Further, revising and drafting are not signs of failure but of success because students' ability to use recursive writing processes in response to feedback is, itself, a threshold concept and not a signal that a writer has failed. We also want to be careful with how the concept of failure is used in a classroom: a subconcept in *NWWK*, for example, *failure can be an important part of writing development* (Brooke and Carr 2018), is one our students know all too acutely. For this reason, it is very difficult to frame failure as an opportunity. Instead, as our student reflections show, failure is perceived as yet another sign that they do not belong in college or aren't good at writing. Instructional approaches that frame writing as a teachable process that supports growth are often the pedagogical differences between students' retention in college and dropping out. It is this experience that leads us to suggest this threshold concept not be framed as dependent upon failure but rather upon movement and progress that varies for each student writer.

Some students in this section of our study enacted this threshold concept, commenting on how much they still needed to learn, as well as how willing they were to do so. Britney wrote, "Writing is an activity that can never be perfected. For all the different styles of writing, there is always room for improvement and growth." In her self-assessment, Joanna noted, "Yes, it's important to have an open mind but along with that, because when people are willing to change some of their weakness, they are more likely to become a better writer." Warren explained, "I was in English 098 [developmental writing], and I thought it went quite well and that the next class was not going to be too difficult. I felt ready for the first essay and quite frankly thought it was going to be similar to those I completed last semester. That assumption was the problem: I brought basic reading skills, the ability to write straightforward essays and fundamental computer skills to a class that demanded much more." In these reflections, students show how they have worked with the threshold concept for first-year writing, *writing can be taught and learned*. All these students acknowledge that they require more practice and experience with different writing situations. Warren's comment that he thought he knew something but then realized he didn't demonstrates a metacognitive understanding of, as well as a liminal relationship to, these concepts when he recognizes his mastery is context specific.

A reworking of this threshold concept from *failure* to *teaching and learning* would also support students who did *not* demonstrate an understanding that writing can be learned. They lamented their lack of prior writing experience, their frustration with their own low skill levels, or their negative emotional experiences of reading and writing instruction and practice. Shane's self-assessment writing reveals how previous negative experiences with writing influenced his identity as a college writer: "People do not always enjoy writing. Some people can't stand the thought of reading and writing. People will do whatever they can to try and avoid doing either of these tasks. Some, think that writing and reading is too much. They don't want to take the time to do either of them. I am most defiantly[5] one of those people. My past experiences have not been very pleasant. I have not had fun with my past writing. For that reason I do not enjoy it now, and don't look forward to it." Shane's reflection draws from his own experience as a writer to generalize about other writers with similar experiences who view writing and reading as tasks to avoid. He does not seem to believe reading and writing are skills that can be developed through practice or have a sense that his prior efforts have resulted in success. Instead, Shane describes writing as an activity or pastime and not as part of his identity, and that self-assessment seems final. He assumes writing is enjoyable for those who are more successful and that his lack of success is because it is not enjoyable to him. As Jan Meyer and Ray Land (2006) write, of great interest to teachers is "what it means, for example, when a student for the first time becomes conscious of the fact that they are, or are beginning to *think* like, an accountant, chemist, economist, historian, lawyer, mathematician, physicist, statistician, and so on" (23). In our framework, thinking like a writer—not like a writing studies scholar or a compositionist but like someone who is actively engaged in making conscious decisions about writing choices (the beginning of moving toward disciplinary competence)—starts with students' belief that they can be writers regardless of their past academic experiences. At open-admission institutions, the belief that writing can be learned regardless of background and (lack of) experience is a transformative threshold concept.

FIRST-YEAR WRITING THRESHOLD CONCEPT 2: WRITERS WRITE FOR DIFFERENT PURPOSES AND AUDIENCES, OFTEN USING GENRES WITH PREDICTABLE CONVENTIONS

Based on our analysis of student work, understanding that purpose and audience interact with rhetorical conventions and genres is a threshold concept for the first-year writing students in our open-access institution. Because there are common genres and conventions outside the five-paragraph essay that many students in open-admissions contexts have not previously encountered, the idea that conventions and genres of writing can be taught, learned, recognized, practiced, and mastered as part of building rhetorical knowledge and rhetorical adaptability is key for writing development (see Hassel and Giordano 2009).

Several students from our analysis illustrate the value of this first-year writing threshold concept. Mark, who ultimately did not complete the course, actually moved *further* away from the concept throughout the course, despite metacognitive reflection on his knowledge of choices among genres based on an analysis of purposes and audiences. Mark showed an initial cognitive and metacognitive understanding of the threshold concepts *writing speaks to situations through recognizable forms* and *genres are enacted by writers and readers*. For example, he discussed his prior learning experiences with writing in his first self-assessment paper in the course. There, he reflects on prior coursework that helped him address what he saw as a litany of problems with his writing in past courses and contexts. He explains, "[One] problem I took care of was what was called the five-paragraph three-part paper. I would break the paper up into five paragraphs and each paragraph would have three parts. This proved to be thought of negatively by instructors because it was to structured and some papers needed a different flow." But when it came to putting together a position essay, a later assignment in the first-year writing course, he organized his ideas around three main points with a five-paragraph essay structure. Mark's initial understanding of rhetorical choices about form, as demonstrated in his first paper, reflected thoughtful consideration of the relationship between the structure and the ideas presented in the paper, with the content demanding a "different flow." He realized he needed to vary the structure of his writing depending on a college writing purpose. However, in the next assignment, rather than building on his understanding of form, he reverted back to a five-paragraph paper.

This reversion to a more basic writing strategy is not unusual for students who have a general sense that there are a wide range of rhetorical genres but whose prior experience exposed them to a narrow range of forms (see Hassel and Giordano 2009). Mark's experience also exemplifies Meyer and Land's (2006) notion of liminality, in particular what they call "oscillation"—noting that "transformation can be protracted, over periods of time, and involve *oscillation* between states, often with temporary regression to earlier status" (24). Mark's efforts in this English 101 course thus speak to progress, not failure, aligned with Meyer and Land's assertion that "in student learning terms mimicry, it seems, may involve both attempts at understanding *and* trouble misunderstanding, or limited understanding" (24). While Mark was able to use a familiar genre, it was disconnected from the purpose and audience of the assigned writing task.

Although Mark struggled with the concept *writers write for different purposes and audiences, often using genres with predictable conventions,* evidence from other students' writing suggests this concept is an important foundation for basic writing and first-year writing instruction. Warren describes his understanding that there are distinctions between his high-school learning, his basic writing course, and the subsequent first-year writing sequence he will need to complete:

> The biggest difference between high school essays and college essays is the time between each essay. In high school, we waited at least a couple weeks before we even started the next essay, in college we wait maybe a week before we move on to a new topic and start the next essay. Another difference is the actual length of the essays. When in high school the required length was generally two or three pages, in college that required length went up to a bigger range in length, anywhere from two pages to sometimes ten or more pages. The third biggest difference is editing because college is way more in depth when it comes to editing than high school ever was.

Warren's comments suggest that he understands the ideas about purposes and conventions associated with this threshold concept but that he needs to work on articulating the specifics of those differences (he refers at one point to "straightforward essays"), and his primary understanding of those differences is related to length, amount of time to complete the assignment, and sentence-level correctness instead of rhetorical considerations. Warren showed progress in understanding genre and purpose by the end of the course, noting, "This trap of always writing reports was definitely a struggle to overcome, but the assignments we completed in this class helped me appreciate different writing formats and change my approach to meet the professor's requirements." For students like Warren, the process of working with threshold concepts associated with purposes and conventions is iterative and liminal, requiring a series of varied experiences with employing rhetorical knowledge for college writing tasks.

The roadblocks students in our research encounter with the threshold concept focused on audience, purpose, and genre may help writing studies scholars more accurately capture the ways college writers, especially those in institutions like ours, become familiar with ways of disciplinary thinking, seeing, and knowing. Conrad, who did not ultimately complete the course or the writing assignments, notes, "In previous writing courses through high school we went over many of the things we talk about on a daily basis in our current English 101 class, however, we did not talk about audience, stance, purpose, genre or media." Conrad is able to identify the new rhetorical content of the course yet is unable to connect those concepts to previous writing experiences. Moreover, his perception that these foundational concepts are new in English 101 suggests that identifying writing studies concepts (like the ones Conrad cites) must be part of, for many underprepared and at-risk students who attend two-year and open-admission campuses, an extended learning process—as many as four or five semesters of college writing.

Tim's reflective writing reveals that he, too, felt his high-school experience focused on writing concepts that don't relate to what he is being asked to do in English 101. For example, in his reflective writing, Tim laments, "I personally feel that I was set up for failure in my previous high school English classes due to the lack of quality, lack of motivation, and the actual fact that teachers did not want to take the time to sit down to thoroughly grade essays." He describes the evaluation criteria of high-school English as "proper grammar, at least two pages, and double spaced," echoing Warren's understanding of how writing works. Tim's comments likewise reveal a frustration with his perceived lack of preparation, which he assigns to former instruction he sees as focused on lower-order conventions.

Whether Tim's assessment is accurate or not, the insights provided by students like him and Warren suggest to us that some students interpret high-school writing as a single kind of genre—or as "genreless" writing, in which they are not being asked to consider audience and purpose.

Consequently, students starting college composition after one or more semesters of basic writing need scaffolded and specific opportunities to cross the threshold for writing in genres with predictable conventions. A first-year writing curriculum that reflects disciplinary knowledge and prompts students to think like college writers presents a particular challenge for these students because they struggle to reconcile their previous writing experiences and prior learning with college-level rhetorical requirements and adaptability.

FIRST-YEAR WRITING THRESHOLD CONCEPT 3: READING AND WRITING ARE INTERCONNECTED ACTIVITIES

The threshold concepts in *Naming What We Know* do not directly address the relationship between reading and writing. However, this relationship is gaining greater visibility in the curriculum, particularly in two-year college developmental English programs using integrated reading and writing (IRW). Patrick Sullivan's chapter in this book also both addresses the absence of threshold concepts focusing on writing in *NWWK* and defines "deep reading" as a threshold concept, as he has done in his earlier work (Carillo 2015, 2016; Sullivan 2017; see also Sullivan, Tinberg, and Blau 2017). To complement the one Sullivan describes in this volume, we see the need for another first-year writing threshold concept focused on reading: *reading and writing are interconnected activities*. This concept acknowledges the mutually informing relationship between reading and writing—the texts students read both inform and enrich their composing products and processes; their writing tasks inform their selection of texts and the reading strategies they employ to address them. We extend the threshold concept of deep reading so that it makes more visible the relationship between the practice of reading and the practice of composing. This relationship is troublesome, transformative, and integrative because it allows students to make more conscious connections between prior coursework and learning and the current academic writing tasks they face.

In their self-assessments, students were asked to reflect on their prior writing experiences and how they had prepared them for the expectations of the English 101. Students showed a disconnection between reading and writing in three ways. Some explicitly stated that some of their previous classes focused on reading and therefore, in their view, were not connected to their writing class; others omitted discussion of prior courses with reading content altogether; still others discussed reading in the context of learning literary analysis or even research skills but not within a context of seeing strong relationships between those literacy activities and composing.

In her reflective writing, Amelia initially expresses frustration at what she perceives to be a gap between her prior learning experiences and the expectations of English 101: "I had very little writing experience in high school—only having completed two major papers. I hated writing and would do it only when forced. This did not prepare me well for college English, where I was expected to complete five papers throughout the semester." In her introductory self-assessment, she does not address reading at all, instead focusing on outlines, procrastination, and wordiness as areas for improvement and referencing a creative short story she wrote about the Vietnam War. Later she says this experience reflected research skills she developed, observing, "Research was critical to creating an accurate and well documented story since it took place in a convulsive and troubled time. By using critical thinking and reading, I was able to properly research different sources and use them correctly in my story. I feel my preparation for college writing in this aspect is complete based on my past experiences with properly researching." In her final assessment, she writes, "Reading has always been important to me, so I was okay at critical reading when I entered college." Amelia's multiple opportunities to reflect on the interconnected nature of reading and writing helped her identify relationships between her research and critical-reading experiences. However, Amelia does not demonstrate she understands the relationship between reading and the writing tasks in English 101 that do not resemble her prior learning experiences. At the end of the semester, the instructor reported, "I remember her telling me she was homeschooled. She focused more on reading than writing papers." Because her prior learning experiences emphasized reading but not academic writing and analysis of texts, Amelia experienced difficulty when asked to write formal source-based essays for varying purposes, but also, her comments show she saw reading and writing as two different kinds of activities rather than interrelated ones. Amelia was not able to make progress with this threshold concept until she began to see the connections between reading and writing.

Tanner and Mack also show through their reflective writing how they struggled to see connections between reading and writing in their literacy growth. Tanner writes, "My high school English courses were not focused on writing. The main focus was on understanding literature and creating presentations," while Mack remembers, "Coming into college English I never took many writing classes. I took a lot of reading classes which gave me some strength in reading text, but I was weak when it came to writing an essay." Tanner's and Mack's experiences are reflected in Alice Horning and Elizabeth Kraemer's "Reconnecting Reading and Writing: Introduction and Overview" (2013): "The tacit goals of critical literacy—including the integration of ideas in a larger context and applying reading material to the writer's own rhetorical purpose—are neither stated explicitly nor taught in a reading and writing context" (10). Instead of understanding reading and writing as mutually informative, some students can perceive these components of their learning as discrete activities that may even compete with one another.

The vexed relationship for many students between reading and writing is similarly captured in Conrad's powerful self-assessment of his experiences with literacy:

> Overall my reading skills are that of an 8th grader. I barely read and when I do it is either an assignment or something I have actually found interest in which is very rare. All in all I can assume that I still as of yet have not read over a 100 books. I am a really slow reader so when it comes to reading something I actually have to sit down and read it. I know that it is true that reading helps improve your writing process, and maybe that is why I have always struggled with English. It has only been recent for me to write a good essay.

Conrad explicitly states that he understands the relationship between reading and writing, saying "reading helps improve your writing process," and yet the challenges he articulates have presented barriers to his success as a writer, consistent with Horning and Kraemer's (2013) observation that "it might be fair to say that a linchpin in the array of academic writing is the ability to call on and engage with source materials to enter ongoing conversations on issues and topics. Because academic writing so often entails the use of what students have read, the need to reconnect reading and writing is clear" (11). Sullivan (2017) adds that we must "frame deep reading as a form of intellectual inquiry" (165), cognitive and rhetorical work that bridges students' writing and reading activities, illuminating how they are interconnected processes whether writing about reading or reading one's own writing in a "readerly" way.

The students in Rachel's class demonstrate how the interconnected nature of reading and writing is a critical threshold concept for first-year writing. Making the reading-writing relationship a central component of first-year composition courses has a specific value to students whose engagement with reading has been difficult or unrewarding. Directly articulating the mutually enriching functions of reading and writing is of specific benefit to students starting their college studies in developmental reading and writing—or working their way through a multicourse sequence.

FIRST-YEAR WRITING THRESHOLD CONCEPT 4: WRITING PROCESSES ARE INDIVIDUALIZED, REQUIRE READERS, AND REQUIRE REVISION

The final threshold concept we propose for first-year writing, especially in open-access institutions, takes into account the individualized nature of students' writing processes and the importance of peer feedback and revision. This broad concept relates to but condenses the writing studies concepts in *NWWK* and builds on the previous three concepts in our sequence and on two threshold concepts from *NWWK*: *all writers have more to learn* and *writing is always (also) a cognitive activity*. Our analysis of student writing suggests that these writers are extremely well acquainted with some of the *NWWK* threshold concepts relating to revision but that these concepts are inflected differently for writers who have been underserved by or alienated from formal schooling, as is the case for the students in our study and in many open-access institutions. Collin Brooke and Alison Carr's subconcept, *failure can be an important part of writing development*, serves as an important model for us here (Brooke and Carr 2015). Our revised fourth threshold concept, *writing processes are individualized, require readers, and require revision*, reframes failure in a way that reflects the experience of struggling writers and is also a building block that will offer a productive intellectual and emotional reorientation to writing and the writing process.

As our table at the start of this chapter demonstrates, a quarter of the students in our study started in basic writing, while two-thirds of the participants repeated at least one if not two of the courses in the first-year writing sequence. A threshold concept for first-year writing in the open-access context, then, must identify in specific ways how learning happens and go beyond acknowledging the idea that failure helps one learn: there are writing processes, and they can be deployed in multiple ways for success on writing tasks. Additionally, many open-access students see revision as optional or as a sign of failure; threshold concept 4 makes explicit that revision is a signal of a writer's successful process, not a failed one. Our analysis of student work coupled with our students' perceptions of failure reveals the importance of a threshold concept for first-year writing focusing directly on writing process for the purposes of revision.

Many of Rachel's students struggle to articulate and reflect on their writing processes and sometimes are limited by their prior experiences with writing. Damien, Shane, Britney, and Tim, for instance, did not reference revision or the role of feedback from readers. Says Damien, "To me, the process of writing was somewhat mystical. There was no secret formula to writing; it seemed to be just a spectacular act of pure creation. That was the approach that made writing difficult for me, and this is the approach that I grew out of this semester. Good writing definitely requires a bit of creativity, but it also needs a rational foundation. By learning to apply solid structural elements to my writing, I was able to demystify the creative process." Shane's struggle was similar to Damien's, if expressed differently: "The biggest one [of things he needed to work on] being the writing process I always just threw a paper together last minute and would hope for the best. I also knew I had to work on taking points and putting them together properly in my paper." In their reflective pieces, each of these writers is expressing openness to learning something more than "writing happens" and moving beyond the idea that writing processes are "somewhat mystical," to use Damien's phrase. While it is clear both students have learned structure is important, it is unclear how their understanding of structure fits into an overall writing process.

Rachel's English 101 students often wrestled with the complexities of writing processes, specifically their individualized and context-specific nature. Ideally, the curriculum aims to teach students to recognize that there is not a single process but rather that a process can be specific to them, even if that process is guided. For example, Britney reflects on a transformative moment in the course when she says, "As the weeks slowly went by, I became more comfortable with my abilities, but I did everything my professor asked of me. In high school, teachers never suggested writing an outline to use as a guide. I tried this for my first paper and it was incredible. I was able to organize my thoughts and when it came time to write the actual paper, I had a guide which helped me stay organized in my writing." For Britney, being introduced to specific process-supporting tools at this moment was important to her growth as a writer—being provided with options for approaching a writing task beyond rough draft/final draft and seeing her writing process as multistage.

When students begin to see writing processes as multistaged, it can become easier for them to see how reader feedback can inform those stages and subsequent revisions. For example, Tim's comment encapsulates this revised threshold concept about writing processes in a comprehensive way; at least in terms of his reflections on the writing process, his learning seems to demonstrate he is crossing the threshold associated with this concept. Tim writes:

> Last but certainly not least is the whole "writing process" from the Learning Outcomes packet. This process was brand new to me this semester. Of course, previous years I have written a rough draft and then the final draft. In English 101 however, I created working thesis statements,

outlines, rough drafts, peer review drafts, revisions, and then the final version of the essay. I love the "writing processes" because I can clearly see my progress from draft to draft; also peer review days gave me the opportunity to gather more ideas from friends on ways to improve my essay. Most of the time my peers came up with ideas that were brand new and made more sense than what I wrote at first. From this point forward I plan to incorporate the writing processes for all of my future papers along with using it in the workplace for my job.

Tim's reflection shows how the idea of a writing process was new to him and that learning a process that worked for him was important to his growth as a writer. In addition, his reflection shows he understands how reader feedback can inform further work on a piece of writing. And perhaps most important, it shows a commitment to drawing on his new understanding of writing process in future writing contexts.

These students' reflections showed us how important a concept specific to teaching writing process clearly is in ways useful and empowering for first-year writers. Students come into our classrooms with varied perceptions about writing, and often those perceptions are influenced by feelings of inadequacy and even failure. Those perceptions influence their willingness to share their work and to believe they can revise and improve. Defining and using this threshold concept for first-year writing as part of a framework for thinking about curricular and pedagogical practices can help students understand that thinking like a writer means employing a writing process, seeking and using feedback from readers, and revising and improving their work.

LOOKING AHEAD: REMAINING ISSUES AND ONGOING WORK

We are eager to see how threshold concepts, which across disciplines seem to function as an agreed-upon but open-to-evolution way of articulating how experts in those fields see, know, and think, might be potentially transformative ways of approaching college writing instruction in open-access institutions. The concepts we outline here seem to have particular value to student populations for whom the expectations of college literacy are unstated, unfamiliar, and even hidden. Given that tens of thousands of students take first-year writing in two-year colleges and four-year open-access institutions, in order for disciplinary knowledge to be inclusive and representative of the whole of disciplinary work, it is critical that study and analysis of student learning and teaching at open-access institutions are included in disciplinary conversations.

To accurately articulate disciplinary knowledge, threshold concepts must be revisited and tested through evidence of student learning and a deep understanding of the needs of a wide range of student writers, especially first-year writers. Writing studies will benefit from continuing the process of *NWWK* by including more systematic analysis of student writing and writers from representative student populations. Doing so bridges a gap between threshold concepts defined by experts in the field and how students approach and pass the thresholds to disciplinary ways of knowing and thinking like writers.

NOTES

1. A 2014 report examining trends in dual-enrollment data found that "over 70 percent of students who took college courses through dual enrollment programs used a two-year institution, and programs are available through 96 percent of two-year institutions" while "only 7 percent of students who took college courses through a dual enrollment program used a nonprofit four-year institution" (Hanover Research 2014).
2. This study was approved by the institution's Institutional Review Board. Student names are pseudonyms. A forthcoming book project reports on our analysis of the larger pool of student and instructor participants from a cross-section of composition courses offered at multiple campuses. As part of this work, participating instructors contributed student writing (with consent) to a repository of first-year composition texts.
3. For example, a recent analysis of four of the major journals in the field (*College English*, *WPA*, *CCC*, and *Composition Studies*) by Hassel and Phillips shows that just 5 percent of articles published over the last fifteen years address students in two-year college contexts.
4. The Community College Research Center shows that 68 percent of students at two-year colleges take one or more remedial courses (compared with 40 percent in four-year institutions). A plurality of black (44 percent) and Hispanic (46 percent) students enroll in two-year colleges (Community College Research Center 2018; Hispanic Association of Colleges and Universities 2018). College Board data compare the population of returning adult students, noting that "while about 80% of public and private nonprofit four-year students started postsecondary education while they were under the age of 20, only 58% of students in the public two-year sector were this young when they first enrolled. Twenty-two percent of public two-year students began their postsecondary studies between the ages of 20 and 24, and 20% began after they turned 25" (Ma and Baum 2016).
5. We preserved the students' original language, including typos and grammatical errors.

REFERENCES

Adler-Kassner, Linda, and Elizabeth Wardle, eds. 2015. *Naming What We Know: Threshold Concepts of Writing Studies*. Logan: Utah State University Press.

Brooke, Collin, and Allison Carr. 2015. "Failure Can Be an Important Part of Writing Development." In *Naming What We Know: Threshold Concepts of Writing Studies*, edited by Linda Adler-Kassner and Elizabeth Wardle, 62–64. Logan: Utah State University Press.

Brown, Sarah. 2018. "A Veteran President Calls on Colleges to Stop the Snobbery." *Chronicle of Higher Education.* https://www.chronicle.com/article/A-Veteran-President-Calls-on/244230.

Calhoon-Dillahunt, Carolyn. 2018. "Returning to Our Roots: Creating the Conditions and Capacity for Change." Chair's address at the Annual Convention of the Conference on College Composition and Communication, Kansas City, MO.

Carillo, Ellen. 2015. *Securing a Place for Reading in Composition: The Importance of Teaching for Transfer.* Logan: Utah State University Press.

Carillo, Ellen. 2016. "Creating Mindful Readers in First-Year Composition Courses: A Strategy to Facilitate Transfer." *Pedagogy* 16 (1): 9–22. http://teaching.lfhanley.net/wp-content/uploads/2016/03/Carillo-Mindful-Reader.pdf.

Community College Research Center. 2018. "Community College FAQs." https://ccrc.threshold concept.columbia.edu/Community-College-FAQs.html.

Conference on College Composition and Communication. 2017. "CCCC Writing Program Certificate of Excellence." http://cccc.ncte.org/cccc/awards/writingprogramcert.

Cousin, Glynis. 2006. "An Introduction to Threshold concepts." *Planet* 17 (1): 4–5. https://www.ee.ucl.ac.uk/~mflanaga/Cousin Planet 17.pdf.

Downs, Doug, and Liane Robertson. 2015. "Threshold Concepts in First-Year Composition." In *Naming What We Know: Threshold Concepts of Writing Studies,* edited by Linda Adler-Kassner and Elizabeth Wardle, 105–21. Logan: Utah State University Press.

Hanover Research. 2014. *Dual Enrollment: Models, Practices, and Trends.* https://www.hanoverresearch.com/wp-content/uploads/2017/08/Dual-Enrollment-ModelPractices-and-Trends.pdf.

Hassel, Holly, and Joanne Giordano. 2009. "Transfer Institutions, Transfer of Knowledge: The Development of Rhetorical Adaptability and Underprepared Writers." *Teaching English in the Two-Year College* 37 (1): 24–40.

Hassel, Holly, and Cassandra Phillips. Under review. *Materiality and Writing Studies: Aligning Labor, Pedagogy, and Scholarship.*

Hispanic Association of Colleges and Universities. 2019. "2019 Fact Sheet: Hispanic Higher Education and HSIs." https://www.hacu.net/hacu/HSI_Fact_Sheet.asp.

Horning, Alice, and Elizabeth Kraemer. 2013. "Reconnecting Reading and Writing: Introduction and Overview." In *Reconnecting Reading and Writing,* edited by Alice Horning and Elizabeth Kraemer, 5–25. Boulder, CO: WAC Clearinghouse.

Land, Ray, Glynis Cousin, Jan H. F. Meyer, and Peter Davies. 2005. "Threshold Concepts and Troublesome Knowledge (3)*: Implications for Course Design and Evaluation." In *Improving Student Learning: Diversity and Inclusivity,* edited by Chris Rust, 53–64. Oxford Center for Staff and Learning Development. https://www.ee.ucl.ac.uk/~mflanaga/ISL04-pp53-64-Land-et-al.pdf.

Lovas, John. 2002. "All Good Writing Develops at the Edge of Risk." *College Composition and Communication* 54 (2): 264–88.

Ma, Jennifer, and Sandy Baum. 2016. "Trends in Community Colleges: Enrollment, Prices, Student Debt, and Completion." College Board Research, Research Brief. https://trends.collegeboard.org/sites/default/files/trends-in-community-colleges-research-brief.pdf.

Meyer, Jan H. F., and Ray Land. 2006. *Overcoming Barriers to Student Understanding.* New York: Routledge.

Rodrigo, Rochelle, and Susan Miller-Cochran. 2018. "Acknowledging Disciplinary Contributions: On the Importance of Community College Scholarship to Rhetoric and Composition." In *Composition, Rhetoric, and Disciplinarity,* edited by Rita Malenczyk, Susan Miller-Cochran, Elizabeth Wardle, and Kathleen Blake Yancey, 53–69. Logan: Utah State University Press.

Smith, Ashley. 2015. "Community College to Bachelor's." *Inside Higher Ed.* https://www.insidehighered.com/news/2015/03/26/nearly-half-four-year-college-graduates-attended-two-year-college.

Snyder, Thomas D., and Sally Dillow. 2013. *Digest of Education Statistics 2012*. Washington, DC: National Center for Educational Statistics. https://nces.ed.gov/pubs2014/2014015.pdf.

Sullivan, Patrick. 2017. "'Deep Reading' as a Threshold Concept in Composition Studies." In *Deep Reading: Teaching Reading in the Writing Classroom*, edited by Patrick Sullivan, Howard Tinberg, and Sheridan Blau, 143–71. Urbana, IL: NCTE.

Sullivan, Patrick, Howard Tinberg, and Sheridan Blau. 2017. *Deep Reading: Teaching Reading in the Writing Classroom*. Urbana, IL: NCTE.

Wardle, Elizabeth, and Doug Downs. 2017. *Writing about Writing: A College Reader*. 3rd ed. Boston: Bedford/St. Martin's.

Yancey, Kathleen Blake, Liane Robertson, and Kara Taczak. 2014. *Writing across Contexts: Transfer, Composition and Culture of Writing*. Logan: Utah State University Press.

4
WRITING AS PRACTICED AND STUDIED BEYOND "WRITING STUDIES"

Doug Hesse and Peggy O'Neill

What are the borders of "writing studies?" We ask this question in light of ongoing thoughtful efforts to establish threshold concepts of this discipline. We ask because some writing sites and traditions don't seem to be represented in the definitional work done so far. A consideration of two of those sites—creative writing and journalism—will illustrate our point and, if we're successful, suggest a couple of options. One would be to add new threshold concepts within or adjacent to writing studies, an addition to accommodate more inhabitants under the roof of writing, although we aren't suggesting we (or others whose primary identification is in composition and rhetoric) are the ones who should be making decisions about threshold concepts from other areas. The other would be to adopt a different name, perhaps *composition studies*, recognizing that writing has many addresses in different departments, programs, and professions.

Discussions of threshold concepts consider how disciplines function in the academy, how knowledge is made, what students need to learn, and how faculty are educated and prepared. According to Jan Meyer and Ray Land (2006), threshold concepts tend to be transformative, irreversible, integrative, bounded, and troublesome. Sometimes these concepts are academic, in the best sense of the term, shaping scholarly membership to a discipline. Sometimes, however, concepts are grounded less in scholarly identity than in professional practitioner identity. After all, psychologists, engineers, chemists, economists, historians, and writers practice in the world beyond universities. Many fields, in fact, aim to prepare students to practice in that world, not within the academic one. For example, *Threshold Concepts in Practice* (Land, Meyer, and Flanagan 2016) devotes nine chapters to specific professions, including engineering, medicine, nursing, computer science, law, teaching, and architecture. The two-way link between the profession and the academy is fluid, and the degree to which one site exerts more influence than the other in generating threshold concepts varies. In the introduction to this volume, Linda Adler-Kassner and Elizabeth Wardle recognize this link, noting they "tend to use the term 'community of practice' (Wenger 1999) rather than 'discipline' since disciplines can be understood as communities of practice, and threshold concepts are also operative in sites well beyond academic disciplines" (4). Composition studies, for example, is heavily shaped by professors' knowledge, while creative writing and journalism take their leads from writers' experience itself. Writing is fundamental to all three areas, which surely share many threshold concepts, such *as writing speaks to situations through recognizable forms* (Bazerman 2015, 35) or *revision is central to developing writing* (Downs 2015, 66). But creative writing and journalism have emphases beyond those endemic to composition.

One implication is that readers of volumes like *Naming What We Know* (Adler-Kassner and Wardle 2015) should take care not to assume the threshold concepts of writing studies now being articulated stand for all of writing. After all, *writing studies* claims a big domain, transcending more focused terms like *composition studies*. Adler-Kassner and Wardle acknowledge that "the threshold concepts of writing studies speak both to and beyond our disciplinary community . . . because the subject of our discipline—composed knowledge—is widely relevant" (3). This interdisciplinarity—or transdisciplinarity—has long generated considerable discussion within the field, as elaborated, for example, in Janice Lauer's 1984 conception of composition as a dappled discipline.

In her introduction to *Naming What We Know*, Kathleen Blake Yancey (2015) provides an historical overview of the disciplinary core of rhetoric and composition, or composition studies, tellingly using those more limited names. The prior question about how we should name *who* we are (or what we ought to be called) isn't asked in Adler-Kassner and Wardle's own introduction to *Naming What We Know*. For some people, *composition studies* might seem an inferior term. The gravitational force of composition as merely a first-year requirement is strong, after all, and many thus see it as limiting. Coupling composition with rhetoric, as many in the field do, is one way of addressing some of the limitations suggested by composition, but rhetoric comes with its own concerns, as Jennifer Maher (see ch. 5, this volume) argues. Maher contends that "rhetoric is one of our essential threshold concepts, but one not merely initially troublesome to learners but persistently troublesome for both learners and experts in the discipline" (99). The term *writing* opens a wider domain than *composition*, even when *composition* is partnered with *rhetoric*, one arguably more vital and important. Clearly, we ought to imagine our province as fully as we can claim professional knowledge for doing so. But if we're going to claim writing—all of it—we ought to make sure we actually account for everything and include those who work in writing outside the typical bounds of composition studies. We should also include voices from those areas more interested in questioning the status quo than normalizing it, as well as those perspectives that have been marginalized in the dominant discourse (see, for example, the critiques in chs. 1 and 2 of this volume).

Adler-Kassner and Wardle (2015) wisely insist on the provisional nature of their enterprise. They contend that the emerging threshold concepts present "not a canonical statement" but "an articulation of shared beliefs providing multiple ways of helping us name what we know and how we can use what we know in the service of writing" (xix). Naming and sharing, Yancey (2015) notes, provide an opportunity "to uncover and interrogate assumptions" and to help us engage with "our colleagues in general education and writing across the curriculum" (xix). Adler-Kassner and Wardle (2015) share this stance, explaining that the "threshold concepts from writing studies can assist writers and teachers of all sorts, whatever their disciplinary or professional affiliations" (3). Adler-Kassner and Wardle, in both the introduction to this volume and with coauthors in chapter 1, acknowledge the critiques and limitations of a threshold concepts framework but argue that while these may be valid to some extent, the "the potential benefits outweighed the risks" (23).

While threshold concepts offer analytic and explanatory benefits, Meyer and Land (2006) explain that a "non-trivial" issue is the possibility that "they might become part of a 'totalising' or 'colonising' view of the curriculum," exerting a "normalising function in a Foulcaldian sense" (16). They can become unproductively ossified. As the sixteen authors of chapter 2 (this volume) argue, literacy, which includes writing, has been used to oppress and to liberate. Adler-Kassner and Wardle (2015) recognize the danger, explaining their goal as is to identify and explore "final-for-now definitions of *some* of what our field knows" (4). In the introduction to this new volume, they reaffirm that "the threshold concepts are contingent, contextual, and threshold-for-now," acknowledging that "there are always more concepts to be named, additional exploration of the boundaries surrounding the realms where these concepts are operative, and discussions to be had about the relevance of the concepts named" (9). In that spirit, we have been thinking about how some others think about writing, especially those coming from outside composition studies, and how they might help us think about writing.

Specifically, we focus on creative writing and journalism, disciplines that feature writing as a subject of study, as a teaching subject, and as an extra-academic professional practice. We explore these fields as informed colleagues who have shared our academic homes (as well as our personal lives) with creative writers and journalists, as professors who have directed creative theses and dissertations and taught creative writing, and as writers who have quite modestly published creative and journalistic work. We consider whether some ideas about writing from creative writing and journalism should be folded into writing studies, recognizing that members of these fields might embrace or reject such folding, either as colonizing or corrupting. Our goal is not to stake a claim in either of these fields or to annex their territory for compositionists. Rather, we aim to interrogate the contours of writing as mapped by these different communities in their scholarship and professional documents to consider the complications of claiming writing studies for ourselves.

THE CASE OF CREATIVE WRITING

Just as there are composition and composition studies, so there are also creative writing and creative writing studies. In both cases, the single extra word opens different emphases, as Tim Mayers (2009) has outlined. Composition (without studies) traditionally has referred to the required academic course or sequence, so well established (and often critiqued) that it's earned the shorthand FYC. Add *studies*, and a different lens opens, one focusing on research and scholarship that ranges from the pedagogical and the applied to the historical, critical, and theoretical; that scholarship substantially includes the acts, sites, and status of writing beyond the first year.

Creative writing similarly points to broad introductory-level courses that parallel (but for the requirement) composition, but creative writing further leads into intermediate and advanced fiction, poetry, or creative nonfiction, or into genres or subgenres. Adding *studies* again opens a scholarly terrain "about" those courses, especially regarding pedagogy but also about writing itself. Dianne Donnelly (2012) summarizes the distinction this way: "Creative writing and *creative writing studies* are two distinct enterprises.... Whereas the curricular design of creative writing programs continues (and plans to continue) to offer value-added writing and reading strategies for students who want to develop their writing/reading skills and improve their works-in-progress, the ascending field of creative writing studies—as a separate program track—rethinks its pedagogy and scholarship and shifts its educational goals." Creative writing has paralleled composition in asserting a content needing to be defined and recognized. When Graeme Harper and Jery Kroll (2008) ask of creative writing, "What is its *specific* subject matter and what is related to it, but perhaps not core to its interests?" (2), they take on a familiar task. For both composition and creative writing, *studies* claims a scholarly identity. Many fields have made this move with varying degrees of staying power: women and gender studies, aging studies, Judaic studies, cultural studies, American studies, even English studies, and more. However, while people teaching (and teaching about) composition generally agree it should be researched, creative writing studies has faced skepticism from writers themselves. Status in creative writing comes through publication, and some snidely whiff that those who can't do "real writing" (that is, publish stories, poems, memoirs, etc.), instead write about teaching or do lit crit.

Of course, creative writing and its teachers have long been marginalized in many English departments. Some in literary studies, especially in the shadow of high theory, have scoffed at its perceived lack of intellectual rigor (Graff 2009). Some in composition studies, especially in the shadow of social constructivism, have questioned creative writing's naïve romanticism, shallow theorizing, and ideological/political naïveté; James Berlin's 1996 *Rhetoric and Poetic* exemplifies this perspective. In turn, many creative writers have associated "mere composition" with formalistic scullery work that's less about "real" writing than about providing service from teaching outposts writers might endure on the way to worthier territories.

Those viewpoints have significantly softened, especially in recently constituted departments of writing that marry composition and creative writing (and technical, professional, and other species). Creative writing has embraced nonfiction. Composition has begun taking seriously forms of discourse that privilege rhetorical tools beyond logos. Both enterprises have substantially been transformed from their common Cinderella status in English-department kitchens. Thirty years ago, Bob Scholes (1985) sketched how English valued "literary" texts over nonliterary ones and reading/consumption over writing/production. Scholes established four hierarchized domains of English departments: reading literature, reading nonliterature, writing literature (a.k.a. creative writing), and writing nonliterature (a.k.a. composition). The last two Scholes waggishly called "writing pseudo literature" and "writing pseudo non literature" (7). Scholes fought this hierarchy.

Since then, creative writing and composition have both ascended, even triumphed. Production has gained favor for students who increasingly want to make, not consume, perceiving more careers, skills, opportunities, and interests in writing than they do in reading, resulting in more significant enrollments in writing than in reading, attended by tracks, majors, minors, and separate departments. At the same time, composition's longstanding commitments to pedagogy, assessment, and applied research enjoy new status as higher education "discovers" teaching. Some proponents of creative writing studies believe that advocating parallel scholarly approaches about creative writing courses offers similar access to respectability. Conversely, critics from within creative writing believe courses and programs are doing just fine without, thank you, and worry about corrupting the field's identity, promise, and spirit. That's a position eloquently sketched by Anna Leahy (2016), a writer thoroughly affiliated with creative writing studies, in "Against Creative Writing Studies and for Ish-ness."

We cite status parallels between composition (studies) and creative writing (studies) to ask what threshold concepts might be claimed for writing versus for composition or for creative writing. After all, the term *writing* umbrellas both. It's odd to imagine a house (or office building or apartment) named *writing* beyond whose threshold lies *creative writing*. We might, then, build an addition to writing studies that makes room for creative writing, knowing the latter may not welcome the space. Donnelly (2012) implies as much when she writes, "The academic goal of creative writing studies is to stand alongside composition studies and literary studies and any other university field of study as a separate-but-equal [ouch!] discipline" (2).

We aren't the first to consider which threshold concepts might define creative writing. In "The Writer and Meta-knowledge about Writing: Threshold Concepts in Creative Writing," Janelle Adsit (2017) cites *Naming What We Know*, quoting several propositions as preamble to her own list of creative writing concepts (305). As a single voice among a vast field of writers, no more, no less, Adsit generates a dozen thematic areas: attention, creativity, authorship, language, genre, craft, community, evaluation, representation, resistance, theory, and revision. Several resonate with those in *Naming*, such as "There are no universal standards for 'good writing'; however, there are conventions that are particular to established genres" (309) or "All forms of representation, including literary production, can be interrogated for assumptions, values, and ideologies" (311).

Other concepts diverge. For example, Adsit (2017) asserts that "writers learn to be responsive to what emerges in the process of creation, as they also bring comparative literary analysis to bear on their revision process" (313). The first clause suggests a rather organic dynamic for revision, a Romantic notion that the emerging text cues possibilities. The second clause mitigates that dynamic by assigning a role to the extratextual knowledge of literary analysis. Neither clause invokes the dynamics of reader needs/responses, rhetorical situation, or authorial purpose that are vital in composition studies.

Some of Adsit's (2017) concepts are controversial to writers themselves. For example, she offers, "Historical knowledge of aesthetic theories is important to the practice and craft of writing" (313). Although a sense of tradition matters to most poets, novelists, and essayists, Adsit overstates the significance of theory for many writers. Her qualifying restriction of theory to that "written by writers, for writers" (313) somewhat redeems it.

To press further the kind of thinking Adsit (2017) began, we reviewed three broad bodies of work about creative writing. One—from which we've primarily drawn so far—is the literature of creative writing studies, found in a burgeoning series of books and at least two journals: the well-established *New Writing: The International Journal for the Practice and Theory of Creative Writing* and the more nascent *Journal of Creative Writing Studies*. Stephanie Vanderslice's 2012 *Rethinking Creative Writing in Higher Education* contains a brief narrative bibliography of a field that is now sufficiently venerable to invite both canonical analyses, such as Mary Hedengren's 2015 "The Necessity of Influence: *New Writing* Articles and Establishing Creative Writing Scholarship," and pedagogical axiologies, such as Alexandra Peary and Tom Hundley's 2015 *Creative Writing Pedagogies for the 21st Century*. The last parallels early works like Tim Donovan and Ben McClelland's 1980 *Eight Approaches to Composition* or, more recently, Gary Tate, Amy Rupiper, Kurt Schick, and Brooke Hessler's 2014 *A Guide to Composition Pedagogies*.

Our second body of sources is authors writing about their own writing, their writing lives, their peers' work, and writing in general. This corpus is most famously embodied in the *Paris Review* interviews of poets, fiction writers, and novelists, hundreds of them since 1952. Author interviews are a mainstay of literary magazines and trade/scholarly magazines such as the Association of Writers and Writing Programs' *Writer's Chronicle*. These publications also feature craft essays and essays/memoirs on the writing life. Books in the genre, such as Stephen King's 2000 *On Writing: A Memoir of the Craft* or Annie Dillard's 1989 *The Writing Life*, provide advice but also constitute identity, figuring ways of being a writer.

Finally, there are advice books and textbooks. By the former, we mean the vast self-help industry, once led by *Writer's Digest* and *Writer's*

Market but now more diffuse, calculated to help aspiring writers, from journaling to publishing. Academic writers mostly scorn it, though they tolerate advice from "serious" writers, such as John Gardner's *The Art of Fiction: Notes on Craft for Young Writers*. Creative writing textbooks are accepted as a necessary evil for introductory classes but dismissed thereafter. Still, just as composition textbooks constituted a body of knowledge for the field in its infancy, so have creative writing texts. A bestseller like Janet Burroway's 2015 *Imaginative Writing* establishes the parameters of craft in six ideas—image, voice, character, setting, story, development and revision—which Burroway deploys, in modes-of-discourse fashion, across the genres of creative nonfiction, fiction, poetry, and drama.

From this literature, we offer four commonplaces within creative writing, an inexhaustive list that we're confident, with more exploration, would constitute a set of threshold concepts. The first: *writing requires mastering craft*. Craft refers to a host of techniques and strategies that can be identified, manipulated, practiced, taught, acquired. These include everything from point of view to characterization to emplotment to meter and rhyme to, the most sacred of all, show, don't tell; that last is nearly a threshold concept in its own right. Craft is related to but different from—bigger than—style. But while craft can be taught (in fact, in some traditions, it's the only—and least important—thing that can be), mere technicians aren't necessarily good writers.

From this precept follows a second: *there is tradition (and craft), and there is talent (and art)*. Creative writing values writers being familiar with the literature that preceded and contemporarily surrounds them. Writers derive craft insights from successful writers. The cynical side of this, as Chad Harbach (2014) notes, is that writers need to create readerships and these readerships consist mainly of other writers, embodied in legions of little magazines and reviews (28). However, beyond tradition and craft are talent and art. Crucial aspects of writing are imagination, creativity, insight, spirit, and so on. These are ineffable—or at least that's at the heart of the venerable position that creative writing (as opposed to more workaday and servile kinds) can't be taught but, rather, only invited, encouraged, and coached on its margins. Creative writing studies mostly rejects that view, as, for example, in Kelly Ritter and Stephanie Vanderslice's 2007 *Can It Really Be Taught: Resisting Lore in Creative Writing Pedagogy*. Still, someone "in" creative writing understands the dynamics and tension between what aspects of writing can be rendered explicit and coaxed and what lie somehow beyond. For example, David Foster Wallace (2014) noted that professional writer/teachers "must teach the practice of art, which by its nature always exists in at least some state of tension with the rules of its practice, as essentially an applied system of rules" (77).

A third: *writers are writers*. This tautology invokes a prevalent assumption that there is some unique, vital identity of "real" writer as opposed to "mere" writer. While of course everyone writes, not least because school and work compel them, there is a difference between people who write and people who are writers. The difference is expressed in the need and desire to write when not compelled. By this way of thinking, writers have a particular allegiance to cultivating a writerly persona, to developing particular work habits, and so on. The identity of writer needn't (and generally can't) be manifested in making a living as a writer. What matters is manifesting passions and commitments (and perhaps insights and abilities) beyond those in people for whom writing is an aspect of their identities—but not a centrally defining one. We acknowledge the deconstruction-begging Romanticism of this identity, but the noble isolated artist is only one aspect. Affiliation with community is essential, especially given the current state of publishing.

That brings us to the last, most important: *authors' reports on their own writing are privileged forms of knowledge*. While critics and theorists may generate useful insights, essential knowledge derives from practitioners themselves: from poets, novelists, and essayists. Patrick Bizzaro (2009, 258) affirms Wendy Bishop's belief that "the teaching of writing should reflect what writers actually do and that our research methods should permit us to collect that information by studying writers at work: 'The writer-teacher-who-writes (and teaches writing out of that writing).'"

We realize our exploration into creative writing studies as a territory within the larger landscape of writing studies is brief, and even contentious for some, but it maps some of the overlap between the ground occupied by creative writing studies and that claimed by composition studies. Our point is not to stake a claim on creative writing but rather to think about what it means to name the field *writing studies*, and then to articulate that field's threshold concepts requires us to think about writing in more expansive ways. With that view in mind, we turn to a different field, journalism.

THE CASE OF JOURNALISM

Journalism is not limited to writing (there are television and radio, for example, with live reporting), but it has writing as a significant focus. With schools of journalism established over a century ago, and the

Associated Press founded in 1846, journalism has a long history as both an academic discipline and profession, and as with creative writing, there often is tension between these two aspects of it. Even though there exists a field of journalism studies (parallel to composition and creative writing and marked by books, journals, textbooks, and conferences) with journalists and journalism scholars that attend to writing, the field tends not to study writing in the ways composition scholars do. In fact, distinctive principles of journalism—which fit threshold concepts as Meyer and Land (2006) define them—constitute a framework beyond writing. An ethos, as it were, for the profession. While journalism practitioners and educators care about issues of style, structure, and other textual features, that ethos focuses more on truth and accuracy (Craft and Davis 2013, 33; Society of Professional Journalists).

Journalism is defined both in terms of what journalists do—"gathering, assessing, creating, and presenting news and information" and what they produce (American Press Institute 2017). There are "recognizable forms" with different genres for different outlets, purposes, and audiences. Writing is a technology journalists employ in the service of their primary purpose, which is to inform (Craft and Davis 2013; Fink 2003).

Journalism distinguishes itself "from other activities and products by . . . identifiable characteristics and practices . . . that separate journalism from other forms of communication" (American Press Institute). Among these practices, defined in textbooks such as *Principles of American Journalism: An Introduction* (Craft and Davis 2013) and *Elements of Journalism* (Kovach and Rosenstiel 2007), are newsgathering and reporting with the purpose of seeking and reporting the truth. Professional journalists identify the role of the press, especially in the United States, as central to a democratic society. This ethos is apparent in foundational documents like the mission statement of the American Press Institute: "For democracies to thrive, people need accurate information about the problems of civil society and the debates over how to solve them. That requires an economically sustainable, independent and free press that is vested in the values of verification and monitoring the powerful, and is dedicated to putting citizens first, ahead of political faction" (2017). We want to be clear that we're characterizing the ethos and guidelines of professional journalism, not the advocacy forms of writing some want to pass as journalism, the pages of Breitbart or MoveOn, for example. Within the Society of Professional Journalists Code of Ethics are four principles, the first of which is to "Seek Truth and Report It," to "be accurate and fair" and "honest and courageous."

Eighteen behaviors range from the rather lofty and abstract—such as "Take responsibility for the accuracy of their work" or "Support the open and civil exchange of views, even views they find repugnant"—to the more mundane—such as "Label advocacy and commentary" or "Never plagiarize. Always attribute."

The American Press Institute (2017), drawing on Kovach and Rosenstiel's (2007) popular book, identifies ten elements of "good journalism":

1. Journalism's first obligation is to the truth.
2. Its first loyalty is to citizens.
3. Its essence is a discipline of verification.
4. Its practitioners must maintain an independence from those they cover.
5. It must serve as an independent monitor of power.
6. It must provide a forum for public criticism and compromise.
7. It must strive to keep the significant interesting and relevant.
8. It must keep the news comprehensive and proportional.
9. Its practitioners must be allowed to exercise their personal conscience.
10. Citizens, too, have rights and responsibilities when it comes to the news.

Kovach and Rosenstiel (2007) emphasize the personal ethics of journalists as key to the integrity of the field. Because no formal regulations credential journalists, they explain, and "since by its nature [journalism] can be exploitive, a heavy burden rests on the ethics and judgment of the individual journalist and the individual organization where he or she works" (230). This ethos is found across journalism textbooks, as, for example, Craft and Davis (2013) affirming journalism's role as a watchdog requiring fairness and independence. The Associated Press defines its role as bringing "truth to the world." In fulfilling this goal, the AP explains that today "news is transmitted in more ways than ever before—in print, on the air and on the Web, with words, images, graphics, sounds and video. But always and in all media, we insist on the highest standards of integrity and ethical behavior." More specifically, for example, "That means we abhor inaccuracies, carelessness, bias or distortions." This level of attention to ethics and the formation of students' and professionals' ethos surpasses what we see in other writing-related fields. Granted, all teachers, disciplines, and professions value integrity and ethics, but journalism considers it essential.

Despite the differences, professional journalists and theorists share several tenets with writing studies. They emphasize that learning to write requires learning about writing but, most important, doing it. They emphasize revision, audience and purpose, storytelling, style, structure, and genre expectations. But what is paramount is journalism's expectation of veracity. An engaging, interesting story must be accurate, must report the truth, must create meaning. Sensationalism, or "infotainment" as Kovach and Rosenstiel (2007, 191) call it, is not to be confused with effective journalism.

A defining feature of journalism writing is the style guide. The most popular is the *Associated Press Stylebook and Briefing on Media Law* (Associated Press 2018). The text, in its fifty-second edition, claims to be "the industry's best selling reference." It is considered the go-to guide for grammar, mechanics, and usage, and it also includes guidelines for different types of journalism, with sections, for example, on broadcast, business, food, and religion. While all writers and presses abide by style guides, the reverence for the style guide in journalism surpasses those for composition studies (although one might argue that many in literary studies approach the MLA handbook with equal zeal).

Echoing the importance of tradition in creative writing, Elliot King and Jane Chapman (2012) propose that journalism students should develop more than just skills related to gathering information and writing; they should understand different components of the discipline: its history, its practice, key works produced by journalists, key figures, and critical analysis of it and its impact (4). Their position reflects standards articulated by professional organizations such as the Association for Education in Journalism and Mass Communication and the Accrediting Council on Education in Journalism and Mass Communications (ACEJMC), which is responsible for evaluating college journalism and mass communications programs. Many competencies and values for accreditation are broader than writing, such as the injunction that students should "understand and apply the principles and laws of freedom of speech and press, for the country in which the institution that invites ACEJMC is located, as well as receive instruction in and understand the range of systems of freedom of expression around the world, including the right to dissent, to monitor and criticize power, and to assemble and petition for redress of grievances" (Accrediting Council on Education in Journalism and Mass Communications 2018). Other competencies, more specific to writing, resonate with those of us in composition studies:

- demonstrate an understanding of the history and role of professionals and institutions in shaping communications;
- understand concepts and apply theories in the use and presentation of images and information;
- think critically, creatively and independently;

- conduct research and evaluate information by methods appropriate to the communications professions in which they work;
- write correctly and clearly in forms and styles appropriate for the communications professions, audiences and purposes they serve;
- critically evaluate their own work and that of others for accuracy and fairness, clarity, appropriate style and grammatical correctness;
- apply tools and technologies appropriate for the communications professions in which they work. (Accrediting Council on Education in Journalism and Mass Communications 2018)

A discipline with journals, books, and organizations devoted to teaching and education, journalism scholarship often views issues similar to those in composition, although through a different lens. For example, journalism scholars may study a story to parse the coverage or the reporting, as in three papers at the Association for Education in Journalism and Mass Communication 2017 conference: "The Nation's Stamp of Approval: The 1976 Women's-Magazine Campaign for the ERA," "Misconception of Barack Obama's Religion: A Content Analysis of Print News Coverage of the President," and "Framing Drunken Driving as a Social Problem." Or, scholars may focus on the content of particular publications, as in other papers from the same conference: "On the Cover of the Rollin' Stone: How *Rolling Stone* Magazine Frames Politics and News" or "PolitiFact Coverage of Candidates for U.S. Senate and Governor 2010–2016." With creative writing, journalism shares a tradition of interviewing journalists about their work (e.g., Robert Boynton's 2005 *The New Journalism: Conversations with America's Best Nonfiction Writers on Their Craft*) or featuring key journalists and their influence (e.g., Kate McLoughlin's 2007 *Martha Gellhorn: The War Writer in the Field and in the Text*).

Although composition studies may have some features in common with journalism, defining concepts in and about journalism differ from how we define them in writing studies. A key distinction is that for journalism, the profession is the primary guide for education. To a large extent, creative writing shares that orientation, its goal being to produce publishing writers, not academics (although cynics might say otherwise). At the level of application, writing studies does not aspire to create certain kinds of professional writers but rather a broader repertory of transferrable knowledge and skills. The purpose of the undergraduate degree in journalism is to prepare students for careers, but, certainly, journalists would agree with the sentiment of many threshold concepts of writing studies articulated in *Naming What We Know*. Consider a substitution, which would likely be uncontroversial.

Metaconcept: *Journalism* is an activity and a subject of study.
1. *Journalism* speaks to situations through recognizable forms.
2. *Journalism* enacts and creates identities and ideologies.
3. All *journalists* have more to learn.

However, journalists would not likely list precepts like these as their primary threshold concepts. More likely, the concepts for journalism would reflect the ten elements we quoted above from the American Press Institute (2017)—such as "Journalism's first obligation is to the truth," "Its first loyalty is to citizens," and so on. Our point is not to claim journalism as our own, or to critique it, but rather to illustrate that some key concepts of journalism may overlap in some ways with those identified with writing studies because writing is an essential element of journalism.

CONCLUSIONS

Our purpose in characterizing concepts from creative writing and journalism is to point out how the threshold concepts canon of writing studies, as articulated by those who work in composition and rhetoric, may not account for concepts important in other domains of writing, domains that seem to fit within the purview of writing, especially with characteristics of professions. From our depictions above, for example, we note how creative writing and journalism both insist on writing as ethos formation. Creative writing prizes fealty to tradition and craft, with a writer's own experiences as paramount. Journalism prizes fealty to truth above all, the formation of a personal identity that collectively constitutes the field's identity.

Some creative writing precepts likely would have been less troubling within composition studies just two or three decades ago. Then, the presence of "creative writers" at the CCCC convention and in the field's journals exemplified a less problematic expressivist tradition. Belletrism was a reasonable aim alongside academic discourse and argument, and creative nonfiction wasn't yet fully claimed by creative writing per se. Wendy Bishop was this movement's avatar, and her extensive works, beginning with *Colors of a Different Horse* (Bishop and Ostrom 1994), inflected composition studies until the highwater mark of her 1999 *CCC* essay "Places to Stand." But already by then, the field was moving in a different direction, signaled by the nature (if not exactly the ferocity) of Gary Olson's (2000) rebuke of that essay, concluding, "Wendy wants creative writers to 'matter,' and I want composition studies to matter as an intellectual discipline" (40). It's clear composition studies has gone a different direction from Bishop's since then (and arguably from Olson's high theory, too). In any case, the territory of academic creative writing was being staked out as AWP went from conferences of several hundred members to conferences of ten thousand or more.

The journalistic potential of composition studies had its own avatar, Donald Murray, celebrated through the 1980s and 1990s as having been a Pulitzer Prize-winning journalist for the *Boston Globe*. But Murray was known in the field much less for his advice on journalism (like his 2000 *Writing to Deadline: The Journalist at Work*) than for his work on process, craft, and teaching. Like Bishop, Murray ultimately came to be associated with a denigrated expressivist tradition. More widely, however, the journalistic orientation to reporting has enjoyed comparatively little favor in a composition studies tradition that has favored academic argument and analysis. The editorial and Op Ed may have some valence as civic discourse within composition studies, but the news story largely may not. Composition's studies may admire journalism's professional ethics, but in curious ways, this ethic, with its fealty to objective, discoverable truths, is antithetical to rhetorical roots. While journalism's information dynamic perhaps intersects with technical writing, its storytelling dynamic—to create interest that turns attention rather than to meet a given rhetorical situation—finds less home within writing studies as currently constituted.

Furthermore, journalism's focus on codified styles and practices seeks to map circumscribed, vocational target discourse. Still, it's valuable for writing studies to embrace some journalistic practices and genres. For example, when John Duffy (2017) asks us to "understand our work as the teaching of . . . 'trustful talk among strangers'" (244), journalism's calls for accuracy, verification, and trust are useful compass points. We understand how journalism's orientation to creating career identities rather than to cultivating general writing sensibilities doesn't quite fit composition, but certain of its practices and assumptions do. Other areas of journalism seem to overlap with creative writing, such as long-form literary journalism, as published in the *New Yorker* and other magazines, and the new journalism of writers such as Truman Capote and Ken Kesey.

Our point, finally, is that in developing helpful and generative threshold concepts about writing, we should not inadvertently ignore "outside" professional bodies of knowledge and practice about writing. As Adler-Kassner and Wardle note in their introduction to this volume, "Naming the discipline, naming threshold concepts, and naming activities that stem from those concepts have consequences for those we consider to be at the center of all of this work: our students, instructors in our programs and centers, colleagues in our institutions" (10). We might understand how to build bridges for students and others between the kinds of writing they do in school and composition courses and the kinds that exist in the world beyond our classrooms.

One possibility—a bad one, we think—would expand the catalog of writing studies to include those concepts that are transformative, irreversible, integrative, bounded, and troublesome to creative writers and journalists. Such an expansion might strike the latter as an appropriating, even colonizing, move. More sensibly, we should keep in mind that writing exists in practices beyond those of focal concern in rhetoric and composition doctoral programs. We should acknowledge those practices and what might be useful in them, including their key terms and definitions of shared terms, as Chris Anson, Chen Chen, and Ian Anson have explored in their chapter in this collection. And, at the very least, we should refer to and value those "other" domains as we teach teachers, lest in constructing threshold concept knowledge with them (Timmermans and Meyer 2017), we stop short of writing's full potential.

REFERENCES

Adler-Kassner, Linda, and Elizabeth Wardle, eds. 2015. *Naming What We Know: Threshold Concepts of Writing Studies*. Logan: Utah State University Press.

Adsit, Jannell. 2017. "The Writer and Meta-knowledge about Writing: Threshold Concepts in Creative Writing." *New Writing* 14 (3): 304–15.

Accrediting Council on Education in Journalism and Mass Communications. N. d. "Principles of Accreditation." Accessed January 10, 2018. http://www.acejmc.org/policies-process/principles/.

American Press Institute. N.d. "The Elements of Journalism." Accessed December 15, 2017. www.americanpressinstitute.org/journalism-essentials/what-is-journalism/elements-journalism/.

Associated Press. 2018. *The Associated Press Stylebook and Briefing on Media Law*. New York: Basic Books.

Associated Press. N.d. Associated Press Statement of News Values and Principles. Accessed January 10, 2018. https://www.ap.org/about/news-values-and-principles/downloads/ap-news-values-and-principles.pdf.

Association for Education in Journalism and Mass Communication Conference. N.d. "2017 Abstracts." Accessed January 10, 2018. www.aejmc.org/home/2017/06/2017-abstracts/.

Bazerman, Charles. 2015. "Writing Speaks to Situations through Recognizable Forms." In *Naming What We Know: Threshold Concepts of Writing Studies*, edited by Linda Adler-Kassner and Elizabeth Wardle, 35–37. Logan: Utah State University Press.

Bishop, Wendy. 1999. "Places to Stand: The Reflective Writer-Teacher-Writer in Composition." *College Composition and Communication* 51 (1): 9–31.

Bishop, Wendy, and Hans A. Ostrom, eds. 1994. *Colors of a Different horse: Rethinking Creative Writing Theory and Pedagogy*. Urbana, IL: NCTE.

Berlin, James. 1996. *Rhetorics, Poetics, and Cultures: Refiguring English Studies.* Urbana, IL: NCTE.

Bizzaro, Patrick. 2009. "Writers Wanted: A Reconsideration of Wendy Bishop." *College English* 71 (3): 256–70.

Boynton, Robert S. 2005. *The New Journalism: Conversations with America's Best Nonfiction Writers on Their Craft.* New York: Vintage.

Burroway, Janet. 2015. *Imaginative Writing.* 4th ed. New York: Pearson.

Craft, Stephanie, and Charles N. Davis. 2013. *Principles of American Journalism: An Introduction.* New York: Routledge.

Dillard, Annie. 1989. *A Writer's Life.* New York: Harper and Rowe.

Donovan, Timothy R., and Ben W. McClelland, eds. 1980. *Eight Approaches to Teaching Composition.* Urbana, IL: NCTE.

Donnelly, Dianne. 2012. *Establishing Creative Writing Studies As an Academic Discipline.* New Writing Viewpoints 7. Bristol: Multilingual Matters.

Downs, Doug. 2015. "Revision Is Central to Developing Writing." In *Naming What We Know: Threshold Concepts of Writing Studies,* edited by Linda Adler-Kassner and Elizabeth Wardle, 66–67. Logan: Utah State University Press.

Duffy, John. 2017. "The Good Writer: Virtue Ethics and the Teaching of Writing." *College English* 79 (3): 229–50.

Fink, Conrad C. 2003. *Writing to Inform and Engage: The Essential Guide to Beginning News and Magazine Writing.* Cambridge, MA: Westview.

Gardner, John. 1991. *The Art of Fiction: Notes on Craft for Young Writers.* New York: Random House.

Graff, Gerald. 2009. "What We Say When We Don't Talk about Creative Writing." *College English* 71 (3): 271–79.

Harbach, Chad. 2014. "MFA vs NYC." In *MFA vs NYC: The Two Cultures of American Fiction,* edited by Chad Harbach, 9–28. New York: n+1/Faber and Faber.

Harper, Graeme, and Jeri Kroll, eds. 2008. *Creative Writing Studies: Practice, Research, and Pedagogy.* Bristol: Multilingual Matters.

Hedengren, Mary. 2015. "The Necessity of Influence: New Writing Articles and Establishing Creative Writing Scholarship." *New Writing* 13 (2): 218–33.

Hessler, Brooke, and Joe Lambert. 2017. "Threshold Concepts in Digital Storytelling: Naming What We Know About Storywork." *In Digital Storytelling in Higher Education,* edited by Grete Jamisson, Pip Hardy, Yngve Nordkvelle, and Heather Pleasants, 19–35. New York: Palgrave Macmillan.

King, Elliot, and Jane L. Chapman. 2012. *Key Readings in Journalism.* New York: Routledge.

King, Stephen. 2000. *On Writing: A Memoir of the Craft.* New York: Scribner.

Kovach, Bill, and Tom Rosenstiel. 2007. *The Elements of Journalism: What Newspeople Should Know and the Public Should Expect.* New York: Three Rivers.

Land, Ray, Jan H. F. Myer, and Michael T. Flanigan, eds. 2016. *Threshold Concepts in Practice.* Rotterdam: Sense.

Lauer, Janice M. 1984. "Composition Studies: Dappled Discipline." *Rhetoric Review* 3 (1): 20–29.

Leahy, Anna. 2016. "Against Creative Writing Studies (and for Ish-ness)." *Journal of Creative Writing Studies* 1 (1): n.p.

Mayers, Tim. 2009. "One Simple Word: From Creative Writing to Creative Writing Studies." *College English* 71 (4): 217–28.

McLoughlin, Kate. 2007. *Martha Gellhorn: The War Writer in the Field and in the Text.* Manchester: Manchester University Press.

Meyer, Jan H. F., and Ray Land. 2006. "Threshold Concepts and Troublesome Knowledge: An Introduction." In *Overcoming Barriers to Student Understanding,* edited by Jan H. F. Meyer and Ray Land, 3–18. London: Routledge.

Murray, Donald M. 2000. *Writing to Deadline: The Journalist at Work*. Portsmouth, NH: Heinemann.

Olson, Gary A. 2000. "The Death of Composition as an Intellectual Discipline." *Composition Studies* 28 (2): 33–41.

Peary, Alexandra, and Tom C. Hunley, eds. 2015. *Creative Writing Pedagogies for the 21st Century*. Carbondale: Southern Illinois University Press.

Ritter, Kelly, and Stephanie Vanderslice, eds. 2007. *Can It Really Be Taught? Resisting Lore in Creative Writing Pedagogy*. Portsmouth, NH: Heinemann.

Scholes, Robert. 1985. *Textual Power: Literary Theory and the Teaching of English*. New Haven, CT: Yale University Press.

Society of Professional Journalists. "SPJ Code of Ethics." Updated September 6, 2014. https://www.spj.org/ethicscode.asp.

Tate, Gary, Amy Rupiper, Kurt Schick, and H. Brooke Hessler, eds. 2014. *A Guide to Composition Pedagogies*. New York: Oxford University.

Timmermans, Julie A., and Jan H. F. Meyer. 2017. "A Framework for Working with University Teachers to Create and Embed 'Integrated Threshold Concept Knowledge' (ITCK) in Their Practice." *International Journal for Academic Development*: 1–15. http://doi.org/10.1080/1360144X.2017.1388241.

Vanderslice, Stephanie. 2012. *Rethinking Creative Writing in Higher Education: Programs and Practices That Work*. Creative Writing Studies.

Wallace, David Foster. 2014. "The Fictional Future." In *MFA vs NYC: The Two Cultures of American Fiction*, edited by Chad Harbach, 73–80. New York, NY: n+1/Faber and Faber.

5
RHETORIC AS PERSISTENTLY "TROUBLESOME KNOWLEDGE"
Implications for Disciplinarity

Jennifer Helene Maher

Disciplinary histories serve the important function of legitimizing the identity and work of a discipline. In their discussion of disciplinary histories in the sciences, Loren Graham, Wolf Lepenies, and Peter Wingart (1983) note distinctions between the internal and external orientations of these histories. The former orientation serves to enculturate newcomers and create a shared sense of identity rooted in the innate value of its disciplinary knowledge (8–10). The latter orientation aims to generate legitimation for the discipline and its knowledge beyond the discipline itself (e.g., the public, the government, funding organizations). Yet, histories of rhetoric and composition are often rooted in what David Fleming (2009) identifies as a "self-consciousness of its own history" (25), in spite of the field's disciplinary rise over the last fifty years. While a number of factors likely contribute to this state (e.g., marginalization in many English departments, the "pedagogical imperative" of composition, an overdependence on contingent labor), it is perhaps the question of our own disciplinarity that too often lies at the heart of such insecurity.

The story of rhetoric and composition's disciplinarity seems always on the edge of a precipice, and that is if it exists as a discipline at all. For example, Robert Connors (1997) warned over twenty years ago, "We are already pursuing research paths so disparate that many thoughtful people have feared that the discipline may fly apart like a dollar watch" (18). Twelve years later, Fleming (2009) observed in his own history, "If, as a discipline, we display extraordinarily avid interest in and knowledge about our history, the actual narratives we relate often differ radically from one another, so much so that they sometimes seem to leave us in different fields altogether" (25). And more recently, John Duffy (2014) assessed the state of the discipline in this way: "We offer no common vision, no shared rationale for our work. We are constrained in telling our story because we are not agreed on just what that story is" (213). And making the matter of our disciplinarity even more tenuous are questions of whether we are, ever have been, or should even desire to be a discipline (Kristensen and Claycomb 2010; Claycomb and Riedner 2004; Horner 2014).

As Maureen Goggin (2000) remarked almost twenty years ago, "Debates over the status of rhetoric and composition as a discipline reveal that *discipline* is a highly contested term in the field" (xix). A significant reason for this contestation, which simultaneously catalyzes the delegitimizing of our disciplinarity not just from outside but also from within, is rhetoric, which I identify as an essential threshold concept in and to the discipline in its various namings (e.g., composition; writing studies; technical communication; professional writing; composition and rhetoric; rhetoric and composition; rhetoric, writing, and composition). Rhetoric has alternately been defined as "the faculty of observing in any given case the available means of persuasion" (Aristotle 1984, 1355b 26–27); "the science of speaking well" (Quintilian 2001, II: xv, 35); "the use of words by human agents to form attitudes or to induce actions in other human agents" (Burke 1969, 51); "the study of how we use language and how language uses us" (Ratcliffe 2003); "just another way to name our laboring with words, with students, with community members, with texts" (Inoue 2017); and "the kind of study one has to perform in order to effect persuasion, the traditional end of rhetoric" (Bizzell 1992, 218). This rhetoric about *rhetoric* may seem so varied and ambiguous as to preclude the term from functioning as a threshold concept, but this is not the case. Threshold concepts function, in the words of Jan Meyer and Ray Land (2003), as "'conceptual gateways' or 'portals' that lead to previously inaccessible, and initially perhaps 'troublesome', ways of thinking about something" (Meyer and Land 2003, 1). And although *rhetoric* is understandably troublesome to newcomers, whose meaning of the word is typically limited at best to the pejorative, it is what I identify as *persistently troublesome* not only to what I refer to in the remainder of this chapter as the *discipline of rhetoric and composition* but also in its very nature, which is perhaps best illustrated in the opening line of classicist George A. Kennedy's (1992) "A Hoot in the Dark: The General Evolution of Rhetoric": "After spending much of my professional life teaching rhetoric, I began to wonder what I was talking about" (1). In fact, in understanding rhetoric as a threshold concept not merely initially but persistently troublesome, we stand to crystallize out of these competing, even antithetical, narratives of our history what

Chris Anson (2015) describes as "a kind of metaknowledge that brings together fundamental principles of discipline-based communication" (204). Consequently, identifying and exploring threshold concepts constitute important and much-needed disciplinary work that, at the same time, highlights the consequences that arise when a threshold concept, for varied reasons, remains persistently troublesome. Just as important, we also stand to reassert the importance of rhetoric to the construction of not only the discipline but also the world.

FROM INITIALLY TO PERSISTENTLY TROUBLESOME

In their earliest discussion of threshold concepts, Meyer and Land use the example of cooking to explain how these concepts work (2003, 1). While cooking at the most elemental level is simply the use of heat to effect an outcome, in the discipline of physics, this process is understood through the concept of heat transfer. Formalized through mathematical expression as an equation, heat transfer is thus known through its function of measuring the temperature gradient, meaning the direction and rate of change in heat. To illustrate how heat transfer works, Meyer and Land use the following example:

> Imagine that you have just poured two identical hot cups of tea (i.e., they are at the same temperature) and you have milk to add. You want to cool down one cup of tea as quickly as possible because you are in a hurry to drink it. You add the milk to the first cup immediately, wait a few minutes and then add an equal quantity of milk to the second cup. At this point which cup of tea will be cooler, and why? (The answer is the second cup, because in the initial stages of cooling it is hotter than the first cup with the milk in it and it therefore loses more heat because of the steeper temperature gradient.) (2003, 1)

To make or even drink a cup of tea safely, one need not understand or even know of the concept of heat transfer. But, as Meyer and Land explain, once you have crossed the liminal threshold of the concept, "it alters the way in which you think about cooking" (2). The process of cooking and the means by which to cook are transformed. When, for example, a person comes to know the threshold concept of heat transfer, even the act of watching a popular cooking show occurs in a new light: "a focus on the pots and pans that are selected by the chef in context (the heat source in relation to the cooking process to be applied as a function of time and its regulation to the ingredients) rather than simply on the ingredients and, superficially, the 'method'" (2003, 1). Thus, the threshold concept rewrites a person's knowledge of the world in ways Meyer and Land (2005) describe as transformative, irreversible, and integrative (373).

In unique constellations, threshold concepts create a necessary and inevitable gateway newcomers must travel through on the path to some degree of disciplinary knowledge and eventual expertise. Essential to establishing and maintaining disciplines, these concepts are also what Meyer and Land identify as bounded and troublesome. The notion of boundedness, described as "possessing terminal frontiers, bordering with thresholds into new conceptual spaces" (2005, 374), may conjure the worst notion of disciplinarity, what Steven Fuller (2007) describes as "a necessary evil of knowledge production" (19). Threshold concepts in this view are obstacles to "holding patterns in the dynamic of enquiry"; they are the first markers of "'well-boundedness'" (Fuller 1991, 310) in a terrain of knowledge. Yet, boundedness does not necessitate impermeability, as interdisciplinary endeavors so well illustrate. Most simply, threshold concepts initially and significantly signal there is something to be known, a feature especially important in a time characterized, particularly in the United States, by what Tom Nichols (2017) identifies, in the book of the same name, as "the death of expertise." While externally oriented legitimation of disciplinary expertise demands engagement with a public on a level made accessible to that public, David Perkins (2006) points out, "Threshold concepts are pivotal but challenging concepts in disciplinary understanding. They act like gateways. Once through the gate, learners come to a new level of understanding central to the discipline" (43). Consequently, threshold concepts are initially troublesome because the knowledge they foster strikes learners as "conceptually difficult," "alien," or "tacit" (38–41).

Identifying threshold concepts can be particularly useful to a discipline like rhetoric and composition, which is not only relatively new to disciplinarity in the context of the modern university but also has a history of struggling with what, if anything, constitutes its disciplinarity. Forty years ago, for example, Douglas Park (1979) lamented, "What composition studies now offer is a potpourri of theory, research, speculation, some of it close to pedagogy, some far removed, some of it speculative and contemplative, some scientifically and experimentally oriented, some of it jargon-ridden and pretentious, enough of it so provoking and stimulating that the pervading sense of excitement and challenge seems justified. What composition research does not offer is a shapely coherence that makes it definable as a discipline" (47). More recently, Kathleen Blake Yancey (2015) has echoed a similar concern: "What seems to be missing, since the beginning of the field and even in this late age of print, is any consensus in the field on what we might call the *content of composition*: the questions, the kind of evidence, and materials that define the disciplines and would thus define us as well" (xviii). Given that a key element to disciplinarity is internal legitimation, the fact that what constitutes our "disciplinary core" (xvii) continues to be unclear is troubling.

Through Linda Adler-Kassner and Elizabeth Wardle's (2015) edited collection *Naming What We Know: Threshold Concepts in Writing Studies*, the coherence and definition needed by the discipline take shape through the identification and explanation of some of its threshold concepts. As they explain, "Whatever we call ourselves, wherever we may be on the continuum of disciplinarity, fifty (plus) years of research has led us to know some things about the subject of composed knowledge" (2). Among the threshold concepts discussed are *writing is a social and rhetorical activity* (Roozen 2015, 16), *writing is not natural* (Dryer 2015, 27), and *writing involves ethical choices* (Duffy 2015, 31), all of which Adler-Kassner and Wardle, as well as contributors, identify as part of the metaconcept *writing is an activity and a subject of study* (15). For many in the discipline, the response to these concepts is likely to be either one of agreement to the point of an indifferent shrug or protest for the sake of what is not identified as a threshold concept. The first response is a result of these concepts identifying a tacit knowledge that those with disciplinary expertise take for granted to such an extent that the concepts hardly seem worth articulating in such an obvious way. The second response stems from the kind of contestation common regarding what knowledge is central to disciplinary identity. Our ongoing struggle with who we are and what it is we do as a discipline necessitates this kind of reverse engineering in order to identify those gateways so fundamental, yet still too often alien, to the tacit and problematic knowledge about "good writing" (see Ball and Loewe 2017, 7–50) both students and the general public possess. As Perkins notes, "The role of tacit knowledge is one of those good news bad news stories. On the good news side, it is often very efficient for knowledge to function tacitly. . . . On the bad news side, learners' tacit presumptions can miss the target by miles, and teachers' more seasoned tacit presumptions can operate like conceptual submarines that learners never manage to detect or track" (2006, 40). Articulating our threshold concepts can therefore be seen as a necessary move to stifle the negative effects of the tacit knowledge of *good writing* that appear in many of the 5.37 million Google results of the term. To this end, "An effort to name what we know to ourselves and to students and faculty new to the discipline . . .

is also an effort and a call to extend discussions about what we know to audiences beyond ourselves" (9). (For a concise example of such an effort, see Roberts-Miller 2017.)

To contribute to this effort and call in our own discipline, I contend that rhetoric is one of our essential threshold concepts but one not merely initially troublesome to learners but persistently troublesome for both learners and experts in the discipline. This is most obvious in the ongoing naming conundrum (Detweiler 2015; Haynes 2003; Phelps and Ackerman 2010) whereby *rhetoric* is partnered with *composition*, sometimes appearing first, sometimes second, or sometimes erased altogether, as demonstrated in the use of *writing studies* or *composition*. What makes the naming issue particularly problematic is the significance of language, particularly in the form of threshold concepts, to signaling that gateways exist. Land (2015) explains, "The conceptual transformation and shifts in subjectivity students experienced in various disciplines . . . were invariably and inextricably accompanied by changes in their use of discourse" (xi). Our own trouble naming the discipline is therefore not only a problem for the discipline itself but also for the students we hope will find the knowledge we have to impart transformative.

In sum, rhetoric is troublesome for two reasons. The first is the positioning of rhetoric as somehow supplemental and not necessarily central to the work of our discipline. The second relates to how rhetoric functions beyond not just our own discipline but beyond disciplines themselves. As Meyer and Land point out, "Language itself, as used within any academic discipline, can be another source of conceptual troublesomeness" (2003, 6). With this, they point to the unique nature of rhetoric in that language is always a constitutive part of every discipline. Even more significantly, rhetoric is an essential way of being in the world. As Thomas Rickert (2012) summarizes, "Rhetoric accomplishes its work by inducing us to shift, at least potentially, how we dwell or see ourselves dwelling in the world. Rhetoric does not just change subjective states of mind; it transforms our fundamental disposition concerning how we are in the world, how we dwell" (xiii). To this end, we must recognize, understand, and embrace the fact that rhetoric is persistently troublesome—necessarily so—because of its complexity and vastness.

DISCIPLINARY TROUBLE

As a sort of twin to disciplinary angst about what we *are*, our discipline has been fraught, to varying degrees over the years, with an anxiety over the significance of what we *do*, not just in relation to other disciplines but also to one another. In 1990, Richard Young, noting the success of our endeavor into disciplinarity, nonetheless warned, "What we are doing today often seems more like building subdivisions than dragon hunting. And the neighbors are getting quarrelsome" (331). Sharon Crowley (2001) argued a decade later, "Increasingly rhetoricians are threatened inside the university by our very own colleagues, those folks who have built an empire in first-year composition" (165–66). But because "composition, as it has been practiced in the required first-year course for more than 100 years, has nothing whatever to do with rhetoric" (Crowley 2003), rhetoric is left struggling (again) to find its real place in the discipline beyond its (sometimes) titular prominence. According to Karen Kopelson (2008), in her research on graduate-student perceptions of the field of rhetoric and composition, rhetoric's position in the field is tenuous to varying degrees: "The field of rhetoric and composition is, in the most extreme cases, gradually evacuating itself of its first term (if not explicitly in name, then implicitly in institutional practice) or, in other cases, is undergoing an interesting inversion of its titular terms" (770). But the marginalization of rhetoric is evident, even in the nascency of the discipline. In a reading of James Britton's foundational work, Russell Durst (2015) concludes, "While Britton pursued scholarship that helped to establish a discipline, he himself was a profoundly anti-disciplinary figure; he studied the role of language in teaching and learning in order to construct a pedagogical framework, but he opposed the idea of developing an academic area" (385). With his attention focused on what he thought really mattered—student learning and the teaching of writing—Britton held "a dismissive attitude toward classical and other forms of rhetorical study" (386). This dismissal has continued in the often-subtle politics of naming, as Krista Ratcliffe (2003) revealed in a discussion of the editorial process at the discipline's flagship journal: "In 1999 Joe Harris sent me page proofs for my *CCC*'s article on rhetorical listening, and I noticed that all my uses of the phrase 'rhetoric and composition studies' had been changed to 'composition studies.' That was the first time I seriously wondered about the absence of rhetoric in the term composition studies; I chalked the absence up to the editor's wanting to save space or perhaps to achieve a more elegant styling, but afterwards, I kept noticing this absence in other journals and books." Although easily read as an attempt to erase rhetoric, the situation is much more complex. When, for instance, efforts to revitalize rhetoric in the 1960s and 70s are described as attempts to "inoculate composition with rhetoric" (Crowley 2003), it is not hard to understand the suspicion, even disdain, some have had and may continue to have for rhetoric, whether in name or in practice. In a blistering critique of *The Prospects of Rhetoric*, edited by Lloyd Bitzer and Edwin Black, W. Ross Winterowd wrote in 1972 of the danger of "cozy clubbiness" in rhetorical studies, an effect he attributed to the Speech Communication Association and "even more so" to the Rhetoric Society of America. Due to this club mentality, "The total impression that one gets from the Conferences is that they were a Mutual Protections, if not a Mutual Admiration, Society" (5).

From a disciplinary perspective, rhetoric has historically raised suspicion either because of its often-conservative reliance on its classical roots in the Western tradition or because of its potentially traitorous appeal to a more palatable kind of scholarly work. What Susan Jarratt (2003) identifies as "classicizing" is evident in Richard Coe's comments, which appeared in the Rhetoric Society of America's newsletter in 1974: "It should be noted first, of course, that rhetoric is an ancient field; predating by more than a millennium even the English language; despite its recent (and temporary?) eclipse by English departments, rhetorical study was for centuries the foundation of education in Europe and elsewhere. Rhetorical study was a sensible foundation because it embraces all forms of symbolic exchange and communication: the use of symbolic concepts and modes of communication is one of the basic defining characteristics of human beings" (1). Though accurately pointing to rhetoric's expanse, the appeal to its ancient roots can appear to smack of a kind of elitism that has traditionally propelled the distinction between the lofty study of literature and the lowly teaching of writing, to say nothing of the privileging of the Western European tradition at the expense of Other rhetorics (e.g., indigenous, queer, Asian, and African American, to name but a few) and rhetorical intersectionalities. But, in *On African-American Rhetoric*, Keith Gilyard and Adam Banks argue, "Rhetoric has set in motion too many positive actions by African Americans to belittle the art categorically, or at the least that should be the case" (10).

Similarly problematic is a justification of rhetoric as more overtly theoretical than the first-year composition classroom typically belies. In a 2001 review of Goggin's edited collection *Inventing a Discipline*, Winterowd noted that purity of scholarship could only occur by "virtually outlawing any work that has even a hint of application. . . . The fear among old-timers in composition-rhetoric is that the field is becoming like literary studies, valuing 'pure' scholarship and devaluing application" (371). This fear was undoubtedly stoked by the fact that the discipline of literature embraced rhetoric in a way that could presumably never occur with composition. George Gopen (2017) highlights a key moment in this embrace: "In 1984, Terry Eagleton published a widely read and well received book on literary theory, *The Function of Criticism*, in which he declared, near its end, with a sense of surprise, that, when you come right down to it, Theory was all about Rhetoric. This was what the high end of the English profession decided to do in response to the crisis. Those new theorists became the people who produced the majority of the most highly regarded books published in the field on a yearly basis for the next three decades" (359). And rather than creating some sort of affinity among the disparate factions in English, the ultimate ignominy was the fact that "those who write about rhetoric of various sorts in contemporary literary theory do so, for the most part, in ignorance of the field of rhetoric and composition" (Jarratt 2003). If rhetoric was ever thought to be a bridge that could heal a historical rift in English between its most warring factions—literature and composition—this illusion ceased long ago.

Even among less combative relations, the connection of rhetoric to composition has ceased to exist as it might have once, regardless of Crowley's (2003) insistence that the "yoking" of the two has largely been artificial. For example, Christine Farris (2003) reflected, "When I entered the field of composition in the 1980s . . . the connections to rhetoric, indeed, went without saying." However, twenty years later, this was no longer the case: "The 'rhetoric' shaping the freshman writing course familiar to our current graduate students *is* perhaps less recognizable *as rhetoric* than it was." Undoubtedly the relationship of rhetoric to the discipline continues to be troublesome, with Lisa Ede (2009) observing, "For some, rhetoric is foundational. . . . For others, however, rhetoric represents only one of a number of possible subfields or emphases in the discipline" (W484). And even among those for whom rhetoric may be understood as foundational, what constitutes rhetoric is a source of much contentious, albeit generative, debate, as histories examining rhetorics about rhetoric so well illustrate (see Baliff 2013 and Vitanza 1994, in particular). So although rhetoric is certainly prominent in *rhetoric and composition* or *composition and rhetoric*, its actual function in productively centering and propelling the discipline is too often problematically contingent.

Because of the troubled history of rhetoric in the discipline, the alternate use of or move to something like *writing studies* to identify the discipline might appear to avoid a whole host of long-held issues with *rhetoric, composition,* and the relationship of the one to the other. In the introduction to *Keywords in Writing Studies*, a new iteration of their 1996 publication *Keywords in Composition Studies*, Paul Heilker and Peter

Vandenberg (2015) locate writing studies as "an increasingly global construct of academics comprising methodological diversity and linguistic orientations scarcely considered in the mid-1990s" (xiii). Grounded in Charles Bazerman's (2002) "The Case for Writing studies as a Major Discipline," they identify three trajectories in writing studies: "massively interdisciplinary," "an extensive and extending field, with composition at its conceptual center," and "a serious intellectual discipline worthy of professional respect, power, and resources" (xiv). Because "writing is powerful along many dimensions, various in its manifestations, and composed of many elements and processes" (Bazerman 2002, 38), a project like Heilker and Vandenberg's can be seen, somewhat similarly to Adler-Kassner and Wardle's, as a way of controlling for the messy unwieldiness inherent to the discipline while also improving our station among (or even beyond) the disciplines.

However, *writing studies* is hardly unproblematic because of the many tacit presumptions associated with *writing*. These kinds of presumptions are evident in Jody Shipka's (2011) account of the questioning that often undergirds reactions to unconventional final products, such as a pair of pink of ballet shoes, but could just as easily apply to assignments stemming from other postprocess pedagogies and approaches, like writing about writing: "'How is *that* college-level academic writing?,' 'How can *that* possibly be rigorous?,' or 'How can allowing students to do *that* possibly prepare them for the writing they will do in their other courses?'" (2). And given the not unproblematic staffing (and sometimes administration) of first-year composition, which, according to Doug Hesse (2004), "tradition and necessity suggest can passably be taught by most anyone beyond the bachelor's degree" (ix–x), the presumptions that undergird such questions are likely even among seasoned teachers of writing, especially those who do not have expertise in the discipline (see Hammer 2010; Maher 2018; Robertson and Taczak 2018; Wardle and Scott 2015). *Rhetoric*, in contrast, does the essential work of denaturalizing writing and signals that there are principles and practices that must be learned beyond and possibly in contrast to the lessons of high-school writing instruction or, as in the case made by Hesse and Peggy O'Neill in this collection, conceptions of writing and ethics in the profession of journalism. Like the concept of heat transfer in physics, rhetoric stands to transform how individuals understand a symbol system like writing and the kind of work it does not just in their classroom compositions but in almost every aspect of their lives. What is more, rhetoric can start to push newcomers to think of how meaning is made and how persuasion exists beyond written language. As Kenneth Burke (1969) explains, "Wherever there is persuasion, there is rhetoric. And wherever there is 'meaning' there is persuasion" (172). Because meaning exists beyond written language, even in its most dynamic forms, rhetoric as threshold concept more obviously points to the ever-complex, ever-unfolding ways meaning is made beyond writing or composition. (See, for example, Scot Barnett and Casey Boyle's 2016 edited collection *Rhetoric, Through Everyday Things*.) Yet, this is another reason rhetoric is persistently troublesome. Whereas *writing*, and *composition* in particular, provide well-boundedness that can be seen as useful both disciplinarily and pedagogically—a fact that obviously influences Bazerman's decision to put composition at the discipline's center—*rhetoric* is and always has been inherently troublesome due to its dangerous plasticity and its immense interstitiality.

A TROUBLESOME NATURE

At the risk of being accused of classicizing, I begin my discussion of the troublesome nature of rhetoric with a brief foray into Aristotle's work. Unlike in matters that "cannot now or in the future be, other than they are," Aristotle (1984) argues that rhetoric addresses questions regarding what is probable among alternative possibilities (1356a25). It is for this reason we can understand how, in the founding of the modern university, rhetoric was left out because "rhetoric did *not* fit in" (Connors 1997, 60). Part of the reason was simply that rhetoric was not an object of PhD study in the German educational system upon which the modern university system in the United States was modeled. As Connor (1997) explains, "To the increasingly powerful acolytes of the German system . . . rhetoric was at best a suspect and unscientific study, one seemingly unredeemable by research, and at worst simply unscholarly drudge work. It could not be buried and it would not go away, but neither could it be saved as 'real scholarship'" (62–63). Simply put, rhetoric denied the very kind of clarity and certainty demanded of knowledge and its production. Even in the mid-twentieth century, such frustration with rhetoric continued. Writing in 1965 of rhetoric's revival, Wayne Booth wrote of his frustration with the various ways *rhetoric* was being utilized: "As applied to art, the term is today given every conceivable degree of narrowness and generality, meaning anything from mere ornamental figures that can be tacked on a discourse or subtracted at will to the whole range of all possible forms of discourse; as systematic study, rhetoric may be anything from a classification of ornamental figures to the theory of man as a logos-possessing animal. What is worse, one cannot even now, after nearly a decade of revived popularity, predict whether the term will be used to refer to something good or something bad" (8). In spite of his admitted preference for new systematic approaches akin to those of ancient Greeks who sought the "discovery of truth," Booth nonetheless pointed out that "duty" compelled such study because "our lives are permeated by rhetoric" (9).

Part of this duty undoubtedly arises from the fact that rhetoric is not just troublesomely but dangerously plastic, a quality about which Plato warned. In Plato's dialogue *Phaedrus* (1997b), Socrates notes that in the hands of most, rhetoric is aimed at nothing more than enchantment so that the audience is compelled to believe what is being said, in spite of what is actually true: "'Is not rhetoric, taken generally, a universal art of enchanting the mind by arguments; which is practiced not only in courts and public assemblies, but in private houses also, having to do with all matters, great as well as small, good and bad alike, and is in all equally right and equally to be esteemed?'" (261a–b). Elsewhere, in *Gorgias*, Socrates further argues that rhetoric is like cookery, too easily concerned with producing "gratification and pleasure" so that the orator, like the cook unconcerned with the health of the body, "ignores the care of the soul" (Plato 1997a).

Not to be mistaken as an argument limited to classical rhetoric, we can see in Margaret Kantz's (1990) "Helping Students Use Texts Persuasively" an important extension of rhetoric's creative potential and implicit danger. Compelled to move students beyond the limited way they so often read and produce texts (i.e., looking for and reproducing what is true), she wants us to encourage students "to think rhetorically," meaning to recognize that "facts and opinions are essentially the same kind of statement: they are claims" (81). But what separates the one from the other is reception by an audience, a connection she attributes to Steven Toulmin but that we can just as easily connect back to Aristotle's conception of the *enthymeme* (1984, 1354a15). Without going further into the nuances of the enthymeme (see instead Bitzer 1959 and Walker 1994), we can identify that rhetoric itself is persistently troublesome because it deals in probability and therefore not only offers no assurance of truth but challenges the very nature of truth. This is why, for Kantz (1990), borrowing from Christina Haas and Linda Flower (1988), "rhetorical reading," of others' texts as well as one's own, offers a way to foreground differences among claims and how those claims are constructed and consumed.

But the interstitial quality of rhetoric makes knowing how rhetoric works in different situations persistently troublesome, so much so that knowledge of rhetoric at work not just in specific disciplines but in the world at large must always be treated as partial and contingent. Even genres must be considered, according Catherine Schryer (1993), as "stabilized-for-now or stabilized enough" (204) rather than fixed. Due to rhetoric's interstitiality and ubiquity, rhetoric is therefore both bound and unbound, with John Gage noting in 1973 in the Rhetoric Society of America newsletter, "[Aristotle's] rhetoric was the first example of the latest 'revolution': interdisciplinary studies" (22–23). Of importance, rhetoric as a persistently troublesome threshold concept encourages seasoned experts to see the multitude of ways meaning-making works in and beyond what might be for many the bounded comfort of the composition classroom, the discipline of rhetoric and composition, and even academic disciplines. Analyses of how rhetoric works has occurred in such varied areas as medicine (Graham 2015; Jack 2014; Lay 2000; Teston 2017), software (Brown 2015; Maher 2015; Ridolfo 2015; Vee 2017), and the workplace (Faber 2002; Peeples 2002; Spinuzzi 2015). Yet, these studies can sometimes seem far afield from the "real work" of researching and teaching writing and composition. For instance, in response to Bazerman's January 15, 2016, WPA-L listserv announcement of a special issue on rhetoric and computation, edited by Annette Vee and James J. Brown Jr. for the journal *Computational Culture: A Journal of Software Studies*, Pat Belanoff responded, "I thought you might enjoy this; remember when literary theorists were accused of abstruse language? I think the comp people have done them one better. I haven't the slightest idea what any of these articles are about!" Because rhetoric lives in intricate ways everywhere and among not only people but also places (Rai 2016; Rice 2012), animals (Gordon, Lind, and Kutnicki 2017; Hawhee 2016), and things (Barnett and Boyle 2016; Lynch and Rivers 2015), its scope can be overwhelming, even for those in the discipline. Yet, crossing the threshold that allows one to see rhetoric as inherently and persistently troublesome is something that benefits not only those in the discipline of rhetoric and composition but also the rhetorical readers and rhetorical writers we aim to cultivate and support in our classrooms, in the workplace, and in civic life.

DROWNING IN RHETORIC

Just a few recent examples of the use of rhetoric, not as a threshold concept but in popular publications, illustrate just how important it is that we see the conceptual core of our discipline as grounded in essential ways in the threshold concept of rhetoric: "Trump's Rhetoric of White Nostalgia" (Brownstein 2016); "Donald Trump May Sound Like a Clown, But He Is a Rhetoric Pro Like Cicero" (Romm 2016); "Trump's Rhetoric: A Triumph of Inarticulacy" (Leith 2017); "Senator Flake Compares Trump's Rhetoric to Joseph Stalin" (Hunt 2018); and "Trump's Love of Dictatorial Rhetoric" (Giroux 2018). Although such articles reify Booth's critique of rhetoric—narrow and general, good and bad—its increasing and sometimes more complex use in the perfect, rhetorical storm that is Donald Trump, Twitter, Facebook, and Russian trolls and bots serves as a propitious moment by which to signal how inescapable and powerful rhetoric is, but in ways more complex than a nonexpert expert might understand. In *Win Bigly: Persuasion in a World Where Facts Don't Matter*, Scott Adams (2017), creator of the comic *Dilbert*, celebrates his prognostication that Trump would win the 2016 presidential election. Particularly noteworthy in Adams's discussion is the way he identifies both himself and his work: "Keep in mind that I'm a trained persuader and a professional writer. Objectively speaking, my opinions will usually be more persuasive than the opinions you see from people with less training. Training makes you better at most skills, and persuasion is no different. I've been training in the combined arts of writing and persuasion for about forty years. You should expect me to be far more persuasive than the average pundit, based on practice alone" (245). While "rhetoric" itself only appears twice, *Win Bigly* testifies to the importance of persuasion while also propagating problematic, tacit knowledge someone who knowingly engages in the work of persuasion as enchantment but who has not passed through the conceptual gateway of rhetoric might be expected to have.

I raise the example of Adams's (2017) *Win Bigly* not to suggest we pander to legitimate ourselves and the discipline through the external circumstances of the current sociopolitical climate but because we know how dangerous rhetoric can be. Although Aristotle grounds rhetoric as an "offshoot of ethical studies," the always-looming opaqueness of rhetoric can easily mask evil. Steven Katz (1992) illustrates just this in his rhetorical reading of what initially appears as a simple memo addressing changes that should be made to vans to enhance their functionality. From a purely instrumental analysis, the memo "is an almost perfect document" in terms of its style and function (256). However, in what Katz identifies as an "ethics of expediency," the memo is "*too* technical, *too* logical" because "the writer shows no concern that the purpose of his memo is the modification of vehicles not only to improve efficiency, but also to exterminate people" (257). That the vans were being used in Nazi Germany to carry not "loads" but people to their deaths is masked by instrumental choices in language and adherence to genre conventions for this type of text.

The persistently troublesome nature of rhetoric is not something that is solvable, and to have such a disciplinary aim would be futile. Instead we should see our mission as helping our students, those in other disciplines, and the general public see the importance of rhetoric in all they produce and consume, including but not limited to reading and writing. However, the persistent trouble that comes from arguments about the proper place of rhetoric in the discipline all too often serves to distract us. For example, in his 2019 CCCC call for proposals on the "terminological and theoretical functions of performance-rhetoric and performance-composition," Vershawn Ashanti Young (2018) wrote, "Rhetoric is one of the peas—composition is the other—in our disciplinary pod." In a WPA-L discussion of the racialized politics of performance in the call itself, which included African American Vernacular English, Alex Reid responded in part on March 22, 2018, "I do get the concerns expressed here about teaching code-meshing in FYC (or other gen ed writing curricula) and how this plays in Peoria or the business school or wherever. I can see how it's a conversation worth having. . . . What I do find curious in the call is the peas in a pod metaphor. In terms of our disciplinary structure, that's not how I see rhetoric and composition at all." A moment such as this illustrates how our rhetoric too often propagates the disciplinary trouble with *rhetoric* and ensures "we are continuing to preoccupy ourselves with ourselves" (Kopelson 2008, 770). By instead recognizing rhetoric as an essential threshold concept to the whole of our discipline and acting from that recognition, including in our first-year composition and technical communication classrooms, we can then get on with productively troubling how people understand rhetoric and how rhetoric, in the form of language and other symbols, works in varied, situated ways in the world in which we all dwell.

REFERENCES

Adams, Scott. 2017. *Win Bigly: Persuasion in a World Where Facts Don't Matter*. New York: Portfolio/Penguin.

Adler-Kassner, Linda, and Elizabeth Wardle, eds. 2015. *Naming What We Know: Threshold Concepts of Writing Studies*. Logan: Utah State University Press.

Anson, Chris. 2015. "Crossing Thresholds: What's to Know about Writing across the Curriculum." In *Naming What We Know: Threshold Concepts of Writing Studies*, edited by Linda Adler-Kassner and Elizabeth Wardle, 203–19. Logan: Utah State University Press.

Aristotle. 1984. "Rhetoric." In Volume 2 of *The Complete Works of Aristotle: The Revised Oxford Translation*, edited by Jonathan Barnes, 1729–1867. Princeton, NJ: Princeton University Press.

Ball, Cheryl E., and Drew M. Loewe, eds. 2017. *Bad Ideas about Writing.* Morgantown: West Virginia University Libraries, Digital Publishing Institute. https://textbooks.lib.wvu.edu/badideas/badideasaboutwriting-book.pdf.
Ballif, Michelle. 2013. *Theorizing Histories of Rhetoric.* Carbondale: Southern Illinois University Press.
Barnett, Scot, and Casey Boyle, eds. 2016. *Rhetoric, through Everyday Things.* Tuscaloosa: University of Alabama Press.
Bazerman, Charles. 2002. "The Case for Writing Studies as a Major Discipline." In *Rhetoric and Composition as Intellectual Work,* edited by Gary Olson, 32–39. Carbondale: Southern Illinois University Press.
Bitzer, Lloyd F. 1959. "Aristotle's Enthymeme Revisited." *Quarterly Journal of Speech* 45 (4): 339–408.
Bizzell, Patricia. 1992. "Foundationalism and Anti-Foundationalism in Composition." In *Academic Discourse and Critical Consciousness,* 202–20. Pittsburgh: University of Pittsburgh Press.
Booth, Wayne C. 1965. "The Revival of Rhetoric." *PMLA* 80 (2): 8–12.
Brown, James J. Jr. 2015. *Ethical Programs: Hospitality and the Rhetorics of Software.* Ann Arbor: University of Michigan Press.
Brownstein, Ronald. 2016. "Trump's Rhetoric of White Nostalgia." *Atlantic,* June 2. https://www.theatlantic.com/politics/archive/2016/06/trumps-rhetoric-of-white-nostalgia/485192/.
Burke, Kenneth. 1969. *A Rhetoric of Motives.* Berkeley: University of California Press.
Claycomb, Ryan, and Rachel Riedner. 2004. "Cultural Studies, Rhetoric Studies, and Composition: Toward an Anti-Disciplinary Nexus." *Enculturation* 5 (2). http://www.enculturation.net/5_2/claycomb-riedner.html.
Coe, Richard. 1974. "Rationale for the Independence of Rhetoric Programs." *Newsletter: Rhetoric Society of America* 4 (3): 1–3.
Connors, Robert J. 1997. *Composition-Rhetoric: Backgrounds, Theory, and Pedagogy.* Pittsburgh: University of Pittsburgh Press.
Crowley, Sharon. 2001. "Judith Butler, Professor Rhetoric." *JAC* 21 (1): 163–67.
Crowley, Sharon. 2003. "Composition Is Not Rhetoric." *Enculturation* 5 (1). http://enculturation.net/ 5_1/ractic.html.
Detweiler, Eric. 2015. "'I' 'And' '-' ? An Empirical Consideration of the Relationship between 'Rhetoric' and 'Composition.'" *Enculturation* 20. http://enculturation.net/an-empirical-consideration.
Dryer, Dylan. 2015. "Writing Is Not Natural." In *Naming What We Know: Threshold Concepts of Writing Studies,* edited by Linda Adler-Kassner and Elizabeth Wardle, 27–29. Logan: Utah State University Press.
Duffy, John. 2014. "Ethical Dispositions: A Discourse for Rhetoric and Composition." *JAC* 34 (1–2): 209–37.
Duffy, John. 2015. "Writing Involves Making Ethical Choices." In *Naming What We Know: Thresholds Concepts of Writing Studies,* edited by Linda Adler-Kassner and Elizabeth Wardle, 31–32. Logan: Utah State University Press.
Durst, Richard K. 2015. "British Invasion: James Britton, Composition Studies, and Anti-Disciplinarity." *College Composition and Communication* 66 (3): 384–401.
Ede, Lisa. 2009. "What's in a Name? The Uncanny Relationship of Rhetoric and Composition and Cultural Studies." In "At the Intersections: Rhetoric and Cultural Studies as Situated Practice." *College Composition and Communication* 61 (2): W483–90.
Faber, Brenton D. 2002. *Community Action and Organizational Change.* Carbondale: Southern Illinois University Press.
Farris, Christine. 2003. "Where Rhetoric Meets the Road: First-Year Composition." *Enculturation* 5 (1). www.enculturation.net/5_1/pdf/farris.pdf.

Fleming, David. 2009. "Rhetoric Revival or Process Revolution?: Revisiting the Emergence of Composition-Rhetoric as a Discipline." In *Renewing Rhetoric's Relation to Composition: Essays in Honor of Theresa Jarnagin Enos*, edited by Shane Borrowman, Stuart C. Brown, and Thomas P. Miller, 25–52. New York: Routledge.

Fuller, Steve. 1991. "Disciplinary Boundaries and the Rhetoric of the Social Sciences." *Poetics* 12 (2): 301–25.

Fuller, Steve. 2007. *The Knowledge Book: Key Concepts in Philosophy, Science and Culture*. New York: Routledge.

Gage, John. 1973. "Inside Rhetoric at Berkeley." *Newsletter: Rhetoric Society of America* 3 (3): 22–23.

Gilyard, Keith, and Adam Banks. 2018. *On African-American Rhetoric*. New York: Routledge.

Giroux, Henry. 2018. "Trump's Love of Dictatorial Rhetoric." *U.S. News & World Report*. https://www.usnews.com/news/best-countries/articles/2018-01-11/president-donald-trump-loves-the-rhetoric-of-dictators.

Goggin, Maureen Daly. 2000. *Authoring a Discipline: Scholarly Journals and the Post–World War II Emergence of Rhetoric and Composition*. Mahwah, NJ: Erlbaum.

Gopen, George D. 2017. "Marginalization on the Home Front: The Curious Sibling Relationship between English Studies and Composition Studies. A Personal Account." In *A Minefield of Dreams: Triumphs and Travails of Independent Writing Programs*, edited by Justin Everett and Christina Hanganu-Bresch, 351–70. Logan: Utah State University Press.

Gordon, Jeremy G., Katherine D. Lind, and Saul Kutnicki, eds. 2017. "A Rhetorical Bestiary." Special issue, *Rhetoric Society Quarterly* 47 (3).

Graham, S. Scott. 2015. *The Politics of Pain Medicine: A Rhetorical-Ontological Inquiry*. Chicago: University of Chicago Press.

Graham, Loren, Wolf Lepenies, and Peter Wingart, eds. 1983. *Functions and Uses of Disciplinary Histories*. Boston: D. Reidel.

Haas, Christina, and Linda Flower. 1988. "Rhetorical Reading Strategies and the Construction of Meaning." *College Composition and Communication* 39 (2): 167–84.

Hammer, Brad. 2010. "From the Editor: The Multiple Voices of Compositionist Labor." *Forum: Newsletter for Issues about Part-Time and Contingent Faculty* 13 (2): A1–A5.

Hawhee, Debra. 2016. *Rhetoric in Tooth and Claw: Animals, Language, Sensation*. Chicago: University of Chicago Press.

Haynes, Cynthia. 2003. "Rhetoric/Slash/Composition." *Enculturation* 5 (1). http://enculturation.net/ 5_1/index51.html.

Heilker, Paul, and Peter Vandenberg, eds. 2015. *Keywords in Writing Studies*. Logan: Utah State University Press.

Hesse, Doug. 2004. Forward to *The End of Composition Studies*, by David. W. Smit, xi–xiii. Carbondale: Southern Illinois University Press.

Horner, Bruce. 2014. "Grounding Responsivity." *JAC* 34 (1–2): 49–61.

Hunt, Kasie. 2018. "Senator Flake Compares Trump's Rhetoric to Josef Stalin." MSNBC. https://www.msnbc.com/kasie-dc/watch/sen-flake-compares-trump-s-rhetoric-to-josef-stalin-1137050691575.

Inoue, Asao B. 2017. "CCCC 2018 Call for Program Proposals: Languaging, Laboring, and Transforming." http://cccc.ncte.org/cccc/conv/call-2018.

Jack, Jordynn. 2014. *Autism and Gender: From Refrigerator Mothers to Computer Geeks*. Champaign: University of Illinois Press.

Jarratt, Susan. 2003. "Rhetoric in Crisis? The View from Here." *Enculturation* 5 (1). http:// enculturation. Net/5_1/ractic.html.

Kantz, Margaret. 1990. "Helping Students Use Textual Sources Persuasively." *College English* 52 (1): 74–91.

Katz, Steven B. 1992. "The Ethic of Expediency: Classical Rhetoric, Technology, and the Holocaust." *College English* 54 (3): 255–75.

Kennedy, George A. 1992. "A Hoot in the Dark: The Evolution of General Rhetoric." *Philosophy & Rhetoric* 25 (1): 1–21.

Kopelson, Karen. 2008. "Sp(l)itting Images: or, Back to the Future of (Rhetoric and?) Composition." *College Composition and Communication* 59 (4): 750–80.

Kristensen, Randi Gray, and Ryan Claycomb, eds. 2010. *Writing against the Curriculum: Anti-Disciplinarity in the Writing and Cultural Studies Classroom.* Lanham, MD: Lexington Books.

Land, Ray. 2015. Preface to *Naming What We Know: Threshold Concepts of Writing Studies,* edited by Linda Adler-Kassner and Elizabeth Wardle, x–xiv. Logan: Utah State University Press.

Lay, Mary M. 2000. *The Rhetoric of Midwifery.* New Brunswick, NJ: Rutgers University Press.

Leith, Sam. 2017 January 13. "Trump's Rhetoric: A Triumph of Inarticulacy." The *Guardian.*

Lynch, Paul, and Nathaniel Rivers, eds. 2015. *Thinking with Bruno Latour in Rhetoric and Composition.* Carbondale: Southern Illinois University Press.

Maher, Jennifer. 2015. *Software Evangelism and the Rhetoric of Morality.* New York: Routledge.

Maher, Jennifer. 2018. "Embracing the Virtue in Our Disciplinarity." In *Composition, Rhetoric, and Disciplinarity,* edited by Rita Malenczyk, Susan Miller-Cochran, Elizabeth Wardle, and Kathleen Blake Yancey, 161–84. Logan: Utah State University Press.

Meyer, Jan H. F., and Ray Land. 2003. *Threshold Concepts and Troublesome Knowledge: Linkages to Ways of Thinking and Practising within the Disciplines.* Enhancing Teaching-Learning Environments in Undergraduate Courses Project Occasional Report 4, University of Edinburgh, May. http://www.etl.tla.ed.ac.uk/docs/ETLreport4.pdf.

Meyer, Jan H. F., and Ray Land. 2005. "Threshold Concepts and Troublesome Knowledge (2): Epistemological Considerations and a Conceptual Framework for Teaching and Learning." *Higher Education* 49 (3): 373–88.

Meyer, Jan H. F., and Ray Land, eds. 2006. *Overcoming Barriers to Student Understanding: Threshold Concepts and Troublesome Knowledge.* New York: Routledge.

Nichols, Tom. 2017. *The Death of Expertise: The Campaign Against Established Knowledge and Why It Matters.* New York: Oxford University Press.

Park, Douglas B. "Theories and Expectations: On Conceiving Composition and Rhetoric as a Discipline." *College English* 41 (1): 47–56.

Peeples, Tim. 2002. *Professional Writing and Rhetoric: Notes from the Field.* New York: Pearson.

Perkins, David. 2006. "Constructivism and Troublesome Knowledge." In *Overcoming Barriers to Student Understanding: Threshold Concepts and Troublesome Knowledge,* edited by Jan H. F. Meyer and Ray Land, 33–47. New York: Routledge.

Phelps, Louise Wetherbee, and John M. Ackerman. 2010. "Making the Case of Disciplinarity in Rhetoric, Composition, and Writing Studies: The Visibility Project." *College Composition and Communication* 62 (1): 180–215.

Plato. 1997a. "Gorgias." In *Plato: Complete Works,* edited by John M. Cooper, 791–879. Indianapolis: Hackett.

Plato. 1997b. "Phaedrus." In *Plato: Complete Works,* edited by John M. Cooper, 506–66. Indianapolis: Hackett.

Quintilian. 2001. *Quintilian: The Orator's Education.* Edited and translated by Donald A. Russell. Cambridge, MA: Harvard University Press.

Rai, Candice. 2016. *Democracy's Lot: Rhetoric, Publics, and the Places of Invention.* Tuscaloosa: University of Alabama Press.

Ratcliffe, Krista. 2003. "The Current State of Composition Scholar/Teachers: Is Rhetoric Gone or Just Hiding Out?" *Enculturation* 5 (1). http://www.enculturation.net/5_1/ratclifee.html.

Rice, Jenny. 2012. *Distant Publics: Development Rhetoric and the Subject.* Pittsburgh: University of Pittsburgh Press.

Rickert, Thomas. 2012. *Ambient Rhetoric: The Attunements of Rhetorical Being.* Pittsburgh: University of Pittsburgh Press.

Ridolfo, Jim. 2015. *Digital Samaritans: Rhetorical Delivery and Engagement in the Digital Humanities*. Ann Arbor: University of Michigan Press.

Roberts-Miller, Patricia. 2017. "Rhetoric Is Synonymous with Empty Speech." In *Bad Ideas about Writing*, edited by Cheryl E. Ball and Drew M. Loewe, 7–12. Morgantown: West Virginia University Libraries, Digital Publishing Institute.

Robertson, Liane, and Kara Taczak. 2018. "Disciplinarity and First-Year Composition: Shifting to a New Paradigm." In *Composition, Rhetoric, and Disciplinarity*, edited by Rita Malenczyk, Susan Miller-Cochran, Elizabeth Wardle, and Kathleen Blake Yancey, 185–205. Logan: Utah State University Press.

Romm, Joe. 2016. "Donald Trump May Sound Like a Clown, But He Is a Rhetoric Pro Like Cicero." Think Progress. https://thinkprogress.org/donald-trump-may-sound-like-a-clown-but-he-is-a-rhetoric-pro-like-cicero-ac40fd1cda79/.

Roozen, Kevin. 2015. "Writing Is a Social and Rhetorical Activity." In *Naming What We Know: Threshold Concepts of Writing Studies*, edited by Linda Adler-Kassner and Elizabeth Wardle, 17–19. Logan: Utah State University Press.

Schryer, Catherine F. 1993. "Records as Genre." *Written Communication* 10 (2): 200–234.

Shipka, Jody. 2011. *Toward a Composition Made Whole*. Pittsburgh: University of Pittsburgh Press.

Spinuzzi, Clay. 2015. *All Edge: Inside the New Workplace Network*. Chicago: University of Chicago Press.

Teston, Christa. 2017. *Bodies in Flux: Scientific Methods for Negotiating Medical Uncertainty*. Chicago: University of Chicago Press.

Vee, Annette. 2017. *Coding Literacy: How Computer Programming Is Changing Writing*. Cambridge: MIT Press.

Vee, Annette, and James J. Brown, eds. 2016. "Rhetoric and Computation." Special issue, *Computational Culture* 5. http://computationalculture.net/issue-five/.

Vitanza, Victor J., ed. 1994. *Writing Histories of Rhetoric*. Carbondale: Southern Illinois University Press.

Walker, Jeffrey. 1994. "The Body of Persuasion: A Theory of the Enthymeme." *College English* 56 (1): 46–65.

Wardle, Elizabeth, and J. Blake Scott. 2015. "Defining and Developing Expertise in a Writing and Rhetoric Department." *WPA: Writing Program Administration* 39 (1): 72–93.

Winterowd, W. Ross. 1972. "The Prospect (and the Future) of Rhetoric." *Newsletter: Rhetoric Society of America* 2: 4–5.

Winterowd, W. Ross. 2001. "Essay Review: Inventing a Discipline." *Rhetoric Review* 23 (3/4): 2001.

Yancey, Kathleen Blake. 2015. "Coming to Terms: Composition/Rhetoric, Threshold Concepts, and a Disciplinary Core." In *Naming What We Know: Threshold Concepts of Writing Studies*, edited by Linda Adler-Kassner and Elizabeth Wardle, xvi–xxxi. Logan: Utah State University Press.

Young, Richard. 1990. "Working on the Margin: Rhetorical Studies and the New Self-Consciousness." *Rhetoric Society Quarterly* 20 (4): 325–32.

Young, Vershawn Ashanti. 2018. "CCCC 2019 Call for Program Proposals: Performance-Rhetoric, Performance-Composition." http://cccc.ncte.org/cccc/conv/call-2019.

6
THE WORLD CONFRONTS US WITH UNCERTAINTY
Deep Reading as a Threshold Concept

Patrick Sullivan

Historically, composition and rhetoric have devoted only intermittent attention to reading as a critical component of literacy development, preferring to cede reading instruction to K–12 reading specialists. Meanwhile, national standards like the Common Core, which shape the reading experiences of students before they arrive at college, have generally rendered reading into a mechanical cognitive process focused primarily on decoding texts (Carillo 2016; Dole et al. 1991; Hillocks 2002; Ravitch 2013; Tucker 2011; Wolf 2008, 226). Recent collections such as *Deep Reading: Teaching Reading in the Writing Classroom* (Sullivan, Tinberg, and Blau 2017) and *What Is College Reading?* (Horning, Gollnitz, and Haller 2017) have attempted to reframe and retheorize the role of reading instruction in the composition classroom, but it is by no means clear our discipline is ready to acknowledge that reading—and reading instruction—should be core activities in the writing classroom. The omission of references to reading activities in *Naming What We Know* (Adler-Kassner and Wardle 2015) suggests perhaps that our discipline may not view reading as the creative, disruptive, and transformative act it is, despite a robust body of research that demonstrates precisely this understanding of reading. This chapter theorizes an approach to teaching writing that positions *deep reading* at the heart of meaning-making in the composition classroom, proposes we embrace deep reading as a threshold concept in our discipline, and conceptualizes reading as a luminous, creative, and profoundly generative meaning-making activity.

DEFINING DEEP READING

Mariolina Salvatori and Patricia Donahue (2012) suggest that the key question related to the role of reading in the composition classroom is a complex one: "What does it mean to teach a particular kind of reading, and how is that reading to be connected to which kind of writing?" (206; see also Bean 2011; Horning and Kraemer 2013; Horning and Gollnitz 2014). Deep reading is, indeed, a particular kind of reading (transactional) linked to a specific kind of writing (reflective). It is an active, generative process of intellectual inquiry built around engagement with texts and complex, ill-structured problems (Baxter Magolda 2001; King and Kitchener 1994; Perry 1999). Deep reading is a process in which readers engage texts from the position of a conversational partner or interlocutor. The reader's job is to proceed with humility and open-mindedness, suspend judgment, and read for the purpose of engaging new ideas, perspectives, and understandings. One reads, in this model, for the purpose of exploration and "conversation"—in the way Kenneth Bruffee (1984) uses this term, as shorthand for a constructivist theory of knowledge. This reading process is built around mature meaning-making practices described by learning theorists where individuals must make commitments within complex systems and under complicated conditions, in which the footing is unsure and contingencies abound (Baxter Magolda 2004; Kegan 1994; King and Kitchener 1994; Perry 1999; see also Fogarty et al. in this volume). Reflection is foundational to this model because, as Kara Taczak (2015) and others have noted, "reflection is critical for writers' development" (78–79; see also Schön 1983; Sullivan 2014; Yancey 1998). For these reasons, deep reading is an academic activity that privileges caution, humility, curiosity, flexibility, persistence, and open-mindedness. It is a form of inquiry that invites readers to acknowledge *what they don't know* and to employ humility as an essential tool of mature meaning-making.

Louise Rosenblatt's (1995) model of "transactional" reading provides one of the primary theoretical foundations for this process. Building on John Dewey's ideas about "transaction" as designating "relationships between reciprocally conditioned elements" (291), Rosenblatt's transactional theory of reading is built on the core belief that "there are no generic readers or generic interpretations but only innumerable relationships between readers and texts" (291; see also Rosenblatt 1978). Transactional reading, therefore, "places the stress on each reading as a particular event involving a particular reader and a particular text recursively influencing each other under particular circumstances" (Rosenblatt 1995, 292). This type of reading is a "constructive, selective process over time in a particular context" (26).

Deep reading produces troublesome knowledge because, through this process, reading becomes a profoundly creative, disruptive, and transformative activity. *How* we read, *how* we listen, and *how* we model, frame, and theorize engagement with others in our classrooms, then, becomes a high-stakes enterprise. We cannot be content with superficial decoding skills or the ability to select the right answer on multiple-choice tests (Carillo 2016; Felten 2016; Roberts and Roberts 2008; Sacks 1999). Transactional theory liberates us to theorize reading as a complex human activity luminous with promise, opportunity, and challenge—an affective and cognitive activity shaped by memories, prior knowledge, past experiences, historical contexts, situational conditions, cultural knowledge, communities of practice, sponsoring agents, culturally inscribed and culturally sponsored reading practices, socially sanctioned interpretive conventions, ideologies, politics, power relationships, material conditions, social customs, other texts, genre, agency, rhetorical situations, and other variables as well. Perhaps most important, a transactional understanding of reading invites students to ask, following Kylene Beers and Robert E. Probst (2017), "not only 'What does this text say?' but also 'What does it say to me? How does it change who I am? How might it change what I do in the world?'" (22; see also Atwell 2014, 2016). Deep reading is troublesome knowledge because it challenges the idea that texts have a stable meaning and that the act of reading is a simple process of information gathering where the role of the reader is to try to determine an author's intention and meaning.

Because deep reading positions students within liminal ontological spaces, this process creates confusion, doubt, and uncertainty (Blau 2003a, 21–22; Dewey 1997; Sommers 1982). Deep reading proceeds from the understanding that readers have agency (Blau 2003a, 2003b, 2017; Carillo 2015, 2016; Rosenblatt 1978, 1995; Wolf 2008; and others) to construct meaning collaboratively with an author as they read. Agency here is a function of a particular positionality. Readers suspend judgment of a text and an author and seek to engage dialogically with a reading and the context in which it was produced. This type of reading is *liminal* because it "involves messy journeys back, forth and across conceptual terrain" (Cousin 2006, 5; Land 2016; Salvatori and Donahue 2005; Sweeney and McBride 2015; Weissman 2016). This liminality is generated by the questions students are asked to engage as readers—ill-structured problems (defined below)—and by the responsibility put on students as cocreators and conversational partners in this meaning-making process. This type of reading is also *integrative* because it theorizes the primary activities in the writing classroom—reading, writing, and thinking—as interrelated forms of the same cognitive activity: problem solving, knowledge building, and meaning-making (see Phillips et al. in this volume).

Deep reading is *transformative* because it opens up a new and previously inaccessible way of thinking about the role of reading in the construction of knowledge and the process of self-authorship (Baxter Magolda 2011). Deep reading requires that students create new mental models, new understandings of meaning-making and knowledge building, and a transformed understanding of the world and their place in it (Land et al. 2006; Meyer and Land 2006a, 2006b; Meyer, Land, and Baillie 2010, ix; Perkins 2006). Deep reading is transformative in this way because it requires students to become, borrowing language from Jack Mezirow (1990), "critically aware of how and why our presuppositions" about reading, typically based on the traditional decoding model, "have come to constrain the way we perceive, understand, and feel about our world" (14; see also Carillo 2015, 2016; Sullivan 2014, 2017). Deep reading helps students reformulate "these assumptions to permit a more inclusive, discriminating, permeable and integrative perspective" about reading and meaning-making and helps them understand the value of "making decisions or otherwise acting on these new understandings" (Mezirow 1990, 14). Because threshold concepts are statements that distill what is commonly accepted knowledge within a bounded space—in this case, the bounded space of writing studies and composition—deep reading is a threshold concept because it reflects decades of research and practice with reading and writing by Rosenblatt (1978, 1995), David Bartholomae and Anthony Petrosky (1986); Salvatori and Donahue (2005, 2012, 2016, 2017), Sheridan Blau (2003, 2003b, 2017), Alice Horning and Elizabeth Kraemer (2013), Horning and Deborah-Lee Gollnitz (2014), Horning, Gollnitz, and Cynthia Haller (2017), David Jolliffe (2007), Ellen Carillo (2016), and Maryanne Wolf (2008).

Deep reading also extends beyond engagement with the text, theorizing the world as a complex, dynamic domain characterized by high degrees of change (Heraclitus 2003; *I Ching* 1967; Ovid 2005), uncertainty (Einstein 1920; Gleick 2008; Heisenberg 2014; Langer 2014; Trungpa 2007), and mystery (Chödrön 2002; Dickinson 1976; Hubble; the Book of Job; Lao Tzu 2007). As such, deep reading prepares students for the many cognitive challenges that await them after high school and college—as professionals, as adults and parents, and as citizens of the world. Educational psychologist Robert Kegan's (1994) book *In Over Our Heads: The Mental Demands of Modern Life* provides a comprehensive overview of the complex cognitive terrain adults navigate *after they leave school* (13; see also Ariely 2010; Kahneman 2011; Nisbett 2016; Wilson 2004). Kegan examines the private domains of parenting and partnering, along with the public domains of work, dealing with difference, and citizenship. Deep reading is a learning activity designed to help students develop the habits of mind necessary to productively engage complexity, change, and uncertainty. These habits of mind include flexibility, open-mindedness, humility, curiosity, creativity, persistence, responsibility, and metacognition (Costa and Kallick 2008; Council 2011; Facione 1990).

UNCERTAINTY

At the operational and theoretical core of deep reading is engagement with uncertainty in the form of ill-structured problems. Interest in uncertainty among educators dates back to John Dewey. It is one of the key elements of Dewey's (1997) "reflective thinking" pedagogy he develops in *How We Think* and *Democracy and Education*. For Dewey, reflective thinking requires "a state of perplexity, hesitation, and doubt," as well as a problem that "perplexes and challenges the mind so that it makes belief at all uncertain" (9; see also Dewey 2008, 159–70). Ray Land (2016) suggests that threshold concepts themselves constitute a "pedagogy of uncertainty."

The distinction between well-structured and ill-structured problems is central to deep reading. Well-structured problems have correct and undisputed answers. Ill-structured problems are more complex, conditional, and contingent. They do not have easy, final, or agreed-upon solutions, and they require reflection, evaluation of a broad range of evidence, and engagement with often conflicting and competing claims. Patricia King and Karen Kitchener (1994) note that ill-structured problems, by definition, "cannot be resolved with a high degree of certainty" (110). In fact, "experts often disagree about the best solution, even when the problem can be considered solved" (110). King and Kitchener suggest that "ill-structured problems should be viewed as essential aspects of undergraduate education" because they help students build new mental models and develop a "more complex epistemological framework" with which to engage the world (236). Building student reading experiences around ill-structured problems allows us to acknowledge and embrace the radical contingency of all human knowledge. What we think we know about the world is always being revised, reformed, and reimagined.

Texts themselves are ill-structured problems, and that is why we need to engage reading in the composition classroom in the ways we are theorizing here. Texts are ill-structured problems because they are rhetorical artifacts and because they are always the product of a particular historical moment and a unique conjunction of ideologies, power relationships, material conditions, and political, economic, psychological, personal, and social variables. Even textbooks, which are routinely regarded as simply presenting "the facts," have been designed, organized, and executed in strategic and intentional ways—for particular purposes for a particular audience (see, for example, Wineburg 2001, 63–88). Perhaps most essentially, texts are ill-structured problems because, following Mikhail Bakhtin, "'language lies on the borderline between oneself and the other. The word in language is half someone else's'" (quoted in Dyer 2015, 24). Deep reading embraces the inescapably complex nature of the communicative act as individuals engage text, language, intersubjectivity, and the Other. For this reason, it is an academic activity that positions itself in opposition to more instrumentalist understandings of reading, like those embodied in the Common Core, which theorizes readers not as "active participants in the creation of knowledge or insight, but as scavengers who must 'draw' knowledge and 'gain' insight from the text where this knowledge and insight is contained" (Carillo 2016, 31; see also Blau 2003b).

DEEP READING ACROSS THE DISCIPLINES

Professionals across a wide variety of subject areas, specialties, and professions routinely use deep-reading practices to create new knowledge and conduct the business of their discipline. This list of professions includes law, medicine, healthcare, sociology, psychology, science, business, government, history, economics, philosophy, engineering, and many others. Deep reading can therefore be theorized as providing "doors between disciplines" through which we can build solidarity with our colleagues across professions (Blaauw-Hara et al. in this volume).

Science

One paradigmatic example of this practice is provided by Thomas Kuhn (1990) and the story he tells about the genesis of his landmark theoretical work, *The Structure of Scientific Revolution*. This important book is a meditation on the creation of new knowledge in the sciences, built around what Kuhn calls "paradigm change" or "paradigm shifts"—key moments in the history of science when new conceptual, theoretical, and procedural frameworks emerge to replace outmoded forms of knowledge. Kuhn's thinking about this subject emerged from his own process of deep reading while he was preparing to teach a history of science class for non–science majors. As he began to immerse himself in ancient scientific texts he would soon need to teach, many of which he was unfamiliar with, his intellectual footing became unsure and uncertain. His engagement with Aristotle's *Physics* proved especially problematic. Kuhn's ill-structured problem was trying to understand a great thinker who inhabited a completely different conceptual world than he did—one that was pre-Newtonian.

At first, Kuhn (1990) notes, "Aristotle appeared not only ignorant of mechanics, but a dreadfully bad physical scientist as well" (8). Kuhn's strategy for resolving this dilemma was to engage in a deep-reading process, working from the perspective of a conversational partner or interlocutor who suspended judgment, sought to listen and explore, and remained open to new ideas, complexities, and perspectives. Eventually, Kuhn's persistence, rereading, reflection, and capacity for sustained focused attention paid off with understanding: "Suddenly the fragments in my head sorted themselves out in a new way, and fell into place together. My jaw dropped, for all at once Aristotle seemed a very good physicist indeed, but of a sort I'd never dreamed possible. Now I could understand why he had said what he'd said, and what his authority had been. Statements that had previously seemed egregious mistakes, now seemed at worst near misses within a powerful and generally successful tradition" (9).

In addition to resolving this impasse related to Aristotle, Kuhn's (1990) deep reading produced an additional, historically important collateral benefit—a new theoretical model for how science progresses (Kuhn 2012). "That sort of experience—the pieces suddenly sorting themselves out and coming together in a new way," Kuhn reports, "is the first general characteristic of revolutionary change" (8–9). This insight formed the basis for Kuhn's famous theory: "Though scientific revolutions leave much piecemeal mopping up to do, the central change cannot be experienced piecemeal, one step at a time. Instead, it involves some relatively sudden and unstructured transformation in which some part of the flux of experience sorts itself out differently and displays patterns that were not visible before" (9). Kuhn's deep-reading practices, which were instrumental for the production of this new knowledge about the nature of scientific revolution, links his work to ours in the writing classroom in paradigmatic ways because it provides an exemplary model of the skills we are teaching in the writing classroom—reading, writing, and thinking, along with persistence, curiosity, reflection, metacognition, and rereading—at work in highly integrative and purposeful ways and shows how these skills transfer to other disciplines beyond the writing classroom. Reflection was one of Kuhn's primary tools in this process, as was his willingness to suspend judgment, explore and listen, and read for the purpose of discovery and exploration.

History

Another illustration of deep reading that we can draw inspiration from comes from the work of Sam Wineburg (2001), who has defined mature historical thinking in his book *Historical Thinking and Other Unnatural Acts* in ways analogous to deep reading. Wineburg's work also demonstrates how deep reading can be used not only to generate cutting-edge theory at the highest levels of disciplinary knowledge building, as we see in the example of Kuhn, but also in middle-school and high-school classrooms to teach history, critical inquiry, and the habits of mind essential for a healthy and vibrant democracy (Wineburg 2001; Wineburg, Martin, and Monte-Sano 2013; see also Harpham 2017). Wineburg defines historical thinking not as an answer-getting activity but as a problem-exploring enterprise built around engagement with ill-structured problems through deep reading. Echoing Kegan's claims about the cognitive complexity of adult life, Wineburg theorizes history as "a storehouse of complex and rich problems, not unlike those that confront us daily in the social world" (51). Contending with these richly complex problems, Wineburg suggests, helps us develop "the invaluable mental power which we call judgment" (5).

In the first chapter of *Historical Thinking*, Wineburg (2001) reports on a protocol analysis (Ericsson and Simon 1993) he conducted with a professional historian at work engaging an ill-structured problem. Bob Alston, the professional historian, is given a group of primary-source documents by Abraham Lincoln and some of his contemporaries, including Stephen Douglas, John Bell Robinson, Jon Van Evrie, and William Lloyd Garrison. Wineburg invites Alston to examine these texts in order to understand Lincoln's positions on slavery and race and to determine whether Lincoln was a "Great Emancipator" or a "White Supremacist" (18). As Wineburg tracks Alston's reading protocols and his engagement with these texts, he describes Alston's reading process as "a prolonged exercise in the 'specification of ignorance'" (20). Alston asked, "on average, 4.2 questions per document, and underscored what he did not know with markers such as 'I don't have enough to go on' or 'This makes no sense to me' a total of fourteen times" (20). This deep-reading process ultimately produces, in the end, "a nuanced and sophisticated understanding of Lincoln's position" (21).

As Alston engaged this ill-structured problem and the uncertainty it brought with it, he attempted to understand both the historical context of that time and Lincoln's positions about slavery and race in the United States within that context. Curiosity, flexibility, caution, and humility were essential tools in Alston's meaning-making process, aligning his approach with foundational critical- and creative-thinking practices (Facione 1990). Wineburg (2001) concludes this chapter by defining mature historical thinking not as an activity defined by bold claims and strong thesis statements but by curiosity, openness, flexibility, engagement with context, and a candid assessment of all an individual *does not know*. The questions Alston asks and his willingness to be confused and *to not know* are essential to his deep-reading process (20; see also Sullivan 2014, 2017). Alston is very attentive to context and disciplinary concerns—hallmarks of all skilled readers, regardless of discipline. Reflection is one of Alston's primary tools in this process, as is his willingness to suspend judgment, to explore and listen, and to read for the purpose of discovery, exploration, and conversation. Alston is also an active participant in this meaning-making activity, a cocreator with his primary sources.

DEEP READING IN THE COMPOSITION CLASSROOM

Given the importance of deep reading for students, it's imperative to consider how we might incorporate this approach to teaching writing in composition classrooms. Assignment design is crucial to this process. Four key elements are essential for deep-reading activities: (1) building assignments around ill-structured problems; (2) embracing a transactional theory of reading; (3) privileging reflection as essential to mature meaning-making; and (4) reading for the purpose of discovery and exploration. For my FYC course at my home institution, an open-admissions community college in Connecticut, I have developed a number of deep-reading assignments that explore knowledge domains. This class is built around excerpts from Paul Hirst's (1973) essay, "Liberal Education and the Nature of Knowledge." During the course of the semester, we explore three different knowledge domains: history, the fine arts, and the human sciences. The history unit is built around an ill-structured problem in the form of two questions: What is history good for? And Why should we bother studying it? (see app. 6.1 for the full assignment). The primary texts for this unit are two chapters from Wineburg's (2001) book and Maya Angelou's (2009) *I Know Why the Caged Bird Sings*. Students are positioned as transactional readers whose job is to suspend judgment, seek to explore and listen, and open themselves to new ideas, complexities, and perspectives. Reflection is built into the assignment design:

> **Essay #1: History as a Knowledge Domain! Genre: Reflective Essay.** For this essay I would like you to use the introductory exercise we completed (the history quiz on dates and names), our class discussions, and the texts

we have read and discussed in order to explore what you've learned about history as a knowledge domain. There are two central questions, drawn from Wineburg's work, that I would like you do consider: **1. What is history good for?; and 2. Why should we bother studying it?** Please feel free to call it like you see it as you discuss this.

Important note: Reflective focus! This essay is designed to be reflective, so please focus your work in this essay on "listening" carefully to our assigned readings and then reflecting on what you've learned from these readings and our discussion. Please note that it is not our goal here to arrive at any definitive or final answer to the questions we are exploring. Instead, our goal is simply to encounter and engage these readings and the questions they raise in ways that are exploratory, thoughtful, and collaborative. I am not interested in having you formulate a thesis and supporting it. I am interested in having you respond thoughtfully, deeply, and creatively to the questions we are exploring. Feel free to acknowledge what you don't know as well as what you do know. Please also feel free to use personal experience as you discuss these questions if you wish. And feel free to be as creative as you feel you can be/would like to be. Images and pictures welcome in whatever writing you do.

The effectiveness of this approach is evident in the writing students often produce in response to these assignments. Here is a brief excerpt from a successful essay authored by one of my students in this class, Leah McNeir:

> There is, of course, significant value in having a common historical lexicon that citizens can draw from, and value in developing a student's ability to identify important figures and events from our shared heritage. However, what is missing from the traditional approach is the syntax of historical discussion; or, that is to say, a focus on understanding historical contexts, connections, and perspectives. To achieve a deeper historical understanding, students must be given the chance to develop the reasoning skills that help them to appreciate and compare diverse historical and modern perspectives; examine both historical and their own biases, and support their interpretations with well-analyzed evidence. In addition to this, providing opportunities for students to connect to material would support student's ability to recall information in its fuller context and to derive richer meaning and applicability from material. History, as part of the humanities, should embrace the human stories, dramas, emotional and psychological intrigues that are axiomatic to history. To quote Maya Angelou, *"People will forget what you said, people will forget what you did, but people will never forget how you made them feel."* As natural mental storytellers, people become more engaged in material that is presented in its richer human context, as opposed to dry material devoid of emotion, humanity, story, and related associations. An engaged student is one who is more likely to be intrinsically motivated to learn, willing to put in the effort to develop historical empathy and is one who will recall learned information better.

Although this is a short excerpt from a longer essay, Leah is engaging in deep reading to answer the core questions for this assignment (What is history good for? And Why should we bother studying it?). She has engaged our assigned texts from the perspective of a conversational partner, interlocutor, and cocreator—suspending judgment, seeking to explore and listen, and opening herself to new ideas, complexities, and perspectives. Leah is also demonstrating characteristics researchers have identified as essential for strong critical and creative thinking. Using categories drawn from the American Philosophical Association's "Critical Thinking: A Statement of Expert Consensus for Purposes of Educational Assessment and Instruction: Executive Summary" (Facione 1990), these include open-mindedness regarding divergent worldviews; flexibility in considering alternatives and opinions; honesty in facing one's own biases, prejudices, stereotypes, egocentric or sociocentric tendencies; and a willingness to reconsider and revise views where honest reflection suggests change is warranted ("To achieve a deeper historical understanding, students must be given the chance to develop the reasoning skills that help them to appreciate and compare diverse historical and modern perspectives; examine both historical and their own biases, and support their interpretations with well-analyzed evidence") (15; see also Costa and Kallick 2008; Council 2011). This assignment requires students to engage complex questions (Bain 2004), grapple with uncertainty (Perry 1999), embrace the value of multiple perspectives (Langer 2014), and participate in academic practices that promote self-authorship (Baxter Magolda 2004). Artifacts like this can help us provide students with a clear definition of what "good writing" is, regardless of subject area, grades six through fourteen: a nuanced and sophisticated understanding of a complex problem.

NONACADEMIC EXAMPLES OF DEEP READING

Deep reading also has applications well beyond the classroom. Theorizing deep reading as a threshold concept—in composition and in other areas of life as well—supports Peter Felten's (2016) call for us to identify threshold concepts that reach "beyond individual disciplines" (7). Two recent examples from my personal life may serve as illustrations. Driving home from work recently, my Check Engine light clicked on. I took the car to our neighborhood mechanic, and the diagnostic instrument indicated I needed a new air-flow sensor. We installed a brand-new sensor, but two days later the Check Engine light came on again. Before I could get back to the mechanic, this condition caused me to fail our state-mandated emissions test required of all Connecticut vehicles. The mechanic and I were both stymied. We tried resetting the car's diagnostic computer, but that yielded the same result. We had followed the standard protocol for diagnosis and replacement, and yet the car was still malfunctioning. We found ourselves confronting an ill-structured problem.

Undaunted, the lead mechanic at my garage indicated he would "do some research" and said he was going to dig into mechanics' discussion boards and dealer forums to see whether there was any conversation about this problem. The mechanic engaged in this reading activity from the perspective of a conversational partner and cocreator who suspended judgment and sought to explore, listen, and open himself to new ideas and perspectives. He was also reading for the purpose of discovery, exploration, and conversation. He conducted this process collaboratively with mechanics from across the nation on trouble-shooting websites. These interactive discussion boards are sites where automotive wisdom is stored, shared, and created, and where ill-structured problems are discussed and resolved collaboratively. Through his reading and research on this subject, my mechanic discovered a number of anomalies that suggested a potential solution for my 2008 Toyota Corolla. Apparently, there is sometimes a compatibility or tolerance issue with non-Toyota parts for some applications (often involving electronic systems), and he suggested we try replacing the aftermarket part (a new replacement part but one made by a company other than the vehicle's original manufacturer) with an original part manufactured by Toyota. Most mechanics don't routinely use these because they are much more expensive than aftermarket versions. Once the Toyota part was installed, we had no more trouble with the air-flow sensor.

This mechanic's deep-reading process included immersion in confusion and uncertainty and a problem-solving process that relied heavily on caution, humility, open-mindedness, collaboration, and conversation. The answer my mechanic was looking for wasn't in any of the standard repair handbooks. He had to read carefully and extensively to assemble enough clues to piece together and create a solution. As a reader, he positioned himself as a conversational partner with his colleagues and fellow mechanics. He was an active participant in this meaning-making process, a cocreator with other members of his community of practice, solving a particular problem involving a specific vehicle on a given day under particular circumstances. Reflection was one of his primary tools, which allowed him to piece together disparate data points into a solution that worked. This is deep reading practiced at a small rural town's garage and gas station—suggesting that the work of the world may perhaps not be that far removed from the academy, after all (see Rose 2004). (This mechanic, by the way, is beloved in our community.)

My second example involves the highest stakes possible—deep reading with a life hanging in the balance. In the summer of 2017, my eleven-month-old granddaughter, Marigold Hope, was stricken with HLH, a lethal and mysterious autoimmune disease so rare only one person at the Hartford Children's Hospital, one of the best children's hospitals in the world, had heard of it. He had only seen twenty cases in over twenty-five years of practice. One day Marigold developed a sniffle and then a day or two later cold- and flu-like symptoms. Two days after that, she was in the pediatric intensive-care unit with multiple organ failure. We had only a few days to save her life. Once the HLH diagnosis was made, all of us read everything we could about the disease in order to understand it. Unfortunately, disciplinary knowledge about HLH is meager, so much of our treatment strategy had to be developed creatively and improvisationally, working from what limited knowledge we had. We found ourselves confronting a catastrophic-level ill-structured problem with deep reading.

This deep-reading process involved not only examining all the available scholarship for the purposes of discovery, exploration, and problem solving but also reading and interpreting Marigold's vital signs, blood work, and responses to various treatments. Because we knew so little, we had to construct a treatment strategy within very complex conditions where the footing was unsure and contingencies proliferated everywhere. This process involved high-intensity, high-stakes dialogic and collaborative reading, problem exploring, and decision making among Marigold's team of doctors and nurses.

During one meeting with doctors I attended soon after Marigold was admitted, I saw a profoundly inspiring example of deep reading enacted before me. Marigold's team of about fifteen specialists and nurses was outside her room, and a few of the doctors had printed copies of recent research studies of HLH with them (most of these are descriptive; there is no known cure or treatment for HLH). I saw them discuss a number of key readings and research studies, work carefully as readers through the implications and contradictions within this large body of puzzling data, and collaboratively seek to understand what this published research might be able to tell us about helping Marigold. This deep-reading process included immersion in confusion and uncertainty and a meaning-making and problem-solving process that relied heavily on reflection, humility, and open-mindedness. The doctors had to read carefully and cautiously to assemble enough clues to piece together a treatment strategy. As readers, they positioned themselves as conversational partners or interlocutors with the published research and each other, and the conditions required them to become active participants in this meaning-making activity, cocreators with other doctors and researchers around the world who had encountered HLH.

The team had to invent a treatment strategy *that day* using what they learned from their reading and what they could contribute collaboratively from their accumulated expertise, past experience, and professional specialties. I saw Marigold's team bring all this to bear during forty-five minutes of intense collaborative problem solving and conversation about what they had read and what the published evidentiary record showed. As the days went on, when one treatment strategy didn't work, they tried another. The team remained flexible, open to new information, and ready to reconsider even what they believed the day before. I saw deep reading being employed at the highest levels of disciplinary expertise with the highest stakes imaginable.

I believe Marigold would support my sharing her story with readers because she was very warm hearted and kind (these were the elements of Marigold's character and personality her mother was most proud of), and she would certainly have been proud to share her story to help others learn and grow.

These two nonacademic examples suggest deep reading can be theorized as a threshold concept that crosses disciplinary boundaries and links the work we do in the composition classroom with knowledge-making, meaning-making, and problem-solving activities in many areas of life outside the classroom. Embracing deep reading as a threshold concept, therefore, answers the need in composition for curricular practices that promote transfer of knowledge (Perkins 2006) and reach beyond individual disciplines (Felten 2016).

CONCLUSION

Jan Meyer and Ray Land (2006) famously suggested that a threshold concept is "akin to a portal, opening up a new and previously inaccessible way of thinking about something" (3). Deep reading can serve as this kind of portal for students in writing classes, a disciplinary practice that can help promote deep learning experiences in the composition classroom and align our work with learning theorists, threshold concept theory, and mature meaning-making activities across disciplines, professions, and a wide variety of human activities. Deep reading can also help us theorize in pragmatic and productive ways the role reading should play in the composition classroom—an issue that has a long and contentious history in our scholarship (Blau 2003b; Bunn 2013; Carillo 2015, 2016; Hern 2017; Ihara and Del Principe 2018; Jolliffe 2007; Jolliffe and Harl 2008; Keller 2013, 2014; Morrow 1997; Newkirk 2012; Salvatori and Donahue 2012, 2016, 2017; Smith 2012; Sullivan 2010, 2017; Sullivan, Tinberg, and Blau 2010; Tinberg and Nadeau 2010; Wolf 2018; Wolf and Barzillai 2009). Deep reading can help guide our daily classroom practices, grades six through fourteen, and help us create reading and writing assignments that maximize learning opportunities for our students. Deep reading is an approach to teaching writing that also offers opportunities to colleagues across our discipline, including high-school teachers (Sullivan 2014, 2017), part-time faculty (Tremain et al., this volume), teachers at open-admissions two-year colleges (Phillips et al. and Blaauw-Hara et al., this volume), graduate teaching assistants (Mapes and Miller-Cochran, this volume), and WAC personnel (Wardle, this volume). As we seek to name what we know, let us embrace deep reading as one of the "jewels in our curriculum" (Land et al. 2005, 57).

APPENDIX 6.1

Essay #1: History as a Knowledge Domain! Genre: Reflective Essay.
For this essay I would like you to use the introductory exercise we completed (the history quiz on dates and names), our class discussions, and the texts we have read and discussed in order to explore what you've learned about history as a knowledge domain. There are two central questions, drawn from Wineburg's work, that I would like you do consider: *1. What is history good for?; and 2. Why should we bother studying it?* Please feel free to call it like you see it as you discuss this.

IMPORTANT NOTE: REFLECTIVE FOCUS! This essay is designed to be reflective, so please focus your work in this essay on "listening" carefully to our assigned readings and then reflecting on what you've learned from these readings and our discussion. Please note that it is not our goal here to arrive at any definitive or final answer to the questions we are exploring. Instead, our goal is simply to encounter and engage these readings and the questions they raise in ways that are exploratory, thoughtful, and collaborative. I am not interested in having you formulate a thesis and supporting it. I am interested in having you respond thoughtfully, deeply, and creatively to the questions we are exploring. Feel free to acknowledge what you don't know as well as what you do know. Please also feel free to use personal experience as you discuss these questions if you wish. And feel free to be as creative as you feel you can be/would like to be. Images and pictures welcome in whatever writing you do.

REQUIREMENTS: ESSAYS MUST BE AT LEAST 1500 WORDS IN LENGTH. PLEASE INCLUDE AT LEAST TWO DIRECT QUOTATIONS FROM EACH OF THE WORKS WE ARE DISCUSSING IN THIS UNIT. Make sure that you also discuss the meaning and importance of the quotes you select. Please document these sources appropriately in the body of your text and in your Works Cited list at the end of your essay using MLA format.

HERE ARE SOME QUESTIONS TO CONSIDER:

1. Wineburg suggests that the highest aim of studying history should be to endow us with **"the invaluable mental power which we call judgment"** ("Historical" 5).
   Did our reading and discussion of *I Know Why the Caged Bird Sings* improve our ability to make good judgments? If so, how did it do that exactly? What did it teach us?

2. History's ultimate goal may very well be, as Wineburg suggests (quoting another historian), to **"expand our conception and understanding of what it means to be human"** ("Historical" 6).
   Did our reading and discussion of *I Know Why the Caged Bird Sings* **"expand our conception and understanding of what it means to be human"**? Is this what history should do?

3. Wineburg makes a very interesting and what seems to be a somewhat paradoxical statement about knowing others:
   "Coming to know others, whether they live on the other side of the tracks or the other side of the millennium, requires the education of our sensibilities. This is what history, when taught well, gives us practice in doing. Paradoxically, what allows us to come to know others is our distrust in our capacity to know them, a skepticism about the extraordinary sense-making abilities that allow us to construct the world around us" ("Historical" 23–4).
   What is Wineburg saying here and how might this idea have been in play as we read and discussed *I Know Why the Caged Bird Sings*? Did reading *I Know Why the Caged Bird Sings* educate our sensibilities in any way?

4. Wineburg seems to think "humility" is more important than remembering facts and dates:

"Of the subjects in the secular curriculum, it is the best at teaching those virtues once reserved for theology—humility in the face of our limited ability to know, and awe in the face of the expanse of human history" ("Historical" 23–4).

Why the focus on humility here? Is Wineburg right? Might humility be something that could be valuable to us in life as we interact with others, participate as citizens of the world, and go about the business of living? How might that work, exactly?

Did our reading and discussion of *I Know Why the Caged Bird Sings* "enhance our humility in the face of our limited ability to know" in any way? Did we come out more humble at the end of that book than we were when we began? If so, how did that happen? And is it a good thing?

5. Wineburg seems to favor a particular way to teach history. What is history good for, according to Wineburg? And how does he think we should teach history?

The key passages for this seem to come from the second essay we read:

"History offers a storehouse of complex and rich problems, not unlike those that confront us daily in the real world. Examining these problems requires an interpretive acumen that extends beyond the 'locate information in the text' skills that dominate many school tasks" ("Psychology" 51).

Hmmm. There's no mention of dates and names here. What's so good about "complex and rich problems"? And what, exactly, is this "interpretive acumen" that he's talking about? What is this and why does Wineburg think it is so valuable? Did Angelou's *I Know Why the Caged Bird Sings* give us "complex and rich" problems to consider? What were they? Were they worth thinking about?

6. After reading *I Know Why the Caged Bird Sings*, did anything change in terms of your understanding of the following:
   a. Growing up in the South in the United States.
   b. Growing up in the South in the United States **in the 1930s and 1940s**.
   c. Growing up in the South in the United States in the 1930s and 40s **as a woman**.
   d. Growing up in the South in the United States in the 1930s and 40s as **an African-American woman**.

REFERENCES

Adler-Kassner, Linda, and Elizabeth Wardle, eds. 2015. *Naming What We Know: Threshold Concepts of Writing Studies*. Logan: Utah State University Press.
Angelou, Maya. 2009. *I Know Why the Caged Bird Sings*. New York: Ballantine.
Ariely, Dan. 2010. *Predictably Irrational: The Hidden Forces That Shape Our Decisions*. Rev. and exp. Ed. New York: Harper Perennial.
Atwell, Nancie. 2014. *In the Middle*. 3rd ed. Portsmouth, NH: Boynton/Cook.
Atwell, Nancie. 2016. *The Reading Zone: How to Help Kids Become Skilled, Passionate, Habitual, Critical Readers*. 3rd ed. New York: Scholastic.
Bain, Ken. 2004. *What the Best College Teachers Do*. Cambridge: Harvard University Press.
Bartholomae, David, and Anthony Petrosky. 1986. *Facts, Artifacts, and Counterfacts: Theory and Method for a Reading and Writing Course*. Upper Montclair, NJ: Boynton/Cook.
Baxter Magolda, Marcia. 2004. *Making Their Own Way: Narratives for Transforming Higher Education to Promote Self-Development*. Sterling: Stylus.
Bean, John C. 2011. *Engaging Ideas: The Professor's Guide to Integrating Writing, Critical Thinking, and Active Learning in the Classroom*. 2nd ed. San Francisco: Jossey-Bass.
Beers, Kylene, and Robert E. Probst. 2017. *Disruptive Thinking: Why How We Read Matters*. New York: Scholastic.
Blau, Sheridan. 2003a. *The Literature Workshop: Teaching Texts and Their Readers*. Portsmouth: Heinemann.
Blau, Sheridan. 2003b. "Performative Literacy: The Habits of Mind of Highly Literate Readers." *Voices from the Middle* 10 (3): 18–22.
Blau, Sheridan. 2017. "How the Teaching of Literature in College Writing Classes Might Rescue Reading as It Never Has Before." In *Deep Reading: Teaching Reading in the Writing Classroom*, edited by Patrick Sullivan, Howard Tinberg, and Sheridan Blau, 265–90. Urbana, IL: NCTE.
Bruffee, Kenneth. 1984. "Collaborative Learning and the Conversation of Mankind." *College English* 46 (7): 635–52.
Bunn, Michael. 2013. "Motivation and Connection: Teaching Reading (and Writing) in the Composition Classroom." *College Composition and Communication* 64 (3): 496–516.
Carillo, Ellen C. 2015. *Securing a Place for Reading in Composition: The Importance of Teaching for Transfer*. Logan: Utah State University Press.
Carillo, Ellen C. 2016. "Reimagining the Role of the Reader in the Common Core State Standards." *English Journal* 105 (3): 29–35.
Chödrön, Pema. 2002. *The Places That Scare You: A Guide to Fearlessness in Difficult Times*. Boston: Shambhala.
Costa, Arthur L., and Bena Kallick, eds. 2008. *Learning and Leading with Habits of Mind*. Alexandria, VA: Association for Supervision and Curriculum Development.
Council of Writing Program Administrators, National Council of Teachers of English, and the National Writing Project. 2011. *Framework for Success in Postsecondary Writing*. http://wpacouncil.org/framework.
Cousin, Glynis. 2006. "An Introduction to Threshold Concepts." *Planet* 17 (1): 4–5.
Dewey, John. 2008. *The Middle Works of John Dewey, 1899–1924*. Vol. 9, *Democracy and Education, 1916*. Edited by Jo Ann Boydston. Carbondale: Southern Illinois University Press.
Dewey, John. 1997. *How We Think*. New York: Dover.
Dickinson, Emily. 1976. *The Complete Poems of Emily Dickinson*. Edited by Thomas H. Johnson. New York: Back Bay Books.
Dole, Janice A., Gerald G. Duffy, Laura R. Roehler, and P. David Pearson. 1991. "Moving from the Old to the New: Research on Reading Comprehension Instruction." *Review of Educational Research* 61 (2): 239–64.
Dyer, Dylan B. 2015. "Words Get Their Meanings from Other Words." In *Naming What We Know: Threshold Concepts of Writing Studies*, edited by Linda Adler-Kassner and Elizabeth Wardle, 23–25. Logan: Utah State University Press.

Einstein, Albert. 1920. *Relativity: The Special and General Theory*. Translated by Robert W. Lawson. New York: Holt. https://www.ibiblio.org/ebooks/Einstein/Einstein_Relativity.pdf.

Ericsson, K. Anders, and Herbert A. Simon. 1993. *Protocol Analysis: Verbal Reports as Data*. Rev. ed. Cambridge: MIT Press.

Facione, Peter. 1990. "Critical Thinking: A Statement of Expert Consensus for Purposes of Educational Assessment and Instruction: Executive Summary." The Delphi Report Executive Summary: Research Findings and Recommendations Prepared for the Committee on Pre-College Philosophy of the American Philosophical Association. ERIC Doc. No. ED 315.

Felten, Peter. 2016. "On the Threshold with Students." In *Threshold Concepts in Practice*, edited by Ray Land, Jan H. F. Meyer, and Michael T. Flanagan, 3–9. Rotterdam: Sense.

Gleick, James. 2008. *Chaos: Making a New Science*. New York: Penguin.

Harpham, Geoffrey Galt. 2017. *What Do You Think, Mr. Ramirez?* Chicago: University of Chicago Press.

Heisenberg, Werner. 2014. "The Physical Content of Quantum Kinematics and Mechanics" [Über den anschaulichen inhalt der quantentheoretischen racticin und ractici]. In *Quantum Theory and Measurement*, edited by John Archibald Wheeler and Wojciech Hubert Zurek, 62–86. Translated by John Archibald Wheeler and Wojciech Hubert Zurek. Princeton: Princeton University Press.

Heraclitus. 2003. *Fragments*. Translated by Brooks Haxton. New York: Penguin.

Hern, Katie. 2017. "Unleashing Students' Capacity through Acceleration." In *Deep Reading: Teaching Reading in the Writing Classroom*, edited by Patrick Sullivan, Howard Tinberg, and Sheridan Blau, 210–26. Urbana, IL: NCTE.

Hillocks, George. 2002. *The Testing Trap: How State Writing Assessments Control Learning*. New York: Teachers College Press.

Hirst, Paul H. 1973. "Liberal Education and the Nature of Knowledge." In *Philosophy of Education*, edited by Richard Stanley Peters, 87–111. New York: Oxford University Press.

Horning, Alice, and Elizabeth W. Kraemer. 2013. *Reconnecting Reading and Writing*. Anderson, SC: Parlor.

Horning, Alice, and Deborah-Lee Gollnitz. 2014. "What Is College Reading? A College–High School Dialogue." *Reader* 67: 43–72.

Horning, Alice, Deborah-Lee Gollnitz, and Cynthia R. Haller. 2017. *What Is College Reading?* Fort Collins, CO: WAC Clearinghouse.

Hubble Space Telescope. "Top 100 Images." Accessed September 15, 2018. https://www.spacetelescope.org/images/archive/top100/.

I Ching, or, Book of Changes. 1967. Translated by Richard Wilhelm and Cary F. Baynes. Princeton: Princeton University Press.

Ihara, Rachel, and Ann Del Principe. 2018. "Encountering Internationalizing in the Writing Classroom: Resistant Teaching and Learning Strategies." *Across the Disciplines* 15 (2). https://wac.colostate.edu/docs/atd/articles/ihara-delprincipe2018.pdf.

Jolliffe, David A. 2007. "Learning to Read as Continuing Education." *College Composition and Communication* 58 (3): 470–94.

Jolliffe, David A., and Allison Harl. 2008. "Texts of Our Institutional Lives: Studying the 'Reading Transition' from High School to College: What Are Our Students Reading and Why?" *College English* 70 (6): 599–607.

Kahneman, Daniel. 2011. *Thinking, Fast and Slow*. New York: Farrar, Straus and Giroux.

Kegan, Robert. 1994. *In Over Our Heads: The Mental Demands of Modern Life*. Cambridge: Harvard University Press.

Keller, Daniel. 2013. "A Framework for Rereading in First-Year Composition." *Teaching English in the Two-Year College* 41 (1): 44–55.

Keller, Daniel. 2014. *Chasing Literacy: Reading and Writing in an Age of Acceleration.* Logan: Utah State University Press.

King, Patricia, and Karen Strohm Kitchener. 1994. *Developing Reflective Judgment.* San Francisco: Jossey-Bass.

Kuhn, Thomas S. 2012. *The Structure of Scientific Revolutions.* 50th anniversary edition. Chicago: University of Chicago Press.

Kuhn, Thomas S. 1990. "What Are Scientific Revolutions?" *The Probabilistic Revolution.* Vol. 1, *Ideas in History,* edited by Lorenz Kruger, Lorraine J. Daston, and Michael Heidelberger, 7–22. Boston: MIT Press.

Land, Ray. 2016. "Toil and Trouble: Threshold Concepts as a Pedagogy of Uncertainty." In *Threshold Concepts in Practice,* edited by Ray Land, Jan H. F. Meyer, and Michael T. Flanagan, 11–24. Rotterdam: Sense.

Land, Ray, Glynis Cousin, Jan H. F. Meyer, and Peter Davies. 2005. "Threshold Concepts and Troublesome Knowledge (3): Implications for Course Design and Evaluation." In *Improving Student Learning—Equality and Diversity,* edited by Chris Rust, 53–64. Oxford: Oxford Centre for Staff and Learning Development.

Land, Ray, Glynis Cousin, Jan H. F. Meyer, and Peter Davies. 2006. "Conclusion: Implications of Threshold Concepts for Course Design and Evaluation." In *Overcoming Barriers to Student Understanding,* edited by Jan H. F. Meyer and Ray Land, 195–206. New York: Routledge.

Langer, Ellen J. 2014. *Mindfulness.* 25th anniversary ed. Boston: Da Capo.

Lao Tzu. *Tao Te Ching.* 2007. Translated by Stephen Addiss and Stanley Lombardo. Boulder, CO: Shambhala.

Meyer, Jan H. F., and Ray Land, eds. 2006a. *Overcoming Barriers to Student Understanding.* New York: Routledge.

Meyer, Jan H. F., and Ray Land. 2006b. "Threshold Concepts and Troublesome Knowledge: An Introduction." In *Overcoming Barriers to Student Understanding,* edited by Jan H. F. Meyer and Ray Land, 3–18. New York: Routledge.

Meyer, Jan H. F., Ray Land, and Caroline Baillie, eds. 2010. *Threshold Concepts and Transformational Learning.* Rotterdam: Sense.

Mezirow, Jack. 1990. "How Critical Reflection Triggers Transformative Learning." In *Fostering Critical Reflection in Adulthood,* edited by Jack Mezirow and Associates, 1–20. San Francisco: Jossey-Bass.

Morrow, Nancy. 1997. "The Role of Reading in the Composition Classroom." *JAC* 17 (3): 453–72.

Newkirk, Thomas. 2012. *The Art of Slow Reading.* Portsmouth, NH: Heinemann.

Nisbett, Richard E. 2016. *Mindware: Tools for Smart Thinking.* New York: Farrar, Straus and Giroux.

Ovid. 2005. *Metamorphoses: A New Translation.* Translated by Charles Martin. New York: W. W. Norton.

Perkins, David. 2006. "Constructivism and Troublesome Knowledge." In *Overcoming Barriers to Student Understanding,* edited by Jan H. F. Meyer and Ray Land, 33–47. New York: Routledge.

Perry, William. 1999. *Forms of Ethical and Intellectual Development in the College Years: A Scheme.* San Francisco: Jossey-Bass.

Ravitch, Diane. 2013. *Reign of Error: The Hoax of the Privatization Movement and the Danger to America's Public Schools.* New York: Knopf.

Roberts, Judith C., and Keith A. Roberts. 2008. "Deep Reading, Cost/Benefit, and the Construction of Meaning: Enhancing Reading Comprehension and Deep Learning in Sociology Courses." *Teaching Sociology* 36 (2): 125–40.

Rose, Mike. 2004. *The Mind at Work: Valuing the Intelligence of the American Worker.* New York: Viking.

Rosenblatt, Louise. 1978. *The Reader, the Text, and the Poem: The Transactional Theory of the Literary Work.* Carbondale: Southern Illinois University Press.

Rosenblatt, Louise. 1995. *Literature as Exploration.* 5th ed. New York: MLA.

Sacks, Peter. 1999. *Standardized Minds: The High Price of America's Testing Culture and What We Can Do to Change It.* New York: Da Capo.

Salvatori, Mariolina Rizzi, and Patricia Donahue. 2005. *The Elements (and Pleasures) of Difficulty.* New York: Pearson/Longman.

Salvatori, Mariolina Rizzi, and Patricia Donahue. 2012. "What Is College English? Stories about Reading: Appearance, Disappearance, Morphing, and Revival." *College English* 75 (2): 199–217.

Salvatori, Mariolina Rizzi, and Patricia Donahue. 2016. "Guest Editors' Introduction: Guest Editing as a Form of Disciplinary Probing." In "Reading," special issue, *Pedagogy* 16 (1): 1–8.

Salvatori, Mariolina Rizzi, and Patricia Donahue. 2017. "Unruly Reading." In *Deep Reading: Teaching Reading in the Writing Classroom,* edited by Patrick Sullivan, Howard Tinberg, and Sheridan Blau, 313–36. Urbana, IL: NCTE.

Schön, Donald. 1983. *The Reflective Practitioner: How Professionals Think in Action.* New York: Basic Books.

Smith, Cheryl Hogue. 2012. "Interrogating Texts: From Deferent to Efferent and Aesthetic Reading Practices." *Journal of Basic Writing* 31 (1): 59–79.

Sommers, Nancy. 1982. "Responding to Student Writing." *College Composition and Communication* 33 (2): 148–56.

Sullivan, Patrick. 2002. "'Reception Moments,' Modern Literary Theory, and the Teaching of Literature." *Journal of Adolescent and Adult Literacy* 45 (7): 568–77.

Sullivan, Patrick. 2010. "What Can We Learn about 'College-Level' Writing from Basic Writing Students? The Importance of Reading." In *What Is "College-Level" Writing?* Vol. 2, *Assignments, Readings, and Student Writing Samples,* edited by Patrick Sullivan, Howard Tinberg, and Sheridan Blau, 233–53. Urbana, IL: NCTE.

Sullivan, Patrick. 2014. *A New Writing Classroom: Listening, Motivation, and Habits of Mind.* Logan: Utah State University Press.

Sullivan, Patrick. 2017. "'Deep Reading' as a Threshold Concept in Composition Studies." In *Deep Reading: Teaching Reading in the Writing Classroom,* edited by Patrick Sullivan, Howard Tinberg, and Sheridan Blau, 143–71. Urbana, IL: NCTE.

Sullivan, Patrick, and Howard Tinberg, and Sheridan Blau, eds. 2010. *What Is "College-Level" Writing?* Vol. 2, *Assignments, Readings, and Student Writing Samples.* Urbana, IL: NCTE.

Sullivan, Patrick, Howard Tinberg, and Sheridan Blau, eds. 2017. *Deep Reading: Teaching Reading in the Writing Classroom.* Urbana, IL: NCTE.

Sweeney, Meghan A., and Maureen McBride. 2015. "Difficulty Paper (Dis)Connections: Understanding the Threads Students Weave between Their Reading and Writing." *College Composition and Communication* 66 (4): 591–64.

Taczak, Kara. 2015. "Reflection Is Critical for Writers' Development." In *Naming What We Know: Threshold Concepts of Writing Studies,* edited by Linda Adler-Kassner and Elizabeth Wardle, 78–79. Logan: Utah State University Press.

Tinberg, Howard, and Jean-Paul Nadeau. 2010. *The Community College Writer: Exceeding Expectations.* Carbondale: Southern Illinois University Press.

Trungpa, Chögyam. 2007. *Shambhala: The Sacred Path of the Warrior.* Boston: Shambhala.

Tucker, Marc S., ed. 2011. *Surpassing Shanghai: An Agenda for American Education Built on the World's Leading Systems.* Cambridge: Harvard Education Press.

Weissman, Gary. 2016. *The Writer in the Well: On Misreading and Rewriting Literature.* Columbus: The Ohio State University Press.

Wilson, Timothy. 2004. *Strangers to Ourselves: Discovering the Adaptive Unconscious.* Cambridge, MA: Belknap.

Wineburg, Sam. 2001. *Historical Thinking and Other Unnatural Acts*. Philadelphia: Temple University Press.

Wineburg, Sam, Daisy Martin, and Chauncey Monte-Sano. 2013. *Reading Like a Historian: Teaching Literacy in Middle and High School History Classrooms*. New York: Teachers College Press.

Wolf, Maryanne. 2008. *Proust and the Squid: The Story and Science of the Reading Brain*. New York: Harper.

Wolf, Maryanne. 2018. *Reader, Come Home: The Reading Brain in a Digital World*. New York: Harper.

Wolf, Maryanne, and Mirit Barzillai. 2009. "The Importance of Deep Reading." *Educational Leadership* 66 (6): 32–37.

Yancey, Kathleen Blake. 1998. *Reflection in the Writing Classroom*. Logan: Utah State University Press.

7
EXPANDING THE INQUIRY
What Everyday Writing with Drawing Helps Us Understand about Writing and about Writing-Based Threshold Concepts

Kathleen Blake Yancey

Although the writing studies threshold concepts identified in *Naming What We Know* (Adler-Kassner and Wardle 2015) describe a good deal of what we know about writing, the applications thus far are to school contexts, which is not surprising given that writing in school continues to focus the discipline of rhetoric and composition. At the same time, given the discipline's interest in everyday writing and the value of having writing studies threshold concepts describe all kinds of writing, a good question is what we might learn about the capacity of the current threshold concepts to address everyday writing. Put as a set of questions: How well do these threshold concepts describe the texts of everyday writing? Might an exploration of everyday writing lead to revision of some threshold concepts, and if so, how? Alternatively, given this exploration, might we need to add new threshold concepts to the current list? As a means of beginning to think about these questions, I here define and analyze several examples of everyday writing; in doing so, I focus especially on the role of drawing, and the relationship of drawing and language, in much everyday writing. I then consider more generally how one threshold concept, as exemplar, might be revised to accommodate a fuller set of texts, including those of the everyday, and more accurately describe them. In taking up these tasks, my larger intent is to demonstrate that by engaging in this kind of process, we concurrently refine writing, and writing studies as a disciplinary umbrella, as we conceptualize writing more capaciously.

We begin with a definition. In defining everyday writing, we have many scholars to draw on. Anne Gere (1994), for example, frames writing in both the San Francisco Tenderloin and an Iowa writers workshop as the extracurriculum, while literacy scholars David Barton and Mary Hamilton (2012) conceptualize it according to purpose(s), among

DOI: 10.7330/9781607329329.c007

them organizing life and participating in social communities. Others like historian Martyn Lyons (2012), calling it "ordinary writing," point to the influence of large-scale migrations like those prompted by World War I on the development of everyday writing, with this purpose for everyday writing maintaining contact with loved ones. Still others like Jennifer Sinor (2002) see everyday writing as the canvas wherein domestic life and identity can be constructed, represented, and preserved; in addition, everyday writing as preservation and memory adjunct may be increasingly important for older writers, as I have argued elsewhere (Yancey 2019). Like other writing, everyday writing is situated, but as these brief accounts make clear, everyday writing as a category of writing shares three defining features: it is purposeful, self-sponsored, and action-oriented (Yancey et al., forthcoming).

In this chapter, then, drawing on different examples of everyday writing operating in very different contexts, I propose that two semiotic modes—the linguistic and the visual, the latter as instantiated in drawing—inform a good deal of everyday writing in print.[1] I also outline an emerging taxonomy articulating the role drawing plays in relationship to the linguistic in everyday writing, in the process demonstrating how ubiquitous such writing-drawing composing is. Not least, given these examples and observations, I raise questions about what this writing-drawing practice in everyday writing means for a threshold concepts–informed understanding of composing.

THE ROLE OF THE VISUAL IN WRITING

In *Naming What We Know*, two threshold concepts point explicitly to the role of the visual in composing. The first of these, *all writing is multimodal*, addresses the role various modes, or resources, play in composing. Drawing on a definition created by the New London Group, Cheryl Ball and Colin Charlton (2015) explain that texts are composed and take on meaning through an *ensemble* of modes:

> *Multimodal* means multiple + mode. In contemporary writing studies, a mode refers to a way of meaning-making, or communicating. The New London Group (NLG) outlines five modes through which meaning is made: linguistic, aural, visual, gestural, and spatial. Any combination of modes makes a multimodal text, and all texts—every piece of communication a human composes—use more than one mode. Thus, all writing is multimodal (42).

In addition, Ball and Charlton (2015) note that mode has thus shifted from its earlier use in categorizing texts (e.g., narrative, expository) to one signaling "equal emphasis on how meanings are created, delivered, and circulated through choices in design, material composition, tools and technologies, delivery systems, and interpretive senses" (42). Not least, Ball and Charlton address two misconceptions of multimodality. First, multimodal texts are not exclusively digital; rather, all texts are multimodal (a point others have made likewise: see, for example, Shipka 2011). Second, "there is no such thing as a monomodal text" (43). What people tend to mean when they claim that a text is monomodal, as Ball and Charlton explain, is that one mode, especially the linguistic, is "*privilege*[d] . . . over [others like] spatial or visual modes" (3).[2] Put another way, other modes in addition to the linguistic are always a part of composing.

A second threshold concept, *texts get their meaning from other texts*, also speaks to the visual in writing, approaching it not through the lens of multimodality, but rather through the lens of intertextuality. In explaining *texts get their meaning from other texts*, Kevin Roozen (2015) begins with a common key term in writing studies: *intertextuality*: "Although we commonly refer to *a* text or *the* text, texts are profoundly intertextual in that they draw meaning from a network of other texts. As a field, writing studies has developed a number of names for the networks of texts that writers and readers create and act with, including *landscapes, sets, systems, ecologies, assemblages, repertoires,* and *intertexts*" (44–45). The reference to intertextuality, as represented here, tends to mean that linguistic texts refer to or are embedded in other linguistic texts. But as Roozen points out, such intertextual texts can also be what he calls "nonwritten."

> Texts even rely upon a range of nonwritten texts. Readers and writers, for example, might draw upon visual images as they engage with a focal text. The child's reading of *Winnie the Pooh* might be informed by pictures or video images she has seen of the characters and scenes from the book. The shopper might use the images on coupons as a way to remember which items to include on next week's grocery list. Texts might also be linked to inscriptions such as charts, diagrams, and tables. Adjusting the insurance claim might involve the processor in looking up pricing data in a set of Excel charts, creating a digital drawing of an automobile accident, or interpreting schematics of automobile parts. (45)

In this conception of writing, the visual informs various texts, including children's books and coupons for shopping. Likewise, many texts, especially in disciplines like biology and engineering, include what Roozen (2015) refers to as "inscriptions such as charts, diagrams, and tables" (45), but that many others, from scholars like Gunther Kress to programs like the University of Minnesota writing-enriched curriculum (WEC), consider part and parcel of composing itself. In that sense, they are not the nonwritten, though they are nonlanguage; they too contribute to

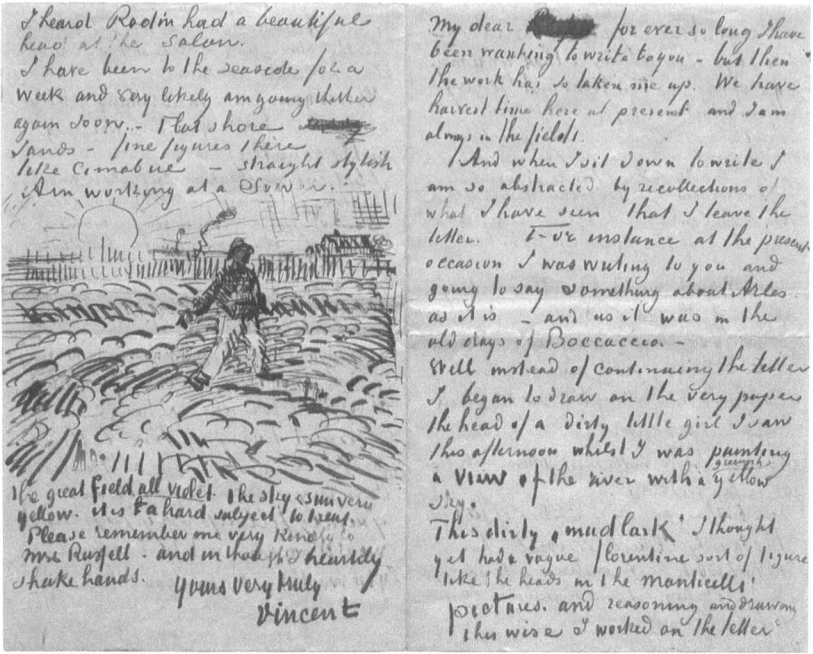

Figure 7.1

multimodal composing. In addition, while the focus in this threshold concept is on the reader, that reading was of course created by a writer; by inference, writers are creating such texts. Not least, Roozen includes a provision for drawings as another kind of intertext when he includes the example of the "digital drawing of an automobile accident" (45), one similar to the kind of writing-drawing exploration outlined in this collection by Rebecca Nowacek, Aishah Mahmood, Katherine Stein, Madylan Yarc, Saul Lopez, and Matt Thul.

The idea of drawing, which as related to writing has received attention largely in emergent literacy, is also, as we shall see, a practice informing a good deal of everyday writing.

DRAWING IN WRITING

It's commonplace for some writers to use drawing and writing together, even as a routine practice. Artists like Vincent Willem van Gogh, for example, include drawings in their letters; the drawings in his letters seem like rough drafts of paintings that later become famous. But writers-who-are-not-artists also include drawings in their writing, as the

Figure 7.2

journals of composition scholar Eli Goldblatt demonstrate. Some of his writing can be seen in the Museum of Everyday Writing, whose purpose is to collect and showcase many kinds of mundane, nonacademic, and nonworkplace writing and to provide a site for research into everyday writing. In explaining the writing he contributed to the museum, Goldblatt (2016) notes that when he travels, he keeps a journal in which writing and drawing are intermixed.

> Two of [the museum artifacts] are [journal] entries at 3:31 PM & then again at 7:40 PM on Friday, 9/23/16 from our rented cottage on the Isle of Mull in Scotland during a recent trip my wife, Wendy Osterwell, & I took to the UK. The other is an image from an earlier entry at 3:18 PM, Saturday 9/17 on a walk above the small town of Coniston in the Lake District of England. I keep a journal while I travel & often draw as well as

write. My notes are about what we've done & seen, what I'm thinking as we move through the landscape, & what I'm dreaming.

In still other cases, writers include drawings quite intentionally because other forms of visual recording have been banned: such was the case for interned Japanese Americans during World War II. On December 27, 1941, nearly two months before Japanese Americans were evacuated to reassembly camps (and then later to internment camps), the federal government ordered all suspected "enemy aliens" in the Western United States to surrender both short-wave radios and cameras. Consequently, much of internment-camp writing—like that of Stanley Hayami's—is filled with drawings recording what took place in both reassembly and internment campus and bringing those experiences to life (Gesensway and Roseman 1987; Oppenheim 2008).

Interestingly, however, most of what we know about the relationship of drawing and writing comes not from the composing practices of adults, but rather from studies of children's emergent literacy. The writing of children is, of course, often filled with drawings, but it's also the case that there has been a working assumption that as they mature, children shift, or make a transition—from (1) drawing to (2) language *and* drawing and then into (3) language exclusively. In this model of developing literacy, drawing functions only as a preparatory practice to the more important practice of using language. More recent research into the writing of elementary-school children aged seven to twelve conducted in Brazil, however, indicates that children themselves don't want to grow out of drawing, but rather want to continue drawing even as they compose with language. In this study, children continued drawing and did so (1) when no direction to draw was provided and sometimes (2) at the risk of seeming to defy their elders (Collelo 2001). As important, drawing on the analysis of these children's texts, researcher Sylvia Collelo (2001) provides a schema of how drawing informs writing, one instructive for the everyday writing of adults as well. Collecting 623 texts from the students, half of which included "drawings, doodles and illustrations," Collelo theorizes that "developing tendencies in the relationship of drawing and writing [sprang] from three basic types: 'drawings on their own', 'drawings connected with writing' and 'parallel drawings.'" The second two relationships, drawing connected with writing and parallel drawings, involved the intermixing of drawing and writing, much as Goldblatt does in his journal and Van Gogh did in his letters. The first type, Colello explains, includes "'drawings to say', in different degrees of efficiency and with communicative value." All drawings declined as children matured, at least in part because the school suggested that, in effect, the children should move on, although children persisted in drawing even if in a limited way—primarily to contribute to "informative texts."

THE ROLE OF LANGUAGE AND DRAWING IN EVERYDAY WRITING

Outside the boundaries of school and the workplace, writers can choose to write with drawing, and they do so in several ways. To demonstrate such drawing-writing, I here outline an emerging taxonomy of the uses of drawing in everyday texts and then consider the implications of this analysis for threshold concepts describing writing. What's especially relevant in this demonstration is how very often everyday writing includes drawing, especially for certain rhetorical purposes. In other words, as the threshold concept *all writing is multimodal* stipulates, all writing is multimodal, but some writing, specifically everyday writing in print, exhibits a special relationship between the linguistic and the visual of drawing. Thus, taking a cue from the writing-drawing relationships articulated in Colello's (2001) schema, I have identified a taxonomy of five types of relationships between drawing and writing in everyday writing. In these relationships, drawing

- complements language;
- responds to an idea or text;
- complements *and* responds to an event, occasion, or text;
- elaborates writing; and/or
- works symbolically with language to respond to political events.

Complementing Language

Complementing language with drawing seems, at least in part, a classic kind of multimodality, though the multimodality in this instance privileges language and drawing, as four examples—a note left on a car, a message left in a book holding receipts for a meal, and two texts providing directions to guests attending baby showers—suggest.

One is a simple note left on Linda Adler-Kassner's car in the wake of the 2016 presidential election. According to the Facebook post Adler-Kassner included when she uploaded this photo, she was out of town, but her spouse had driven the car to UC Santa Barbara (where they both work) and had texted the note to her. As her Facebook post explained, "I'm at NCTE in Atlanta, but someone left this note on our car at UCSB today. A great reminder: hope is us, here, now. Thank you, kind and gracious anonymous person." As the photo demonstrates, the handwritten

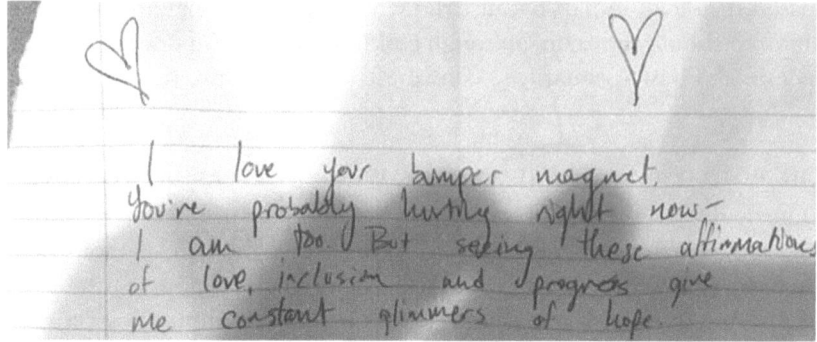

Figure 7.3

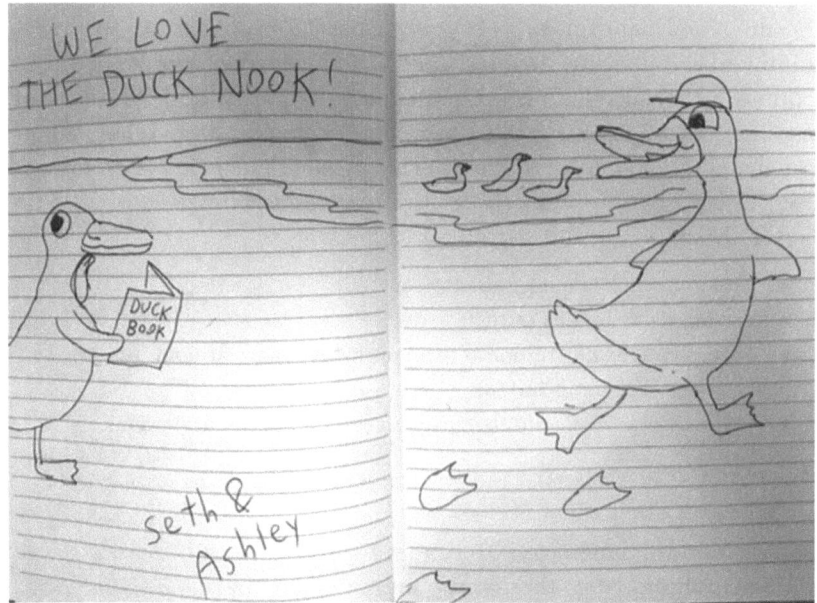

Figure 7.4

message is written on a piece of notebook paper, and given the tear on the left, the note itself seems to have been spontaneously written. Transcribed, the note says, "I love your bumper magnet. You're probably hurting right now—and I am, too. But seeing these affirmations of love, inclusion, and progress give me constant glimmers of hope." At the top of the note are two hearts, one on each side of the note, the hearts both complementing the message of "love, inclusion, and progress" and framing it for the reader.

Expanding the Inquiry 143

Figure 7.5

A second example comes from a guestbook at a bed and breakfast; at this inn, each room is named, and when reserving rooms, guests choose the specific room. One of the rooms, named Duck Nook, prominently displays a guestbook including comments from earlier guests and inviting comments from others. In the case of this entry, the verbal enthusiasm for the Duck Nook—"WE LOVE THE DUCK NOOK"—is complemented with a drawing of several ducks, three in a pond, one walking away and looking behind, and a third who is reading *Duck Book*, which may be the guestbook itself, the duck holding it representing the guest who created the illustration—which functions much as do the images in *Winnie the Pooh* invoked by Roozen (2015). In this case, the drawing, playing off the name of the room, complements the idea of loving the room itself in a somewhat cartoonish way by invoking the ducks as characters.

A somewhat different purpose informs notes used at two different baby showers. The first, a yellow Post-it Note, asks guests to "Please Remove Your Shoes," a request that may be unwelcome to some, but that is softened by an accompanying smiley face. A second note at another baby shower signals guests that cats may be underfoot and what to do about

144   YANCEY

Figure 7.6

it. This note is announced by the word "<u>WARNING,</u>" which is also underlined so no reader will miss it. Under that header, an observation is made and a call to solidarity issued: "Cats are stealthy and will sneak into rooms. <u>DO NOT</u> LET THEM. (Bathroom is ok)." Pointing from "LET THEM" are two arrows leading to drawings of the cats, one with pointy ears, the other with more rounded ears further apart and a spray of black descending from her crown. This message, like the Post-it Note, also makes a request, but does so by characterizing cats, with the drawings themselves complementing the note as they particularize the cats. Seeming to echo an **FBI** wanted poster,[3] the note is purposefully funny: most people know that cats are stealthy, and unless there are other cats in the household, guests won't need the drawings of the cats to recognize them.

In notes like these, then, composers use drawing to complement a verbal message and for diverse purposes—to articulate shared values, to express enthusiasm, and to direct guests.

Drawing as a Response

In other examples of everyday writing, composers use drawing-working-with-writing as a kind of response, in the examples here to thank

Expanding the Inquiry 145

Nancy Elizabeth Markovich ▸ Betton Hills Neighborhood
40 mins · Tallahassee, FL

Figure 7.7

anonymous others and to build on others' responses in a kind of print network.

One way writing-drawing works as a response is exemplified by a sign expressing thanks to utility workers assisting in the aftermath of a hurricane. This handwritten and illustrated sign, posted in front of a house, has a simple message: "Thank You Guys!" followed by a heart, with another heart fronting the signature, Betton Hills, which is the name of a neighborhood in Tallahassee, Florida. The hearts here, of course, also complement the words, much as in the message to Adler-Kassner (above), but the message itself is a response to an event, in this case Hurricane Hermine in 2016. As important, this response, which is heartfelt, as the drawing suggests, is also deliberately anonymous; it's not particular people who send thanks but the entire neighborhood, and it's not specific utility workers who are thanked but all of them, and perhaps others besides. Such a text seems especially appropriate when audience members are unknown; moreover, using a universal drawing like a heart, in this case twice, sends a message most if not all

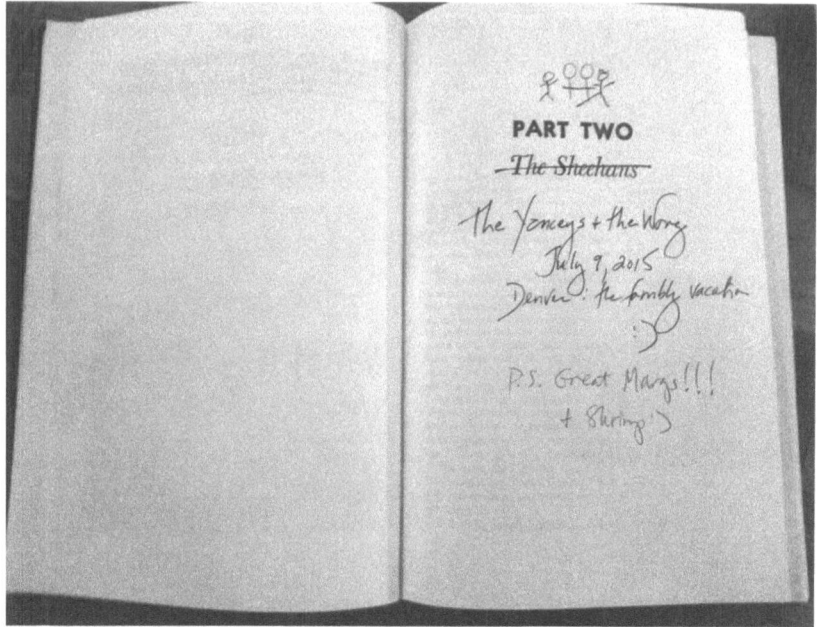

Figure 7.8

understand, which may be particularly important in a world increasingly multilingual and global.

A second example, a comment in a book, isn't the ordinary annotation;[4] the book itself is used to convey bills for meals to customers, who are also invited to write in the book as they pay their bills. Because diners can compose in books, even scratching out items in the book (as in the example here), this composing task feels a bit transgressive. In this particular example, one composer has added four stick figures at the top, indicating the number of diners; has replaced the name of the family that is the focus of "PART TWO" of the book with another name, "The Yanceys and the Wong," and a date, "July 9, 2015"; and has added an annotation, "Denver: the family vacation," closing it with a smiley face whose genesis is likely email. This drawing-inscription is a response to the experience of dining together, and it's the first response; the second, taking the form of a P.S. in a letter, comments, "Great Margs!!! + shrimp" with another emoji-styled happy face. This second response is thus a twofold response: to the meal and to the first response. It is also a collective response in that it contributes to the other responses in the now-being-rewritten book. Both the need and the desire to respond motivate drawing-writing responses.

Figure 7.9

Complementing and Responding

Some everyday writing texts use both writing and drawing to respond and drawing to complement the language. At Agnes Scott College in Atlanta, Georgia, students are invited to make requests in the cafeteria by completing a form. What many students do is personalize the form in some way, often through drawing.[5] One student, for example, wrote to endorse the recently instituted Meatless Monday dinner, recommending that the dining service "Ignore the haters! Stay you, stay true, stay meatless Monday!" There is a "K" that might represent the composer's name, and there are two drawings representing people: a smiley face—which may be something of a visual trope in everyday writing—and a "cool" smiley face created by a pair of sunglasses and a smile. Here, then, the drawings complement the language as they respond to the new Monday dinners.

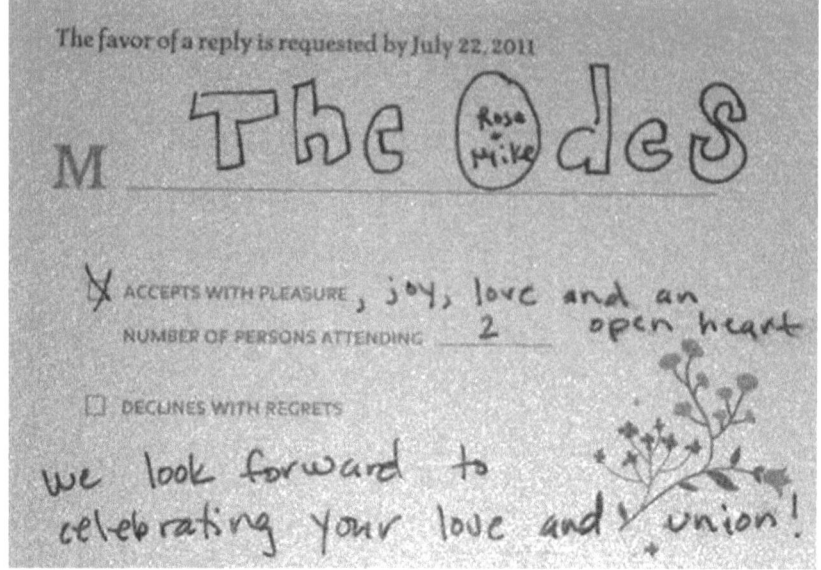

Figure 7.10

The second example is literally a response, in this case to a wedding invitation. Using the form as a prompt, the composer adds to the conventional "accepts with pleasure" the attributes "joy, love, and an open heart." Likewise, the composer adds, "We look forward to celebrating your love and union." The couple's name is drawn in block letters, and in the middle of the "O" is placed the names of the couple. The drawing of the block letters, with the names included in one of them, complements the added line "your love and union," as it identifies who is attending the event. In these examples, the drawing complements the language as they work together in response.

Elaborating Language

In some cases, however, the drawing is more prominent than the language, and the drawing could be said to elaborate the language. For example, someone learning flower arranging, as the composer here is, may be copying a floral design presented in a book or one appearing in a room. In a case like this, the drawing helps the composer complete the task of representing the design, and it's probably at least as easy to draw as it is to describe verbally: the drawing presents something of a model, which might be especially important in three-dimensional

Figure 7.11

work. The flowers are identified verbally as "left bud [and] podocarpus branches + anemones in white vase," with their arrangement articulated in the drawing; depending on a person's knowledge of plants and interpretation of the drawing, they might, or might not, need the language. Moreover, in a reverse of the notes above, which used the drawing of a smiley face to soften a verbal message and the format of an FBI wanted poster to amuse readers, this writing-drawing provides direction through the drawing. The only way to understand how the flowers are arranged is through the drawing. As important, the drawing functions as a kind of unified memory device: one look at it, and the composition of the arrangement is clear.

Another example of such elaboration can be geographical directions. For example, when people are asked to provide directions from one place to another, they often (perhaps typically) write them verbally, which can include noting the starting point and destination; naming streets and

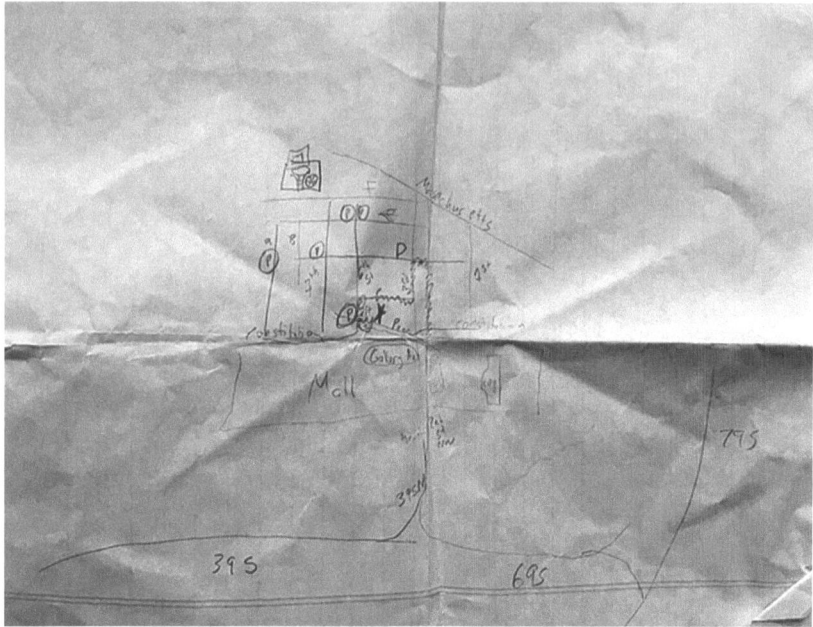

Figure 7.12

kinds of streets (e.g., interstate, one-way); identifying landmarks along the way; and marking the left- and right-hand turns as well as compass directions (e.g., south, northwest). Another approach in response to the same task is to draw the directions. As we see in the example here, of directions from Maryland into Washington DC's Newseum, words still play a role: the streets Massachusetts and Constitution are named; the street Pennsylvania Avenue is abbreviated to "Penn"; the landmark Mall is identified; and directions, as with "1st NW," are noted. The words thus locate specific places on the drawing, mostly the major thoroughfares, but the drawing provides the directions visually. And again, like the design drawing above, the drawing represents three dimensions, which is in part why it is an intuitive and useful approach. This everyday writing uses drawing to make sense of and elaborate on language.

Responding Politically

Writing has been important for political action, as the US Declaration of Independence and the Emancipation Proclamation suggest; everyday writing using writing and drawing together also plays a role in such writing, and as we see here, it can be planned and/or spontaneous.

Figure 7.13

At first glance, the welcome signs greeting refugees at the Denver International Airport are all words, even if colorful words, which in some cases—the yellow of "no ban, no wall" on black, for instance, and the red "RESIST IGNORANCE, NOT IMMIGRANTS" on white—make effective use of color contrast in a classic move characteristic of multimodality. But the drawing identifying which "IMMIGRANTS" and "REFUGEES" are particularly welcome is part of the word "WELCOME": the "C" in "WELCOME" has become a crescent and next to it is a star, which together represent Islam. Drawing, in other words, isn't always separate from language but can be a particularly important part *of* language.

Another planned example, a poster from the 2018 Women's March in Dayton, Ohio, makes the claim "'STRONG MEN DON'T NEED TO PUT DOWN WOMEN TO FEEL POWERFUL," with the words "MICHELLE OBAMA" acting as the signature. The fonts and their colors on the pink poster, with pink the traditional color used to signal a girl child, are varied for emphasis, with "POWERFUL" in block letters of two colors. Adjacent to the signature is a silhouette, presumably of Obama, but the crown on the head, combined with the silhouette, evokes other historically powerful women who were queens (e.g., Queen Elizabeth I), thus making the historical point: strong men have supported women for quite some time.

Figure 7.14

Figure 7.15

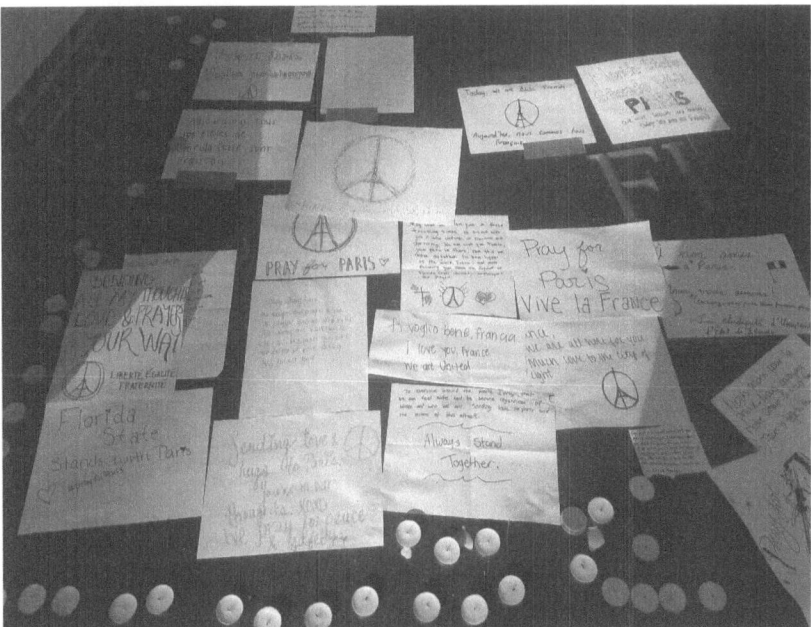

Figure 7.16

A third example, more spontaneous, includes many examples of everyday writing composed in response to the November 2015 terrorist attacks in Paris. Those examples were taped to the fountain in front of Wescott, the administration building at Florida State University, the fountain a central meeting site for students. It's also a canonical site in that it provides the backdrop for graduation photos and other celebratory events, but as the photo suggests, it can be repurposed, in this case as something of a memorial for Paris and the lives lost in this terrorist attack. In addition to messages of empathy, solidarity, and hope, the memorial includes several material artifacts, among them bunting, flowers, and candles. The messages are largely conveyed in language, but the languages are multiple—English, French, Spanish, Italian, Arabic, and Chinese—and expressed in multiple colors, often the red, white, and blue of France. The drawings included in the messages are also diverse, although there are two repeated drawings: (1) hearts and (2) the more specific drawings of a peace sign enclosing an Eiffel tower. This collection of everyday texts includes other drawings as well, including of a French flag and flowers.

In all three of these political examples, the drawing is symbolic. In the planned signs at the Denver airport, the drawing uses a symbol to welcome one group of refugees particularly while welcoming all; in the case of the Women's March poster, Michelle Obama is both author of the quotation and representative of the claim; in the case of the spontaneous memorial at Florida State, the drawings employ an historic sign for peace to frame a specific landmark identifying France that becomes a symbol of the event itself.

THRESHOLD CONCEPTS, WRITING, AND DRAWING

As the examples here indicate, everyday writing—writing that is purposeful, self-sponsored, and action-oriented—serves many purposes, from providing directions to expressing sorrow and solidarity, and inhabits many spheres, both public and private. More specifically, the everyday writing analyzed in this chapter privileges two modes, language and the visual of drawing: working together, language and drawing often appear in different kinds of relationships—with drawing complementing language; working with language in responding to an idea, text, or event; complementing *and* responding to an idea, text or event; elaborating language; and working symbolically with language to respond to political events—although which mode predominates varies.

What's particularly relevant here is also how this analysis might contribute to a threshold concepts–informed conception of writing: should some threshold concepts be amended and/or might other threshold concepts be added? For example, the threshold concept *words get their meanings from other words*, although working somewhat differently than the earlier-discussed threshold concept *texts get their meaning from other texts*, also speaks to the intertextuality of composing, but in this case to language exclusively. As Dylan Dryer (2015) explains, words have no inherent meanings; rather, they are meaningful as they interact with other words and with context.[6]

> While the realization that words cannot be permanently linked to specific meanings can be disconcerting, the effects of this threshold concept are familiar. Most of us, for example, have had the unpleasant feeling that someone else has twisted our words or taken them out of context; we might have bristled at an excessively technical loophole someone finds in seemingly sensible and obvious rule; we might have been startled by an interpretation of familiar poem or a text we hold sacred (Meyer and Land, 2006: 5). These experiences are reminders that the relations that imbue a sentence with particular meanings come not just from nearby words but also from the social contexts in which the sentence is used. . . .

"Language," says Mikhail Bakhtin, "lies on the borderline between oneself and the other. The word in language is half someone else's" (Bakhtin 1981, 293). (24)

Words do get their meanings from other words and contexts, at least in the cases examined here, *and* words get their meaning from accompanying drawings. The immigrants especially welcome at the Denver International Airport are Muslim; the stealthy cats, as the drawing on the notice makes clear, are ordinary cats, which makes the notice amusing; the Yanceys and the Wong are four in number, as the stick figures show; the Burkean identification between the composer and Adler-Kassner is expressed in two hearts; Michelle Obama is both quoted author and synecdoche; the bombing of Paris-as-Eiffel Tower is framed in a peace symbol made famous during the Vietnam War.

The question is, What might writing studies teachers, scholars, and researchers of threshold concepts make of these examples? One could make the case, for example, that what these examples demonstrate is a variant of the threshold concept addressing multimodality. It's accurate, I think, to frame these examples this way; the problem in doing so is all it leaves out—the materiality of the composing, the embodiedness of the drawing, and the fundamental role in meaning-making drawing in particular plays in texts like these. Alternatively, one might review current threshold concepts to see how they could be revised, in a twofold way. First, threshold concepts, especially those too absolute, can be modified: thus, the threshold concept *words get their meanings from other words* might be revised to something more nuanced and accurate like *words get their meanings from other words, from visuals, and from context.* In this new version, it's clear that words and contexts aren't the only source of meaning for other words. Second, all writing threshold concepts might be reviewed to see where everyday writing fits or matches; where it does not, new threshold concepts might be nominated.

In sum, there is more work to do, especially as writing studies threshold concepts continue to be refined: another question is how such a refining process might be prompted or staged. One approach might involve investigations into writing that explicitly intend to break new ground. Charles Bazerman, Arthur Applebee, Virginia Berninger, Deborah Brandt, Steve Graham, Paul Kei Matsuda, Sandra Murphy, Deborah Wells Rowe, and Mary Schleppegrell's (2017) recent project on lifespan writing provides a useful case in point; the scholars involved in this project might return to the contemporaneous list of threshold concepts to inquire as to their capacity and their accuracy: do they describe what the new scholarship shows, and might some of them need to be revised to accommodate new insights? Another approach to assuring that writing studies threshold concepts are as comprehensive and accurate as possible might be a variant of the original semi-crowd-sourced effort: a wiki or other platform, also focusing on capacity and accuracy, could be established, its purpose to welcome new voices and new insights. And yet another approach might be more systematic and directive: establishing a SIG at CCCC for this specific purpose, to ensure that writing studies threshold concepts are as comprehensive and accurate as possible. It might also be that teachers who have used threshold concepts in their classes could be consulted on what if anything in the current list should still be addressed. And I could also imagine that this book, in partnership with the earlier book on threshold concepts, in retrospect, comprises the first of a series of books on writing studies threshold concepts, with a new book in the series released at five-year intervals, the purpose of each new volume to take up, probably in different forms, questions about the comprehensiveness and accuracy of writing studies threshold concepts.

In sum, there are many ways to go about this continuing effort, one this volume participates in. What's important about the chapters in this volume, and the proposals above, is that they bring threshold concepts to life, making them as useful as possible. Likewise, in the process, they assure that our threshold concepts not only name what we (already) know but also explore and theorize what we are still learning.

NOTES

Photo Credits. Linda Adler-Kassner, for the photo of two hearts, posted originally on Facebook. Elizabeth Wardle, for the Michelle Obama poster at the 2018 Women's March. Kathleen Blake Yancey, for all the others.

1. Although digital writing includes many visuals and many kinds of visuals, including drawing, the focus here is on print. As the examples of everyday writing here attest, print, and handwritten print, is very much alive and serves a variety of rhetorical purposes and, in some cases, is the only available resource for the task.
2. Gunther Kress (2009) argues that texts were principally linguistic until relatively recently: for a counterargument, see Kathleen Blake Yancey's (2016) "Print, Digital, and the Liminal Counterpart (in-between): The Lessons of *Hill's Manual of Social and Business Forms* for Rhetorical Delivery."
3. What is obvious in many of these examples is how clever and creative composers are, even in creating a note for an informal occasion. Although I haven't interviewed the writers of these texts, my sense is that their own pleasure—both in creating these notes and in the anticipated pleasure of their audience—is part of the exercise, which leads to another observation about writing: composing can be a very pleasurable experience and, on some occasions, even fun.
4. Although many annotations include drawings. For a widely historical selection, visit the Oxford University Marginalia Facebook group.

5. Personalizing forms is a characteristic of much everyday writing since a good deal of it, as we see here, begins with a form.
6. And there's another issue at play here. Dryer's argument is largely located in the distinction between the sound of language and its meaning, as he says, "Saussure meant that because that there is no necessary connection between any sounds or clusters of symbols and their referents (otherwise different languages would not exist), the meaning of words is relational—they acquire their meanings from other words" (23). That's a fair point, but as Lester Faigley has argued, the oral narrative of language overlooks the historical role of the visual in composing: see Faigley 1999.

REFERENCES

Adler-Kassner, Linda and Elizabeth Wardle. 2015 *Naming What We Know: Threshold Concepts of Writing Studies*. Logan: Utah State University Press.

Ball, Cheryl, and Colin Charlton. 2015. "All Writing Is Multimodal." In *Naming What We Know: Threshold Concepts of Writing Studies*, edited by Linda Adler-Kassner and Elizabeth Wardle, 42. Logan: Utah State University Press.

Bakhtin, Mikhail M. 1981. "Discourse in the Novel." In *The Dialogic Imagination*, translated by Caryl Emerson and Michael Holquist, 259–422. Austin: University of Texas Press.

Barton, David, and Mary Hamilton. 2012. *Local Literacies: Reading and Writing in One Community*. Abingdon: Routledge.

Bazerman, Charles, Arthur N. Applebee, Virginia W. Berninger, Deborah Brandt, Steve Graham, Paul Kei Matsuda, Sandra Murphy, Deborah Wells Rowe, and Mary Schleppegrell. 2017. "Forum: Taking the Long View on Writing Development." *Research in the Teaching of English* 51 (3): 351–60.

Colello, Silvia M. Gasparian. 2001. "The Role of Drawing in Children's Writing." 13th COLE Congresso de Leitura do Brasil, in Campinas (SP). http://www.hottopos.com/rih6/silvia.htm.

Dryer, Dylan. 2015. "Words Get Their Meanings from Other Words." In *Naming What We Know: Threshold Concepts of Writing Studies*, edited by Linda Adler-Kassner and Elizabeth Wardle, 23. Logan: Utah State University Press.

Faigley, Lester. 1999. "Material Literacy and Visual Design." In *Rhetorical Bodies*, edited by Jack Selzer and Sharon Crowley, 171–201. Madison: University of Wisconsin Press.

Gere, Anne Ruggles. 1994. "Kitchen Tables and Rented Rooms: The Extracurriculum of Composition." *College Composition and Communication* 45 (1): 75–92.

Gesensway, Deborah, and Mindy Roseman. 1987. *Beyond Words: Images from America's Concentration Camps*. Ithaca, NY: Cornell University Press.

Goldblatt, Eli. 2016. "Copper Mine's Valley." Museum of Everyday Writing. https://museumofeverydaywriting.omeka.net/items/show/241.

Kress, Gunther. 2009. *Multimodality: A Social Semiotic Approach to Contemporary Communication*. London: Routledge.

Lyons, Martyn. 2012. "New Directions in the History of Written Culture." *Culture and History Digital Journal* 1 (2): 1–9.

Oppenheim, Joanne. 2008. *Stanley Hayaimi, Nisei Son*. New York: Brick Tower.

Roozen, Kevin. 2015. "Texts Get Their Meaning from Other Texts." In *Naming What We Know: Threshold Concepts of Writing Studies*, edited by Linda Adler-Kassner and Elizabeth Wardle, 44. Logan: Utah State University Press.

Shipka, Jody. 2011. *Toward a Composition Made Whole*. Pittsburgh: University of Pittsburgh Press.

Sinor, Jennifer. 2002. "Reading the Ordinary Diary." *Rhetoric Review* 21 (2): 123–49.

Yancey, Kathleen Blake. 2016. "Print, Digital, and the Liminal Counterpart (in-between): The Lessons of *Hill's Manual of Social and Business Forms* for Rhetorical Delivery." *Enculturation* 23. http://enculturation.net/print-digital-and-the-liminal-counterpart.

Yancey, Kathleen Blake. Forthcoming. "The Composing of Seniors: Navigating Contexts, Texts, and Practices." In *Talking Back: Senior Scholars Deliberate the Past, Present, and Future of Writing Studies*, edited by Norbert Elliot and Alice Horning. Logan: Utah State University Press.

Yancey, Kathleen Blake, Joe Cirio, Jeff Naftzinger, and Erin Workman. Forthcoming. "Defining Everyday Writing: Theories, Scenes, and New Directions for Research." *South Atlantic Review.*

PART 2

Using Threshold Concepts to Engage with Writing Teachers and Students

8
DOORS BETWEEN DISCIPLINES
Threshold Concepts and the Community College Writing Program

Mark Blaauw-Hara, Carrie Strand Tebeau, Dominic Borowiak, and Jami Blaauw-Hara

INTRODUCTION

Integrating threshold concepts into a departmental curriculum can be a daunting project, particularly at a community college where writing faculty hail from nearly every degree program related to English. Because threshold concepts of writing draw from the discourse community of rhetoric and composition, they might at first seem alien to faculty from other subdisciplines. Yet at North Central Michigan College, we have found that threshold concepts offer a rich opportunity to develop a community of practice within the English department that integrates our varying writing identities rather than elides them. We have not eschewed our formative writing identities in exchange for becoming community college English instructors but rather settled into a shared practice in which the language of threshold concepts bridges our fundamental understandings of writing and allows us paths to discuss what we want to teach in more cohesive and unified ways.

We began our project to integrate threshold concepts in 2015, when a team of six writing faculty read *Naming What We Know* and identified the ten concepts they felt best described the knowledge students should gain from first-year composition (Adler-Kassner and Wardle 2015). Based on these initial lists, our WPA, Mark, selected the ten most frequently occurring concepts. Then, we involved the rest of the department, narrowing the list to six:

- *writing is a social and rhetorical activity* (17–19)
- *writing speaks to situations through recognizable forms* (35–37)
- *all writers have more to learn* (59–61)
- *text is an object outside of oneself that can be improved and developed* (61–62)

- *revision is central to developing writing* (66–67)
- *reflection is critical for writers' development* (78–79)

As a department, we challenged ourselves to position the six threshold concepts as core understandings about writing that would serve to guide our essay assignments and activities. Along with brief definitions, the threshold concepts were written into the departmental FYC curricular packet, and Mark began introducing threshold concepts and providing background readings with new faculty during on-boarding sessions. They are discussed at most departmental meetings, and recently, writing faculty journaled (and shared) their own learning of and experiences with the six departmental threshold concepts. We continue to think threshold concepts hold great promise for community college writing programs; however, we would be the first to admit that our own department still needs to grow in its incorporation of them.

In this essay, we summarize scholarship that has helped us understand what has and hasn't worked in our department's uptake of threshold concepts. We also suggest reasons writing-related threshold concept uptake may be particularly challenging in community college programs. Next, we describe our own experiences with the threshold concepts our department identified as central and how those concepts resonated with our disciplinary backgrounds. We then make suggestions for how other community colleges might develop "local teacher-scholar communities of practice" (Toth and Sullivan 2016, 262) to help English faculty from diverse backgrounds experience a "transformed way of understanding, or interpreting, or viewing something" (Meyer and Land 2003, 1)— in this case, the purpose and curriculum of community college writing programs.

FACULTY UPTAKE OF THRESHOLD CONCEPTS

Using threshold concepts as a starting point for instruction functions as a threshold concept itself. Lisa Tremain, Marianne Ahokas, Sarah Ben-Zvi, and Kerry Marsden, in this collection, note that examining the disciplinary assumptions behind classroom practices is challenging work—although, as Ahokas points out in that piece, such work can serve to sharpen one's understanding of one's own pedagogical goals. Similarly to Tremain et al., we think it is useful to view the time faculty spend wrestling with how to integrate threshold concepts as time spent in a liminal state. Ray Land, Julie Rattray, and Peter Vivian (2014) write that "the liminal state can be seen to perform a progressive function which begins with the encountering and integration of something new. This subsequently entails recognition of shortcomings in the learner's existing view of the phenomenon in question and an eventual letting go of the older prevailing view. At the same time this requires a letting go of the learner's earlier mode of subjectivity. There then follows an envisaging (and ultimate accepting) of the alternative version of self which is contemplated through the threshold space" (201). Crucially, they also note that this liminal state is frequently uncomfortable, characterizing it as "unsettling, experienced often as a sense of loss, as prevailing earlier conceptual views, and early states of subjectivity, . . . are relinquished" (201). When applied to teaching, this suggests one should expect a certain amount of confusion and resistance when threshold concepts are introduced to a writing program curriculum because basing one's teaching approach on threshold concepts can seem counterintuitive and challenging to prior understandings or disciplinary preparation. However, a certain amount of departmental discomfort is a normal sign faculty are progressing through the liminal-phase characteristic to learning threshold concepts.

A number of scholars have written about the challenge of teaching from a threshold concept perspective at the university level (Barradell 2013; Harrison, Clayton, and Tilley-Lubbs 2014; Wilcox and Leger 2013). Certain characteristics of many community college writing programs serve to heighten the difficulty of a threshold concepts approach. Chief among these is the diversity of disciplinary preparation faculty in community college writing programs may have. Our program has faculty with degrees in rhet/comp, English education, creative writing, and literature, and our program is not atypical in its disciplinary diversity (Janangelo and Klausman 2012; Klausman 2008). Elsewhere in this collection, Heidi Estrem, Dawn Shepherd, and Susan Shadle point out that such diversity in disciplinary preparation is not limited to the community college and that sometimes that diversity can serve as a stumbling block when faculty try to reach common understandings of writing and how to teach it. In many ways, the diversity of community college writing faculty is a strength, both in terms of spurring robust discussions in department meetings and in offering students a variety of approaches from which to learn. However, it can complicate efforts to reach shared understandings of threshold concepts of writing studies and basic agreement on how to reinforce those concepts with students.

In addition to challenging faculty on a pedagogical level, threshold concepts raise ontological questions. As stated earlier, Land, Rattray, and Vivian (2014) argue that the liminal state is characterized (in part) by the realization of "an alternative version of self" (201). Jan Meyer, Land, and Caroline Baillie (2010) note that "in the liminal phase an ontological shift or change in subjectivity accompanies change in cognitive understanding, often as part of a recognition that such shifts are necessary and appropriate for membership of a given community of practice" (xiii). The liminal phase also connects strongly with Jean Lave and Etienne Wenger's (1991) concept of legitimate peripheral participation, whereby learners gradually become members of a community of practice not only through learning the practices associated with the community but also through adopting identities consistent with that community. Lave and Wenger (1991) write that "activities, tasks, functions, and understandings do not exist in isolation; they are part of broader systems of relations in which they have meaning. These systems of relations arise out of and are reproduced and developed within social communities, which are in part systems of relations among persons. The person is defined by as well as defines these relations. Learning thus implies becoming a different person" (53).

This is relevant to community college writing faculty because it implies faculty need to make an ontological shift from viewing themselves as poets, literary scholars, high-school teachers, or rhetoricians to viewing themselves as community college writing teachers. Such a shift would not necessarily negate other possible identities: scholars generally agree that identity construction is an ongoing, lifelong process and that we can hold multiple identities at the same time, essentially performing different roles as the occasion demands (Goffman 1959; Ivanič 1998; Prior 1998). However, this ontological shift may reveal that some of the ways one approaches writing—as a poet, as a literary scholar—may no longer be appropriate for the new community of practice. This shift entails finding a way to channel one's preexisting pedagogical strengths toward the needs of community college students, a daunting task best supported by a community of practice in which teaching is scaffolded by departmental discussion and idea sharing.

Threshold concepts can be developed as a common teaching language and an accessible place of shared membership among faculty from a range of writing backgrounds. An important step in implementation is to encourage faculty to explore their own understandings of writing from a threshold concepts perspective; because writing fields tend to operate as discrete discourse communities with their own lexes, it would be possible at first to feel threshold concepts are firmly entrenched in rhetoric and ignore the deep understandings of other branches of writing, which members of a diverse community college department bring with them as the underpinning of their personal pedagogies. Instead, the department must acknowledge the varied paths through which faculty discovered their own writing threshold concepts and highlight that these concepts are likely categorized under a different lexis for each branch field of writing. (For more on the diverse identities and preparation faculty bring to the writing classroom, see Estrem, Shepherd, and Shadle in this collection.) The first step, then, is for department members to "name what they know" about writing and to find the commonalities.

In the sections below, each of us discusses our path toward understanding threshold concepts in writing, and we briefly detail our own progress toward using threshold concepts to orient our teaching, as well as our own progression to viewing ourselves as community college writing faculty. Each of us comes from a different area of English and initially approached the teaching of writing from a different perspective. However, we each found that a threshold concepts approach resonates with how we understand writing, and we have found the approach to be useful in our teaching.

INDIVIDUAL JOURNEYS

Mark

I originally trained as a high-school English teacher. Much of my undergraduate education focused on methods rather than theory. However, when we did dip into theoretical texts, I resonated with Paulo Freire's (2000) liberatory pedagogies, Mike Rose's (1989) discussions of socioeconomic class and education, and John Dewey's (1969) arguments for experiential, contextualized learning. During the last few years of my undergraduate education, I worked at my college's writing center, where I learned to focus on the writer rather than the essay. The writing center's consultant-preparation course was also where I first encountered the works of Donald Murray, Peter Elbow, David Bartholomae, Muriel Harris, and more. The writing center was where I learned theory and practice are connected and feed one another and where I tried to make my practice reflect the theories I had begun to hold dear.

My doctoral program solidified my sense that without a strong grasp of writing theory—in fact, not just a grasp, but a conscious alignment of pedagogy with specific theoretical orientations—one is teaching the trees without a sense of the forest. In the writing classroom, this might look like teaching individual essays without any conceptual framework to link them together. I didn't want to teach essays; I wanted to teach *writing*. I think the first time I came across threshold concepts was in Linda Adler-Kassner, John Majewski, and Damian Koshnick's (2012) *Composition Forum* article, and I was intrigued enough to read Meyer and Land's original pieces and to attend a workshop on threshold concepts at the 2014 CCCC. I came out of that workshop convinced that threshold concepts were not only very important to the field but also that they might help me address a growing sense that students' knowledge from writing courses did not transfer to the rest of their coursework. A greater understanding of threshold concepts seemed to hold promise for increasing students' abilities to transfer writing knowledge from their composition courses to their disciplines.

As I learned more about threshold concepts, I wondered whether they could provide an intellectual backbone for first-year writing: a strong, unifying structure on which to hang the essays, readings, and assignments an individual instructor might choose. This question was of particular interest to me as a WPA. If we could settle on a list of departmental threshold concepts and make sure our assignments spoke to them, no matter our backgrounds or pedagogical orientations, it could increase our consistency among sections.

Carrie

I pursued an MFA in poetry for the love of words and the craft of assembling them. My poetry scholarship involved a deep exploration of the meaning of craft; in a workshop-centered curriculum, we practiced writing as a process, allowing our poems to exist as objects outside ourselves as we opened our work to critique and discussion. Revision is a central expectation of MFA programs; they exist on the premise that all writers have more to learn. We worked to uncover the way our voices are shaped by experience, perspective, and other writers; we remixed ideas from the canon into our own work as we experimented with form and meter. Poetic craft is about honing your own writing process and maximizing the constraints of form, meaning, metaphor, and sonics to imbue a small set of words with the largest possible impact. When I moved on from graduate school with the intent of making a life out of writing, I found myself doing so by teaching composition at a community college. I've often encountered the idea that poets teaching composition have "settled" for another field, but this instinct to insulate writing fields from each other seems false to me; the distinction seems less about writing practice and more about the separate languages creative writing and composition use to describe themselves, when in fact both are a practice in making effective meaning out of words. In teaching threshold concepts in composition, I've found deeply familiar writing theory that is applicable to writing, regardless of genre; it is another expression of many of the principles I first learned as poetic craft. What I teach in composition is the assemblage of words, and I follow the guidelines I first learned as a poet, which is to say as a writer—the term does not delineate genre but encompasses everyone who arranges words. In threshold concepts, I find ways to speak the familiar language of craft with my colleagues from different backgrounds and ways to frame what I know from poetry to help my students develop their own compositions. When I begin a semester with the threshold concept *reflection is critical for writers' development* and introduce Deborah Brandt's (1998) ideas of literacy sponsors, it's a touchstone idea from poetry. Those of us who write creatively are keenly aware of the sponsors of our own craft: they're writers who inspired us at critical points of development; the teachers who guided our fledgling attempts; the people, magazines, and groups who told us, explicitly and by implication, that we didn't have a right to speak as poets and inspired us to rebel against that silencing. I can prove to my students that what is formative matters to the entire shape of your voice.

When my students tackle the threshold concept *revision is central to developing writers* and read Nancy Sommers's (1980) work on revision, there's an exact alignment with creative writing: revision is a deep and constant excavation that must be performed under the premise that writing exists outside the self. In poetry this work is intensive and competitive; the drive to be artful requires an absolute rejection of holding onto initial words. It requires a belief that what is sculpted will be better than what is slapdash. When I teach revision to my composition students, it is the poetry talking, but I can access it with composition-centered language by framing it as a threshold concept.

The notion of discourse communities and the threshold concept *writing is a social and rhetorical activity* likewise resonate as a version of poetic craft: a poem's voice determines its audience and locates the gates of its accessibility exactly as an essay must consider the circle within which it speaks. Parallels exist among nearly every threshold concept in composition and element of craft in poetry because ultimately writing is writing, regardless of genre. If we speak a common language, both with each other as writers and as teachers of writing, we can center on the fundamental things we all consider. In this way I am not an interloper in a foreign field; I am teaching what I have learned and loved all along.

Dominic

Composition didn't initially interest me; literature was my passion and comfort zone. This mindset was hard to shake, and I was resistant to the idea of becoming a composition teacher since I couldn't help but feel like an outsider who was ill-prepared or exceedingly ignorant. Thankfully, these feelings lessened over time as I gained experience and confidence in the classroom. After all, I was still being afforded the opportunity to play with language and discuss with students its craft and the effects it could have; yes, the writing we discussed was different than literary analysis, but it still followed all the "rules" I had come to learn. This was a remarkable epiphany and the beginning of my commitment to the field of composition.

After I read the initial work on threshold concepts (Meyer and Land 2003), I began some deeper, more pointed reflection regarding what I thought about writing, and I realized I started to enjoy teaching composition *because of* my work with literature, not in spite of it. For instance, I was invigorated by students creating writing of their own and then thinking about it, talking about it, reshaping it, and talking about it some more; it was interesting for me to listen to students describe themselves as writers (or authors, in a loose sense) and then reflect more on the matter. Understanding all of this was an important step in my development since it started the merging of my literature-based past and my composition-based present and future, even if I still felt a bit disconnected from my rhet/comp colleagues who were (in my mind) so clearly better prepared for the composition classroom.

And then came *Naming What We Know*, and those things that were just beginning to click before really crystallized. I finally felt comfortable with my background in literature and how it prepared me for the composition classroom. All those things I wasn't formally taught but intuitively discovered about writing through my work with literature and literary analysis were articulated as important threshold concepts about writing, and thus, *Naming What We Know* provided me a common language with which I could discuss writing amongst my peers, no matter where they came from or how they learned about writing and its power. My lens was different, but it wasn't worse.

Now, after over a decade of teaching composition classes in community colleges, I fully embrace my literature background and its effect on me as a writing teacher. I was formally trained to look at writing as being open to analysis, discussion, and reflection; I was taught to look at a text as an imperfect object crafted through recognizable forms to communicate with and entertain or enlighten an audience. Writing is craft, and writers are craftspeople. These tenets mirror threshold concepts like *writing is a social and rhetorical activity, writing speaks to situations through recognizable forms,* and *all writers have more to learn.* While threshold concepts theory was certainly emerging during the time of my early teaching career, I was not aware of it or conscious of the fact that my formal education was allowing me access points to teaching composition using concepts similar to literature exploration and analysis, though once that intersection became clear to me, I finally felt at home in the field.

Jami

Writing made sense when I discovered rhetoric. The complexities of writing well, something I had struggled with, began to seem more like a series of decisions embedded in a complex situation rather than a mysterious gauntlet of right or wrong. This realization didn't make writing easy, but it did make it knowable. As a first-generation college student attending a demanding university, I had found myself underprepared for writing. I struggled when I applied the skills for which I'd been rewarded in high school to my more rigorous college writing. I left my undergraduate degree still unclear about whether I was a good writer. This view of writing as identity, as opposed to craft, is something many of my students bring to FYC. They tell me they are not "a writer" or writing is "not my thing," which is really to say they feel they do not fit into a constructed, largely romantic view of writing the field has debunked time and time again.

My master's degree in composition studies introduced me to a rhetorical view of writing. I first started teaching writing as a graduate student, and I taught myself, as I taught my students, to understand the holy trinity of the rhetorical situation as well as exigence and constraint. All were tools to use in crafting a piece of writing. In short, rhetorical theory taught me to understand why writing is hard and also to understand how to break it down into manageable pieces. This insight increased my confidence both as a teacher and as a writer.

When I first read about threshold concepts as part of our English-department project, they made sense. Most of them considered writing rhetorically, which meant the text was a construction, something happening outside myself that could be honed for an audience. This perspective aligned with how I taught composition. Just as I had long ago, my students came to college with a sense of writing developed in literature-based, expressivist-oriented high-school classes. They viewed their writing as an expression of who they were rather than as something outside themselves. Threshold concepts help us see writing as something outside the self, responding to changing situations. This view depersonalizes writing but also makes it more teachable, more a place of intellectual curiosity than a freeing of inner voice. The expressionist school of writing pedagogy has always missed the mark for me, as I found the self I conveyed the wrong sort of self for my professors.

Threshold concepts offered a reaffirmation of what I had already been doing, so teaching with them seemed effortless and interesting. I liked pulling back the curtain on the writing process and welcoming students to the problems and questions any writer, whether skilled or novice, answers when they write. I also enjoyed not teaching the specifics of the rhetorical modes that populate most textbooks. It was a relief to not focus on how to set up a comparison-and-contrast essay or how to punctuate dialogue in a remembered-event essay. The pedagogical options in the expressionist school seemed to far-off, hazy, and idealistic. The textbook model of teaching the nuts and bolts of Aristotle's modes seemed too myopic. A rhetorical/thresholds focus seemed to find the Goldilocks zone for me as a teacher: deep enough for interest but far enough away to be examined and not simply felt.

INTEGRATING A THRESHOLD CONCEPTS APPROACH

As the preceding narratives demonstrate, each of us found that threshold concepts resonated with how we understood writing (and the teaching of writing), despite our different backgrounds. This resonance led each of us to embrace a threshold concepts approach to course design and pedagogy. For writing programs just beginning to explore how threshold concepts might enrich and focus curriculum, we recommend activities and discussions that encourage faculty to explore how threshold concepts articulate understandings about writing they already hold. Rather than asking faculty to set aside their different disciplinary preparations, we think it is helpful to ask them to dive into their understandings of writing and see how threshold concepts connect. However, although this is a good place to start, more must be done to support a full integration of threshold concepts in a community college writing program.

As we argue earlier in this piece, it is paramount to view a threshold concepts pedagogical approach as a threshold concept itself. With this approach, all the characteristics of threshold concepts apply for departmental colleagues encountering this framework for the first time, especially the fact that they are transformative, bounded, and troublesome (Meyer and Land 2003) While most writing instructors will at least tacitly agree with most of the concepts a department might want them to integrate into their teaching, in order for this overlay to be effectively integrated, the concepts must be embraced on a deep level. Furthermore, as Estrem, Shepherd, and Shadle point out in this volume, many instructors need time and space to grapple with the dissonance that can come from reimagining their identities as teachers of community college composition in addition to masters of a particular field of English. Threshold concepts provide a framework for situating ideas and understandings in a way that is transferable among members of the community. When we can discuss our separate understandings using a common language, it is easier to see how they overlap, which strengthens the community and diminishes the dissonance.

While we acknowledge the challenges of implementing this curricular approach, we also argue the benefits far outweigh any obstacles *and* that those obstacles are manageable with planning and effort. Our recommendations for successful implementation follow, formed through research, experience, and reflection on our own approach.

A Robust Community of Practice

The ultimate goal is that the department becomes a unified community with a deep understanding of threshold concepts in writing, as well as their value inside the classroom. Efforts should be made to gradually bring members into the community with special attention to the important role identity plays in the process, initially as a potential obstacle to community membership and then later as a shared element among group members. For institutions with several campus locations, the challenge of a fragmented community is real, though looking for possibilities for overcoming this fragmentation is essential to building a strong foundation on which the community can grow together.

Opportunities for Early and Ongoing Conversation

Within the community of practice, members must have consistent chances to discuss threshold concepts and their applications. We must accept that a threshold concepts curriculum can be troublesome, so staving off frustration and negativity with careful, productive coaching and facilitation is invaluable. In these conversations, leaders and early adopters can model ideas, applications, troubleshooting, and so forth to show the realistic and vastly beneficial ways thresholds concepts can unlock students' learning. Furthermore, community members can explore their identities and be encouraged to look for connections between their disciplinary or personal writing identities and the entrance points into threshold concepts. It is important to note that accepting the identity of a member in the departmental community of practice does not mean that community member must renounce any prior identity as, say, a creative writer or high-school teacher; instead, those identities should be viewed as valuable lenses through which threshold concepts can be filtered and understood.

The Compensatory Value of Intellectual Involvement

As communities of practice, departments can work together to unearth and explore valuable insights into writing. Each member's experience in the discipline is integral in creating a unified, deep understanding of what it means to be a student of writing within that community, and emphasis should be placed on the rewarding nature of this work. While we concede this does not solve the problems of heavy workloads and potential financial strains placed on adjunct faculty, it does address the value this work *adds* to their professional lives. Certainly, as Ahokas and Marsden point out elsewhere in this collection, contingent employment and lack of funding for professional development can serve as counterpressures against the excitement and agency engagement with threshold concepts can bring. However, a robust community of practice acts as a conduit for meaningful, intellectually engaging work, and this engagement can strengthen contingent faculty members' sense of purpose and connection with a writing program.

CONCLUSION

We think threshold concepts hold great promise to improve community college writing programs, primarily because they operate on a macro level: they focus on what we know about writing in a way that overarches more narrow disciplinary understandings. Additionally, in our own engagement with threshold concepts, we have experienced flashes of recognition in which certain threshold concepts have articulated our prior disciplinary understandings of writing in new, powerful ways. Susan Wilcox and Andy Leger (2013) argue that the process of identifying threshold concepts for postsecondary teaching inspires rich discussion about "ideas that matter" (9), and they hold up the process as one of the best professional-development activities for college teachers. We have found this to be the case in our own department.

Selecting threshold concepts to guide our writing classes—and participating in the commensurate discussions about what that means—has served as what Barbara Harrison, Patti Clayton, and Griselda Tilley-Lubbs (2014) call a "threshold experience": "reflective encounters with dissonance that give rise to deeper understanding of threshold concepts" (6). Certainly, as we have engaged with threshold concepts in our department, we have experienced varying degrees of productive dissonance as we have learned what it means to be community college writing teachers. Though adopting threshold concepts as a departmental framework is difficult in that it invites an identity dissonance, as it asks instructors from varied backgrounds to coalesce under a singular composition-centered focus, it provides an opportunity to develop a rich community of practice within the department centered on deeper issues than how to teach a particular type of essay.

We also think our engagement with threshold concepts has pushed us to be more cohesive in our writing instruction—in providing broad, overarching themes to teach to, it has pointed us in the same directions while still providing us the opportunities to teach in ways that play to our individual strengths. Because threshold concepts approach writing from its fundamental underpinnings, they allow many angles of access to instructors from a range of English-related fields. Instructors can use threshold concepts as a lens through which to focus their own understandings of fundamental writing concepts, but because these understandings are translated to a common language, they are easier to discuss, share, and grow. Seeing threshold concepts as a way to center the writing knowledge each instructor possesses allows for academic freedom but simultaneously offers bridges between varied approaches. Finally, threshold concepts provide a path through which faculty who hail from diverse disciplinary backgrounds can embrace the identity of community college writing teachers.

REFERENCES

Adler-Kassner, Linda, John Majewski, and Damian Koshnick. 2012. "The Value of Troublesome Knowledge: Transfer and Threshold Concepts in Writing and History." *Composition Forum* 26. https://compositionforum.com/issue/26/troublesome-knowledge-threshold.php.

Adler-Kassner, Linda, and Elizabeth Wardle. 2015. *Naming What We Know: Threshold Concepts of Writing Studies.* Logan: Utah State University Press.

Barradell, Sarah. 2013. "The Identification of Threshold Concepts: A Review of Theoretical Complexities and Methodological Challenges." *Higher Education* 65 (2): 265–76.

Brandt, Deborah. 1998. "Sponsors of Literacy." *College Composition and Communication* 49 (2): 165–85.

Dewey, John. 1969. *Experience and Education*. New York: Collier-Macmillan.
Freire, Paulo. 2000. *Pedagogy of the Oppressed*. New York: Bloomsbury Academic.
Goffman, Erving. 1959. *The Presentation of Self in Everyday Life*. Norwell, MA: Anchor Books.
Harrison, Barbara, Patti H. Clayton, and Gresilda A. Tilley-Lubbs. 2014. "Troublesome Knowledge, Troubling Experience: An Inquiry into Faculty Learning in Service-Learning." *Michigan Journal of Community Service Learning* 20 (2): 5–18.
Ivanič, Roz. 1998. *Writing and Identity: The Discoursal Construction of Identity in Academic Writing*. Philadelphia: John Benjamins.
Janangelo, Joseph, and Jeffrey Klausman. 2012. "Rendering the Idea of a Writing Program: A Look at Six Two-Year Colleges." *Teaching English in the Two-Year College* 40 (2): 131–44.
Klausman, Jeffrey. 2008. "Mapping the Terrain: The Two-Year College Writing Program Administrator." *Teaching English in the Two-Year College* 35 (3): 238–50.
Land, Ray, Julie Rattray, and Peter Vivian. 2014. "Learning in the Liminal Space: A Semiotic Approach to Threshold Concepts." *Higher Education* 67 (2): 199–217.
Lave, Jean, and Etienne Wenger. 1991. *Situated Learning: Legitimate Peripheral Participation*. Cambridge: Cambridge University Press.
Meyer, Jan, and Ray Land. 2003. *Threshold Concepts and Troublesome Knowledge: Linkages to Ways of Thinking and Practising within the Disciplines*. Enhancing Teaching-Learning Environments in Undergraduate Courses Project Occasional Report 4, University of Edinburgh, May. http://www.etl.tla.ed.ac.uk/docs/ETLreport4.pdf.
Meyer, Jan H. F., Ray Land, and Caroline Baillie. 2010. *Threshold Concepts and Transformational Learning*. Champaign, IL: Sense.
Prior, Paul A. 1998. *Writing/Disciplinarity: A Sociohistoric Account of Literate Activity in the Academy*. Mahwah, NJ: Erlbaum.
Rose, Mike. 1989. *Lives on the Boundary*. New York: Penguin.
Sommers, Nancy. 1980. "Revision Strategies of Student Writers and Experienced Adult Writers." *College Composition and Communication* 31 (4): 378–88.
Toth, Christie, and Patrick Sullivan. 2016. "Toward Local Teacher-Scholar Communities of Practice: Findings from a National TYCA Survey." *Teaching English in the Two-Year College* 43 (3): 247–73.
Wilcox, Susan, and Andy B. Leger. 2013. "Crossing Thresholds: Identifying Conceptual Transitions in Postsecondary Teaching." *Canadian Journal for the Scholarship of Teaching and Learning* 4 (2): 1–11.

9
EXTENDING WHAT WE KNOW
Reflections on the Transformational Value of Threshold Concepts for Writing Studies Contingent Faculty

Lisa Tremain, Marianne Ahokas,
Sarah Ben-Zvi, and Kerry Marsden

NAMING OUR PURPOSE: HOW (CONTINGENT) FACULTY TRANSFORM THRESHOLD CONCEPTS

The threshold concepts of writing identified in *Naming What We Know* (Adler-Kassner and Wardle 2015) were developed by an impressive list of scholars from our field. You know these names; prior to and since *Naming What We Know* (*NWWK*), they present us with extensive and important scholarly projects on writing knowledge and development. These contributions have evolved and shaped the scholarly conversations in writing studies, which spiral out to the everyday writing classroom. But what does it look like when scholarship is taken up and transformed into classroom practice? And who are the people doing this work? While threshold concepts of writing provide a valuable framework for exploring such transformation, no scholarship thus far has drawn connections to how material and labor conditions are always bound up in this process. In this chapter, we examine the extent to which "macro-level knowledge and resolutions from the field," such as threshold concepts of writing, can "inform the micro-level of composition classes" and programs and how working conditions and programmatic and institutional constraints are bound up in this process (Wardle 2013, 1). In describing how our writing program faculty took up threshold concepts of writing in distinct ways, we mirror other discussions of uptake in this volume: Chris Anson, Chen Chen, and Ian Anson, for example, explore how disciplinary faculty identify and use key terms of writing in their courses; through their quilt project at Boise State, Heidi Estrem, Dawn Shepard, and Susan Shadle report on the ways teacher identities influence their manner of engagement in threshold concepts; and Mark Blaauw-Hara, Carrie Tebeau, Dominic Borowiak, Jami Blaauw-Hara

DOI: 10.7330/9781607329329.c009

consider the ontological shifts experienced by writing instructors when threshold concepts of writing move into teaching practice. Each of these investigations, in addition to our own in this chapter, underscore what Adler-Kassner notes in this volume: our colleagues, like our students "are encountering, entering, and engaging in multiple 'liminal thresholds'" (294). In describing writing faculty's uptake of threshold concepts at our institution, we underscore how contingency, authority, and positionality in the broader systems of the writing program, major, institution, and scholarly field were all part of this phenomenon. Our reflective presentations of this work—what we call *reflexive portraits*—illuminate not only how threshold concepts *in*formed curriculum, assessment, and program design but also *trans*formed how we think about teaching, writing knowledge, and our institutional and disciplinary identities.

NAMING OUR FRAMEWORKS: THRESHOLD CONCEPTS, LABOR, AND REFLEXIVITY

In "Extending the Invitation: Threshold Concepts, Professional Development, and Outreach," Adler-Kassner and John Majewski (2015) suggest that engaging with the *concept of* threshold concepts can "change the way faculty think about their teaching." They ask, "How can an introduction to threshold concepts change actual teaching practice?" (196). This is a question at the heart of our reflexive self-portraits. We expand this question to consider the ecological elements that impact or impede such change.

Following Jan Meyer and Ray Land's extensive scholarship on threshold concepts, much of the subsequent research about them concerns identification and teaching of threshold concepts in and across disciplines (see Adler-Kassner and Wardle 2015; Land, Meyer, and Flanagan 2016; Launius and Hassel 2015; Schaub, Bravender, and McClure 2015). The use of threshold concepts as a framework for faculty development is an important anchor across this scholarship. But while some studies frame faculty's uptake of threshold concepts through reflexive practice, reflexivity is not specifically named as an essential step of uptake. This is not the case in Naomi Irvine and Patrick Carmichael's (2009) article "Threshold Concepts: A Point of Focus for Practitioner Research," which explicitly points to the value of reflexivity when faculty formulate and integrate threshold concepts; reflexivity fulfills "the dual role of stimulating reflection ('What is it we do?') and encourage[es] self-conscious consideration of disciplinary distinctiveness ('How might others see us?')" (113). Their findings highlight how reflexive narratives can make faculty's uptake of threshold concepts visible to them; through these narratives, faculty can express "emergent pedagogical positions," which provide a "point of focus for reflection-as-action" (114, 116).

Still, these investigations of how faculty take up threshold concepts do not draw connections to labor or contingency as part of this phenomenon. This absence is especially striking in our discipline since composition scholarship has broadly critiqued the disproportionate relationship between labor conditions for contingent faculty and the necessity of creating space, time, and incentive for professional development (Bousquet 2004; Cucciarre 2014; Kahn, Lalicker, and Lynch-Biniek 2017; McCamley 2014; Mendenhall 2014; Penrose 2012; Schell 1998; Schell and Stock 2001; Wardle 2013). In response, composition scholarship on contingent labor tends to argue that programs, WPAs, and/or tenure-line faculty must create opportunities for contingent faculty to make their thinking, teaching, and value visible within the program, the institution, and the scholarly community. As we argue here, contingent faculty's participation in their programs also includes merging localized practice and expertise with the scholarship from the field.

Our reflexive portraits explore how such merging happened in our own program and how labor conditions, expertise, and authority were bound up in this process. The methodological approaches we used to develop our reflexive portraits were autoethnographic and reflective, but we also we worked collaboratively and collectively. The writers of this work are Sarah, Marianne, and Kerry, all part-time lecturers in the Humboldt State University Writing Program, and Lisa, a full-time, tenure-track faculty member and the WPA. As a group, we met to discuss particular questions that would help us think about what uptake of threshold concepts looked like for each of us; we drafted and discussed responses to these questions; we talked about and read scholarship on threshold concepts and contingent labor; and we collaborated to read, revise, and determine the shape of this chapter. We also drew upon Donna Qualley's (2016) formulation of "retrospective understanding," in which "individuals don't just build on recent, prior knowledge . . . ; they become consciously aware of it" (93). This awareness allowed each of us to reflect on our "identities and relationship to the larger social context" of the program and the broader field, and it reflected back to us our understandings, goals, and ways of knowing (91).

The genre of reflexive portrait is informed by Jane Burke and Sue Dunn's (2006) discussion of reflexive pedagogy, in which reflexivity is a process that encourages reflection but also one that "shifts the focus from the decontextualized, individual learner to the fluid and situated identifications that shape learning and complex pedagogical relations" (221). This reflexivity is coupled with the idea of (written) self-portraiture as a method for self-representation. In *The Situated Self,* J. T. Ismael (2007) points to self-portraiture in art, in which the artist is depicted "in the wide environment, relating themselves to their surroundings . . . like a map with a red dot" (164). Each author of the reflexive portraits in this chapter is the "red dot," and the ecological elements we each capture—the first-year writing program and classroom, the introduction to the English-major course, working conditions, and beliefs about expertise and authority—are features of the broader map.

CONSIDERING WHAT *WE* KNOW: FOUR REFLEXIVE PORTRAITS

The setting for these reflexive portraits is Humboldt State University (HSU), a small institution in the California State University system. HSU was designated a Hispanic-serving institution in 2013, and we have experienced increased enrollment of undergraduate first-generation and Pell-eligible students over the last seven years (57 percent of first-time college students were first-generation and/or Pell eligible in 2017). In the HSU first-year composition and rhetoric program, we offer "stretch" composition (a two-semester, year-long FYC course) or a one-semester "accelerated" course. The current faculty is made up of twelve returning non-tenure-track (NTT) lecturers, of which three-quarters are part-time faculty, and a small contingent of rotating graduate teaching associates. In 2012, the program was approved to hire its first tenure-line WPA; Lisa is the second person to fill this role.

The program uses end-of-course portfolios to assess students' understanding of HSU's FYC outcomes. Through spring 2018, every portfolio was blindly scored by and calibrated across at least two faculty readers, and students needed to pass the portfolio in order to pass the composition course. However, as Lisa, Sarah, and Kerry examine in this chapter, there were problems with this model that stood in contrast to our understandings of threshold concepts. Rather than prioritizing reflection, rhetorical knowledge, or creativity, for example, the portfolio served as a possible obstacle to students' success in our courses due to its strict formatting requirements and pass/fail stakes. Meanwhile, although students could receive a failing score on the portfolio and revise it rather than repeating the entire composition course, it was also the *only* form of writing assessment we used as a program. Using threshold concepts as a framework, we are currently engaging in revision of our portfolio and program assessments.

LISA: RECOGNIZING THE WORK OF PROGRAM TRANSFORMATION: DO ALL OF US HAVE TO TALK ABOUT THRESHOLD CONCEPTS OF WRITING?

I'm currently finishing my second year as tenure-line WPA at Humboldt State. After interviewing at HSU, I was thrilled to be offered the position because I knew I would be coming into a community already thinking and talking about threshold concepts. This was the same powerful scholarly exigency that had inspired me to rethink and reenvision my teaching of first-year writing and how I might direct a program as WPA.

However, I soon learned that only *some*—not all—of the faculty were experimenting with threshold concepts as an approach to curriculum, course assignments, and assessment. This small group of lecturers, which included Sarah, Marianne, and Kerry, had gathered together (informally but consistently) to read and brainstorm together, to pitch ideas about curriculum redesign, and to frame critical questions about how threshold concepts implicated the program's design, in particular its portfolio assessment. This ad hoc (extra) work was important and valuable to this group, and I wanted to validate and foster it across the program. But the faculty who had chosen *not* to participate in these discussions had done so primarily for reasons that concerned other crucial labor conditions: many were teaching five classes each semester, most at very low pay; some taught across multiple institutions or departments to make a living. Meanwhile, there was no established expectation that part-time or NTT faculty "would be involved in a community of teachers/scholars" (Wardle 2013, 9). While I wanted to draw upon the momentum among the group of faculty who were exploring and integrating threshold concepts of writing into curricula, I also needed to acknowledge these lecturers' lived realities: they were underpaid and overworked. If meaningful professional work around threshold concepts *could* happen for the *entire* program, what might this work look like? And how important was it that everyone "talked" threshold concepts of writing?

It was not my goal to strive toward the type of program "utopia" Seth Kahn, William Lalicker, and Amy Lynch-Biniek (2017) have cautioned against but to validate the experience, expertise, and knowledge that was already there. During my first opportunity to work with faculty, I asked them to respond to this question: How do you think individuals move toward increased writing expertise? Opening our conversations through this inquiry allowed faculty to describe what they knew and believed about writing and why they made the choices they did as instructors and curriculum designers. As we collectively mapped the writing knowledge and concepts we believed were important for writing development, we connected our map to the threshold concepts in *NWWK*, and we ultimately checked the results of this conversation against program outcomes. This conversation led to a full-scale revision of our writing outcomes, which now embrace a discourse about writing that is conceptual, developmental, and grounded in threshold concepts. However, once revised, our new outcomes pointed like a proverbial weathervane to how they would be assessed, and they brought our portfolio assessment into sharp focus as a next step for collaborative professional development and work.

From many perspectives, it could be argued that our (now former) portfolio assessment was grounded in best practices. Students selected the texts for their portfolios; faculty read sample portfolios as a norming practice; and we employed calibrated scoring. Kathleen Blake Yancey's (1999) well-known article "Looking Back as We Look Forward: Historicizing Writing Assessment" describes "reading and interpretation and negotiation" as key practices of portfolio assessment; in revising our outcomes, we noticed we had valued and applied practices of "reading" and "negotiation" to our portfolio assessment, but "interpretation[s]" of it were missing in two important ways (491).

First, some mandatory features of the portfolio served as strict gatekeepers: the required cover letter had to be formatted as a business letter; all texts in the portfolio were required to meet spacing and margin requirements, and—most anxiety producing for students and faculty—it needed to include at least fourteen pages of written material, not including citations. Before a faculty reader even looked at content, some portfolios were scored as an automatic zero on the six-point rubric because they were under the page requirement. These constraints led both students and faculty to focus class time leading up to portfolio deadlines on page count and formatting requirements. Even more concerning was that these requirements implied to students that formatting was more valuable than writing knowledge, reflection, or rhetorical awareness. This is to say, though we did not have a standardized curriculum, we did have a standardized competency-based assessment.

The second problem was that the portfolio was not used to strategically assess our outcomes. We also did not use it as an opportunity to share and discuss student work or to simply "get good ideas from other teachers" (Wardle 2013, 11). Instead, it had become an end-of-semester habit, an onerous rating task in which we read and scored every portfolio in the program. It had functioned to give the program a sense of cohesion but without any real rationale for what this cohesion meant to us. As my colleague Marianne says, "It was the hammer that turned all of our issues into nails."

After discussing our values and beliefs about writing, threshold concepts, and the program's outcomes, we began to turn the mirror that is assessment back on ourselves, asking questions like Who is the portfolio for? What does it do? We drew upon threshold concepts of writing, such as Tony Scott and Asao Inoue's (2015) "Assessing Writing Shapes Contexts and Instruction" and Peggy O'Neill's (2015) "Assessment Is an Essential Component of Learning to Write." We read and discussed these and other conceptual frameworks for assessment, and we critiqued the existing portfolio through them. We have recently revised the portfolio's requirements to focus on knowledge making and reflection, and many faculty are experimenting with new assignments that ask students to explore genre, discourse, and rhetoric in creative ways.

But there is more to do, and this work is never seamless. As we continue to work on portfolio and program assessment, only *some* faculty members explicitly draw upon threshold concepts of writing to ground their curricula or their contributions to program work. How much does this matter? As the WPA, how I facilitate program development and contextualize it in the macroknowledge of the field seems paramount. I want to privilege collective knowledge, collaborative decision-making, and faculty ownership of the program and its shape. This more clearly reflects the work I hope our students do as writers—to take up and grapple with new knowledge, to abandon or shift or transform their thinking about writing and their identities as writers with increased agency, voice, and knowledge. In the same way Doug Downs and Liane Robertson (2015) argue that threshold concepts allow for potential "interplay between conceptions of writing" and "the meshing together of conceptions to form . . . theories of writing" for students, I hope to facilitate this same interplay for writing program faculty (120). Still, this approach doesn't mean every member of our program will buy in wholeheartedly to this scholarship, in part because buy-in is inseparable from the labor conditions that shape writing programs. As WPA, I must stay attuned to the tensions between collaborative program development and faculty's working conditions.

SARAH: EMBRACING THE MESS: THRESHOLD CONCEPTS AS A FRAMEWORK FOR TEACHING FIRST-YEAR COMPOSITION

In "Naming What We Know: The Project of this Book," Adler-Kassner and Wardle (2015) stress the "contingent, changing nature of knowledge" (4–5). My own developing knowledge of writing studies has encouraged me to embrace this contingency through a particular "messiness" that has transformed the way I understand the development of teaching expertise. I define *messy* as exploration, process oriented, nonlinear, and not well-aligned to the (former) high-stakes portfolio assessment in our writing program. Genre is often messy, research is messy, and identity is not only messy but complicated. Teaching to these concepts rather than to tidy prescriptive essays can feel like borderline chaos. Yet in developing a threshold concept-anchored FYC curriculum, which has been incredibly and sometimes frustratingly messy, I have been forced to reconsider how students acquire writing knowledge in all the contingency and fluidity associated with both my learning and theirs. Threshold concepts provided me with a framework to deeply examine my own disciplinary values about writing and how I articulate them to students. This transformative work caused me to shift my teaching and students' learning from a skills-based orientation of writing to one that underscores a messy acquisition of writing knowledge.

I first heard about threshold concepts three years ago when our first WPA brought them to my attention. Exposure to resources such as *Naming What We Know* and *Writing about Writing* (*WAW*) (Wardle and Downs 2017), combined with dissatisfaction with HSU's high-stakes, product-based portfolio assessment (which Lisa described earlier), led me to rethink how I'd learned to teach writing. In my stretch FYC course, I experimented with new curriculum and used several new-to-me resources in the classroom. I began to see how activities and lessons centered around *concepts* prompted a shift in student thinking, from seeing themselves as deficient or unskilled at writing to seeing themselves as makers of knowledge and, ultimately, as *writers* able to grapple with and articulate what writing is. Like Wardle (2008), I hoped students would understand that "FYC is a legitimate focus of scholarly and pedagogical inquiry" (177). This possibility, that an FYC class could privilege scholarly concepts of writing as opposed to skills, was enormously attractive. For a few years, my curriculum had felt deeply unsatisfying. A threshold concepts framework permitted me to position students as emergent scholars and to shift my own role from thesis-statement coach (or so it felt some days) to disciplinary professional. I could introduce students to writing studies in ways that could challenge, engage, and foster thinking about how writing worked beyond simply earning a grade.

As part of my curricular revision, I asked students to read and respond to excerpts from *NWWK*, primarily those that explore dispositions, rhetorical knowledge, and the effort and practices of writing. Students wrote reflective pieces about their emerging knowledge in response to these excerpts. Instead of "traditional" thesis-driven papers, I asked students to rewrite and reframe threshold concepts in exploratory ways so they might clarify, interrogate, and develop their existing knowledge about writing. I began to see actual shifts in students' dispositions toward writing and themselves as writers. While tracking their reflections, I noticed that their frustrations about writing began to diminish; some of that frustration was transformed to curiosity. This shift was especially true after they'd explored threshold concepts that focused on dispositions or identity as part of writing. For example, students wrote about ways their literacies and identities are interwoven in response to Yancey's (2015) "Writers' Histories, Processes, and Identities Vary," and they compared and contrasted their knowledge about revision and editing after reading and discussing Charles Bazerman and Howard Tinberg's (2015) "Text Is an Object Outside of Oneself That Can Be Improved and Developed." Students also became more philosophical about what concepts were tricky and what questions they had. Threshold concepts allowed them not only to explore answers to their questions but also to pose answers that led them to *more questions* about writing and themselves as writers. Simultaneously, I saw my *own* perspectives on learning and writing change, which inspired and invigorated me. In conducting these curricular experiments, I felt more like a teacher-scholar; I was experimenting with something that felt epistemologically meaningful, something I could share and explore with my colleagues. But I also had nightmares about how these new methods might not help students produce "portfolio-worthy" pieces. As I recalibrated my sense of what a "successful" writing class could look like, I saw how this curriculum did not privilege the conventions or genres our portfolio assessment called for.

Meanwhile, despite shifts in student dispositions toward and understandings of writing, their writing about these shifts was messy. By no means had they mastered threshold concepts—but I did not expect them to. In fact, while I had envisioned students would attempt to "rewrite" threshold concepts, by reframing them in their own languages and/or for nonscholarly audiences, students actually tended to dissect and unpack them and to think about how they could translate them for and to *themselves*. Their interpretations of threshold concepts were liminal and exploratory, and they sometimes demonstrated misinterpretations, but they also illuminated an eagerness to tackle complicated ideas. I also reflected on and reconsidered this pedagogy in response to the work they did with threshold concepts, especially those concepts I wanted them to revisit or further pull apart. Most anxiety producing was that I had to reflect on how this work might impede their development of the summative portfolios in our program. There was a distinct tension, then, between my emerging values about writing, informed by threshold concepts, and our program's high-stakes, constraint-heavy portfolio assessment. The department's more recent collective decision to remove many of the constraints of the portfolio has allowed me continue to experiment with a threshold concepts approach to curriculum without as much anxiety.

There is still anxiety, of course. For example, the concept of genre has proven itself to be incredibly (and understandably) baffling for many first-year students. But rather than abandoning this concept in my curriculum, I've gone further down the rabbit hole: How might I help students better conceptualize genre? What types of genres do students use or want to use? How can I design learning opportunities that help them investigate genres beyond those typical to academic writing? How can I convince them it's okay to leave a fifty-minute class saying "What the hell is genre?" and to understand that asking this question is part of their developing writing knowledge? So I'm taking this work in small steps. I am also grappling with threshold concepts and how to teach them. Rather than sequencing the course to lead toward a polished, tidy portfolio, I have begun to develop a curriculum that teaches students to see themselves as *writers*, to begin to frame each new writing situation with a critical eye and transferable knowledge. Simultaneously, this new approach to curriculum in FYC has afforded me the space to reconsider and value my development as a teacher-scholar, a curriculum designer, and a professional in the classroom and writing program. As we move forward, I want to continue to add my voice to what we value (and help students value) about writing, especially the liminality and messiness a threshold concepts framework not only permits but privileges.

MARIANNE: THE UTILITY PLAYER AT THE MYSTICAL PORTAL: HOW CAN AN ADJUNCT CONVERT A LITERARY STUDIES PROGRAM TO A THRESHOLD CONCEPTS APPROACH?

I'm the utility infielder of the HSU English department, a contingent faculty member with twenty years' experience teaching first-year composition and with a doctorate in literary studies. I'm assigned whatever courses need staffing. And while my introduction to threshold concepts came by way of writing studies, *my* mind went immediately to their implications for teaching in our undergraduate major.

In "Threshold Concepts and Troublesome Knowledge (2): Epistemological Considerations and a Conceptual Framework for Teaching and Learning," Meyer and Land (2005) focus on the liminal state, the ambiguous identity of novices as they transition from one condition to the next, but what strikes me about their discussion is the seductive nature of this transition; the talk of "portals" suggests neophytes joining secret societies, highlighting a tension in the nature of threshold concepts. In Introduction to the English Major, the first core course in our major curriculum, students discover they *will* be introduced to abstruse and obscure knowledges, both belletristic and theoretical. The appeal for many students, I believe, is precisely this initiation into an occult set of skills. It's maybe paradoxical, then, that reframing the major curriculum around threshold concepts serves not to reinforce this mystification but as a way to make accessible the troublesome and counterintuitive knowledge of the discipline students typically struggle with.

References to threshold concepts as mystical knowledge portals resonate with me. As a working-class, first-generation college graduate myself, I moved through my small liberal arts college feeling conspicuously fraudulent. I identify with my students in the California State University system, the majority of whom are the first in their families to attend a four-year institution. As a result of my own experiences with mystified knowledge, I try to be the teacher I would like to have had—the instructor who explicitly addresses the implicit values and practices of the discipline otherwise hidden to many students. For me, that means acknowledging the difficulty, for *faculty* as well as for students, of specific concepts; highlighting the working assumptions that inform disciplinary practices or beliefs; laying bare the ideological foundations that become invisible to practitioners and making them (even their existence) part of the curriculum.

Historically, for example, I've focused Introduction to the English Major around problems in the construction of meaning: how does meaning presume a familiarity with other texts? How does meaning reflect a text's historical contexts? How does a reader's own historical situatedness inflect the meaning any text will have for them? I'm finding that many of the threshold concepts of writing studies laid out in *Naming What We Know* are equally relevant to my version of Introduction to the English Major: *writing is a social and rhetorical activity; writing expresses and shares meaning to be reconstructed by the reader; texts get their meaning from other texts;* and others. I've also tried to frame threshold concepts specific to literary studies itself, such as *literature itself is a social construct* and *meaning changes across time and cultures.* Some of them are clearly subsets of the writing studies threshold concepts laid out in *Naming What We Know*.

As I develop these threshold concepts, I've found a threshold concepts approach hasn't altered my current curriculum so much as sharpened my understanding of my own goals. I hope to more clearly articulate for my students the motives of particular assignments and class activities that, in turn, will help them understand how and why we do English. For instance, a central text of the class is Milton's pastoral elegy "Lycidas"; we return to it throughout the semester in different contexts, but we consider its genre first, largely because the pastoral elegy is a completely foreign genre for twenty-first-century students. Its conventions are so bizarre that students recognize them pretty quickly *as* conventions rather than inevitabilities. Students research the pastoral elegy specifically as a subgenre of elegy to consider what such a text, with its elaborate conceits, actually *does*—that is, the situations it speaks to and how it speaks to them. Why reimagine the deceased through this archaic and fantastic bucolic ideal? What did such a fiction offer the writers and readers of elegies, at that particular moment? When and why did the pastoral elegy cease to be a viable genre? What ideological and cultural work do literary genres perform? Or, reformulated as a threshold concept, *genres have lifetimes; they rise in response to specific needs, flourish, and disappear when they're no longer ideologically efficacious.* A project of this kind helps students understand better the nature of genres—their flexibility and utility and the ways *writing speaks to situations through recognizable forms* (Bazerman 2015, 35)—and to investigate the role of representation in the invention of the self, the many ways *writing enacts and creates identities and ideologies* (Scott 2015, 48).

If threshold concepts help demystify disciplines and their operating assumptions, they also promote student access to and participation in disciplinary debates. I think it's equally important to emphasize the contingent nature of threshold concepts. Disciplines, after all, are dynamic; Matthew Arnold's threshold concepts are not *our* threshold concepts. If we think of threshold concepts not as defining essences but as snapshots of disciplines at specific moments, they also offer a way to track and investigate disciplinary transformation and to include students in the process of transformation.

Threshold concepts of literary studies now inform my approach to my course assignments, and I would also like to see them prompt a general discussion among our faculty about the discipline as we practice it. Our department currently lacks much consensus about the major curriculum, particularly the core courses; we tend to frame this anarchy as a virtue, but it means students don't always have a particularly coherent sense of the program or the discipline. Identifying and agreeing on sets of threshold concepts for each core course, and indeed across them, would be a major undertaking. But hammering out threshold concepts, however contingent, would force *faculty* to articulate the assumptions that inform their teaching and to discuss how—and whether—those assumptions are articulated in the classroom.

As I think more about the intersections of literary and writing studies threshold concepts, I'm excited, too, about the conceptual bridges they're constructing in my protean life as a literature *and* a composition instructor. I'm beginning now to think in broad terms of *threshold concepts of textual studies* and strategizing how I might persuade my department to embrace threshold concepts and simultaneously recognize the shared intellectual values across literary and writing studies. An adjunct can dream.

Students most likely to find the university governed by unwritten rules and assumptions will likely be the students best served by a threshold concepts approach. Threshold concepts may evoke ineffable knowledge familiar only to those initiated in the sacred mysteries, but they can do so in the service of clarity and accessibility, allowing students to enter and contribute to disciplinary debates. Threshold concepts may be troubling and counterintuitive, but so is much about college generally for those students with no real experience of such places and no mentors who can help them navigate the institution.

KERRY: DO THRESHOLD CONCEPTS REPRESENT AN OPPORTUNITY FOR TRANSFORMATION OF SUBJECT POSITION AND MATERIAL CONDITIONS?

I am a homegrown adjunct, teaching at the same institution I attended as an undergraduate and graduate student pursuing degrees in literature. For the past five years I've taught first-year composition, as well as introductory courses in women's studies and ethnic studies. With work from multiple departments, so far I've been offered enough units each semester to secure health insurance and pay rent. But our university budget has lately been running in deficit and enrollment is down, so I don't yet know if I'll be offered the six units I'll need to qualify for health insurance next semester. I've been pinning my hopes for longer-term stability on colleague retirements. It's a situation that causes me a lot of anxiety. And my dissatisfaction is growing; not because my economic position is any more precarious but because (despite my adjunct status and lack of PhD) I've begun to appreciate the value of my labor as a teacher of writing, as well as my contributions to the writing program here at HSU, since being introduced to and grappling with threshold concepts of writing studies.

In my case, exposure to the concept of threshold concepts, those specifically outlined in *Naming What We Know*, has pushed me to reconceive the way I think about composition and my own value as a writing teacher. Coupled with my position as a relatively new, part-time, contingent faculty member, exposure to threshold concepts has led me to reflect on how engagement with these concepts shapes my identity as a faculty member, as well as my understanding of my authority within the composition program at HSU. Beyond these personal and immediate impacts, however, I also wonder: to what extent will I, as an adjunct working within a capitalist (academic) economy, be able to pivot this change in my view of my own authority and expertise in the local program to one that would be taken up by the larger institution? And how necessary is this institutional change to my continued professional development?

This thinking began in the summer of 2015 when a small group of colleagues and I began an ad hoc reading group that was neither requested nor compensated by the university. Our group was frustrated with curricular stagnation in our classrooms and inspired by the influence of our first tenure-line WPA, who had recently left that position; we wanted to know more about what conversations about curriculum were being had in the field of composition and rhetoric. Starting with a reading of *Writing about Writing*, we moved on to *Naming What We Know*. Our conversations turned from discussions only of curricular changes to talk about changes in how we conceived of the discipline and our program as well as our goals and roles within those sites.

When I first began teaching in composition, I knew little about what it meant to teach writing, and I did not have a clear understanding of the purpose or history of the FYC requirement. Moreover, as a former student of many of my writing colleagues, I wanted to impress them and be accepted as a new peer; however, I saw the path to this acceptance from a position of student/novice (rather than scholar/expert) and understood the *right* way of teaching as following a curriculum as I would a formula. As Lisa explained earlier, the test of my success as a teacher was measured by my students' portfolio pass rate, so I worked to enact the values and definition of good writing created by that powerful summative assessment even as I came to understand the assessment as one that conflicted with my experiences as a writer and developing philosophies as a teacher.

The concept of threshold concepts and those outlined in *Naming What We Know* provided a framework for me to speak to these conflicts of value, identity, and authority. *NWWK* mapped enough of the terrain of writing studies for me to develop an entry path into the discipline. Both overwhelming and validating, this introduction to the field allowed me to see conflicts of value and identity as valid and persistent rather than inconsequential and individual. *NWWK* authorized me to reimagine the focus and possibilities of the FYC classroom. That did not mean simply replacing content, though that did happen, but examining and *valuing* "what [I] know and believe in ways [I] have not before" (Adler-Kassner and Majewski 2015, 189). I spent more time working to understand my goals and motivations, what practices of inquiry and attention I wanted to take up with students in the classroom and with colleagues in the program. In this way, exposure to threshold concepts has not fundamentally transformed my values, but it has transformed how I teach to those values and my ability to advocate for them in my classroom and in our program.

This shift in my identity and authority is particularly visible to me around my changing participation in the HSU composition program and the broader field of composition. I've taken on a new expertise-oriented subject position—participating in original research, writing, conference attendance, and deliberation with colleagues. This new position has been highly gratifying for me even while this work has largely been on my own time and dime. And yet, I have been compensated psychologically by threshold concepts, even while the institution hasn't seen fit to offer matching material compensation. This psychological wage has had a profound impact on my sense of self and the value of my contributions. Still, I'm left with questions: How can I as a contingent faculty member work toward cultivating greater expertise when the larger institution treats lecturers as disposable? To what extent can disciplinary expertise "save" composition lecturers from being treated as disposable in a capitalist system that increasingly relies on contingent labor across the disciplines?

My authority is institutionally constrained based on my tenuous position in the university hierarchy. Yes, I care about and enjoy the work more. I feel more grounded, present, and curious and better prepared to engage students about how to participate in the conversations of their disciplines as I do more of that myself. And yet, I'm no less contingent. Even as I enjoy a greater sense of belonging in my program and the field, my engagement is still curtailed by a lack of stable employment, not to mention a lack of release time for research and sufficient funding to travel to conventions. Curiosity and research interests are not individually sustained. And I wonder how long I can sustain my current sense of excitement and agency as these institutional constraints work, again, to mitigate my knowledge of the field and access to an identity as a writing studies disciplinary member.

CONCLUSION: CONSIDERING THRESHOLD CONCEPTS, TRANSFORMATION, AND CONTINGENCY

Taken together, these reflexive portraits reveal, perhaps unsurprisingly, that we noticed a distinct sharpening of our values about and practices of teaching writing as we took up threshold concepts. We also noticed that the learning of threshold concepts is for us, like our students, liminal, often developed through risk taking and exploration; this learning interacts with how we see *ourselves* as teachers, writers, leaders, and learners. As Marianne points out, threshold concepts can unveil some of the mysteries of disciplinary thinking; they can be used to "inquire, analyze, interpret, and ultimately make knowledge," even in positions of contingency (Yancey 2015, xxviii). Perhaps most important, writing these reflexive portraits helped us engage in "epistemological participation"; we understand more clearly how different communities might engage threshold concepts and how we each can contribute to that engagement (Adler-Kassner and Wardle 2015, 4).

Yet there are tensions working in these portraits, too. Most of these tensions are also a recognition of the constraints presented by labor and the ways programmatic and/or institutional ecologies either encourage or deter contingent faculty from engaging with macrolevel knowledge from the field. Harri Pitkäniemi (2010) argues that there is a type of cognitive fragmentation that occurs when professionals take up new knowledge; these fragments are often in conflict with each other: when "beliefs, images, and mental models that teachers hold about teaching and learning" interact with the uptake of new theory, they "exert important influences on teaching practices and the extent to which changes can be made and sustained" (159). Sarah, for example, describes the conflict between the ways threshold concepts pushed her to allow for more messiness and critical inquiry in her practice and programmatic models for teaching and assessing writing. Kerry's beliefs about teaching and learning were validated by threshold concepts, yet while she feels more agency as a scholar and member of the writing program, her contingent status continues to limit how far she might take such agency.

Our reflexive portraits also identify practices and values—institutional and programmatic—that may be inhospitable to threshold concepts: the perils of teaching first-year writing through them, as Sarah notes, since liminality and experimentation may be less valued in other spaces where students learn; the limited power of adjuncts to affect curricular change, as in both Kerry's and Marianne's portraits; the time it takes to interrogate deeply entrenched practices, such as the program's (former) portfolio, as described by Lisa. Yet while our portraits describe ways programmatic and institutional constraints continue to challenge us, they also underscore the ways threshold concepts of writing have helped us hone and more deeply understand them. As Kerry notes, threshold concepts allowed us "to see these conflicts of value and identity as valid and persistent rather than inconsequential and individual." This aligns with Etienne Wenger's (1998) argument that "we produce meanings that extend, redirect, dismiss, reinterpret, modify or confirm—in a word, negotiate anew—the histories of meanings of which they are a part" (52–53).

It might be argued that the individual factors involved in transforming and being transformed by threshold concepts of writing are too specific to draw any general conclusions about this process, which is perhaps the reason we notice an absence of such examination, so far, in our field. However, by telescoping out to look at the broader elements of program, institution, and labor, then back in to look at values, practices, positionality, and authority, we hope to encourage the usefulness of reflexive uptake of important scholarship like threshold concepts. We argue that creating space for faculty to reflect on and develop awareness of the ecologies in which such concepts are encountered and transformed is a valuable process, and here we hope we've indicated how a reflexive process was particularly revealing for us. We call for additional studies to examine faculty experiences of learning, transforming, and enacting threshold concepts of writing in their programs and institutions, with a particular focus on how labor constrains this work, and we suggest that developing our understandings of localized uptake and transfer of threshold concepts enables us to "extend discussions of what we know" (Adler-Kassner and Wardle 2015, 9).

REFERENCES

Adler-Kassner, Linda, and Elizabeth Wardle. 2015. *Naming What We Know: Threshold Concepts of Writing Studies*. Logan: Utah State University Press.

Adler-Kassner, Linda, and John Majewski. 2015. "Extending the Invitation: Threshold Concepts, Professional Development, and Outreach." In *Naming What We Know: Threshold Concepts of Writing Studies*, edited by Linda Adler-Kassner and Elizabeth Wardle, 186–202. Logan: Utah State University Press.

Bazerman, Charles. 2015. "Writing Speaks to Situations through Recognizable Forms." In *Naming What We Know: Threshold Concepts of Writing Studies*, edited by Linda Adler-Kassner and Elizabeth Wardle, 35–37. Logan: Utah State University Press.

Bazerman, Charles, and Howard Tinberg. 2015. "Text Is an Object Outside of Oneself That Can Be Improved and Developed." In *Naming What We Know: Threshold Concepts of Writing Studies*, edited by Linda Adler-Kassner and Elizabeth Wardle, 61–62. Logan: Utah State University Press.

Bousquet, Marc. 2004. "Academic Labor and the Reflexive Turn in Literature and Cultural Studies." *College Literature* 31 (4): 172–80.

Burke, Jane Penny, and Sue Dunn. 2006. "Communicating Science: Exploring Reflexive Pedagogical Approaches." *Teaching in Higher Education* 11 (2): 219–31.

Cucciarre, Christine. 2014. "Happily and Shamefully Non-Tenure-Track: Hypocrisy in Academic Labor." *College English* 77 (1): 55–63.

Downs, Doug, and Liane Robertson. 2015. "Threshold Concepts in First Year Composition." In *Naming What We Know: Threshold Concepts of Writing Studies*, edited by Linda Adler-Kassner and Elizabeth Wardle, 105–21. Logan: Utah State University Press.

Irvine, Naomi, and Patrick Carmichael. 2009. "Threshold Concepts: A Point of Focus for Practitioner Research." *Active Learning in Higher Education* 10 (2): 103–19.

Ismael, J. T. 2007. *The Situated Self.* Oxford: Oxford University Press.

Kahn, Seth, William B. Lalicker, and Amy Lynch-Biniek. 2017. "Introduction: Paths Toward Solidarity." In *Contingency, Exploitation, and Solidarity: Labor and Action in English Composition*, edited by Seth Kahn, William B. Lalicker, and Amy Lynch-Biniek, 3–12. Fort Collins: WAC Clearinghouse and University Press of Colorado. https://wac.colostate.edu/books/perspectives/contingency/.

Land, Ray, Jan H. F. Meyer, and Michael T. Flanagan. 2016. *Threshold Concepts in Practice.* New York: Springer.

Launius, Christie, and Holly Hassel. 2015. *Threshold Concepts in Women's and Gender Studies: Ways of Seeing, Thinking, and Knowing.* London: Routledge.

McCamley, Michael. 2014. "Unclear, But Not Unclean: Resisting Familiar Binaries in Faculty Labor." *College English* 77 (1): 63–69.

Mendenhall, Annie S. 2014. "The Composition Specialist as Flexible Expert: Identity and Labor in the History of Composition." *College English* 77 (1): 11–31.

Meyer, Jan, and Ray Land. 2003. "Threshold Concepts and Troublesome Knowledge: Linkages to Ways of Thinking and Practicing within the Disciplines." In *Improving Student Learning: Theory and Practice—10 Years On*, edited by Chris Rust. Oxford Center for Staff and Learning Development.

Meyer, Jan, and Ray Land. 2005. "Threshold Concepts and Troublesome Knowledge (2): Epistemological Considerations and a Conceptual Framework for Teaching and Learning." *Higher Education* 49 (3): 373–88.

O'Neil, Peggy. 2015. "Assessment Is an Essential Component of Learning to Write." In *Naming What We Know: Threshold Concepts of Writing Studies*, edited by Linda Adler-Kassner and Elizabeth Wardle, 67–68. Logan: Utah State University Press.

Penrose, Ann M. 2012. "Professional Identity in a Contingent-Labor Profession: Expertise, Autonomy, Community in Composition Teaching." *WPA: Writing Program Administration* 35 (2): 108–26.

Pitkäniemi, Harri. 2010. "How the Teacher's Practical Theory Moves to Teaching Practice—A Literature Review and Conclusions." *Education Inquiry* 1 (3): 157–75.

Qualley, Donna. 2016. "Building a Conceptual Topography of the Transfer Terrain." In *Critical Transitions: Writing and the Question of Transfer*, edited by Chris M. Anson and Jessie L. Moore. Perspectives on Writing. Fort Collins, CO: WAC Clearinghouse. https://wac.colostate.edu/books/perspectives/ansonmoore/.

Schaub, Gayle, Patricia Bravender, and Hazel McClure. 2015. "Teaching Information Literacy Threshold Concepts: Lesson Plans for Librarians." Chicago: Association of College and Research Libraries. http://works.bepress.com/schaubg/3/.

Schell, Eileen. 1998. *Gypsy Academics and Mother-Teachers: Gender, Contingent Labor, and Writing Instruction.* Portsmouth, NH: Boynton/Cook.

Schell, Eileen E., and Patricia Lambert Stock. 2001. *Moving a Mountain: Transforming the Role of Contingent Faculty in Composition Studies and Higher Education.* Urbana, IL: NCTE.

Scott, Tony. 2015. "Writing Enacts and Creates Identities and Ideologies." In *Naming What We Know: Threshold Concepts of Writing Studies*, edited by Linda Adler-Kassner and Elizabeth Wardle, 48–50. Logan: Utah State University Press.

Scott, Tony, and Asao B. Inoue. 2015. "Assessing Writing Shapes Contexts and Instruction." In *Naming What We Know: Threshold Concepts of Writing Studies*, edited by Linda Adler-Kassner and Elizabeth Wardle, 29–31. Logan: Utah State University Press.

Wardle, Elizabeth. 2008. "Continuing the Dialogue: Follow-up Comments on 'Teaching about Writing, Righting Misconceptions.'" *College Composition and Communication* 60 (1): 175–81.

Wardle, Elizabeth. 2013. "Intractable Writing Program Problems, *Kairos*, and Writing about Writing: A Profile of the University of Central Florida's First-Year Composition Program." *Composition Forum* 27. https://compositionforum.com/issue/27/ucf.php.

Wardle, Elizabeth, and Doug Downs, eds. 2017. *Writing about Writing: A College Reader*. 3rd ed. Boston: Bedford/St. Martin's.

Wenger, Etienne. 1998. *Communities of Practice: Learning, Meaning, and Identity*. Cambridge: Cambridge University Press.

Yancey, Kathleen Blake. 1999. "Looking Back as We Look Forward: Historicizing Writing Assessment." *College Composition and Communication* 50 (3): 483–503.

Yancey, Kathleen Blake. 2015. "Coming to Terms: Composition/Rhetoric, Threshold Concepts, and a Disciplinary Core." In *Naming What We Know: Threshold Concepts of Writing Studies*, edited by Linda Adler-Kassner and Elizabeth Wardle, xvii–xxxi. Logan: Utah State University Press.

10
THRESHOLD CONCEPTS AND CURRICULUM REDESIGN IN FIRST-YEAR WRITING

Heidi Estrem, Dawn Shepherd, and Susan E. Shadle

Recent scholarship about writing transfer explores how the content of courses plays a critical role in encouraging or impeding the transfer of knowledge about writing to other rhetorical contexts (see Beaufort 2007; Downs and Wardle 2007; Nowacek 2011; Wardle 2007; Yancey, Robertson, and Taczak 2014). Collectively, these scholars help us reconsider what has long been an assumption underlying many first-year writing programs: that what students write about matters far less than that they are writing, and writing a lot (see Beaufort 2012; Charlton 2009/10; Smit 2004). Instead, this body of writing-transfer research is beginning to indicate writing itself can and should be the *content* of the course as well as its *practice*. When writing is both the content and the activity of the course, the opportunities for writing transfer increase.

How, then, might we identify and teach the central concepts of the field of writing studies, and teach them in a coherent, thoughtful way to first-year students? What does it mean, really, to make writing the central subject of a writing course? The threshold concepts framework provides one especially useful way for both experts and those newer to the field of writing studies to conceptualize the content of the field and, in turn, of the first-year writing classroom. Threshold concepts are disciplinary concepts and practices that serve as a kind of "portal" for students, opening up new and previously inaccessible ways of "thinking and practicing" within an area of study (Meyer and Land 2003, 1, 9). Threshold concepts are commonly identified with at least five key features: they are "transformative, probably irreversible, integrative, often troublesome and often disciplinarily 'bounded'" (Meyer and Land quoted in Irvine and Carmichael 2009, 103–4). These features make threshold concepts a rich entry point for considering what the focus of a curriculum might be.

DOI: 10.7330/9781607329329.c010

With the publication of *Naming What We Know* (Adler-Kassner and Wardle 2015), the field of writing studies now has a starting list of potential content areas for writing courses. While first-year writing instructors sometimes do not have deep disciplinary attachment to the field of writing studies, the idea of threshold concepts can resonate well because threshold concepts focus on student learning. Many first-year writing instructors see destabilizing—or "troubling"—students' previously held ideas about writing as a key component of their pedagogical approach, so the idea of providing a kind of threshold experience in first-year writing courses—one that unsettles students' (mis)conceptions about writing, one that invites them into writing in new ways—can help instructors begin to identify with various threshold concepts of writing studies.

There has been some initial work on threshold concepts and first-year writing courses (see Blaauw-Haara 2014; Downs and Robertson 2016; Rifenburg 2016), but there is still more to learn about the implications of incorporating threshold concepts for professional development in first-year writing programs. Like Mark Blaauw-Hara, Carrie Tebeau, Dominic Borowiak, and Jami Blaauw-Hara in this collection, we embraced the potential of threshold concepts for furthering curriculum work with our colleagues, for threshold concepts "provide a framework for situating ideas and understandings in a way that is transferable between members of the [teaching] community" (171). In this chapter, we (two writing program administrators and a director for a Center for Teaching and Learning) first describe the unique circumstances of first-year writing programs that shape curricular discussions in ways different from other disciplinary areas on campus. Then, we explore the opportunities and challenges threshold concepts provide as a framework for curriculum redesign efforts, focusing on the redesign of first-year writing courses at our institution. The threshold concepts framework can operate as another lens for mapping curriculum, one that acknowledges (and even foregrounds) teaching and learning even as it encourages faculty to identify sometimes-unarticulated disciplinary content that affects learners. We hold that, because of first-year writing's somewhat unique disciplinary history, threshold concepts play a different role in faculty development in first-year writing programs than they might in other disciplines.

TEACHER IDENTITY, DISCIPLINARITY, AND FIRST-YEAR WRITING

In addition to being portrayed as portals to new thinking, threshold concepts are also described, more simply, as "blockages," or "the bits . . . where students get stuck" (Walker 2012, 247). Our curriculum-revision project included some moments when we all got a little stuck. We, too, were having unsettling, perhaps threshold-crossing, learning experiences. We realized, in hindsight, that some of these challenges are related to the intersections of teacher identity and disciplinarity in first-year writing programs. Threshold concepts are inherently disciplinary; in large part, threshold concepts have been developed through gathering faculty in a discipline together and helping them articulate the concepts critical to further progression within that area of study (Land, Meyer, and Flanagan 2016 offers several case studies from different fields). Two issues arise that complicate use of threshold concepts within first-year writing programs: (1) the prevalence of competing definitions of "writing studies" within the discipline itself and (2) the diversity of first-year writing faculty members' disciplinary backgrounds (see Blaauw-Hara, Tebeau, Borowiak, and Blaauw-Hara and Mapes and Miller-Cochran, this collection, for descriptions of how this disciplinary diversity unfolds in first-year writing at a community college and in graduate teaching assistant training, respectively).

The question of writing studies' status and reach as a discipline is beyond the scope of our chapter, but it is important to note that many of us who are steeped in "the" discipline of writing studies have different operating assumptions about what it is and what that means (see Malenczyk, Miller-Cochran, Wardle, and Yancey's 2018 collection *Composition, Rhetoric, and Disciplinarity* for further discussions of this complex history). First, many (perhaps still most) of us experience writing studies as a discipline focused not simply on studying writing but on studying *the teaching of writing*. Indeed, many scholars identify the field explicitly in this way. In his book *A Teaching Subject*, for example, Joseph Harris (2012) offers a description of our field as a "teaching subject," a "loose set of practices, concerns, issues, and problems having to do with how writing gets taught" (xvi). He openly acknowledges his interests lie "less with how knowledge gets made and tested than with how teaching practices are formed and argued for" (xvi). In his summary of developments in the field of composition, Richard Fulkerson (2005) foregrounds that his frustration with trying to "make personal sense" of the field of composition studies led him to his analysis of key changes in how first-year writing is taught—note that this drive to understand the field did not lead, for example, to an analysis of the study of writing itself (654). These identifications of the *discipline of writing studies* with *the teaching of writing* permeate our field and influence our professional identities.

In other words: our field's subject, as it is described in much of our scholarship and as it is experienced, *is* teaching. It is likely that in many MA programs in composition and rhetoric, a good portion of the coursework focuses in some way on the teaching and learning of writing. Those who are awarded graduate teaching assistantships from areas beyond composition and rhetoric (within English departments or from across campus, as is the case in some programs) often take only one, sometimes two, graduate courses within composition and rhetoric, and those courses are most likely to directly serve their development as first-year writing instructors. So, those students are likely to develop an even more limited view of the field as solely concerned with teaching. A graduate teaching assistantship in an English or writing department is just that: teaching writing courses. It is no wonder, then, that many first-year writing instructors identify as *teachers of writing* first. Even if the scope of MA programs is changing within our field, we still focus much more on the teaching of our subject than do faculty in most disciplines.

In contrast, graduate assistantships in other disciplines might include working in a lab, assisting with research, or perhaps assisting a professor in the classroom. Students' graduate coursework focuses on subjects within their fields and not (with rare exceptions, of course) on the *teaching of subjects* within their field. For better or worse, this affects how disciplinarity is experienced and where faculty begin when they consider their teaching. In their study of faculty teaching in biology, for example, Sara Brownell and Kimberly Tanner (2012) explore how professional identity creates critical barriers for large-scale pedagogical change in the sciences. They note, "Scientists' professional identities—how they view themselves and their work in the context of their discipline and how they define their professional status—may be an invisible and underappreciated barrier to undergraduate science teaching reform, one that is not often discussed, because very few of us reflect upon our professional identity and the factors that influence it" (339). Professional identity in STEM fields draws from research areas within that area. For those who teach first-year writing, teaching is likely their primary professional identity, even if they are researchers. After all, much of the field's literature portrays it as a field whose study is the teaching of writing. This perspective, too, might be an "invisible and underappreciated barrier" to curriculum work in first-year writing programs.

Another disciplinary challenge that affects first-year writing programs somewhat differently than other disciplines on campus is that first-year writing instructors do not always share the same disciplinary background. The idea that most faculty have subject-matter expertise that informs curricular decisions is a fundamental premise of the literature about faculty development in higher education; much of that literature glosses over disciplinary content and instead focuses on strategies for supporting student learning. For example, in *Creating Significant Learning Experiences*, Dee Fink (2003) states that "most college faculty members have a good command of their subject matter . . . overall, knowledge of subject matter is not a major bottleneck to better teaching and learning in higher education" (23). While faculty subject-matter knowledge deepens with experience, all faculty are assumed to have it. In contrast, many first-year writing faculty have primary disciplinary identities in other English studies areas. When embarking on curricular change in first-year writing, then, this disciplinary diversity can make the work differently challenging. From our experience, we noticed the discussions about threshold concepts felt different from those that occur in other departments on campus. Those differences are intertwined with these complex, dynamic, disciplinary, and personal identities.

Disciplinarity and the Question of Content in First-Year Writing
The threshold concepts framework was an attractive lens for curriculum revision to us as program administrators because it offered a learning-centered approach for reconsidering our first-year writing curriculum. Threshold concepts center on contextual, discipline-specific content: critical concepts that may unsettle students' previously held notions, will deepen their learning, and will help them move forward as thinkers and writers within a discipline. Because of the recent work on transfer that highlights the ways first-year writing curricula should "focus on the study of and practice with writing knowledge," we wanted to engage with this hard work of identifying not just learning outcomes or teaching strategies but also the content of our courses (Moore 2017, 7). We were confident instructors in our program were regularly engaging their students in practicing "rhetorically based concepts" and writerly behaviors in our first-year writing classes (7); we were less sure these concepts were being *studied* in the course.

The idea that the content of a writing course—the concepts students study, what students read, what they write about—matters is troublesome because so many of us have long believed teaching writing is a matter of teaching writing strategies, processes, and habits of mind. The research on transfer encourages us to rethink this idea. When writing is both the content and the activity of the course, the opportunities for writing transfer increase. In her 2012 keynote address at the Council of Writing Program Administrators' Conference, Linda Adler-Kassner asserted that

> writing classes, especially first year classes, must absolutely and always be grounded in Writing Studies, must always be about the study of writing. They should not, as I heard recently and anecdotally, engage students in writing about vampires—nor about political issues, nor about recent controversies, nor about other things that are not about writing. In Writing Studies classes, students study writing and the intersections between writing and values within specific contexts. (132)

The threshold concept framework could, we hoped, provide a structure for discussing first-year writing course content when many instructors have deep teaching expertise in first-year writing but disciplinary background in other areas, or when they do not have regular access to current conversations about writing, transfer, and the role of first-year writing in a larger institutional context.

THRESHOLD CONCEPTS AND CURRICULUM REDESIGN

Several years ago, we knew our first-year writing curriculum was due for revision. Our goal was to develop a curricular framework that responded to new approaches from our field while honoring local student needs, faculty expertise, and the university's mission. We first briefly describe our context and then explore how threshold concepts functioned within this curriculum project.

First Year Writing Program Context

Our first-year writing program includes a two-semester course sequence, most sections of which are taught by long-term, experienced instructors. The first-semester course, English 101, familiarizes students with university reading and writing practices.[1] The second-semester course, English 102, engages students in inquiry-based research, working from the viewpoint that we produce knowledge by connecting with others' ideas. Between 30 and 50 percent of courses are taught by full-time lecturers, many of whom serve on teaching-and-learning or assessment committees in the English department or hold leadership roles in the university's general-education initiative. In addition, we have several experienced adjunct instructors who consistently teach between a quarter and a third of our courses, depending on the year, and graduate teaching assistants who teach about fifteen percent of the courses.

In 2016, we launched a curriculum-revision project to integrate our courses into a new approach to general education on our campus. We also knew it was time for us to take up, collectively, the field's recent

Table 10.1.

Term	Item	Scope	Purpose
Fall 2015	The Quilt Project inservice: "Embracing Change"	60–70 first-year writing instructors	Commitment to work of revision
	"Quilt Backing" workshops	35 first-year writing instructors (across two meetings)	Threshold concepts introduced, prioritized, and sorted
	Naming What Students Learn reflective survey	60 first-year writing instructors	Threshold concepts further explored, responses used to find key terms for further study in reading groups
Spring 2016	Scholarly reading groups	18 instructors (via application); all instructors through online discussion forum	Six groups meet biweekly in person and in online meetings to facilitate peer-to-peer learning
	First-year writing Committee retreat	6 instructors	Revisited *Naming What Students Learn* Shared survey results, decided on initial key concepts for each course

research on writing transfer. Our outcomes had not been revisited in nearly ten years, and our yearly assessment process pointed to ongoing challenges (similar assignments in both courses, for example).

One of our guiding principles for this curriculum was that we wanted to include everyone's voices in the conversation while also being mindful of the exploitative nature of relying on contingent labor. As table 10.1 demonstrates, we used a variety of meeting formats and modalities to involve as many faculty as possible. These differing meeting formats, patterns, and times were meant to provide various platforms for participation and input. We knew that truly rethinking our courses might be uncomfortable for all of us (although we did not quite anticipate how uncomfortable it would be), so these efforts were an attempt to address the ways we, as instructors, might encounter unsettling threshold experiences of our own.

Another early commitment we made was *not* to begin with revising outcomes but instead to start with understanding student learning within our courses. During the last major revision in 2006–2007, we had begun with rethinking outcomes, and many other pedagogical activities within our department and elsewhere on campus began with the (often fruitful) exercise of identifying course outcomes. However, we believed focusing on our course outcomes would limit a deeper rethinking of the courses overall and might constrain us to just revising around the edges. As Heidi explored in her earlier work about threshold concepts and learning outcomes, starting with outcomes means focusing on "locat[ing] evidence of learning at the end of key experiences—certainly one valuable place to begin understanding learning, but not the only place" (Estrem 2016, 89). Threshold concepts point to student learning in the moment; the threshold concepts framework offers a way to describe and then support students in the messy, uncomfortable work of learning. This time, we wanted to begin in a new place and to unsettle our collective understandings and personal truths about what first-year writing is, what it could be, and what it should be. Our goal was to start somewhere that would help all of us rethink the role, goals, and possibilities of first-year writing.

In addition to beginning in a different *place*, we wanted to proceed in a different *manner* than we had in earlier professional-development efforts. We developed a theme for the curriculum project and launched it as the Quilt Project at our kick-off inservice meeting. We used a quilting metaphor to connect activities. We began the project without a final product or process in mind but rather were dedicated to new ideas and discovery; we wanted to engage our colleagues in professional conversation with good-faith participation.

Threshold Experiences in Curriculum Revision

The first phase of this work was intended to introduce the main threshold concepts as articulated in *Naming What We Know* and to surface our shared values for teaching and learning. Two key moments from the first semester of a four-year project became moments that felt like threshold experiences themselves: we were all unsettled by the intersections of threshold concepts and our local context.

The two "Quilt Backing" workshops in fall 2015 marked the first threshold experience of the project. After launching this project at our annual inservice prior to the semester, we then held two midsemester workshops (with the same content but at different times so as to reach as many instructors as possible) intended to put our values and commitments in conversation with ideas from the field, much like the solid fabric of a quilt's backing holds together its squares and batting. The workshop invited instructors to work with the main threshold concepts identified in *Naming What We Know* and the habits of mind from the *Framework for Success in Postsecondary Writing*. We led instructors through a set of activities. First, in small groups, instructors sequenced threshold concepts and habits of mind over our two courses. Then, groups each chose one concept to dig into further. Finally, instructors used sticky notes to individually rate which concepts they most enjoyed and which they were most unfamiliar with as teachers. The notes were added to a matrix on the wall, thus revealing areas of familiarity and unfamiliarity.

Although this activity was intended to center on local teaching experience and instructor know-how, the process was unsettling for many. We had asked instructors to consider concepts not very familiar to many of them, so we had expected some discomfort. However, some instructors saw little room for their expertise in what had been discussed during the workshops.

In addition to the general unease that can come with large-scale change, the perception some were left with—that their expertise was not accounted for, despite our explicit efforts to account for it—could be the inverse of what Brownell and Tanner (2012) describe about professional identity and faculty's resisting pedagogical change in STEM disciplines. Threshold concepts are, after all, always already about disciplinarity: they identify concepts that are deeply epistemological (Meyer and Land 2003). When we asked our colleagues to engage with threshold concepts of writing studies—threshold concepts that reflect current research in the field within a framework that is about disciplinary knowledge—this request must have struck some of them as unnecessarily academic and distancing. Pedagogical changes based on research in a field with which individuals do not feel closely aligned, or that are part of a field not covered in graduate training, may have fostered anxiety or mistrust of us as WPAs, as well as of the process in general.

While we had intended for the workshops to generate some shared threshold concepts that might propel our conversations in the next semester, we realized we needed to slow down and gather more input through a different venue. Consequently, these workshops led to our second collective threshold experience, a survey for connecting instructors' expertise with threshold concepts in writing studies. To capture more perspectives and voices following workshops, we designed the "Naming What Students Learn" survey. In it, we asked instructors to reflect on threshold concepts for writing at three key writing moments for our students—first-year writing, next stops in college for writing, and lifelong writing. For first-year writing, instructors reflected on troublesome moments for learning in first-year writing and identified key threshold concepts from *Naming What We Know* for our first-year writing courses. Next, they considered learning outcomes and threshold concepts for students' next courses that include written communication as a primary learning outcome. They were asked to describe how the threshold concepts they noted in the first part of the survey help students engage with the outcomes or threshold concepts in specific future courses also aligned with our university's written communication learning outcome. Finally, instructors contemplated the university mission and life after graduation. They were asked to describe how the threshold concepts they identified in the first part of the survey help students engage with the university mission and make their way in the world.

Since we substituted anonymously completing the survey[2] for annual program assessment, nearly all instructors completed this instrument that functioned more like a guided reflection than a survey. We shared key findings from this survey on the project's Google site, and we encouraged instructors to read and reflect on the findings. As WPAs, we were able to analyze results of this programmatic input with the First-Year Writing Committee and use responses to develop a list of six local foundations for writing—concepts that functioned perhaps less as threshold concepts than as subject areas around which instructors had shared interests in learning more: cultural identities in writing, ethics, genre, inquiry, process, writing and/as technology. These concepts became the basis for our spring-semester reading groups and workshops in which teams of instructors explored recent scholarship, made connections with their own teaching practices, and shared results with the program (see table 10.1). The Naming What Students Learn survey felt like a threshold experience because the act of completing it required all of us to think deeply about our personal values, our teaching commitments, and student learning in our context. It also made visible, in writing, our shared values and commitments in ways reflections, workshops, and assessment projects had never quite done before.

Since those early unsettling experiences, we have inched forward, determined to coordinate this effort with open, responsive strategies. We have grown comfortable with discomfort and have attempted to adjust whenever necessary, and we have also worked to keep engaging with our colleagues, in a variety of venues, about the challenging curricular questions surrounding first-year writing.

IMPLICATIONS: AFFORDANCES OF THRESHOLD CONCEPTS FOR PROFESSIONAL DEVELOPMENT IN FIRST-YEAR WRITING PROGRAMS

Threshold concepts offer faculty a way to focus on learners and learning, even as it asks us to identify concepts within the discipline or field that are "troublesome," "liminal," and "transformative" (Meyer and Land 2006). As Adler-Kassner and Wardle explain in the introduction to *Naming What We Know*, threshold concepts "do not just change *what* people know, they change *how* people know because they lead to different ways of approaching ideas" (x). This intersection of the what and the how speaks to the space of the first-year writing curriculum, where practice, craft, and response are critically important to learning about writing—and where we now know the subject material of the course matters as well.

As first-year writing program administrators embarking on a first-year writing curricular-change project, and as scholars interested in threshold concepts, writing transfer, and collaborative writing program administration, the threshold concept framework provided us with an entry point to design professional-development work that foregrounded student learning and experiences while helping us, collectively within our program, name what we know and consider what the content of our classes should be. When we embarked on this project, we deliberately chose to engage with threshold concepts of writing as a way to speak to the space between faculty teaching expertise and disciplinary content. Threshold concepts have informed and enriched our curricular work; at the same time, in ways that resonate with those explored by both Blaauw-Hara, Tebeau, Borowiak, and Blaauw-Hara and Lisa Tremain, Marianne Ahokas, Sarah Ben-Zvi, and Kerry Marsden in their respective chapters in this collection, the uptake and usefulness of the threshold concepts framework has been uneven within our program.

For us, the threshold concept framework provided a grounded, manageable starting point for developing early workshops and for (re)introducing our colleagues to important concepts within the field. However, while we as writing studies faculty and scholars found the threshold concepts of writing studies quite accessible and familiar, our colleagues' perception of them was mixed. Even though many found the threshold concept framework illuminating, it also felt distant and overly academic to some of our colleagues. Early in our project, we imagined threshold concepts might be identified explicitly and then be used to guide curriculum directly; because of the twists and turns in our curricular work, threshold concepts at this point have faded into the background. We still maintain threshold concepts were valuable as a way to initiate and sustain our initial conversations about curriculum and first-year writing, but they have receded in the public-facing drafts of the curriculum. They inform it, but they are not immediately visible.

Invoking the threshold concepts of writing felt invitational to us; they sometimes felt alienating to our colleagues. When instructors have a variety of complex professional identities they are bringing into curricular discussions, as we describe above, it complicates the utility of an approach rooted in the assumption that there is some shared disciplinary experience and knowledge. Threshold concepts that made sense to us were not always intuitive to our colleagues. Certainly they provided a powerful way for all of us to engage with concepts beyond our own teaching and course experiences, and they kept us focused on student learning experiences, something that has continued to inform our work. In this way, threshold concepts productively helped unsettle the substance of what we wanted to change.

While writing this chapter, we have come to realize this curriculum project is not just about what we teach in the classroom but also about how the development of curriculum, when done collaboratively and openly, raises complex issues surrounding faculty identity. We knew this work was as much about people as it was about curriculum, but our threshold moments (and others since that first fall) continue to teach us this fact. Adrianna Kezar's (2014) work on institutional change has helpfully reminded us that opportunities for change are enhanced when we acknowledge the role of prior experience and that people are "more likely to change if they receive feedback and ongoing information" (30). Further, meaningful curriculum change can only be accomplished when we all understand the nature of the sought-after change and/or how the change might be integrated into our work. While this process is still unfolding, one aspect we have tried to maintain is a consistent commitment to visibility and to changing course whenever needed.

We are still a work in progress. So, we offer our experience as a way for other writing faculty to consider how and why articulating threshold concepts can play a productive role in faculty and curriculum development and why they might have a different kind of role within a first-year writing program than they might in writing studies more generally, much less in other disciplines. We now have a revised curricular framework, and the norms around, the norms around participation and communication have changed in our program. Threshold concepts operated within this change-making enterprise as a means for initiating the conversation; they provided a way to frame and understand student learning and disciplinary knowledge. Using (and then adapting and remixing) threshold concepts as part of an unfolding conversation about our curriculum has helped all of us in our program shuttle between content and experience, between what students should, perhaps, know and what they should do.

NOTES

1. Students may also begin in English 101P or English 101M. The former is a four-credit course that supplements a section of English 101 with a one-hour Writers'

Studio with the same instructor. The latter is a six-credit course designed for English-language learners. Both are fully credit bearing.

2. Our program assistant tracked who had completed the survey, but the First-Year Writing Committee and we only saw anonymized results.

REFERENCES

Adler-Kassner, Linda. 2012. "The Companies We Keep or the Companies We Would Like to Keep: Strategies and Tactics in Challenging Times." *WPA: Writing Program Administration* 36 (1): 119–40.

Adler-Kassner, Linda, and Elizabeth A. Wardle. 2015. *Naming What We Know: Threshold Concepts of Writing Studies*. Logan: Utah State University Press.

Beaufort, Anne. 2007. *College Writing and Beyond*. Logan: Utah State University Press. https://compositionforum.com/issue/26/.

Beaufort, Anne. 2012. "*College Writing and Beyond*: Five Years Later." *Composition Forum* 26.

Blaauw-Hara, Mark. 2014. "Transfer Theory, Threshold Concepts, and First-Year Composition: Connecting Writing to the Rest of the College." *Teaching English in the Two-Year College* 41 (4): 354–65.

Brownell, Sara E., and Kimberly D. Tanner. 2012. "Barriers to Faculty Pedagogical Change: Lack of Training, Time, Incentives, and . . . Tensions with Professional Identity?" *CBE—Life Sciences Education* 11: 339–46.

Charlton, Jonikka. 2009/2010. "Seeing Is Believing: Writing Studies with 'Basic Writing' Students." *Council on Basic Writing eJournal* 8/9: 1–9.

Downs, Douglas, and Liane Robertson. 2015. "Threshold Concepts in First-Year Composition." In *Naming What We Know: Threshold Concepts of Writing Studies*, edited by Linda Adler-Kassner and Elizabeth A. Wardle, 105–21. Logan: Utah State University Press.

Downs, Douglas, and Elizabeth Wardle. 2007. "Teaching about Writing, Righting Misconceptions: (Re)Envisioning 'First-Year Composition' as 'Introduction to Writing Studies.'" *College Composition and Communication* 58 (4): 552–85.

Estrem, Heidi. 2015. "Threshold Concepts and Student Learning Outcomes." In *Naming What We Know: Threshold Concepts of Writing Studies*, edited by Linda Adler-Kassner and Elizabeth A. Wardle, 89–104. Logan: Utah State University Press.

Fink, L. Dee. 2003. *Creating Significant Learning Experiences: An Integrated Approach to Designing College Courses*. San Francisco: Jossey-Bass.

Fulkerson, Richard. 2005. "Composition at the Turn of the Twenty-First Century." *College Composition and Communication* 56 (4): 654–87.

Harris, Joseph. 2012. *A Teaching Subject: Composition Since 1966*. 2nd ed. Logan: Utah State University Press.

Irvine, Naomi, and Patrick Carmichael. 2009. "Threshold Concepts: A Point of Focus for Practitioner Researchers." *Active Learning in Higher Education* 10 (2): 103–19.

Kezar, Adrianna. 2014. *How Colleges Change: Understanding, Leading, and Enacting Change*. New York: Routledge.

Land, Ray, Jan H. F. Meyer, and Michael T. Flanagan, eds. 2016. *Threshold Concepts in Practice*. Rotterdam/Boston/Taipei: Sense Publishers.

Malenczyk, Rita, Susan Miller-Cochran, Elizabeth Wardle, and Kathleen Blake Yancey, eds. 2018. *Composition, Rhetoric, and Disciplinarity*. Logan: Utah State University Press.

Meyer, Jan H. F., and Ray Land. 2003. "Threshold Concepts and Troublesome Knowledge: Linkages to Ways of Thinking and Practising." Enhancing Teaching-Learning Environments in Undergraduate Courses Project Occasional Report 4, University of Edinburgh, May. http://www.etl.tla.ed.ac.uk/docs/ETLreport4.pdf.

Meyer, Jan H. F., and Ray Land, eds. 2006. *Overcoming Barriers to Student Understanding: Threshold Concepts and Troublesome Knowledge*. London: Routledge.

Moore, Jessie L. 2017. "Five Essential Principles about Writing Transfer." In *Understanding Writing Transfer: Implications for Transformative Student Learning in Higher Education*, edited by Randall Bass and Jessie L. Moore, 1–12. Sterling, VA: Stylus.

Nowacek, Rebecca. 2011. *Agents of Integration: Understanding Transfer as a Rhetorical Act*. Urbana, IL: CCC and NCTE.

Rifenburg, Michael. 2016. "Student-Athletes, Prior Knowledge, and Threshold Concepts." *Teaching English in the Two-Year College* 44 (1): 32–48.

Smit, David. 2004. *The End of Composition Studies*. Carbondale: Southern Illinois University Press.

Walker, Guy. 2012. "A Cognitive Approach to Threshold Concepts." *Higher Education* 65 (2): 247–63.

Wardle, Elizabeth. 2007. "Understanding 'Transfer' from FYC: Preliminary Results of a Longitudinal Study." *WPA: Writing Program Administration* 31 (1–2): 65–85.

Yancey, Kathleen Blake, Liane Robertson, and Kara Taczak. 2014. *Writing across Contexts: Transfer, Composition, and Sites of Writing*. Logan: Utah State University Press.

11
FRAMING GRADUATE TEACHING ASSISTANT PREPARATION AROUND THRESHOLD CONCEPTS OF WRITING STUDIES

Aimee C. Mapes and Susan Miller-Cochran

Recent research on knowledge transfer has helped writing studies scholars begin to understand the messy nature of writing development, demonstrating that threshold concepts of writing studies are indeed "a productive frame through which to consider questions related to writing and transfer" (Adler-Kassner, Majewski, and Koshnick 2012), especially for undergraduate students. There are compelling studies on transfer and metacognitive practices (Beaufort 2007; Carroll 2002; Driscoll and Powell 2016; Negretti 2012; Nowacek 2011; Rounsaville, Goldberg, and Bawarshi 2008; Sommers and Saltz 2004; Sternglass 1997; Wardle 2007) and in-depth explorations in first-year writing such as Kathleen Blake Yancey, Liane Robertson, and Kara Taczak's (2014) *Writing across Contexts*, as well as Heidi Estrem, Dawn Shepherd, and Susan Shadle in this collection. Only recently, though, has research explored threshold concepts of writing studies in terms of teacher training within writing programs (see, for instance, M. Blaauw-Hara et al., this collection). Threshold concepts scholarship, broadly, pays particular attention to the perplexing nature of troublesome knowledge for professional development (Adler-Kassner, Majewski, and Koshnick 2012; King and Felten 2012). Jan Meyer and Ray Land (2003) often identify threshold concepts expressly as "troublesome knowledge" for professional development. A recent coedited collection *Threshold Concepts in Practice* by Land, Meyer, and Michael Flanagan (2016) includes chapters that explore how threshold concepts instigate feelings for faculty: of ambivalence, being stuck, being transformed, and encountering blockages. In the scholarship, threshold concepts' troublesome blockages are necessary to professionalization.

Correspondingly, research in writing studies on teacher training, and specifically writing-pedagogy education (Reid 2012), portrays learning to teach as a professionalizing process full of ambivalence, resistance, and difficulty. Sidney Dobrin's (2005) edited collection *Don't Call it That*, for example, presents chapters in which teacher training is analogous to coercive acts, unraveling tensions, or a state of being "lost in the composition practicum" (viii). In this chapter, we tell a story of threshold concepts and teacher training in an attempt to clarify the role of writing studies threshold concepts in graduate teaching assistant (GTA) practicum and training.

GTAs are an especially relevant group of professionals to consider in relationship to writing studies threshold concepts since they make up nationally 25 percent of all writing instruction teachers (Gere 2009). The practicum course in which many graduate student writing instructors enroll, often prior to or simultaneously with their first experience as teachers in the composition classroom, can sometimes become a site where complicated tensions with threshold concepts are worked out. In these courses, GTAs encounter a range of challenges: lack of teaching experience, lack of knowledge about the field of rhetoric and composition, and lack of a shared theoretical construct for teaching writing. In many ways, they parallel the faculty about which Chris Anson, Chen Chen, and Ian Anson, as well as Mark Blaauw-Hara, Carrie Tebeau, Dominic Borowiak, and Jamie Blaauw-Hara, write in their respective chapters (this collection) because GTAs have a tacit knowledge of writing but not always a disciplinary knowledge of writing studies. Sometimes, GTAs are selected to teach writing because they are successful writers themselves. And, like the faculty described in the other pieces in this collection, GTAs often lack shared key concepts or terms about writing to which they could refer and build a pedagogy around. As Kristine Hansen (2018) identifies, "High percentages of first-year writing courses are taught by graduate students . . . with, at best, minimal preparation for their jobs" (135). Yet little has been written about how threshold concepts might relate to preparing GTAs for teaching writing. A further complication is that GTAs are often novices themselves—learning in their graduate disciplines and in teaching their own FYC classes. As Dylan Dryer (2012) explains, GTAs experience "their writing confidence and competence undermined in one set of classrooms and faculty offices while being positioned (and positioning themselves) as writing experts in another set of classrooms [their own sections of FYC] and in their own offices [with their own students]" (425). Jessica Restaino (2012) points out that "new teachers, charged with the task of getting students to write and navigating new graduate programs themselves, are largely untrained, unsure of their responsibilities, and equipped with a syllabus they did not design and perhaps a list of pedagogical procedures they do not understand" (1). They don't have a shared theoretical construct for writing pedagogy, either with each other or with the writing program in which they teach. Hansen (2018) explains that a core component of preparation addresses a lack of disciplinary knowledge. We argue in this chapter that a focus on threshold concepts of writing in GTA preparation can help build an understanding of the discipline of writing studies and shape a theoretical construct for teaching writing alongside pedagogical content knowledge.

Much work on writing-pedagogy education has focused on the place of writing studies theory in the GTA practicum course (Goggin and Stancliff 2007) and how to address writing studies theory with new GTAs (Fischer 2005; Hardin 2005; Michel 2005). Although our field often questions the place of theory in teacher training, threshold concepts can provide an essential theoretical precipice upon which professionalizing depends. What's more, scholars of threshold concepts trace their foundation to, among others, Lee Shulman, a curriculum theorist in the United States. Known for his attempt in the 1980s to redress beliefs that teaching has no knowledge beyond content knowledge, Shulman (1987) argued that content knowledge received far too much focus at the expense of teachers' professional ability to internally adapt and present knowledge in a way that helped learners understand. Distinguishing three domains of knowledge relevant to teaching, he emphasized the relationship among content (or subject) knowledge, pedagogical content knowledge, and curricular knowledge. A combination of content knowledge and curricular knowledge, pedagogical content knowledge is a "particular form of content knowledge that embodies the aspects of content most germane to its teachability" (Shulman 1986, 8). When content is germane to its teachability, according to Shulman, there is attention to what is difficult to understand or easy to grasp. Threshold concepts, as they are defined to be alien and troublesome concepts, fall into this *difficult-to-grasp* category. Scholarship on threshold concepts, for instance, specifies the ways new knowledge triggers a liminal, transformative state (Adler-Kassner, Majewski, and Koshnick 2012; Land 2016; Meyer and Timmermans 2016). According to Jan Meyer and Julie Timmermans (2016), these transformations also "create stuck places" (32). Specific to writing studies, coeditors Linda Adler-Kassner and Elizabeth Wardle (2015) lay out the importance of threshold concepts for disciplinary meaning-making that is both transformative and "troublesome" or "alien" knowledge (Meyer and Land 2003). In this collection, Deborah Mutnik characterizes threshold concepts as first unknowable, drawing on Meyer and Land's early work. In this way, threshold concepts seem expressly interested in the intersection of subject knowledge and pedagogy. It is precisely these concepts teachers can identify and think through to develop pedagogical content knowledge. While we oversimplify here, we find it instructive that Shulman wanted to privilege teachers' ways of knowing, and we see insights from Shulman for the practicum, a site of contention for developing teachers. A focus on threshold concepts of writing in the practicum, therefore, can complement providing both an introduction to writing studies and a theoretical foundation for writing pedagogy.

To this end, we offer an account of how we implemented threshold concepts into GTA training in our first-year composition program at the University of Arizona (UA) acting from our belief in their value as an entry point to the discipline when training GTAs with them. We argue they can build a bridge for GTAs to develop foundational knowledge that will help them in the writing classroom. How best to integrate this pedagogical content knowledge in teacher training is not so much to rely on threshold concepts but to offer a preparatory foundation for representing difficult-to-grasp knowledge or to guide GTAs into what Etienne Wenger (1998) might call legitimate peripheral participation in which they see themselves as knowledgeable teachers able to cultivate a supportive writing class using the tools provided through training. In offering theoretically rich frames of writing development, threshold concepts provided our GTAs a way to evaluate various options regarding *what to do* in the classroom (always their most pressing concern). Because this chapter is a descriptive account and not a systematic empirical study, we cannot draw conclusions beyond the context of our program. However, our experience has convinced us threshold concepts can provide a pragmatic and theoretically sound entry point for GTAs in writing instruction and writing studies. In the remainder of this chapter, then, we describe our writing program context and the GTAs who teach in that program. We share how we incorporated threshold concepts into our GTA preparation, and we offer reflections of three of the faculty mentors who help to prepare those GTAs and were working directly with them during practicum. Specifically, we demonstrate how threshold concepts provide a shared lexicon or vocabulary and become a tool for reflection, which, taken together, contribute to pedagogical content knowledge.

THRESHOLD CONCEPTS AND GTA TRAINING AT THE UNIVERSITY OF ARIZONA

The University of Arizona's writing program is housed in the Department of English. While the writing program does offer some sections of writing beyond the 100 level, the vast majority of classes offered are designed to meet the first-year writing requirement. It employs graduate students in applied linguistics, creative writing, English literature, and rhetoric and composition. Given the size of our program, one of the largest in the nation with over 170 current instructors, we practice a distributed administrative model. The program's administrative staff includes a writing program director, three associate directors, and seven assistant directors. The assistant directors[1] are all full-time, career-track faculty who mentor incoming GTAs and help coordinate August orientation and teach practicum throughout the academic year. With over six hundred sections of first-year writing annually, the writing program serves roughly six thousand undergraduate students each semester in two first-year courses, which are collectively referred to as *foundations writing*.[2] During the 2017–2018 academic year, of the 172 instructors teaching foundations writing, 131 were graduate-assistant teachers. Thirty-eight of these were new to the English department and were enrolled in a required presemester orientation and practicum; they also worked with the seven faculty mentors through the entire academic year. New GTAs and their mentors participate in six days of workshops during August orientation. Then GTAs begin teaching within a few days of completing orientation.[3] Not surprisingly (and not unique to UA), GTAs exhibit ambivalence about teaching; sometimes they are enthusiastic, other times petrified.

Mapping Threshold Concepts and Writing Program Objectives

Given how precarious GTAs already feel when arriving to our campus initially, the GTA training team targeted a few writing studies threshold concepts in fall 2017 as a way to ground GTAs' introduction to disciplinary knowledge and to the art of teaching writing. Following a process described by Jessie Moore (2012) for mapping transfer concepts onto curriculum, we identified threshold concepts most relevant for our institutional context while simultaneously anticipating which "big ideas" might be the most troublesome in the context of GTA training (22). First, we turned to the UA writing program's four goals in first-year writing (FYW), each with respective student learning outcomes: (1) rhetorical and genre awareness; (2) research as rhetorical; (3) revision and reflection as a process; and (4) genre conventions. With these categories, we sorted our objectives into two broadly drawn knowledge domains: (1) rhetorical and genre awareness and (2) revision and reflection. After defining our program's context and objectives, we identified threshold concepts in *Naming What We Know* (Adler-Kassner and Wardle

Table 11.1. Mapping threshold concepts to writing program goals

WP objectives	
Genre and rhetorical awareness	Writing is an activity and a subject of study Writing enacts and creates identities Writing is a social and rhetorical activity
Revision and reflection	Writing is not perfectible Writing is impacted by prior experience Writing is a process All writers have more to learn

2015) that best matched the two knowledge domains and seemed most relevant for the purposes of GTA training (see table 11.1).

When considering threshold concepts in the realm of GTA training, our team of trainers consistently pointed out that the term *threshold concept* itself seemed to be troublesome. To many of our seasoned mentors, *threshold concepts* as a label remained needlessly abstract; *principles* communicated a similar idea and seemed more concrete. To address this, we and the GTA mentors decided to refer to threshold concepts as *principles for teaching writing*. Although arguably lacking the connection to research on threshold concepts, we argued that *principles* communicated to GTAs that these were essential elements of their writing classes. In this chapter, we sometimes refer to the threshold concepts we emphasized in the practicum course as *principles* for that reason.

Orientation, Principles, and GTAs' Prior Experience

In the opening session of August orientation, we introduced these seven threshold concepts to GTAs. In a two-part activity, we invited GTAs to select one threshold concept that most resonated with them and to write a short reflection explaining how it resonated, drawing on a past experience. They then formed groups based on the threshold concept they chose. We directed each group of new GTAs to collaboratively rephrase or recreate the statement in their own words or a drawing if preferred (see fig. 11.1). Each group shared their ideas. For the remaining five days, posters remained affixed to the walls of our large meeting space as a reminder of our threshold concepts when planning the course schedule and major activities.

After the introductory activity with threshold concepts, we focused on genre as a key concept. At UA, our first-semester course (English 101) focuses on genre awareness. As homework during orientation, GTAs read Charles Bazerman's (2015) "Writing Speaks to Situations through

Figure 11.1. Threshold concept activity

Recognizable Forms." In the next day's morning session, we introduced genre, building upon ideas from the Bazerman reading. Activities further explored definitions and characteristics of genre:

- A typified response to a recurring rhetorical situation
- A socially/culturally-preferred form for achieving goals and action

- A process, not a product; a "life form," not a formula; a category of action
- Recognizable by community members (but not necessarily by outsiders)
- Texts with obligatory and optional features or elements, but also as situated in context—so some have more freedom than others
- Marked by stability and change, convention and variation; they are not static templates. (Tardy 2017)

Initial orientation training activities translated threshold concepts into statements of principles in language GTAs often generated or, at the least, seemed to understand. A process of application, reflection, and restatement offered a scaffold for GTAs unfamiliar with writing studies' disciplinary language, especially to temper a lack of confidence with highly abstract concepts. The role of reflection seemed an especially useful tool for new GTAs. The reflection on each activity allowed GTAs to connect individually with threshold concepts as they related principles to their own unique prior experiences. In this way, these principles helped GTA trainers provide strategies for effective teaching while simultaneously recognizing the knowledge and experience GTAs—especially those from different areas of English studies—bring to the classroom and the precarious role negotiations they find themselves in as students and teachers.

Threshold Concepts and Practicum: Pedagogical Content Knowledge

Another aspect of GTA training beyond a presemester orientation is practicum—a space designed to support pedagogical content knowledge (Shulman 1986). For Shulman, supporting an understanding of the teachability of a concept starts with an awareness of "useful forms of representation" (8) such as analogies, examples, illustrations, and explanations. These representations are the fundamental habits of establishing strategies for pedagogical content knowledge. For GTA practicum, we see threshold concepts as providing useful principles representing content knowledge in writing studies, even for teachers unfamiliar with writing studies. At our institution, GTA training continues throughout the first semester as a three-credit practicum seminar. Each GTA is assigned to a faculty mentor working with a group of four to six GTAs. In designing strategies for integrating threshold concepts into practicum, mentors named those principles in *NWWK* that seemed, in their experiences, especially relevant to new teachers. Similar to a process described by Blaauw-Hara et al. (in this volume), a team of seven mentors, including

Aimee, identified threshold concepts in *NWWK* that address some of the more common issues emerging in practicum, such as the role of writing assessment, the art of writing feedback, teacher confidence, and disciplinary differences in GTAs' academic programs of study.

Situating UA's writing program goals within pedagogical content knowledge, mentors initially selected as many as eleven threshold concepts from *NWWK*, including at least one threshold concept from each metaconcept, as relevant for practicum. Over time, three threshold concepts seemed to resonate with all seven mentors who began navigating questions from GTAs about the complexities of teaching our genre-informed English 101 curriculum. Mentors described that as GTAs began to assess the first major project, literacy narratives, they felt discomfort evaluating personal experiences. So, too, GTAs seemed to struggle with the purpose of a genre analysis as a heuristic for learning genre. It was while supporting new GTAs across these multifaceted curricular activities that mentors repeatedly mentioned three threshold concepts to emphasize in practicum:

- *writing involves making ethical choices*
- *all writing is multimodal*
- *failure can be an important part of writing development*

WPAs and GTA mentors discussed the relevance of these three threshold concepts for our program, especially connecting them to required assignments for the first-year GTAs. For instance, our community-profile assignment included a dimension of ethics, and our public-argument unit tacitly required multimodality. Most significantly, our use of portfolios and portfolio assessment revealed the importance of failure (and reflection on failure) as a relevant step in writing development. Mentors described how threshold concepts could provide a vocabulary for what we were doing in the program, or as Aimee said, "Threshold concepts provide a way of thinking, a framework for multiple kinds of work."

Our process of integrating threshold concepts into GTA preparation remained consistent with scholarship on threshold concepts, especially for learners coming to terms with difficult knowledge (Land 2016; Meyer and Land 2003; Moore 2012; Mutnik, this collection). Specific stages for GTA training modeled around writing studies threshold concepts at our program may be relevant to other institutional contexts: (1) situating threshold concepts within the institutional context; (2) translating disciplinary language; (3) drawing on GTAs' previous experiences and knowledge; (4) inviting GTAs to restate and illustrate threshold concepts with examples from their own experience; (5) connecting threshold concepts to pedagogical content knowledge. The final step, considering threshold concepts germane to teachability (Shulman 1986), remained the purview of practicum, and mentors continued to integrate threshold concepts in their individual practicum small groups for GTAs. In what follows, we explore insights from perspectives of three GTA mentors who reflected on their process of integrating threshold concepts into GTA preparation.

PEDAGOGICAL CONTENT KNOWLEDGE: INTEGRATING THRESHOLD CONCEPTS IN PRACTICUM

To understand the success, potential, and problems with threshold concepts in practicum, we draw on interviews conducted with three mentors, Dev, Keith, and Terry, who volunteered to share their perspectives. These three mentors have been working with new GTAs for four years and were hired at the same time to focus specifically on GTA mentoring. All have been involved in a curricular revision of first-year writing piloted in fall 2015, and each has continued to help refine the shared curriculum of English 101, especially in relation to GTA training. Dev, Keith and Terry all have doctoral degrees in areas of rhetoric and composition, although we also have mentors who work with our GTAs who come from other disciplinary backgrounds in English (i.e., literature, creative writing, and applied linguistics).

In one mentor practicum group, Terry emphasized ethics, drawing on the threshold concept *writing involves making ethical choices*. In *Naming What We Know*, John Duffy (2015) suggests "writing involves ethical choices because every time we write for another person, we propose a relationship with other human beings, our readers" (31). Terry used this concept to reflect on GTAs' commenting practices. He said, "We talked about what does it mean to have a terse response, even if what you're trying to do is pointing out . . . a simple error, but having that GTA point out an error, there's an ethical way to do it. But there's obviously common mistakes that could shut down a student. That's what we're trying to stave from happening." This developed into a conversation about relationships in the process of responding to student writing, which aligned with some of Terry's beliefs about the significance of teachers connecting with students as the most challenging aspect of training teachers. In this way, threshold concepts offered a useful resource for teasing out the complexity of relationships in the teaching of writing. They offered guidance for making informed decisions for activities like commenting on drafts and writing summative feedback.

Another common approach in practicum was to connect threshold concepts with teaching philosophies. Though each designed different activities, Dev and Keith used threshold concepts to help GTAs articulate their teaching philosophies more clearly, a project required in the program because it helps new instructors deliberately explain why they are doing what they do in the classroom. Previously, though, the project had proven challenging.[4] Working from threshold concepts to help GTAs begin, Dev started a Google Doc in which he listed threshold concepts from part 1 in *Naming What We Know*. After each one, he asked GTAs to (1) summarize the threshold concept in their own words and (2) explain how the threshold concept might fit into a discussion of teaching philosophy. Six GTAs in his small group wrote summaries of the concepts, exploring how these principles might fit in a teaching philosophy. GTAs then used the commenting feature in Google Docs to have a dialogue about their summaries and responses. One GTA talked about how a particular threshold concept created tension for her. Another gave an example of why one was interesting to her, drawing on literary theory she had read.

As another example, Keith also asked GTAs to draw on the threshold concepts from *Naming What We Know* to create a teaching philosophy, but he did so through a multimodal project adapted from Jody Shipka's (2009) discussion of intertextual and multimodal composing demonstrated by a student who submitted the "Child Shaper" packaging as a rhetorical text. In her article, Shipka describes a multimodal piece a student created to an assignment called "The Educational Autobiographic" (W344), which led to a multimodal task-based framework for teaching multimodal composing. Like Shipka, Keith wanted to encourage expression of meaning beyond the constraints of a formulaic teaching philosophy. He asked GTAs to imagine they were creating a writing-teacher doll they would market to consumers; they had to create packaging for the doll that represented their teacher persona and reflected their teaching philosophy. The project gave them a tactile way of thinking through their teaching philosophy before writing it in words, and they realized they would need shared vocabulary to communicate their philosophy and build a teacher persona. Keith explained, "We used threshold concepts [for this activity] because one of the GTAs said, 'Well I feel like if I'm going to be making a philosophy I need some vocabulary to use.'" According to Keith, threshold concepts provided a shared vocabulary or lexicon for thinking through representation. After the GTAs in Keith's group read part 1 of *Naming What We Know*, he instructed them to identify vocabulary they would want to discuss, assuming they would choose words in the major concepts. One GTA highlighted the frequency of the word *ephemeral* from the introduction to *Naming What We Know* and connected *ephemeral* to process-oriented rather than product-oriented instruction. Another focused on the term *threshold concept* and wondered whether genre was a threshold concept. Keith's activity gave GTAs an entry point for thinking through their teaching philosophies in a creative way before articulating those philosophies in prose, but as the GTAs created their packaging, they realized they needed shared language—again, like Anson, Chen Chen, and Anson's (this volume) "key terms"—to talk about their philosophies in the classroom and communicate with each other. Because the packaging is designed for an audience (in this case, the mentor and the other GTAs), they needed language that audience would understand. Threshold concepts gave them an entry point for shared language to discuss their philosophies as they developed a theoretical construct for teaching writing.

Both examples demonstrate how the use of threshold concepts in GTA preparation seemed to address two primary challenges GTAs face when assigned to teach writing classes for the first time: lack of disciplinary knowledge in writing studies and lack of a theoretical construct for teaching writing. Threshold concepts offered a type of bridge in the same way pedagogical content knowledge involves thinking through strategies for how to represent an idea in order to make it teachable. Dev's, Keith's, and Terry's activities provided shared language and introduced GTAs to foundational knowledge in writing studies, and the activities also helped GTAs begin to think about practical applications in their own writing classrooms. This benefit is especially evident in the example from Terry's group. Dev, Keith, and Terry all reported that they appreciated threshold concepts as a resource, and Terry commented that they wished they'd had threshold concepts the first year they were mentors of GTAs in the UA writing program. All recommended we continue using threshold concepts as a basis for GTA practicum moving forward.

THRESHOLD CONCEPTS: A SHARED LEXICON
TO HELP DIVERSE FACULTY REFLECT

We hold that threshold concepts, while abstract for GTAs, can provide an entry point and bridge to disciplinary knowledge many GTAs may lack, if training and development offers optimal conditions for doing so. From our mentors, we learned there are affordances and limitations with threshold concepts in GTA training, based in large part on the commentary mentors offered during follow-up interviews. Though Dev, Keith, and Terry approached threshold concepts from their own unique expertise, all found that threshold concepts—or principles, as we called them—helped GTAs create a shared vocabulary and served as a relevant tool for reflection. They were especially useful for helping mentors work with the diversity in GTAs' academic disciplinary programs of study in creative writing, linguistics, literature, and rhetoric.

One of the most visible benefits mentioned by Dev, Keith and Terry was that a focus on threshold concepts contributed to a shared lexicon for talking about teaching writing. This seemed to help GTAs with a wide range of activities, such as commenting on student writing or composing a philosophy of teaching. Terry mentioned, for example, "I really liked the activity we did at orientation, having those giant Post-it Notes on the wall because what is resonating with them is when they are mulling over some of these concepts." The activity contributed to the lexicon, a vocabulary for identifying these concepts and then understanding what those concepts might look like in action in the classroom setting. For Keith, working with threshold concepts in practicum led to productive conversations. At the end of the semester, Keith noted that—unlike previous years in the GTA practicum—the teaching philosophies his GTAs wrote were more conceptually framed with respect to theories of learning or writing development as opposed to a laundry list of specific class activities. In fact, he noted, one GTA in literature referenced the threshold concept *words get their meanings from other words* as a core principle for writing, which connected to her ongoing interest in theories of language offered by Mikhail Bakhtin. Generally, Keith felt his small mentor group responded positively to threshold concepts, which gave them an introduction to needed disciplinary knowledge: "I think the fact that it gives them a vocabulary to talk about this new subject helps." He elaborated that this common vocabulary set the foundation for thinking about teaching and learning.

Although the mentors described specific applications of threshold concepts in practicum, they also commented that the GTAs from English studies outside writing studies or rhetoric sometimes struggled to access or participate in discussions about threshold concepts. Terry explained how threshold concepts offered a structure for training new teachers: as a primer, these key concepts offered various pathways for teacher development because *Naming What We Know* is a capacious text, open for interpretation. "What I like so much about this reading [*NWWK* classroom edition]," Terry said, "is that there are multiple approaches." Keith said GTAs asked about the term *threshold concept* and wondered whether key terms in our curriculum such as *genre* and *literacy* were also threshold concepts. This comment echoes an earlier study exploring some GTAs' ambivalence about the idea of genre (Mapes et al., forthcoming). Another mentor admitted threshold concepts seemed more approachable than our student learning outcomes, but both remained somewhat mysterious to GTAs and undergraduate students. Instructors needed to understand *why* the program had particular outcomes for first-year writing courses and why we asked them to follow particular practices in their writing classes, yet GTAs reported being resistant to reading the theory that had guided the program's arrival at those outcomes and practices. In essence, many of those GTAs were not familiar enough with some of the key terms used to explain threshold concepts when they attempted to understand the concepts themselves. As a tool for reflection, threshold concepts may offer multiple pathways for GTAs to learning core concepts of writing studies and how to teach those concepts in first-year writing. This insight resonates with Blaauw-Hara et al. in this collection, who conclude, "Rather than asking faculty to set aside their different disciplinary preparations, we think it would be helpful to ask them to dive into their understandings of writing and see how threshold concepts connect" (170). Reflection is fundamental to helping GTAs navigate threshold concepts' troublesome knowledge.

During individual interviews, mentors also expressed benefits of integrating threshold concepts as a tool for reflection. At the same time, mentors suggested that threshold concepts in *Naming What We Know* are highly abstract and difficult for new teachers and new graduate students to engage. Understandably, the threshold concepts of writing in *NWWK* are summaries of disciplinary knowledge. On the one hand, they present disciplinary knowledge more concisely, something many of our GTAs had asked for in previous years when we assigned longer theoretical pieces in the GTA practicum course. But reading threshold concepts can also be confusing without the disciplinary background from which the threshold concepts are drawn. As documented by Estrem, Shepherd, and Shadle, as well as Blaauw-Hara et al. in this collection, sometimes diversity in disciplinary background of faculty (or GTAs like ours) creates an additional stumbling block for development. We are, in many ways, trying to address the gap in disciplinary knowledge Hansen (2018) references. The lack of disciplinary knowledge is challenging to bridge, as so many in our field have already noted. Even so, our mentors found *Naming What We Know* offered room for various interpretations that can lead to different approaches to teacher development. Activities that invite GTAs to rephrase, paraphrase, and translate threshold concepts resonated most with our GTAs.

INSIGHTS AND IMPLICATIONS

Of importance, threshold concepts seem relevant for pedagogical content knowledge as defined by Shulman (1986). In our program, a shared lexicon as a tool for reflection contributed to understanding how to represent an idea to make it teachable. While we recognize the tension surrounding the role of theory in GTA preparation and the balance between theory and practice in practicum (Dobrin 2005; Estrem and Reid 2012; Obermark, Brewer, and Halasek 2015; Reid 2012; Rupiper Taggart and Lowry 2011), threshold concepts provide a primer with different pathways and interests for GTAs and mentors alike. As part of UA's writing program orientation and practicum, our pilot project suggests threshold concepts can provide an accessible entry point for GTAs and their mentors. While threshold concepts cannot resolve every precarious issue of GTA preparation, they offer an accessible structure through which theory can be introduced and fashioned as a topic of inquiry.

In our program, threshold concepts seemed helpful for novice GTAs in tangible ways, but the concepts must be repurposed to address the intersection of content knowledge and pedagogy specific to a GTA preparation course. *NWWK* was not designed as a textbook for teachers new to teaching writing and new to writing studies as a discipline. All new professionals must learn new knowledge, and threshold concepts of writing as they are defined in texts such as *NWWK* offer a scaffold to specify and define our field's knowledge. We have repurposed the text in that way, and we find great benefits in doing so. Specifically as a shared lexicon and a tool for guiding reflection on what's hard to grasp in writing studies, threshold concepts seem to provide an infrastructure for formulating pedagogical content knowledge. When provided as means for thinking through what's difficult to learn or grasp, threshold concepts can be the foundation for defining what's teachable. Starting with threshold concepts as a way to introduce new teachers to a field makes sense to us, but we must also carefully structure that introduction to acknowledge the threshold concepts are a representation of the broader knowledge of a discipline. Given that most GTAs have no prior knowledge of or experience with that discipline, the task of preparing them to teach is herculean and, as Hansen (2018) acknowledges, relatively impossible to do thoroughly in a couple of weeks.

Often scholarship on GTA preparation in writing programs assumes a writing program administrator is leading a seminar of graduate students in a training setting. But in a program that uses a distributed model of leadership, many different people might be helping mentor new teachers in a program. While much research on writing program administration discusses the range of backgrounds GTAs have and the challenges of GTA development, our approach also provides an additional question for those leading GTA preparation in programs like ours in which administrative work is collaborative and distributed. What challenges might be introduced due to the varied backgrounds and training of those who are mentoring the GTAs? Several large universities use models in which experienced faculty mentor graduate students as they teach for the first time (for a detailed description of such a model, see Fedukovich and Hall 2016). In a large program like ours with a collaborative model of administration, for which we would like to develop a more inclusive model of leadership and mentoring that involves faculty from all ranks, having accessible common language is an important, necessary step. We began to realize threshold concepts of writing studies provide common language for those who are training the GTAs as well. This conclusion parallels the work of Anson, Chen Chen, and Anson in this collection; while they focus on faculty participating in WAC initiatives, we find the varied disciplinary backgrounds of our GTAs necessitate similar steps to finding common language.

With the apparent success of asking GTAs to rephrase and translate threshold concepts into their own words and through their own experiences at UA, perhaps this is a useful step in practicum that may work in other programs. Such an exercise could be an important part of addressing major challenges faced in GTA preparation while also making the larger threshold concepts of writing studies meaningful to a local context. Based on our experiences, we have found that new GTAs who come to their writing classrooms from disciplines outsides writing studies (and also those who are in writing studies but are new to the field and/or to teaching) have difficulty making connections between the composition theories they are reading and what they are doing in their own classrooms. GTAs need an entry point for pedagogical content knowledge in order to make sense of *what* theoretical principles they need to know to teach writing effectively (especially within a particular program), *why* those principles are important, and *how* they might put those principles into action in a writing classroom. With this in mind, we recognize threshold concepts of writing studies might provide that entry point, which can offer a bridge for preparing GTAs to grapple with the two big challenges of teaching writing: how to teach writing in terms of both *what to do* and *why* in the classroom.

NOTES

1. We refer to assistant directors as *mentors* in this manuscript.
2. Most undergraduate students complete two semesters of foundations writing, English 101 and English 102.
3. New-GTA orientation involves large-group sessions in the morning in which workshop leaders overview key concepts: (1) writing program goals and student learning outcomes; (2) a brief introduction to principles for teaching writing; (3) English 101 curriculum; (4) lesson plans; (5) institutional policy; and (6) the university learning-management system.
4. All our GTAs must draft a teaching philosophy and add it to a digital teaching portfolio during their first year of teaching.

REFERENCES

Adler-Kassner, Linda, John Majewski, and Damian Koshnick. 2012. "The Value of Troublesome Knowledge: Transfer and Threshold Concepts in Writing and History." *Composition Forum* 26. http://compositionforum.com/issue/26/troublesome-knowledge-threshold.php.

Adler-Kassner, Linda, and Elizabeth Wardle, eds. 2015. *Naming What We Know: Threshold Concepts of Writing Studies*. Logan: Utah State University Press.

Bazerman, Charles. 2015. "Writing Speaks to Situations through Recognizable Forms." In *Naming What We Know: Threshold Concepts of Writing Studies*, edited by Linda Adler-Kassner and Elizabeth Wardle, 35–37. Logan: Utah State University Press.

Beaufort, Anne. 2007. *College Writing and Beyond: A New Framework for University Writing Instruction*. Logan: Utah State University Press.

Carroll, Lee Ann. 2002. *Rehearsing New Roles: How College Students Develop as Writers*. Carbondale: Southern Illinois University Press.

Dobrin, Sidney L. 2005. *Don't Call It That: The Composition Practicum*. Urbana, IL: NCTE.

Driscoll, Dana, and Roger Powell. 2016. "States, Traits, and Dispositions: the Impact of Emotion on Writing Development and Writing Transfer Across College Courses and Beyond." *Composition Forum* 34. http://www.compositionforum.com/issue/34/states-traits.php.

Dryer, Dylan. 2012. "At a Mirror, Darkly: The Imagined Undergraduate Writers of Ten Novice Composition Instructors." *College Composition and Communication* 63 (3): 420–52.

Duffy, John. 2015. "Writing Involves Making Ethical Choices." In *Naming What We Know: Threshold Concepts of Writing Studies*, edited by Linda Adler-Kassner and Elizabeth Wardle, 31–32. Logan: Utah State University Press.

Estrem, Heidi, and E. Shelley Reid. 2012. "What New Writing Teachers Talk about When They Talk about Teaching." *Pedagogy* 12 (3): 447–78.

Fedukovich, Casie, and Megan Hall. 2016. "GTA Preparation as a Model for Cross-Tier Collaboration at North Carolina State University: A Program Profile." *Composition Forum* 33. http://www.compositionforum.com/issue/33/ncsu.php.

Fischer, Ruth Overman. 2005. "Theory in a TA Composition Pedagogy Course: Not If, But How." In *Don't Call It That: The Composition Practicum*, edited by Sidney L. Dobrin, 200–213. Urbana, IL: NCTE.

Gere, Anne Ruggles. 2009. *Initial Report on a Survey of CCCC Members*. Ann Arbor: Michigan State University, Squire Office of Policy Research, http://www.ncte.org/library/NCTE Files/Groups/CCCC/InitialReportSurvey.

Goggin, Maureen Daly, and Michael Stancliff. 2007. "What's Theorizing Got to Do With It? Teaching Theory as Resourceful Conflict and Reflection in TA Preparation." *WPA: Writing Program Administration* 25 (3): 11–28.

Hansen, Kristine. 2018. "Discipline and Profession: Can the Field of Rhetoric and Writing Be Both?" In *Composition, Rhetoric, and Disciplinarity*, edited by Rita Malenczyk, Susan Miller-Cochran, Elizabeth Wardle, and Kathleen Blake Yancey, 134–58. Logan: Utah State University Press.

Hardin, Joe Marshall. 2005. "Writing Theory and Writing the Classroom." In *Don't Call It That: The Composition Practicum*, edited by Sidney L. Dobrin, 35–42. Urbana, IL: NCTE.

Hesse, Douglas. 1993. "Teachers as Students, Reflecting Resistance." *College Composition and Communication* 44 (2): 224–31.

King, Catherine, and Peter Felten. 2012. "Threshold Concepts in Educational Development: An Introduction." *Journal of Faculty Development* 26 (3): 5–7.

Land, Ray. 2016. "Toil and Trouble: Threshold Concepts as Pedagogy of Uncertainty." In *Threshold Concepts in Practice*, edited by Ray Land, Jan H. F. Meyer, and Michael T. Flanagan, 11–24. Rotterdam: Sense.

Land, Ray, Jan H. F. Meyer, and Michael T. Flanagan, eds. 2016. *Threshold Concepts in Practice*. Rotterdam: Sense.

Mapes, Aimee, Brad Jacobson, Rachel LaMance, and Stefan Vogel. Forthcoming. "Troublesome Knowledge: A Study of GTA Ambivalence with Genre-Informed Pedagogy." *WPA: Writing Program Administration*. Spring 2020.

Meyer, Jan, and Ray Land. 2003. *Threshold Concepts and Troublesome Knowledge: Linkages to Ways of Thinking and Practising within the Disciplines*. Enhancing Teaching-Learning Environments in Undergraduate Courses Project Occasional Report 4, University of Edinburgh, May. http://www.etl.tla.ed.ac.uk/docs/ETLreport4.pdf. https://www.colorado.edu/UCB/AcademicAffairs/ftep/documents/ETLreport4-1.pdf.

Meyer, Jan, and Julie Timmermans. 2016. "Integrated Threshold Concepts." In *Threshold Concepts in Practice*, edited by Ray Land, Jan H. F. Meyer, and Michael T. Flanagan, 29–38. Rotterdam: Sense.

Michel, Anthony J. 2005. "From Theory to Theorizing: Rethinking the Graduate Introduction to Composition Course." In *Don't Call It That: The Composition Practicum*, edited by Sidney L. Dobrin, 183–99. Urbana, IL: NCTE.

Moore, Jessie. 2012. "Designing for Transfer: Threshold Concepts." *Journal of Faculty Development* 26 (3):19–24.

Negretti, Raffaela. 2012. "Metacognition in Student Academic Writing: A Longitudinal Study of Metacognitive Awareness and Its Relation to Task Perception, Self-Regulation, and Evaluation of Performance." *Written Communication* 29 (2): 142–79.

Nowacek, Rebecca. 2011. *Agents of Integration: Understanding Transfer as a Rhetorical Act*. Carbondale: Southern Illinois University Press.

Obermark, Lauren, Elizabeth Brewer, and Kay Halasek. 2015. "Moving from the One and Done to a Culture of Collaboration: Revising Professional Development for TAs." *WPA: Writing Program Administration* 39 (1): 32–55.

Reid, E. Shelley. 2012. "Teaching Writing Teachers Writing: Difficulty, Exploration, and Critical Reflection." *College Composition and Communication* 61 (2): W197–W221.

Restaino, Jessica. 2012. *First Semester: Graduate Students, Teaching Writing, and the Challenge of Middle Ground*. Carbondale: Southern Illinois University Press.

Rounsaville, Angela, Rachel Goldberg, and Anis Bawarshi. 2008. "From Incomes to Outcomes: FYW Students' Prior Genre Knowledge, Meta-Cognition, and the Question of Transfer." *WPA: Writing Program Administration* 32 (1–2): 97–112.

Rupiper Taggart, Amy, and Margaret Lowry. 2011. "Cohorts, Grading, and Ethos: Listening to TAs Enhances Teacher Preparation." *WPA: Writing Program Administration* 34 (1): 89–114.

Shipka, Jody. 2009. "Negotiating Rhetorical, Material, Methodological, and Technological Differences: Evaluating Multimodal Designs." *College Composition and Communication* 61 (1): W343–66

Shulman, Lee. 1986. "Those Who Understand: Knowledge Growth in Teaching." *Educational Researcher* 15 (2): 4–14.

Shulman, Lee. 1987. "Knowledge and Teaching: Foundations of the New Reform." *Harvard Educational Review* 57 (1): 1–22.

Sommers, Nancy, and Lisa Saltz. 2004. "The Novice as Expert: Writing the Freshman Year." *College Composition and Communication* 56 (1): 124–49.

Sternglass, Marilyn S. 1997. *Time to Know Them: A Longitudinal Study of Writing and Learning at the College Level.* Mahwah, NJ: Erlbaum.

Tardy, Christine M. 2017. "Genre." Presentation for New GTA Orientation, University of Arizona Writing Program, Tucson.

Wardle, Elizabeth. 2007. "Understanding 'Transfer' from FYC : Preliminary Results of a Longitudinal Study." *WPA: Writing Program Administration* 31 (1–2): 65–85.

Wenger, Etienne. 1998. *Communities of Practice.* Cambridge: Cambridge University Press.

Yancey, Kathleen Blake, Liane Robertson, and Kara Taczak. 2014. *Writing across Contexts: Transfer, Composition, and Sites of Writing.* Urbana, IL: NCTE.

12
THRESHOLD CONCEPTS AND THE PHENOMENAL FORMS

Deborah Mutnick

> *This discourse is a part of me, embedded in me, and makes me who I am. It makes me Oummou Jawara. This discourse is Soninke. The discourse of Soninke has rolled down the tongues of my very first ancestors in Sona of ancient Egypt. Down to the Accra empire of Ancient Ghana. To the Gambia River in the city of Banjul, and now to me, Oummou Jawara.*

Oummou Jawara was a student in an accelerated first-year composition (FYC) class I taught in fall 2017 with a focus on the theme of literacy and identity. That semester, in addition to some commonly taught FYC texts like Malcolm X's "Learning to Read" and Sherman Alexie's "The Joy of Reading and Writing: Superman and Me," I assigned difficult, academic articles, including James Paul Gee's "What Is Literacy?," Deborah Brandt's "Literacy and Sponsorship," and June Jordan's "Nobody Mean More to Me Than You and the Future Life of Willie Jordan." I also introduced threshold concepts in an attempt, together with the articles, to tear away the curtain of educational discourse that maintains myths of linguistic superiority, neutrality, and universality and foster critical consciousness of the social contexts of language and literacy, emphasizing four concepts in Linda Adler-Kassner and Elizabeth Wardle's *Naming What We Know. Threshold Concepts of Writing Studies* (2015): *writing is a social and rhetorical activity; writing is a knowledge-making activity; writing enacts and creates identities and ideologies; and all writers have more to learn.*

Not surprisingly perhaps, it was the last concept students most fully embraced, relieved I didn't expect them to become fully formed writers in one semester. Not so directly stated but evident in their reflective writing was the impact of the other threshold concepts on how they saw themselves as learners, amplified by discussions of "dominant literacy," "powerful literacy" (Gee 1987), "literacy sponsorship" (Brandt 1998), and nonstandard dialects (Jordan 1988). Understanding that "dominant" literacy is related to "the distribution of social power and hierarchical structure of society" (Gee 1987, 22) and that "powerful literacy" (26) can enable a critique of dominant discourses was freeing to these students, most of whose bi- or multilingual, transnational, working-class, immigrant experiences in the United States had undermined their confidence in their linguistic abilities and their desire to read. Though I did not and would not introduce them to Karl Marx's theory of the phenomenal forms, whose relationship to threshold concepts is the subject of this chapter, my preoccupation with its pedagogical effects informed how I revised the course. To briefly explain the phenomenal forms before returning to the concept later in the chapter, Marx (1867b) notes in *Capital* and elsewhere that surface manifestations of reality, or observable phenomena, though neither illusory nor false, contain an "essential relation" hidden by their sensual form and discoverable through scientific or critical processes. In what follows, I argue that in their writing, Oummou and other students enacted a dialectic between their formative discursive selves and their encounters with new knowledge—the "edited-once version" of self, as her classmate Arfa Qadeer put it—through which they began to grasp the "concealed essential patterns" of the phenomenal forms of language and identity in a process that has implications for threshold concepts theory (Marx 1894).

RETHINKING FYC'S TRANSFORMATIVE POTENTIAL

A newly crystallized goal of the fall 2017 class emanating from these theoretical considerations was to help students see the activity of learning in FYC and across the curriculum as a transformative activity that could and should, at least to some degree, change their understanding of the world and the word in relation to themselves. In so doing, I hoped they would begin to see the self as an indissolubly social process of becoming shaped by acquisition of secondary discourses and imagined as doors to new, undiscovered, or partially understood worlds of knowledge and activity. This goal emerged in response to discussions about threshold concepts in writing with colleagues who said the main problem they saw in their first-year students was a failure to grasp what it meant to be in college. Rather than an opportunity for a broad liberal arts education or a deeper understanding of the world around them, including the texts and contexts undergirding disciplinary knowledge, entering students who viewed college as an obligatory rite of passage and/or an instrumental means to a career exhibited a variety of challenging behaviors and attitudes, from an obsessive focus on grades and resentment of required courses to undisciplined responses to reading and writing assignments.

If the problem was how to transform such behaviors and attitudes into curious, vibrant intellectual engagement enabling acquisition of new skills and knowledge through self-motivated practice, a solution lay in the very theories of discourse, rhetoric, and communication that inform FYC instruction. In line with research suggesting that course content matters and that transfer of writing skills and knowledge is supported not only by technical instruction but also by a thematic focus on writing and rhetoric, I aimed to engage students in a study of literacy as discourse that would enable them to reflect on how they themselves are embedded in it, shaped by discursive and ideological forces they have mostly likely never considered, much less understood (Beaufort 2007; Robertson, Taczak, and Yancey 2012; Wardle and Downs 2007). An a priori question centered on why so many entering students resisted disciplined study. Although such questions cannot be fully addressed here, my assumptions are (1) that resistance exists to varying degrees across class and institutional boundaries and (2) that the dispositions of many LIU Brooklyn students, whose median annual family income is $35,000, reflect their specific class and educational backgrounds.

Indeed, the idea that literacy sponsorship as described by Brandt (1998) not only enables and supports but also regulates, suppresses, and withholds literacy resonated with many of my students. Likewise, Gee's (1987) concept of an "identity kit" helped them clarify the relationship between self and society, learning and self-transformation. For this largely immigrant, first-generation student cohort, life-altering circumstances had arguably already raised their critical awareness of history even as the larger definition of discourses in relation to identity explained educational gaps and feelings of shame, anger, and alienation that had previously bewildered them. Along with Oummou, whose family is from The Gambia, and Arfa, whose family is Indian, the class included students from Haiti, the Dominican Republic, Puerto Rico, Pakistan, Serbia, Bangladesh, Palestine, and Guyana. Although I would teach the same curriculum to a more homogenous, middle-class, whiter population, this particular, extraordinarily diverse group embraced the theoretical heart of the course with a poignant eagerness to discover underlying patterns and processes of linguistic realities that explained their own often quite negative experiences of schooling and other social institutions as constituted not by personal or cultural inadequacies but rather by social and political economic relations.

To orchestrate this process of becoming in a short fourteen weeks, students began the semester by composing what I called "Writing the Self—A First Draft." Explaining it would be returned with comments but ungraded and then revised at the end of the semester, I asked them "to write a portrait of yourself as you begin your first semester as a college student at LIU Brooklyn. The idea of 'writing the self' can be thought of as: (1) how we create, invent, or 'write' ourselves consciously or unconsciously; (2) how we use language to discover, invent, and/or express who we are; and (3) how we change or 'rewrite' ourselves through that conscious process." Adjacent to the text was a graphic image depicting identity markers that circulated in various ways throughout the course and that some students referred to in their writing. Students also wrote a literacy autoethnography and a research paper that either explored another person's literacy development, usually that of a family member, or started with a primary text like Malcolm X's "The Ballot or the Bullet" speech and relied on secondary sources to develop an analysis of the rhetorical exigency that gave rise to it. There were multiple goals for students, including for them to develop the critical-reading skills they would need to access complex ideas; to engage in analytical, thesis-driven, evidence-based writing; to begin to grasp threshold concepts in writing studies, particularly that disciplinary, professional, and cultural discourses involve different ways of thinking, behaving, talking, and writing; and to continue to gain critical consciousness, especially in the form of self-reflection and metacognitive awareness of their own experience as college students. In sum, the intent of the redesigned course was to create a context in which students would turn their investigations of literacy on themselves in ways I hoped would enable them to examine their own ontological positions in relation to the course goals, a process I speculated would increase their investment in their studies, contribute to their intellectual development, and only unfold if they undertook it of their own free will.

I had redesigned the course in response to resistance to a very different version of FYC I had been teaching since 2011, which some students felt was overly rigorous and personally irrelevant. It was the problem of resistance and the questions it raised about perceptions of relevance and rigor that intrigued me and contributed to the course redesign. The earlier course, called Pathways to Freedom, was linked to a history class and revolved around rhetorical analysis of Brooklyn's history of slavery, Jim Crow, and resistance to racial repression over three centuries, culminating in the 1960s.[1] I could see the conduciveness of the course theme to rhetorical analysis and its relevance to contemporary issues of mass incarceration, police killings of people of color, and the rise of a new civil rights movement, but many students resented having to read difficult texts and think critically about history's relationship to the present or to them personally. As shall become clear in my discussion of resistance, I believe a key to this pedagogical problem lies in understanding our embeddedness, apropos of the phenomenal forms, in any object of inquiry. In the case of slavery and racism, the power dynamic between white and black Americans created tensions for students with respect to their own racial, ethnic, and class backgrounds that were difficult to confront because they felt personally implicated and because I had set out to cover material that might have enabled a profound reconsideration of this history but required disciplined reading, critical analysis, and openness to rethinking assumptions to do so. The students' embedded response to these historical narratives was most evident and most painful in their use of the plural first-person pronoun to refer to enslaved people or to slaveholders in terms of their own racial identities.

While the subject matter of the history and rhetoric of racism fits within the wide range of thematic content that has been typical of FYC (and can be seen in the new course design vis-à-vis considerations of sponsorship, dominant and nondominant discourses, and nonstandard dialects), I began to wonder if the thematic focus of the Pathways course eluded many students precisely because there was no time to face the other source of their discomfort: their own struggles with intensive, college-level reading and writing—the principal course learning outcomes—and their resentment of critical feedback so unlike what they had received in high school. By insisting they were capable of developing the rhetorical and critical analytical skills needed to grasp the complex texts they encountered in Pathways, I had perhaps elided the very crux of the pedagogical problem: the ontological and epistemological barriers to learning. In the redesigned FYC class on literacy and identity, I aimed to turn the students' gaze back on their own experience of discourse. Though similar to the writing-about-writing (WAW) and teaching-for-transfer (TFT) approaches advocated respectively by Elizabeth Wardle and Doug Downs (2007) and Liane Robertson, Kara Taczak, and Kathleen Blake Yancey (2012), my explicit and somewhat different intent was to engage students in an investigation of their own discursive histories, including their resistance to disciplined reading and writing, and to do so with an overtly materialist perspective that aimed to illuminate the underlying class divisions and political economies of literacy learning that explain disparities in educational access and shifting standards. It is precisely the omission of the conditioning effects of social class, much less a Marxist analysis, in much of composition research, including this volume, that I hope here to rectify by adding a historical materialist account of academic writing instruction to the conversation.[2] Together with the disciplinary turn toward writing as the thematic content of FYC, both threshold concepts theory and Marx's theory of the phenomenal forms helped me rethink the course: by explicitly integrating threshold concepts into the course design, I could bring students into metaconversations about literacy learning; and by considering the pedagogical implications of the phenomenal forms, I would engage them in an investigation of their own discursive practices in order to make their resistance to disciplined reading and writing visible and discussable.

THE TRAUMA OF TRANSFORMATIVE LEARNING

Since its introduction by Jan Meyer and Ray Land in 2003, threshold concepts theory has been widely embraced across disciplinary and national boundaries. Through its focus on core disciplinary concepts, the theory seeks to illuminate how learners acquire "troublesome knowledge" (Perkins 1999, 11) or discard existing knowledge that interferes with crossing learning thresholds (Land, Rattray, and Vivian 2014; Perkins 2009, 14). This process is metaphorically understood in threshold concepts theory as a portal or rite of passage. While the troublesome, even traumatic, aspect of learning has been addressed by threshold concepts theorists (e.g., Adler-Kassner and Wardle 2015; Cousin 2006; Meyer and Land 2006; Perkins 2006), I argue that Marx's theory of the phenomenal forms helps explain *why*, beyond evocations of loss of the familiar or fear of the unknown, that passage can be so difficult. More specifically, the relevance of the phenomenal forms to a threshold approach is that they impede the learning process first by obscuring the "hidden substratum" of surface manifestations of reality *and* then, once these concealed relations are revealed, typically as the inverse of their appearances, by destabilizing ontological and social structures of identity (Marx 1867b).[3]

Although Marx's focus was primarily sociological, concerned with the material social elements of class division and hierarchies of power inherent in stadial political economies, his theory of the phenomenal forms applies as well to cosmic, biological, and psychological realities whose inner relations and patterns are concealed by their surface manifestations. According to Luis S. Villacañas de Castro, whose investigations of the phenomenal forms in relation to pedagogy I draw on throughout this chapter, the Copernican revolutions or Kuhnian paradigm shifts of science exemplify epistemological obstacles to new knowledge that destabilize what we intuitively believe, often invoking the same fierce resistance each transformational discovery met with historically. Examples of these scientific revolutions include Copernicus's heliocentric theory of the solar system, Newton's laws of gravity, Darwin's theory of natural selection and Freud's theory of the unconscious. While phenomenal forms theory is critical to Marxist sociology, its relevance to pedagogical methods and to threshold concept theory both rests on and extends beyond issues of class division and social inequalities. Thus, Villacañas de Castro's investigation of the phenomenal forms illuminates the omission of a critical perspective on troublesome knowledge having to do with the ontological factors affecting the learner's disposition, namely (1) the effects of the observer's relationship to the observed and (2) the impact of socioeconomic stratification on educational outcomes for all learners, regardless of class status. Villacañas de Castro (2015) explains, "Indeed, one such obstacle [to learning] is posed in every class-divided society, and its consequences impinge on the cognition of its individuals. It has to do with the fact that the place they occupy in a given social milieu vis-à-vis the means of production conditions their ability to reach an appropriate representation (a scientific understanding) of the social phenomena that surround them, and of which they form part" (94). At the same time, even as it is important to consider how class stratification conditions individuals, ontological obstacles to learning would likely persist in a classless society insofar as learners are always inscribed in the object of their inquiry.[4]

For Villacañas de Castro (2015), the key question arises at the microgenetic level, "the purely synchronic progress that children may undergo at any given educational site, depending on the features of the instruction they receive" (100), and the crucial problem is the learner's resistance to the trauma of transformative learning. Like many of the students in my fall 2017 FYC class, Oummou's and Arfa's subject positions as first-generation immigrants exposed them to what Arfa called the "grammar police." It also awoke them to the necessity, as Oummou observed, of adding additional languages to "my language," Soninke, the "discourse that is a part of me, embedded in me." Despite the fact that both young women are high academic achievers, they reported painful experiences of writing and speaking in educational settings. Before providing a more detailed account of the phenomenal forms, their impact on learners like Oummou and Arfa, and their relevance to threshold concepts theory, it is helpful to consider what threshold theorists have had to say about resistance to learning and troublesome knowledge.

THRESHOLD CONCEPTS THEORY AND TROUBLESOME KNOWLEDGE

The theories of the phenomenal forms and threshold concepts rest on a similar set of assumptions about the sociocultural basis for learning and the troublesome aspects of disciplinary core concepts. Both suggest encounters with new knowledge decenter the learner, occasioning resistance on the one hand and an unsettling shift in perspective on the other. In the literature on threshold concepts, explanations of epistemological obstacles frequently begin with David Perkins's (2006) definition of "five sorts of trouble—ritual knowledge, inert knowledge, conceptually difficult knowledge, foreign knowledge, and tacit knowledge" (36–37). Also suggestive of phenomenal forms theory, Perkins explains how prior, intuitive conceptions of reality based on "misimpressions" from "everyday experience" and "reasonable but mistaken expectations" lead to a "mix of misunderstandings and ritual knowledge" that impede learning scientific concepts (38). Particularly confusing to "Betty Fable," a student he invokes to make his point, is the distinction between concepts and epistemes, the "activity systems" or "larger conceptual games" of specific discourses (41). Perkins gives the example of how "limit" in mathematics, which "formalizes the intuitive idea of getting closer and closer to a target value" (44), functions as both concept and episteme, noting that "Betty gets befuddled partly because the definition is conceptually complex, but partly because it reflects the foreign episteme of formal Mathematics. Betty expects definitions to make new ideas sensible and accessible, and by this standard the definition of limit appears convoluted and arcane. But the game is different here" (44). This "double trouble" of learning epistemic games, together with threshold concepts, threatens to overwhelm the learner, underscoring for Perkins the importance of threshold theory as "a powerful heuristic for looking at this puzzle" (43).

In addition to the conceptual and epistemic difficulties learners encounter in acquiring new disciplinary ideas and discourses, threshold scholars describe affective and ontological barriers to learning. In their preface to *Overcoming Barriers to Student Understanding*, Meyer and Land (2006) invoke the Limbourg brothers' fifteenth-century tableau of Adam and Eve eating the fruit of knowledge and entering a new and unfamiliar place outside the garden in the context of Freud's discussion of the *unheimlich*, the unhomely or strange, so that now Adam and Eve "have become adult and have left a world of innocence. However, their gain feels like loss. Their new knowledge is troublesome" (xiv). This focus on loss and the ontological and affective dimensions of troublesome learning weaves through the literature on threshold concepts.

In the same volume, Glynis Cousin (2006) observes that "mastery of a threshold concept . . . produces an ontological shift in the learner. New understandings are assimilated into the learner's biography, becoming part of what he knows, who he is and how he feels" (135).

In Cousin's (2006) account of teaching the threshold concept of "Otherness" in cultural studies, she refers to "learner discomfort or even 'trauma'" (136) and the importance of student subject positions in encountering the concept (137). Students' ethnic, racial, gender, sexual, and other markers of identity might make "troubling knowledge . . . a more apt term for the learning of Otherness because everyone, teachers and learners, has an internal relation to it" (136–37). In essence, Cousin's pedagogical argument is that students in closer proximity to those cast as Others are more likely to understand or sympathize with them. She notes as well that "the purpose of multicultural education is 'to get students beyond a world they already know in order to challenge and to provoke their inquiry'" (135) and that studying culture "may enhance but also threaten" cultural identities (137). Her focus on Otherness and analysis of related learners' subject positions underscores the importance of ontological and affective aspects of troublesome knowledge to threshold concept theory. At the same time, she elides underlying questions such as, What besides fear of the unknown makes it difficult to get beyond a world we already know? What sort of threat does new knowledge pose to identity? and How does everyone's "internal relation" to Otherness—and, I argue, all realms of study—create epistemological obstacles to learning?

Meyer and Land (2006) reflect further on "ontological as distinct from epistemological obstacles" (30) in relation to Elizabeth Ellsworth's perspective on barriers to learning "encountered by students who do not fit the 'mythical norm'" (30). Ellsworth (1989) defines that norm as "young, White, heterosexual, Christian, able-bodied, think middle-class, English-speaking, and male" (323), linked to the "rationalist assumptions" of critical pedagogy that perpetuate "repressive myths" and "relations of domination" (297). For Meyer and Land (2006), her "pedagogy of unknowability" corrects an overemphasis on epistemological barriers to troublesome knowledge. They reiterate her call for a "pedagogy of unknowability" responsive to the "incapacity of rationalist approaches to tolerate the unknown and uncertain (because unknowable), the affective (because non-rational) and the contextualized/local (because non-universal)" (30). However, insofar as a pedagogy of the unknowable entails a "never-ending 'moving about,'" (Ellsworth 1989, 321) that unsettles "every definition of knowing." (322), it seems to undermine the whole project of threshold concepts theory in relation to most scientific and pedagogical traditions. In this sense, Ellsworth's poststructuralist belief in "unknowability" fails to grasp the dialectic between epistemological and ontological obstacles to learning and reckon fully with its implications for education, a problem elucidated by the theory of the phenomenal forms.

For Oummou, Arfa, and their classmates, the invitation to investigate their discursive histories through the theoretical lenses of new literacy studies, literacy sponsorship, and historical shifts in writing studies represented by the NCTE 1974 resolution Students' Right to Their Own Language enabled them not only to reconsider their own experience in a new epistemological light but also to enact the self-motivated, repetitive practice Gee (1987) argues leads to discursive mastery. In other words, by studying their own literacy practices through these theoretical lenses, they were able both to comprehend difficult scholarly texts and to apply new knowledge—knowable, potentially transformative theories of discourse—to the specific course goals of developing college-level reading, writing, research, and critical analytical skills. This cohort's experience contrasted sharply with students in the Pathways class in their willingness to engage with difficult content and challenging assignments. While some Pathways students appreciated the course content and approached or even crossed the conceptual threshold of research as a scholarly conversation, many resisted the focus on slavery and racism and the more rigorous expectations of college-level writing, suffering a sort of double trauma that ultimately, even if they became better writers, mired them in the phenomenal forms of a mythical US history and a universalist, oppressive theory and practice of discourse (see Vieira et al., this volume). Villacañas de Castro's (2015, 2016) notion of the phenomenal forms helps explain how the redesigned course created spaces for learning that this one could not.

PEDAGOGY OF THE PHENOMENAL FORMS

In attempting to implement what Villacañas de Castro (2015) calls a "pedagogy of *Erscheinungsformen*" (110), or phenomenal forms, in FYC, I chose the theme of literacy and identity over other thematic content—such as racial injustice, adolescence, gender, and food, which might be the thematic content of a cultural studies approach to writing instruction—to encourage students to investigate, substantively and critically, their own histories as readers and writers and, at least for some, their resistance to rigor in writing and reading and to welcome them into a discourse community as coinvestigators rather than passive recipients of my instructional feedback. Perhaps this shift seems both obvious and belated to those who advocate a writing-about-writing (WAW) approach to FYC (see, e.g., Wardle and Downs 2007; Miles et al. 2008; Bird 2013) or teaching-for-transfer (TFT) approach (see Yancey, Robertson, and Taczak 2014). Like Wardle and Downs (2007), who argue that "writing cannot be taught independent of content" (559) and who introduce students to "readings that report research about writing and theorize ways of thinking about writing" (560), I assigned a mixture of scholarly and nonfiction texts about writing, together with theories of literacy acquisition, sponsorship, and sociological contexts for literacy learning that encouraged students to "test every reading in light of their own experience" (561). And like Yancey, Robertson, and Taczak (2014), I focused on "*specific ideas* in the form of key terms for composition" amplified by "intentionally designed and integrated" reflective writing (131). However, my reasons for turning to WAW are somewhat different, and it is this difference that sheds light on the pedagogical relevance of the phenomenal forms.

The reasons Wardle and Downs (2007) give for their "radical reimagining" (553) of FYC are "to improve writing instruction and to improve the standing of writing studies in the academy" (554). For Yancey, Robertson, and Taczak (2014), the motivation similarly is to help students "intentionally and thoughtfully" transfer writing skills and knowledge from FYC to other disciplinary, workplace, and personal writing domains (132). Adding a critical dimension to these worthy goals of improving writing instruction and transfer of writing skills and knowledge, my main reason for undertaking a WAW or TFT approach is to enable students to question their intuitive understandings and internalized values and beliefs about educational and linguistic realities by gaining awareness of the underlying social, cognitive, and ideological structures that construct and control them. These hidden relations of social and cultural reproduction mystify not only the acquisition of discursive skills and the inequities in educational sponsorship but also the structural basis of individual success and failure. By introducing students to scholarly articles that expose these hidden relations and processes, I aimed to enable them to examine their own experience in light of the readings and thus confront their resistance to disciplined study through new knowledge that explains it. In the Pathways curriculum, I also asked students to approach the course readings in light of their own experience, but the schism between that thematic content and the course goals derailed them. The problem, as suggested above, was not the curriculum's focus on slavery per se but rather the combined effect of the double trauma of racism and literacy development, which shut down inquiry and discussion of both objects of inquiry.

Villacañas de Castro (2016) contends that the theory of the phenomenal forms has crucial educational implications for how teachers address epistemological obstacles to learning in relation to ontological questions of being. He argues that the crux of the matter involves "new knowledge [not only] about particular objects . . . but also about the position that human beings held in relation to those realities, insofar as they formed part of them" (2). This human condition occasions the epistemological break theorized by Guy Bachelard (1938) as a rupture between prescientific and scientific knowledge that can only occur in a dialectical process of ongoing engagement with the observable world. According to Bachelard, the difficulty of scientific thought inheres "in the act of knowing itself" (13), not in the complexity or immensity of the world but in the observer's relationship to the scientific object. Thus, he stated, "one must accept a veritable rupture between sensual knowledge and scientific knowledge" (239).

The challenge in education is to enable the learner to grasp scientific concepts, which requires ontogenetic replication of the phylogenetic process of discovery and understanding. Many Kuhnian paradigm shifts in science continue to stir uneasiness, resistance, and denial for decades, even centuries, after the discoveries were made, not only in the cognitive dissonance experienced by the learner but also in persistent popular beliefs in, say, unscientific concepts like creationism or the harmfulness of vaccines. According to Villacañas de Castro (2016), it is precisely the phenomenal forms that account for the traumatic interaction between the individual and "a theoretical perspective which is radically different from one's own, *yet essential for one's self understanding.* . . . [It is thus] against profound narcissistic blows—to recall Freud's words—[that] the individual resists" (10; emphasis added). This view goes beyond conceptual difficulty and ontological problems of Otherness or loss to expose deeper implications of troublesome knowledge for learners who, embedded in biological, cosmological, psychological, and sociological systems, must wrestle not only with new knowledge but also with their place within these realities and the fields of inquiry to which they give rise.

RELEVANCE OF THE PEDAGOGY OF THE PHENOMENAL FORMS FOR THRESHOLD CONCEPTS THEORY

Villacañas de Castro's interrogation of the phenomenal forms suggests a powerful resonance with threshold concepts theory's interest in troublesome knowledge as a place where learners get "stuck" attempting to grasp threshold concepts. Specifically, phenomenal forms theory explains how the appearance of things—whether societal, natural, or cosmic—conceals their "essential inner pattern" and produces prescientific or unscientific concepts that are implicated in identity formation and can interfere with learning. In other words, we possess two kinds of knowledge, neither of which is false, that reflect different levels of comprehension of reality, variously described as ideological (or intuitive or spontaneous) and scientific (Marx), phenotypic and genetic (Vygotsky), and implicit and explicit (Fals-Borda) (Villacañas de Castro 2016, 6).

How to address these ontological and epistemological obstacles to learning and enable the learner, in the language of a threshold approach, to pass through the portal to postliminal awareness is the question that bedevils us. According to Villacañas de Castro, the answer resides in Freirean dialogue that engages learners in reflective practice in which they conduct their own investigations of reality. Obviously, this does not mean teachers cede their authority or disengage from that process. Instead, Villacañas de Castro argues that there is a "need for the teachers to 'affirm themselves without thereby disaffirming their students' (Freire and Faundez, 1989, 34). Since the task of leaving behind the ideological effects associated with the phenomenal forms always came against solid emotional and conceptual resistances, it was necessary for educators to negotiate very carefully the students' gradual construction of knowledge" (109). This "near mystery" of democratic praxis in teaching (Freire and Faundez 1989, 34) is illuminated by the phenomenal forms. Villacañas de Castro's (2016) central argument, worth reiterating, is that the ontological consequence for all learners, teachers included, of the inseparability of the knower from the object to be known creates a "pedagogical problem . . . if the learning experiences are too negative or traumatic, as they necessarily are from the moment when these theories demand students to push their own narcissism and individualistic perspectives aside, to de-center themselves, and rather think of themselves in terms of being part of . . . concrete subject matters" (8). It is precisely this ontological condition of learning that gives rise to resistance.

The insight afforded by Freirean pedagogy in how to respond to learner resistance caused by the "narcissistic blow" of a familiar world made strange by encounters with the inverse, concealed patterns of things that appear to be real is that genuine learning only occurs through the dialogic *activity* of the learner with the teacher, broadly construed as any discursive partner. For some learners, typically those whose primary discourse is closest to the secondary discourses of school, academic disciplines, and other dominant cultural discourses, this process occurs more easily in traditional forms of educational transmission, although these same students may have more difficulty acquiring critical literacy skills—what Gee (1987) calls "powerful literacy"; for others, such activity may be blocked by myriad factors, including dissonance between primary and academic discourses, class, racial, gender, and other biases of most educational discourses, and, for the purposes of this argument, most significantly, the distortions and deformations of the phenomenal forms in how learners perceive themselves and their worlds.

It is for these reasons Villacañas de Castro (2016) argues with Paulo Freire that "social democracy is the most coherent political model in relation to the tenets of critical pedagogy" (19). New in this formulation to readers familiar with Freire's liberatory pedagogy is the role of the phenomenal forms and their affective and cognitive implications for learners whose negative educational experiences make them resistant. One thinks of Sherman Alexie's (*Los Angeles Times*, April 19, 1998) description of "the sullen and already defeated Indian kids who sit in the back rows and ignore [him] with theatrical precision. They carry neither pencil nor pen. They stare out the window. They refuse and resist." In order to overcome such resistance, Villacañas de Castro (2016) insists on the necessity of both the traumatic confrontation with transformative knowledge and of teachers' respect for students' "algorithms of feeling" (13). The learner's recognition that they are neither autonomous nor wholly self-defined but rather produced by relations and processes that precede their self-awareness can be painful and traumatic. But by repositioning the student from passive receptor of knowledge to active investigator of reality—an approach possible across the disciplines—the pedagogy of the phenomenal forms helps surmount obstacles to learning caused by the sociological impact of class division and the ontological relationship of the observer and the observed upon conditions that impinge on learning at and beyond the site of instruction.

Driving the development of my thematic focus on literacy and identity was the resistance I had encountered in the Pathways curriculum, which indicated a need to open up that discussion publicly rather than push it to the margins of the course. If there was to be resistance to disciplined, rigorous study, I would allow it to become the center of the students' inquiry into their own discursive practices and histories. If students felt oppressed by too much reading and writing about material that seemed distant and unrelated to their current realities, I would change the reading material and offer them opportunities to investigate what it means to acquire new knowledge, enter new discursive worlds, and cultivate the "habits of mind" listed in the syllabus, drawn from the *Framework for Success in Postsecondary Writing*. I would allow them to turn their gaze back on themselves with new critical lenses supplied by Gee, Brandt, Jordan, and other authors, as well as threshold concepts in writing studies, not to encourage them to dwell on the personal but rather to excavate from the phenomenal forms that mystify them the concealed relations that structure identity. As Oummou concludes in her final essay,

> I've come a long way as a writer if I do say so myself. I never listened to the comments left on my papers by professors or other students because I thought to myself, "they just don't understand what I'm trying to say." You can have multiple discourses, which allow you to communicate in different ways, with different people, at different times. My primary discourse was the one I basically "got for free." The one that I spoke when I started babbling my first few words. My primary discourse is my core language, and I never thought about this until we started learning about identity kits in my English Composition class.... This threshold concept of "all writers have more to learn" made me realize that if you graduate college as the same person, providing the same kind of work as you did when you first came in, you've been doing something wrong.

A pedagogy of the phenomenal forms offers insights into the ontological problem of the learner's embeddedness in the object of study and the impact of a class-ridden society on the methods and processes by which knowledge can best be acquired. Specifically, it contributes to threshold concept theories of troublesome knowledge a Marxist analysis of the inverse relationship between surface manifestations of reality and their concealed inner patterns that explains *why* the passage to postliminal understanding of a threshold concept is difficult. It suggests that learner resistance results from narcissistic blows caused by ontological shifts in perspective that decenter the human ego collectively and individually. By turning students' attention to their own identity formation and inviting them to become coinvestigators of the invisible structural, material, sociohistorical forces that shaped them and their educational experience, I aimed to make their resistance an object of study rather than an obstacle to learning. Introducing them to threshold concepts in writing studies and critical theories of literacy acquisition, sponsorship, and nonstandard dialects merged the topic of literacy studies with their own academic literacy development and thus opened a space for resistance to become part of our mutual inquiry.

NOTES

1. For a discussion of the Pathways to Freedom course, see "Pathways to Freedom: From the Archives to the Street" (Mutnick 2018).
2. In this volume, for example, there are very few references to social class (see Vieira et al., chapter 2, and Tremain et al., chapter 10). The discussion in chapter 8 of roadblocks in the context of underprepared students exemplifies the tendency to leave out the question of class division. As I point out in relation to the trauma of transformative learning, while the ontological problem of the learner's embeddedness in the object of inquiry would likely persist even in a classless society, class stratification in a capitalist society is a crucial ontological factor affecting learner disposition.
3. In explaining the transformation of labor-value into wages, Marx (1867b) writes, "In the expression 'value of labour,' the idea of value is not only completely obliterated, but actually reversed. It is an expression as imaginary as the value of the earth. These imaginary expressions, arise, however, from the relations of production themselves. They are categories for the phenomenal forms of essential relations. *That in their appearance things often represent themselves in inverted form is pretty well known in every science except Political Economy*" (emphasis added).
4. In footnote 13 in support of his claim that humans can "work only as Nature does, that is by changing the form of matter," Marx (1867a) cites eighteenth-century economist Pietro Verri: "All the phenomena of the universe, whether produced by the hand of man or through the universal laws of physics, are not actual new creations, but merely a modification of matter. Joining together and separating are the only elements which the human mind always finds on analysing the concept of reproduction and it is just the same with the reproduction of value" ("Commodities"). It is this transformation of matter into different forms that conceals its essential relations.

REFERENCES

Adler-Kassner, Linda, and Elizabeth Wardle, eds. 2015. *Naming What We Know: Threshold Concepts of Writing Studies*. Logan: Utah State University Press.

Bachelard, Guy. 1938. *Formation of the Scientific Mind*. Manchester: Clinamen.

Beaufort, Anne. 2007. *College Writing and Beyond: A New Framework for University Writing Instruction*. Logan: Utah State University Press.

Bird, Barbara. 2013. "A Basic Writing Course Design to Promote Writer Identity: Three Analyses of Student Papers." *Journal of Basic Writing* 32 (1): 62–96.

Brandt, Deborah. 1998. "Sponsors of Literacy." *College Composition and Communication* 49 (2): 165–85.

Cousin, Glynis. 2006. "Threshold Concepts, Troublesome Knowledge and Emotional Capital: An Exploration into Learning about Others." In *Overcoming Barriers to Student Understanding: Threshold Concepts and Troublesome Knowledge*, edited by Jan H. F. Meyer and Ray Land, 134–37. London: Routledge.

Ellsworth, Elizabeth. 1989. "Why Doesn't This Feel Empowering? Working Through the Repressive Myths of Critical Pedagogy." *Harvard Educational Review* 59 (3): 297–324.

Freire, Paulo, and Antonio Faundez. 1989. *Learning to Question: A Pedagogy of Liberation*. New York: Continuum.

Gee, James Paul. 1987. "What Is Literacy?" *Teaching and Learning: The Journal of Natural Inquiry* 2 (1): 3–11.

Jordan, June. 1988. "Nobody Mean More to Me Than You And the Future Life of Willie Jordan." *Harvard Educational Review* 58 (3): 363–74.

Land, Ray, Julie Rattray, and Peter Vivian. 2014. "Learning in the Liminal Space: A Semiotic Approach to Threshold Concepts." *Higher Education* 67: 199–217.
Marx, Karl. 1894. "Supplementary Remarks." Vol. 3, Part 2 of *Capital*. Marx Engels Archive, Marxists Internet Archive. https://www.marxists.org/archive/marx/works/1894-c3/ch12.htm.
Marx, Karl. 1867a. "Commodities." Vol. 1, Part 1 of *Capital*. Marx Engels Archive, Marxists Internet Archive. https://www.marxists.org/archive/marx/works/1867-c1/ch01.htm #13b.
Marx, Karl. 1867b. "The Transformation of the Value (and Respective Price) of Labour-Power into Wages." Vol. 1, Part 1 of *Capital*. Marx Engels Archive, Marxists Internet Archive. https://www.marxists.org/archive/marx/works/1867-c1/ch19.htm.
Meyer, Jan, and Ray Land. 2003. "Threshold Concepts and Troublesome Knowledge: Linkages to Ways of Thinking and Practising." Enhancing Teacher-Learning Environments in Undergraduate Courses Project Occasional Report 4, University of Edinburgh, May. http://www.etl.tla.ed.ac.uk/docs/ETLreport4.pdf.
Meyer, Jan H. F., and Ray Land. 2006. *Overcoming Barriers to Student Understanding: Threshold Concepts and Troublesome Knowledge*. London: Routledge.
Miles, Libby, Michael Pennell, Kim Hensley Owens, Jeremiah Dyehouse, Helen O'Grady, Nedra Reynolds, Robert Schwegler, and Linda Shamoon. 2008. "Commenting on Douglas Downs and Elizabeth Wardle's 'Teaching about Writing, Righting Misconceptions.'" *College Composition and Communication* 59 (3): 503–11.
Mutnick, Deborah. 2018. "Pathways to Freedom: From the Archives to the Street." *College Composition and Communication* 69 (3): 374–401.
Perkins, David. 1999. "The Many Faces of Constructivism." *Educational Leadership* 57 (3): 6–11.
Perkins, David. 2006. "Constructivism and Troublesome Knowledge." In *Overcoming Barriers to Student Understanding: Threshold Concepts and Troublesome Knowledge*, edited by Jan H. F. Meyer and Ray Land, 33–47. London: Routledge.
Perkins, David. 2009. "Tomorrow's Learning: The Place of Information, Knowledge and Wisdom." Wenner-Gren International Series 85, *From Information to Knowledge; from Knowledge to Wisdom*: 5–17. http://www.portlandpresspublishing.com/content/wenner-gren-international-series-volume-85.
Robertson, Liane, Kara Taczak, and Kathleen Blake Yancey. 2012. "Notes toward A Theory of Prior Knowledge and Its Role in College Composers' Transfer of Knowledge and Practice." *Composition Forum* 26. https://compositionforum.com/issue/26/prior-knowledge-transfer.php.
Villacañas de Castro, Luis S. 2015. "A Critique of Vygotsky's Misapprehension of Marx's 'Phenomenal Forms.'" *Science & Society* 79 (1): 90–113.
Villacañas de Castro, Luis S. 2016. *Critical Pedagogy and Marx, Vygotsky, and Freire: Phenomenal Forms and Educational Research*. New York: Palgrave Macmillan.
Wardle, Elizabeth, and Doug Downs. 2007. "Teaching about Writing, Righting Misconceptions." *College Composition and Communication* 58 (4): 552–84.
Yancey, Kathleen Blake, Liane Robertson, and Kara Taczak. 2014. *Writing across Contexts: Transfer, Composition, and Sites of Writing*. Logan: Utah State University Press.

13
GRAPPLING WITH THRESHOLD CONCEPTS OVER TIME
A Perspective from Tutor Education

Rebecca Nowacek, Aishah Mahmood, Katherine Stein, Madylan Yarc, Saul Lopez, and Matt Thul

At their core, threshold concepts help illuminate the complicated phenomenon of expertise. When described, threshold concepts also provide a powerful vocabulary for conceptualizing the transformative nature of expertise. For this reason, our university writing center has used the language of threshold concepts in general—and the threshold concepts of writing identified in *Naming What We Know* (*NWWK*) (Adler-Kassner and Wardle 2015) in particular—as the anchor for educating peer writing tutors over the past four years.

Undergraduate students who become peer writing tutors begin by taking a course foregrounding threshold concepts of writing, then work as tutors for at least two and sometimes six additional semesters. While these undergrad tutors may not be "typical" students—they self-select to apply to become tutors and after being selected have unusually robust engagement with writing across disciplines—*they are still students*. Thus the experiences of these student-tutors offer a powerful insight into how students' understandings of threshold concepts evolve over time. In this chapter we (the faculty director of our writing center and five undergraduate tutors) draw on data gathered from multiple cohorts of tutors to better understand both *what* and *how* student-tutors learn about threshold concepts of writing.

LEARNING THRESHOLD CONCEPTS

Research with an extended focus on how students learn threshold concepts is relatively underdeveloped. A considerable body of scholarship seeks to identify threshold concepts in various disciplines, including geography (Fouburg 2013), history (Díaz et al. 2008), and business (Bolinger and Brown 2015). Also common are proposals for how to incorporate threshold concepts into courses (e.g., Meyer et al. 2015; Vidal, Smith, and Spetic 2015). Although there are fewer examinations of how individuals learn (or don't learn) threshold concepts, the studies that do generally adopt one of two foci.

First, some studies track the quality of students' understandings of threshold concepts over a single semester. Such scholarship often hearkens back to the various forms of troublesome knowledge identified by Jan Meyer and Ray Land (2006). Particularly relevant are their descriptions of ritual knowledge (which has a "routine and rather meaningless character" [9]) and conceptually difficult knowledge (in which intuitive beliefs often result in misunderstandings [9]). Typically, researchers conducting such studies code students' responses using categories such as preliminal, liminal, and postliminal (Vidal, Smith, and Spetic 2015), then track their changes or stagnation over time. Research of this sort often has pedagogical implications: Martin Shanahan and Jan Meyer (2006), for instance, argue that if initial exposure to a threshold concept is oversimplified, students may acquire it as ritual rather than transformative knowledge (100) and Natalia Vidal, Renae Smith, and Wellington Spetic (2015) speculate on why certain demographics of students seemed to achieve postliminal status more frequently. However, these studies have done little to establish the precise mechanisms through which students' knowledge of threshold concepts becomes postliminal or self-expressed.

A second set of studies highlights the influence of experiences on students' understandings of threshold concepts. Erin Fouberg (2013), for instance, argues for the importance of students "personalizing" knowledge. Nicola Reimann and Ian Jackson (2006) argue students' "relevant personal experience[s]" (125) significantly influence engagement with class prompts and perhaps thus with concepts themselves. Multiple scholars have argued that students' personal experiences mediate evolving understandings of threshold concepts (Ashworth 2016; Vidal, Smith, and Spetic 2015; Cousin 2006). And Alexander Bolinger and Kory Brown (2015) argue that students' personal experiences can "motivat[e] [them] to more carefully process and scrutinize the information" (458), which allows students to develop "more thoughtful, complex representations" (454) of threshold concepts. These studies, however, are rarely able to sketch out specific pathways through which experience shapes students' evolving understandings of threshold concepts.

One important exception is the work of Max Scheja and Kerstin Pettersson. In a series of studies on the development of threshold concepts in mathematics, they argue that how students *contextualize* concepts is central to how their understandings of those concepts develop over time. In a case study of how one student's understanding of the mathematical threshold concept of *function* evolves, Pettersson (2012) articulates developmental stages, moving from connections to everyday life, to a more abstract conceptualization that contradicts *and* exists concurrently with the initial conceptualization, and eventually into a "new and unified understanding" (6). More generally, their work explores how students' understandings of threshold concepts evolve over time, sometimes in unpredictable or self-contradictory ways.

Eager to better understand this process of contextualization and track how students' understandings of threshold concepts develop over time, we began with three research questions: (1) How do student-tutors articulate their understanding of threshold concepts of writing, long after their initial exposure? (2) How do their understandings of threshold concepts change over time? and (3) How do tutors' experiences (in the initial class, in subsequent writing center work, and in their other classes) help them understand the threshold concepts of writing? Unlike studies that focus on a single class, our study follows student-tutors over time and across contexts. By tracking how students grapple with threshold concepts in a context where the concepts may be directly applicable, we offer an important complement to the existing classroom-focused research.

CONTEXT AND RELEVANT BACKGROUND INFORMATION

More than forty undergraduate tutors work in Marquette University's Ott Memorial Writing Center. After students are hired, they take a semester-long class organized into five units, each focused on one of the five threshold concepts of writing identified in *NWWK*.

This study was conducted during the fall 2017 semester; thirty of our forty undergraduate tutors elected to participate. Participants include fifteen tutors were in their first semester of tutoring, eight tutors with three semesters' experience, two tutors with four semesters' experience, and one tutor with six semesters of experience. We drew on three types of data: reflections composed over a series of staff meetings going back several years, archived discussion posts posted during the required class via our campus learning-management system (LMS), and discourse-based interviews.

In our central set of reflections, student-tutors were prompted: "What threshold concepts of writing (if any) have stayed with you over time? Please draw a picture and describe in words your understanding of/

relation to those threshold concepts." We coded reflections by reading through them, then generating first-pass codes (Saldaña 2015). Many reflections were easy to group because they used the same language, often taken directly from course readings (e.g., "writing enacts and creates identities and ideologies"). In other cases, we generated categories to encompass several different reflections that appeared to reference a similar concept (e.g., we used *peerness* to describe nondirective tutoring and the peer-on-peer tutoring). In all cases, the entire research team talked to consensus on both the categories and the placement of individual reflections.

During discourse-based interviews, we asked student-tutors about the list of threshold concepts generated through their staff-meeting reflection, as well as other documents. After compiling the threshold concepts student-tutors named in their reflections (see table 13.1), we asked interviewees to place the different threshold concepts into categories: (1) ideas that were never troublesome and didn't require a transformation in their way of thinking, (2) ideas that were troublesome but eventually transformative, (3) ideas that were so troublesome they never felt transformed, and (4) threshold concepts the interviewee thought should not be considered a threshold concept. We also asked interviewees to elaborate on their own reflections and LMS posts. We have drawn on all three sources—reflections, LMS posts, and interviews—to develop our analyses.

WHICH THRESHOLD CONCEPTS DO TUTORS REMEMBER—AND WHY?

To gauge which threshold concepts tutors remembered several months or years after their initial exposure, we drew on a piece of reflective writing completed during a staff meeting held during the first week of classes. The results of our analyses are presented in table 13.1. Two trends in this table are linked to ideas we develop later in this chapter.

First, four of the five threshold concepts of writing articulated in *NWWK* were identified by at least one student-tutor; however, no one alluded to the fifth threshold concept: *writing is (also always) a cognitive activity*. This absence gave us a window into understanding the particular ways students might experience threshold concepts as conceptually difficult.

Second, most student-tutors named only one or two threshold concepts: approximately half the respondents (n=13) named one threshold concept and approximately one-third (n=8) named two. Only two

Table 13.1. Threshold concepts named by our tutors

Threshold concepts named (n=25 tutors)	# times named
THRESHOLD CONCEPTS OF WRITING	
Writing enacts and creates identities and ideologies*	9
Genre *(writing speaks to situations through recognizable forms)**	6
Revision is important/good	3
Writing is a social and rhetorical activity*	2
Writing isn't linear	2
Everyone's writing process differs and they're always subject to change.	2
All writers have more to learn*	1
Boundary crossers/guarders	1
No writing is perfect	1
No writing is in a vacuum. All writing is a response	1
Writing is (also always) a cognitive activity*	0
THRESHOLD CONCEPTS OF TUTORING	
Peerness	3
Cognitive scaffolding	3
Motivational scaffolding	2
We can't entirely understand someone else's experiences	2
Transfer	1
Scaffolding	1
THRESHOLD CONCEPTS ARE A THRESHOLD CONCEPT	5

* *One of the five central threshold concepts identified in* Naming What We Know.

tutors named three threshold concepts in their reflection, while one tutor named six and another seven. The trend to name only one or two concepts may be due to the time constraints of the prompt. However, because some student-tutors did name six or seven concepts, we suspect most were simply unable to articulate more than one or two concepts. This trend may suggest students have forgotten many of the threshold concepts—but some students, as we argue later, may also have internalized the threshold concepts to such an extent that they could no longer readily articulate them. Concepts named by tutors as "threshold" are identified in table 13.1.

The threshold concepts listed in table 13.1 emerged from in vivo coding; they do not correspond neatly with the concepts in *NWWK*, and some readers might object that they are not threshold concepts as Meyer and Land (2006) define them but instead core concepts or simply things students remembered learning. However, our analyses did not seek to establish what the threshold concepts of writing "truly" are; we merely sought to determine how student-tutors articulate their understanding of threshold concepts of writing several months or years after their initial exposure. We were also not trying to characterize expert views of writing; instead, we aimed to surface how student-tutors, while working to cultivate expertise, articulate threshold concepts over time.

WRESTLING WITH THRESHOLD CONCEPTS: CONTEXTUALIZATION AND INTERNALIZATION

Our analyses of the written reflections document how even students in the same classroom recall the threshold concepts discussed in that class very differently. We argue that one cause of this variation is the types of knowledge students build around those threshold concepts, types of knowledge strongly influenced by experiences prior and subsequent to initial exposure to the threshold concept. We argue that the student-tutors we observed passed through as many as three stages of grappling with threshold concepts over time: initial exposure, recontextualization, and (in some cases) internalization.

The bottle-shaped image in figure 13.1 offers a visual representation that highlights several important dimensions of that process. We have come to see the bottle as a metaphor for students' passage into the more rarified space of expertise, a space in which—perhaps as in a wine bottle—various elements and experiences can be transformed through interaction and over the passage of time. The entailments of the bottle metaphor are far from perfect (we recognize moving *into* a bottle could seem more constraining than illuminating and think here of work in Decoding the Disciplines by Díaz et al. 2008), but we hope this visual representation nevertheless helps readers synthesize several claims we explore through the remainder of the chapter.

How People Take Up Threshold Concepts During Their Initial Exposure

Each of the student-tutors included in this study first encountered the threshold concepts of writing—and indeed the very idea of threshold concepts—in the tutor-education course; thus, for this group of students, we can very clearly identify a moment of initial exposure to the threshold concepts. On the left-hand side of our diagram, we have positioned Initial Exposure to a threshold concept within the neck of

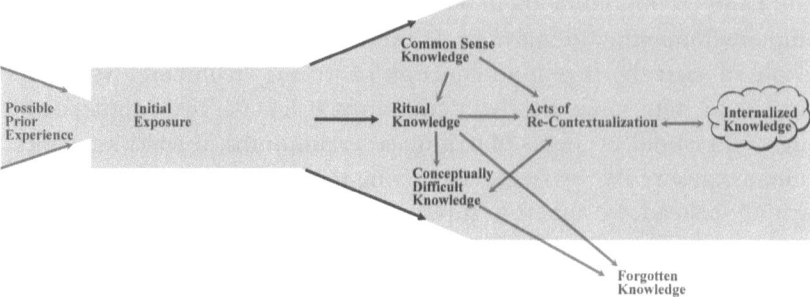

Figure 13.1. Three stages of grappling with threshold concepts over time

the bottle, suggesting the ways threshold concepts can be seen as a gateway into emergent expert understandings of a phenomenon. We place Possible Prior Experiences in a funnel position to indicate the ways prior experiences influence what students bring to that initial exposure. As the bottle widens away from Initial Exposure, we identify three types of knowledge—Common Sense, Ritual, and Conceptually Difficult—which we define and illustrate below. These three types of knowledge branch off with solid lines because our research suggests students *must* process their initial exposure to the threshold concept in one of these three ways. (Dotted lines, which we discuss in the next section, represent *possible* paths.)

Common-Sense Knowledge

When asked to define threshold concepts, student-tutors inevitably described them as "difficult to understand," "an a-ha moment," something that "sticks with you and shifts how you think about an idea." Yet after initial exposure to the language of threshold concepts of writing, student-tutors did not experience *all* of them as troublesome or transformative. Some concepts identified in *NWWK* did not invite such a shift because they already seemed (based on student-tutors' previous experiences before the course began) obvious. Glynis Cousin (2006) found a similar trend, noting that the degree to which a concept is "counterintuitive and alien . . . may be related to the learner's subject position" (137). Table 13.1, then, perhaps reflects inevitable variation in which threshold concepts required more engagement and therefore remained memorable over time.

Within our interviews, the three threshold concepts student-tutors most often described as common sense constellated around processes of writing and revising: "revision is important/good," "everyone's writing process is different and they're always subject to change," and "all writers have more to learn." Students described their initial encounters with these threshold concepts:

- I feel like that [concept] is pretty self-explanatory. I don't think anyone would ever argue that it's not. So it seems to me that it's pretty much something that everyone always understands. (Brandon)
- I think I came in knowing these. And maybe the class when we talked about these things was me confirming what I'd already experienced. (Donna)

In some cases, student-tutors were so accustomed to this way of thinking that, like Brandon, they saw the threshold concept as "self-explanatory" and struggled to imagine anyone wouldn't look at writing this way. In many other cases, though, students recognized their perspective was strongly shaped by experiences previous to the course—most often in high-school classes.

Conceptually Difficult Knowledge

While student-tutors may have found some of the threshold concepts obvious, they experienced many others as troublesome but (in some cases) eventually transformative. They described such concepts as "weird," "abstract," and "hard." In Meyer and Land's (2006) terms, they experienced these threshold concepts as "conceptually difficult."

In some cases, student-tutors offered a narrative of struggle and triumph. Kelly, for instance, described peerness as a concept that didn't click immediately: "I think that took time and practice to understand. So in that way it was troublesome. In my shadowing, watching [my mentor] work, it just took time. So it wasn't necessarily troublesome, but I needed to really understand how that worked and it wasn't just a one time—oh I get it now. It was a process of learning it over time." In other cases, the struggle with conceptually difficult knowledge remained unresolved. Shirley spoke repeatedly of her uncertainty about what "scaffolding" meant. She had read about it, she even asked her dad (a teacher) to explain it, but still, she noted, "I just always struggle with it."

One concept that particularly illuminates the experience of conceptual difficulty is *writing is (also always) a cognitive activity*. This was the only one of the five main threshold concepts articulated in *NWWK* that was not named in any of the twenty-five student-tutor reflections. We asked students why this might be. Some tutors described this threshold concept as "obvious," a common-sense concept that didn't leap to mind;

another student confessed she'd simply forgotten about this threshold concept. But others had experienced the threshold concept quite differently, attributing its absence not to common sense or forgetfulness but to the concept's abstract and puzzling nature.

Brandon, for instance, suggested it was at a "higher level" and harder to recall than concrete strategies like scaffolding; Kelly noted that "thinking about your thinking, it's just kind of meta and not applicable. It's more abstract" and therefore less memorable than concepts she felt herself putting into practice regularly. Two other student-tutors described ways this concept was in tension with other understandings of writing. For Phillip, "The connotation of cognitive kind of seems like it's independent and alone, which kind of completely opposes the idea of social writing." Michelle expressed a similar cognitive dissonance, but for different reasons: "Hearing writing is *always* cognitive takes away a lot of the emotional aspects of writing. I think one of my big objections is that I journal a lot and I don't think that's cognitive, I think that's me vomiting on the page. . . . When I hear the word cognitive that sounds very official and I think that supersedes the emotional, when maybe that's the reason you write." In some cases, then, student-tutors were less likely to recall threshold concepts they found conceptually difficult—either because they were more abstract or because they contradicted their other (perhaps "common-sense") beliefs about writing.

Ritual Knowledge

Finally, some student-tutors' initial exposure to a threshold concept resulted in what Meyer and Land (2006) describe as ritual knowledge, knowledge with a "routine and rather meaningless character" (9). Ritual understandings are often simply parroted; students may be able to reiterate the concept but lack any deep understanding of the concept or its implications. In many cases, student-tutors developed ritual understandings when they had little direct experience to either perceive the threshold concept as common sense or grapple with it as conceptually difficult. And in some cases, ritual knowledge persisted in a complicated relationship with conceptually difficult knowledge—as suggested by reactions to the threshold concept *writing enacts and creates identities and ideologies.*

While *identities and ideologies* was the threshold concept most frequently named by our student-tutors (n=9), there are several possible reasons for that frequency, all linked to how the concept was incorporated into the required course. First, it could be this is the concept students most often truly came to understand and remember; three weeks

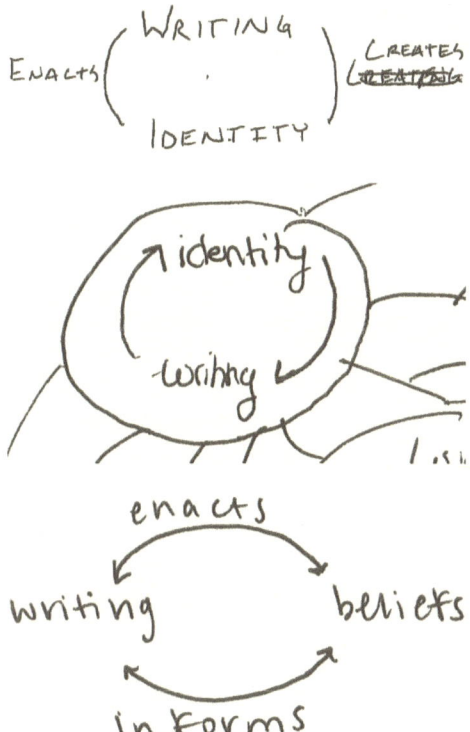

Figure 13.2. Illustrations from Scott (top), Heather (middle), and Jennifer (bottom)

of the semester—and ten assigned readings—were dedicated to helping students wrestle with this threshold concept. Consequently, that unit may have felt more focused, and student-tutors may have learned about identities and ideologies more deeply.

Another explanation, however, connects to the idea of ritual knowledge. Like Reimann and Jackson (2006), we believe classroom discourse might play a significant role in how students grapple with threshold concepts. Specifically, during the spring 2017 semester, in order to help student-tutors see the common thread running through readings that might have otherwise seemed quite disparate, Rebecca drew a picture on the board nearly every day of the unit on identities and ideologies. This picture—which may exemplify Kathleen Blake Yancey's point in this collection about the frequency of drawing in everyday writing—reappeared, in nearly identical formats, in approximately half the reflections that named identities and ideologies. (See Figure 13.2 for three examples.)

For many, the diagram seemed to operate as a visual remnant that allowed them to remember the concept even if they didn't fully understand it. Eric articulated a ritual understanding when he said, "I get it, but it'd be tough for me to recognize outside of Rebecca telling me what it is over and over again." Eric recognized the concept but admitted it was only through repetition that he "understood" it. The constant repetition and illustration of this threshold concept made it the most-often remembered—even if tutors didn't fully understand it. This hypothesis is supported by the fact that student-tutors from earlier cohorts who didn't experience the constant repetition of that image in class never drew such a picture; indeed, in many cases, students from earlier cohorts admitted to having forgotten this threshold concept.

Revising and Recontextualizing Initial Understandings of Threshold Concepts
The center of the bottle diagram highlights the ongoing importance of experience for deepening understandings of threshold concepts. The particular demographic of our research participants—undergraduate students who study threshold concepts of writing, then spend years talking about writing as part of their work as student-tutors—offers us certainty that these students have ongoing experiences with writing. These experiences might affirm or challenge student-tutors' initial understandings of those threshold concepts. Experience, therefore, is the unlabeled liquid sloshing around in the bottle. Our figure represents three important insights about the role of experience in how students grapple with threshold concepts over time.

First, relationships among the three types of initial understandings of threshold concepts are extremely dynamic. A series of dotted arrows points between these types of knowledge and what we have labeled Acts of Recontextualization. Our interviews indicate that student-tutors' initial understandings of threshold concepts can ferment over time, developing along a number of identifiable routes. Whereas the three solid lines splaying out from Initial Exposure indicate an individual will certainly take one of those three paths, the dotted lines represent possible (not inevitable) change. For instance, threshold concepts initially perceived as mere ritual knowledge could, through experience, be reconsidered and become conceptually difficult knowledge. In other cases, threshold concepts students initially perceive as common sense might conceivably devolve into ritual knowledge (although we did not document any such cases in our interviews).

Second, it's entirely possible for threshold concepts to be forgotten. We saw this repeatedly during our interviews: when sorting out the threshold concepts listed in table 13.1, students would confess to having no idea what a particular concept meant. They would say things like, "I'm gonna be honest: I don't remember what this is." Because most of our data were collected retrospectively, we are not able to establish how these students initially took up those forgotten threshold concepts, but we suspect forgotten knowledge most often begins as ritual or conceptually difficult knowledge. We have positioned Forgotten Knowledge outside the bottle within which experiences ferment and possibly change students' understandings of threshold concepts.

Finally, students who demonstrate a deep engagement with a particular threshold concept often contextualize, and then recontextualize, that concept among prior and subsequent experiences. Our understanding of this process of recontextualization—which we've included as Acts of Recontextualization in our figure—is strongly informed by the work of Pettersson and Scheja (2008), who argue that "the study of how students understand . . . concepts will essentially become a study of how students pull together the information provided in a particular learning environment and create personal contexts for understanding that information" (771). Their definition of contextualization also resonates with Rebecca Nowacek's 2011 model of transfer as an act of recontextualization, a process through which individuals take knowledge or skills or even identities associated with one context and repurpose them for use in another context. Our interviews illuminated how powerful that process of recontextualization could be for deep engagement with threshold concepts over time.

Brandon, for instance, identified the concept of boundary crossers versus boundary guarders as his "favorite" threshold concept, describing it as "a big deal for me." Indeed, his reflection consisted solely of a picture of this threshold concept (see fig. 13.3) and he said, in an interview, that this threshold concept was the only one he remembered. Brandon's initial exposure to this threshold concept was profoundly influenced by his identity as an engineer who loves writing: "It stuck with me because I felt it was very applicable to my experience." Boundary crossing became "a running joke" with friends and was something he elected to write about in LMS posts.

Beyond the initial exposure, Brandon continued to draw on experiences to contextualize and recontextualize his understanding of this threshold concept. He described this concept as one he was continuing to "test" in subsequent semesters, as he shifted between his work on high-stakes engineering projects and other writing in his humanities classes. Without the concept of boundary crossers/boundary guarders, Brandon argued, he still would have understood that writing for

Figure 13.3. Brandon's response to the reflective prompt What threshold concepts have stayed with you over time?

engineering projects and writing in his literature class were different kinds of writing, but, he told us, now "I am way more aware of how I need to alter my approach from the beginning based on the different genres." Brandon's extended engagement with the concept of boundary crossers/boundary guarders illustrates how students' previous and subsequent experiences can deepen their understandings of threshold concepts through processes of recontexualization.

Other students didn't have the same positive response to their initial exposure but described a process of revisiting and recontextualizing a threshold concept later. Rose, for instance, explained that coaching tennis over the summer helped her understand a concept: "[Coaching was] definitely where I recognized and would classify threshold concepts as a threshold concept the most. Because I was able to conceptualize it with this language. It was honestly running through my head verbatim: Oh, this is their threshold concept"—especially when helping baseball players learning tennis distinguish between forehand and backhand. Similarly, Angela explained that she "started to get really interested" in the idea that "writing is (also always) a cognitive activity" several semesters after her initial exposure to that threshold concept during a capstone course on intellectual property.

In short, by including Acts of Recontextualization in our figure, we hope to highlight that it's not merely the passage of time and subsequent experiences but an active process of recontextualizing, of, as Scheja and Pettersson (2010) argue, "creating personal contexts" (771), that helps student-tutors grapple with and deepen their understanding of threshold concepts over time.

Internalized Knowledge and Emerging Expertise

Finally, our figure highlights the particular value we place on internalized knowledge. Although Meyer and Land (2006) don't taxonomize this particular type of knowledge, we see it as roughly equivalent to what Shanahan and Meyer (2006) describe as "accurate and self-expressed" knowledge of threshold concepts (113). Internalized knowledge is a type of expert knowledge, seeing through and with the threshold concepts. But we also believe this internalized knowledge remains dynamic and is not always fully self-aware and articulable; it is not unlike the "conditionalized" knowledge cognitive psychologists describe as increasingly routinized, even automatic (Bransford, Brown, and Cocking 2000, 43–44). Indeed, while the ability to recite the threshold concept as presented in class was often typical of new tutors grappling with threshold concepts as conceptually difficult or tucking them away as ritual knowledge, more experienced tutors often seemed to lose their ability to name the threshold concept as a threshold concept. It simply became something they knew and that tacitly informed their tutoring practice.

Whereas student-tutors in their first semester of tutoring tended to identify class discussions and readings as most helpful to their understandings of threshold concepts, student-tutors who'd worked for three or more semesters identified subsequent experiences (in the writing center and elsewhere) as most crucial to their understandings. For instance, both Angela and Melissa emphasized how working as a tutor had deepened their understandings of "writing as a social and rhetorical act." And their understandings of the concept of peerness had been profoundly changed by their experiences working in the writing center. Melissa explained, "When I was originally going to sign up for this class . . . [I thought it would be] closer to editing than the conversational stuff that we do now. And so the idea of being just readers not experts is something that I've had to learn." Her work with writers in STEM disciplines was particularly transformative. Angela, however, drew on her writing center experiences to resist this articulation of peerness: "I *don't* just read, I *don't* just say 'that's great.' No, I have to be aware of what this writer needs. I'm not just reading, I'm part of a collaboration." Angela expanded with several stories of successful collaboration that hinged on expert knowledge she had cultivated over time, concluding that a focus on peerness "takes away our agency" and diminishes the importance of her accrued tutoring expertise.

Angela was also particularly vocal about the importance of tutoring experiences for truly understanding threshold concepts: "Yeah I think you can write about [threshold concepts] all day and all night, but you have to live them." Because Angela so frequently referenced her conference experiences (at one point even apologizing for having "so many conference flashbacks"), she clearly illustrates the crucial role ongoing experiences play for helping student-tutors recontextualize and deepen their engagement with threshold concepts. Recently, R. Mark Hall, Mikael Romo, and Elizabeth Wardle (2018) offered a detailed case study of a single student and drew a similar conclusion about the power of tutoring experiences to invite "deep learning" of threshold concepts. In addition, Dana Driscoll (2016) documents how a transfer-oriented tutor-education class seemed to facilitate a wide range of future connections—both to tutoring work and to work beyond the writing center. We are especially struck by Driscoll's (2016) analysis of how one tutor describes using knowledge and skills she acquired through the course without being able to articulate the "course-specific language" (168).

As in Driscoll (2016), the experienced student-tutors in our study were not only more likely to invoke their subsequent tutoring experiences as more important than readings or class discussions for understanding threshold concepts, they also alluded to a process of internalization that made the threshold concepts they had embraced more difficult to articulate. While discussing threshold concepts generally, Angela admitted, "Some of these [concepts], I think they're threshold concepts, but that doesn't mean that I've thought about them recently." Melissa, a tutor with more than two years of experience, similarly revealed, "Before we started talking about TCs again this semester, I couldn't really recall any TCs by name or detail." But as she discussed what initially appeared to be forgotten knowledge (because she felt unable to name any threshold concepts in her written reflection), it became clear not all these threshold concepts had been forgotten. Instead, her knowledge had been internalized, playing out as part of her expertise: "I can't really recall any TCs by any name or particular detail, but I understand a lot of these, [even though] I wouldn't be able to name these as a concept. . . . That's the way I feel about English grammar. I can't explain why it is the case, but I understand it." This pattern of internalization potentially casts new light on findings like those of Linda Bergmann and Janet Zepernick (2007), whose student interviews document how students often forget or minimize an initial context for learning about writing (like FYC) and focus on subsequent contexts of repurposing. Our study of these tutors—because it tracks how student-tutors repurpose and internalize specific threshold concepts—reaffirms the importance of that initial learning working in concert with subsequent experiences.

In this way, undergraduate tutors like Melissa and Angela make visible how student-tutors who have grappled with threshold concepts over time may, as they recontextualize their initial understandings through subsequent experience, lose their ability to name what they know, even as they grow in their tacit knowledge, confidence, and expertise. By attending more carefully—in our future research and pedagogical practices—to the stages of development we have proposed in this chapter, we may better help students engage in deep and transformative learning.

REFERENCES

Adler-Kassner, Linda, and Elizabeth Wardle, eds. 2015. *Naming What We Know: Threshold Concepts of Writing Studies*. Logan: Utah State University Press.

Ashworth, Helen. 2016. "Students' Acquisition of a Threshold Concept in Childhood and Youth Studies." *Innovations in Education and Teaching International* 53 (1): 94–103.

Bergmann, Linda, and Janet Zepernick. 2007. "Disciplinarity and Transfer: Students' Perceptions of Learning to Write." *WPA: Writing Program Administration* 31 (1–2): 124–39.

Bolinger, Alexander R., and Kory D. Brown. 2015. "Entrepreneurial Failure as a Threshold Concept: The Effects of Student Experiences." *Journal of Management Education* 39 (4): 452–75.

Bransford, John D., Ann L. Brown, and Rodney R. Cocking. 2000. *How People Learn: Brain, Mind, Experience, and School*. Washington, DC: National Academy Press.

Cousin, Glynis. 2006. "Threshold Concepts, Troublesome Knowledge and Emotional Capital." In *Overcoming Barriers to Student Understanding: Threshold Concepts and Troublesome Knowledge*, edited by Jan Meyer and Ray Land, 134–47. London: Routledge.

Díaz, Arlene, Joan Middendorf, David Pace, and Leah Shopkow. 2008. "The History Learning Project: A Department 'Decodes' Its Students." *Journal of American History* 94 (4): 1211–24.

Driscoll, Dana. 2016. "Building Connections and Transferring Knowledge: The Benefits of a Peer Tutoring Course Beyond the Writing Center." *Writing Center Journal* 35 (1): 153–81.

Fouberg, Erin H. 2013. "'The World Is No Longer Flat to Me': Student Perceptions of Threshold Concepts in World Regional Geography." *Journal of Geography in Higher Education* 37 (1): 65–75.

Hall, R. Mark, Mikael Romo, and Elizabeth Wardle. 2018. "Teaching and Learning Threshold Concepts in a Writing Major: Liminality, Dispositions, and Program Design." *Composition Forum* 38. http://compositionforum.com/issue/38/threshold.php.

Meyer, Jan H. F., and Ray Land. 2006. "Threshold Concepts and Troublesome Knowledge." In *Overcoming Barriers to Student Understanding: Threshold Concepts and Troublesome Knowledge*, edited by Jan Meyer and Ray Land, 3–18. London: Routledge.

Meyer, Jan H. F., David B. Knight, David P. Callaghan, and Tom E. Baldock. 2015. "Threshold Concepts as a Focus for Metalearning Activity: Application of a Research-Developed Mechanism in Undergraduate Engineering." *Innovations in Education and Teaching International* 52 (3): 277–89.

Nowacek, Rebecca S. 2011. *Agents of Integration: Understanding Transfer as a Rhetorical Act.* Carbondale: Southern Illinois University Press.

Pettersson, Kerstin. 2012. "The Threshold Concept of a Function—A Case Study of a Student's Development of Her Understanding." *Eighth Swedish Mathematics Education Research Seminar,* Umeå, Sweden.

Pettersson, Kerstin, and Max Scheja. 2008. "Algorithmic Contexts and Learning Potentiality: A Case Study of Students' Understanding of Calculus." *International Journal of Mathematical Education in Science and Technology* 39 (6): 767–84.

Reimann, Nicola, and Ian Jackson. 2006. "Threshold Concepts in Economics: A Case Study." In *Overcoming Barriers to Student Understanding: Threshold Concepts and Troublesome Knowledge,* edited by Jan Meyer and Ray Land, 115–33. London: Routledge.

Saldaña, Johnny. 2015. *The Coding Manual for Qualitative Researchers.* Thousand Oaks, CA: SAGE.

Scheja, Max, and Kerstin Pettersson. 2010. "Transformation and Contextualisation: Conceptualising Students' Conceptual Understandings of Threshold Concepts in Calculus." *Higher Education* 59 (2): 221–41.

Shanahan, Martin Peter, and Jan Meyer. 2006. "The Troublesome Nature of a Threshold Concept in Economics." In *Overcoming Barriers to Student Understanding: Threshold Concepts and Troublesome Knowledge,* edited by Jan Meyer and Ray Land, 100–114. London: Routledge.

Vidal, Natalia, Renae Smith, and Wellington Spetic. 2015. "Designing and Teaching Business & Society Courses from a Threshold Concept Approach." *Journal of Management Education* 39 (4): 497–530.

14
"I CAN'T GO ON, I'LL GO ON"
Liminality in Undergraduate Writing

Matthew Fogarty, Páraic Kerrigan,
Sarah O'Brien, and Alison Farrell

According to Jan Meyer and Ray Land (2006), along with being troublesome, integrative, transformative, and probably irreversible, threshold concepts are characterized as liminal. Their liminal nature is summarized by Linda Adler-Kassner and Elizabeth Wardle (2016): "Threshold concepts involve what the name implies—thresholds. But the movement toward and the (hopeful) crossing of those thresholds isn't straightforward; instead, it happens in a two-steps-forward-one-step-back kind of way as learners push against troublesome knowledge" (ix). Glynis Cousin (2006) observes that the idea of liminal states aids "our understanding of the conceptual transformations students undergo" in challenging learning situations, like the grasping of threshold concepts (4). And yet, Ray Land, Julie Rattray, and Peter Vivian (2014) suggest that the liminal space "has remained relatively ill-defined, something of a 'black box' within the conceptual framework of Threshold Concepts" (201).

This chapter focuses on this liminal space. Specifically, we wanted to better understand the nature, occurrence, and impact of liminality in undergraduate writing through the lens of threshold concepts of writing, through which those concepts could in turn provide an effective theoretical and pedagogical framework for our particular context. Our setting is a relatively new writing center (established 2011) in an Irish university that has an undergraduate population of 10,050 students and a postgraduate enrollment of 1,900. Following a presentation of our distilled findings, we explore and contextualize one key action-oriented insight about undergraduates' experiences with threshold concepts of writing that emerged from the data, that of the coexistence of apparent liminality, a stage that can be paralyzing for students, and authentic liminality, a stage that is important for students grappling with threshold concepts and that is therefore productive and potentially transformative.

DOI: 10.7330/9781607329329.c014

In the next section, we review literature that has contributed to these ideas of liminality; following that review, we describe the research that led us to these definitions.

RESEARCH CONTEXT—LIMINALITY IN UNDERGRADUATE WRITING

> *This is a world that is radically unknowable: even though we may make modest gains here and there, our ignorance expands in all kinds of directions.*
>
> —Ronald Barnett

Ronald Barnett's (2012) observation is both reassuring and devastating for researchers. For us, it suggests that despite our most virtuous and rigorous efforts, all our research, thinking, and writing is infused with uncertainty, not least because of the overwhelming quantity and breadth of scholarship that makes it an impossibility to have an entirely comprehensive knowledge of any field. Against this reality, we echo the words of our colleagues in *Naming What We Know* by "stressing the contingent changing nature of knowledge" (Adler-Kassner and Wardle 2015, 4).

The growing body of work in higher education around threshold concepts includes a range of interpretations, practical applications, and reflections on how seeing one's discipline in this manner can be illuminating, specifically with regards to curriculum design and assessment (Cousin 2006; Land 2011; Meyer and Land 2006; Meyer, Land, and Baillie 2010; O'Mahony et al. 2014; Peter et al. 2014). The majority of colleagues researching liminality with reference to threshold concepts cite Victor Turner's (1969, 1979) work on rites of passage as providing foundations in this area. With regard to writing and liminality, researchers have approached this topic from various perspectives including postgraduate writing (Kiley 2009; Kiley and Wisker 2009), academic literacies (Gourlay 2009), L2 writers (Das Bender 2016), comparisons across disciplines (Peter et al. 2014), and with direct reference to writing transfer (Adler-Kassner et al. 2016). In the work on this topic one theme persists: the uncertainty associated with liminality. And though a sense of arrival and comprehension can be achieved in this liminal space, this sense is frequently counteracted by the doubt and confusion of grappling with troublesome, complex ideas. Land, Rattray, and Vivian (2014) note that these thresholds, or "conceptual gateways," often involve "a letting go of customary ways of seeing things" (200). Land (2011) continues, describing this as "a space of transformation in which the transition from an earlier understanding (or practice) to that which is required is effected" (200). Liminality in learning is described in the threshold concepts literature using a host of terms, many of which encapsulate the essence of uncertainty: *troublesome, liquid space, problematic, suspended, unsettling, oscillative, out of focus, sense of loss, nonlinear, recursive, messy, abstract, mimicry, difficult, mystery.* Generally, this language points to an academic rabbit hole that may end in anxiety of an intolerable kind and/or failure.

Threshold concept scholars also have a keen awareness of the uncomfortable nature of liminality. Patrick Sullivan (this volume), for instance, remarks that the liminal space of deep reading produces confusion, uncertainty, and chaos. Similarly, Margaret Kiley and Gina Wisker (2009) observe that in the liminal space "doctoral students are often likely to feel 'stuck', depressed, unable to continue, challenged and confused" (432). They suggest that an inability to move from this space is damaging for early career researchers: "While it is acknowledged that being in the liminal state and even being stuck . . . are probably necessary stages . . . we would argue that it is damaging for research students to remain stuck to the extent that they lose confidence and seriously question their identity as researchers" (434).

An important counterpoint, however, is also noted in the scholarship that acknowledges the potential in the liminal space and time. This idea of potential is especially important for the idea of authentic liminality we describe later in this chapter. Belinda Allen (2014), as an academic, artist, and designer, encourages us to "re-envision liminality as an authentic creative space for learners and teachers, a space for unknowing and unlearning, a disorienting and productive space" (31). Allen asserts that if the process of entering liminality "is deliberate, 'jumping' rather than 'falling' or 'being pushed', there is potential to develop confidence and self-efficacy" (33). Land, Rattray, and Vivian (2014) also remark on how the liminal space can foster creativity, a site where "students' thinking and practice would stay emergent and fresh, without becoming stylised" (2). Similarly, Beverly Hawkins and Gareth Edwards (2015) suggest when writing about liminality and leadership learning that the experience of doubt in liminality "is a central thread through the processes of *learning about* and *doing* leadership" (27). They note that the "liminal context . . . is vital because it provides a place in which students can experiment with ideologies, identities and practices that differ from those they employ teleologically in their lives outside the classroom" (34). Lesley Gourlay (2009) also sees emotional struggles as "a normal part of the academic process" (189), whereas Jason Sunder (2017) goes a step further, noting that his work around supporting this area "proceeds from the premise that it is precisely by remaining open to uncertainty, contingency, and complexity that humanities research maintains its purchase" (1).

But while the research literature on liminality seems to introduce and consider to some extent what we call *authentic liminality*, there is still a gap around explorations of the essence of liminality, a factor that especially emerged in our study. In "Liminality Close-Up," Land (2014) discusses three analyses by Peter Vivian, Guy Walker, and Caroline Baillie, John Bowden, and Jan Meyer that "[throw] helpful light on the nature of [the liminal space]" (3). All three analyses have assisted us in our efforts to detect what our data suggest about students' experience of liminality in writing. Similar to Vivian (2012), we believe in starting where students are and recognizing the uniqueness of that point for each student. Like Walker (2013), in turn influenced by Paul Salmon, Neville Stanton, Guy Walker, and Daniel Jenkins (2009) and indeed echoing Vivian (2012), we advocate for providing students with an opportunity not only "to relate concepts and ideas to everyday experience and raise students to the level of 'compatible' understanding" but to conspicuously build on what they already possess in terms of writing knowledge, skills, and processes, thus helping students navigate liminality, whether apparent or authentic (261). Indeed, Walker's and Vivian's studies resonate with Alison Farrell, Sandra Kane, Cecilia Dube, and Steve Salchak's (2017) work on writing transfer, which notes the importance of "recognizing what students are bringing to college," particularly those processes and attitudes that are useful and that, "where acknowledged and built on, could contribute to greater success for students and improved retention for institutions" (81–82). Finally, Baillie, Bowden, and Meyer's (2013) view of "continual variation in liminality as new concepts are grasped" was something we also identified with regards to liminality in undergraduate writing (241).

Research Approach

Using threshold concepts of writing as our theoretical framework, we pursued our curiosity around liminality and undergraduate writing by exploring three key questions:

1. Do students experience uncertainty in their academic writing?
2. In what aspects of writing do they experience uncertainty?
3. What are their strategies for both tolerating and navigating their way through uncertainty in academic writing?

The research setting was the Maynooth University (Ireland) writing center, which itself embodies liminality, existing as it does apart from the disciplines, devoid of the tradition of writing studies typical in the

United States, unsupported by WAC/WID programs and their associated pedagogies, and in an infrastructural no-man's land (Farrell and Tighe-Mooney 2015; O'Brien 2017; Riedner 2015). In Irish universities, generally, writing programs are a rarity, and where modules do have an identified focus on writing, they do not necessarily have an institutional designation as writing programs. Given this context, our research into liminality using threshold concepts of writing required the provision of a locally navigable channel into this world. We provided this by enquiring into uncertainty in undergraduate writing with our students. We underpin this approach with the assertion that undergraduate writing is imbued with uncertainty and that that uncertainty is *amplified* within liminal spaces. These spaces include undergraduates' own experiences, which mirror many elements of the research summarized earlier. Because of the way our writing center is situated, uncertainty may have been amplified in that physical space, as well.

Indeed, it is precisely the liminal nature of this space that allows us to decipher the epistemological and ontological challenges associated with being a writer. In other words, we see the undergraduate writing process as having an inherent unavoidable uncertainty due in no small part to its creative essence. While it has predictable elements and features (in terms of recognizable forms, knowable rules, conventions and strategies, familiar tools/technology, learnable patterns, declarable goals, etc.) at its core, the enactment involves uncertainty and/or unpredictability, not least because of the multiplicity of possible writing moves and the uniqueness of each writing act. We argue that in addition to this suffusion of uncertainty that exists across undergraduate writing, uncertainty is accentuated in the liminal space because that space is remarkably complex, unknown, and brimful of possibilities. Given our situation, threshold concepts of writing offer both a theoretical framework and a pedagogical bridge that faculty and students can use to explain and explore writing in general, particularly in instances of liminality.

Our research methodology further reinforces the "betwixt and between" nature of the enquiry. We chose action research that blends "practical and theoretical concerns" (Cohen, Manion, and Morrison 2011, 357), incorporates intentions "to change and improve" (Open University 2005, 4), and "offers a means of providing an understanding to a problematic situation" (Opie 2004, 79). This intentionality "that the research will inform and change" one's practice (Ferrance 2000, 1) is a defining characteristic of the approach also described in the literature as both collaborative and individualistic, practitioner based, cyclical, incorporating critical analysis and self-reflection, and having the potential to be emancipatory and empowering (Grundy 1987; Kincheloe 2003; McNiff 2002; Stenhouse 1975; Whitehead 1985; Zuber-Skerritt 1996).

Site and Research Participants

In order to answer our questions, we surveyed undergraduate students who had visited the writing center. An online questionnaire was employed as an efficient way to gather and process anonymous data from a potentially large number of respondents; questionnaires would also facilitate the identification and subsequent exploration of patterns or trends in the data. The research cohort, undergraduates who had visited the writing center between September 2015 and June 2017, was chosen for its representation across the disciplines and across the undergraduate-year groups. In total, 334 students were invited to participate in the research; 93 students completed the questionnaire, which was designed to gather descriptive quantitative and qualitative data using a Likert scale and open-response questions. The Likert scale data were initially analyzed within the online questionnaire tool, while the open-response questions were interrogated using thematic analysis, specifically the model described by Virginia Braun and Victoria Clarke (2006).

EXPLORING STUDENTS' EXPERIENCES OF UNCERTAINTY IN UNDERGRADUATE WRITING

While one questionnaire cannot comprehensively answer our research questions, the responses we gathered did yield useful data. The findings indicate that the vast majority of our research participants experience the uncertainty that is an intrinsic part of undergraduate writing, hint at the magnified uncertainty that occurs in instances of liminality, and are largely aware of their strategies for coping with uncertainty in writing. All these findings also point to the revised conceptions of liminality we focus on here, apparent and authentic liminality. In the remainder of this chapter, we use threshold concepts of writing as a lens with our data in order to gain theoretical and pedagogical insights specifically into the liminal space in undergraduate writing. First, we present the thematically distilled data.

Where, What, and When of Uncertainty for Undergraduate Writers

The majority of students in this research reported they experience uncertainty because they find writing in university more various and complex than the writing they did before college. They also remark that disciplinary differences contribute to this variety and complexity. Specifically, many students experience confusion when sourcing evidence, composing through the discourse of the discipline—achieving the appropriate academic tone/register, clarifying and meeting audience expectations, crafting an argument, reliably sourcing and effectively using evidence, and conforming to the conventions of the genres required, including referencing. Students' uncertainty is reinforced by a lack of understanding around how to interact with disciplinary scholarship and ideas—interrogating, discriminating, and integrating this thinking; having some sense of what "good" university writing looks like; and having an inability to articulate and/or find a place for one's voice.

The idea of disciplinary deciphering towards argumentation was a theme distilled from this data that captures key aspects of the confusion respondents reported with regard undergraduate writing. Students reported having difficulty clarifying and understanding what is expected of them in terms of academic writing processes and outputs in the university. They remarked on the challenges of "trying to fully understand what the lecturer expects from the essay" and faculty "being unclear about what they want." This uncertainty is captured in data extracts: "The most confusing thing is how different things are expected of you from different disciplines"; "Often the lecturers do not specify what kind of a piece they want from a student and hence leaves one confused"; "Different disciplines have different writing styles and expectations." The variation among disciplines is perceived to play out also within disciplines and between faculty in a manner that can be incomprehensible to students; one respondent used words and phrases such as "inconsistencies," "ambiguous," "you have to second guess," "no uniformity," and "chaotic system."

The concerns around argument related largely to using evidence, what students described as "backing up" opinions, and sourcing what writers need in the "overwhelming information available." These concerns also included the notion of voice and the challenge of how and where one's opinion can gain a foothold amongst the other voices and within the disciplines; this concern is captured in this extract from the data: "The difficulty I often have is that I read extensively and consequently have difficulty synthesizing the information and formulating a cogent argument in a timely manner. The second difficulty is finding the balance between adequately referring to relevant literature and finding my own voice. The emphasis can be different between various departments." Other related issues included using the appropriate tone, saying "exactly what I want to say," knowing "if I am going in the right direction," the need for critical engagement/thinking, and structuring.

Students' Strategies for Coping with Uncertainty in Undergraduate Writing

The diversity inherent in these students' experience of uncertainty in undergraduate writing is reflected in their strategies for coping with it. Students employ a range of strategies when it comes to coping with uncertainty; these may or may not involve other people and could be classed as inactive, reactive and proactive. Uncertainty prevents some, but not all students, from writing: some students see uncertainty as a site of opportunity; for some, uncertainty encourages writing risk taking; for others, it is a precursor to possible failure. Hence, uncertainty prompts low-risk behavior, such as choosing the "easiest" topic/assignment.

Specifically, the questionnaire data provide answers to our research questions around what students do to mitigate feelings of uncertainty. Through our thematic analysis, we delineated their responses under two main themes: seek help—expert/other, and writer resilience. Faced with uncertainty in writing, the most common action noted by students was to seek either expert help from faculty or the writing center, or to seek help from peers; students mentioned looking for assistance from other unspecified people, but this response was in the minority. According to our data, students who pursue expert help use that opportunity to talk about the writing task, to seek specific guidance, to find inspiration and encouragement, to grow in confidence, to experience success, to gain knowledge, and to get feedback. One student noted, "I spoke to my tutors in first year about the feedback from my essays and I was able to use some of the feedback into my writing. However, I didn't fully grasp the argument structure. So, I examined one particular essay with the help of my lecturer and I understood exactly where I was going wrong." Where undergraduates talk to peers about their writing, they report they bounce ideas off each other, articulate what they want to say in their writing, clarify whether they are going in the right direction, ask for advice, and seek help with proofing. Some students also mentioned seeking help online, and some contact the library.

Of greater interest to us than the somewhat predictable, albeit sound, strategy of asking for help were the other ways students addressed or ignored their uncertainty with regards to writing. This theme has been named *writer resilience*, and we informally trace the responses along a continuum of doing nothing to doing something. A small minority of students noted that they do not do anything to mitigate feelings of uncertainty; we return to this data specifically in the next section. Moving from that point towards doing something, a variety of strategies were employed by students, all of which we would categorize under the broader 'internal' heading. Students mentioned dithering and procrastinating, taking a break, staying positive / hoping for the best, journaling, planning, mind mapping, starting/making an attempt at the assignment, working hard, reading, researching, and writing. Writing itself emerged as the most often employed self-reliance strategy for respondents. In their comments students hint at how writing helps them to move through the uncertainty: "I keep writing and rewriting until I am happy with the work that I produced. And I also read a lot"; "I try focus on making important points in my writing and try create flow"; "I just keep writing and hope for the best." Some students noted a combination of techniques they use to address uncertainty as captured in this response: "Procrastination. . . . Although I do think that in this case the best course of action is to brainstorm for your assignment the day you get it and let it mull over in your mind for a few days and let it grow itself. . . . Sometimes you just have to go for it though, you need to take risks sometimes." Others noted that the uncertainty persists: "No, I am always uncertain until I get my grades"; "Often feel uncertain about writing pieces but have to submit them anyway."

APPARENT AND AUTHENTIC LIMINALITY IN UNDERGRADUATE WRITING

When we explored our findings through the lens of threshold concepts of writing, one key insight emerged: the notion of the coexistence of apparent and authentic liminality. This insight is rhizomatic in character with synergistic, complementary strands. We explore it in the following section.

While Patricia Claudette Johnson's (2010) work in "writing liminal landscapes" includes the idea of the "'apparently' real" (522), we recognized in our research an apparent liminality that coexists with an authentic liminality; we suggest that both liminality types exist for undergraduates and that they manifest themselves in two corresponding types of uncertainty. What we call *apparent liminality* is the unnecessary and potentially paralyzing uncertainty that materializes whenever students' knowledge and skills are inadequate to the task and/or students are entirely unsure of what is required, whereas authentic liminality is the necessary, productive, and potentially transformative uncertainty that exists in some writing processes. Johnson (2010) argues that an apparent reality prevails in which the viewer claims "mastery" over a place by bringing a particular ideology and/or perspective, historical, political or otherwise, to it in order not to "reflect reality but reproduce the 'apparently' real" (522). Similarly, what undergraduates bring to academic writing influences their perceptions and experiences of it, including their interpretation of its liminal quality. Given our context, with its absence of immediately identifiable theoretical and pedagogical writing frameworks, it can be very difficult for undergraduates to distinguish between apparent and authentic liminality. Using threshold concepts of writing can help both our students and faculty decipher the liminal space.

Though apparent liminality can cause confusion and frustration for undergraduates, its essence is tangible and negotiable. The disorientation of apparent liminality is akin to that one might experience in completing a complicated, many-pieced jigsaw. If, for example, one had never attempted such a task, it may appear that the jumbled pieces simply pass through some mystical space only to reappear postprocess as a perfectly coherent whole; in reality, the making involves having a clear sense of the final product and a knowledge of the processes required to reach the end goal. In writing, a process for which students lack both the knowledge and skills required, the task can seem insurmountable. However, the apparent liminality associated with the threshold concept *writing speaks to situations through recognizable forms* (Bazerman 2015, 35), in this instance the forms or genres associated with undergraduate academic writing, can be diminished for students so they know the approach to take and so they have a sense of what the finished product should look like. Our research suggests students are actively seeking information about these processes and the final outcome. What emerges from the data is that the students want clarity in terms of writing outputs. This clarity is required not least because they assume, quite rightly in some cases, that these outputs can be somewhat fixed and that the process is one through apparent liminality to a predictable end product—not unlike the picture on the jigsaw box. Hence, sharing the threshold concept *writing is a social and rhetorical activity*, which Kevin Roozen (2015) explains as "writers are engaged in the work of making meaning for particular audiences and purposes" (17), should prove more effective when our writers have a relatively clear sense of what their imagined reader is looking for. Gourlay (2009) echoes this, noting from her data that "some of the confusion and worry experienced by these students might have been avoided, and that even tentative attempts to discuss requirements might have (at least partially) illuminated the scene" (189). Equally, students want to know how to meet the audience's expectations. Pauline Ross, Shelly Burgin, Claire Aitchison, and Janice Catterall (2011) suggest students are concerned with writing processes, and they report that in their research with doctoral candidates, "Students . . . experienced the benefits of the process of writing as a way of connecting 'doing' and 'knowing'" (25).

On the other hand, considering authentic liminality emphasizes the point that writing is in every conceivable way a malleable and developmental process, which brings sharply into focus the threshold concept *all writers have more to learn* and the elaboration that "writers never cease learning to write, never completely perfect their writing, as long as they encounter new or unfamiliar life experiences that require or inspire writing" (Rose 2015, 59–61). When our students experience this type of liminality again, they feel "pressurized," "overwhelmed," "frustrated," "confused," "lacking in confidence," and "filled with doubt." These all-too-familiar experiences are not just epistemological but intensely ontological. This is the liminality associated assuredly with the threshold concept *all writers have more to learn* but also *writing enacts and creates identities and ideologies* (Scott 2015, 48). In this liminality, we are not hampered by a fixation on those facets of uncertainty for which there are black-and-white answers; rather, we experience "writing as a creative activity, inextricably linked to thought," and we understand that "we write *to* think" (Estrem 2015, 19). When we and our students can tolerate, navigate, and perhaps even relish this authentic liminality, there is the possibility for the writer to develop in conjunction with the individual writing processes and the text.

Using our data, threshold concepts, and the extant literature, we suggest that negotiating authentic liminality in undergraduate writing is (1) a process of constant change as much as it is one of irreversible transformative learning; (2) a unique process for each student—there is no universal undergraduate writing liminality; and (3) concerned as much with thinking and becoming as it is with writing. We look at each of these in turn.

In the scholarship in this area, the sense of constant change appears sometimes alongside and sometimes in opposition to the idea of transformation. Gourlay (2009) argues that the "threshold" notion "is not without its own weaknesses . . . it can be misleading. . . . There is a danger that the metaphor can lead to an oversimplified notion of a clear transition point" (189). She suggests it might be "more useful to use the notion as one means of understanding aspects of a messy and complex process of learning and transformation over time" (189). Similarly, Baillie, Bowden, and Meyer (2013) suggest the experience of "continual waves of less and more comfortable liminality" (243). And Pauline Ross, Shelly, Burgin, Clair Aitchison, and Janice Catterall (2011) point out that "transformation has to be understood as a matter of shifting subjectivity, not as deep changes to an essential selfhood. Subjectivity is best understood as always in process, and so shifts are commonplace, part of the negotiations that take place as a result of the discursive nature of subjectivity" (quoted in Land 2014). Our research and experience lead us to suggest that authentic liminality in undergraduate writing is closer to a process of constant change with occasional breakthrough moments, which may feel transformative. Within authentic liminality, the writer necessarily changes throughout.

How this change occurs is a unique process. Mira Peter, Ann Harlow, Jonathan Scott, David McKie, E. Marcia Johnson, Kirstine Moffat, and Anne McKim (2014) observe the individual nature of students negotiating liminality, commenting that students "vary in how fast they come to fully grasp these troublesome ideas" (18). Moving through the liminal space as a writer compares well with the liminality experienced by a traveler, "which is personal and deeply influenced by preconceived notions about place" (Johnson 2010, 508). For this reason, we must connect with what students bring to writing and value their existing knowledge, skills, and dispositions. James Purdy and Joyce Walker (2013) make an echoing claim in their consideration of liminal space and research identity when they contend that "students' ability to continue the process . . . of building adaptive, flexible researcher identities can be significantly damaged if our instructions, methods and tools ignore, disregard, or even suppress the knowledge on which their existing identities are based" (10). This thinking in turn prompts us to return again to the area of writing transfer around which there has been much research.

Undergraduate students, we suggest, recognize the need for change and how personal this experience is when they comment on finding space for their voices in the undergraduate writing they do. The comments noted here capture the struggle associated with this process: "I continue to struggle in composing an argument that is not personally opinionated. Drawing arguments for and against from resourced material is frustrating; it is merely constructing ideas that have already been said/written. One either agrees with them or not thereby one is giving a hidden personal opinion"; "Originality is possibly the hardest part"; "While we are told we cannot give our own opinions, everything must be backed up by research, but then to be critical we have to have an opinion." The unique nature of negotiating liminality emerged from our data in the themes around argumentation and writer resilience. The individual behavior associated with these themes, including writing avoidance, low-risk adequate writing, and risk-taking writing, makes a decisive impact on the trajectory of the student's intellectual development and their success. Academic writing work is genuinely complex, and though we know and accept that "the relationship between disciplinary knowledge making and the ways writing and other communicative practices create and communicate that knowledge are at the heart of what defines particular disciplines" (Lerner 2015, 40), still it is a constant challenge for many of us to connect our voices with those of others in our field. For our students, the initiation into a discipline, through engagement in the community's discourse, routes them through a cacophony of others' voices amongst which "my voice" fraught with doubt is called on to begin to articulate a solid argument in a balanced and critical manner. The negotiating of this no-man's land is critical for our students' development as writers, not least because it represents the first step in recognizing the stage of the writing process about which our participants expressed the least awareness; namely, much like their texts, they too are works in progress. In addition, crucially, our students often do not know it is *how* they structure and arrange the key points formulating their argument that makes it *their original argument.*

The development of voice and self as a writer reinforces the unique experience of liminality and the key existential dynamic of the writing process. Mira Peter Ann Harlow, Jonathan Scott, David McKie, E. Marcia Johnson, Kirstine Moffat and Anne McKim (2014) also record "the interaction between the epistemological and ontological aspects of learning" (18) as a part of negotiating the troublesomeness in the liminal space, which involves both "a conceptual and an ontological shift" (Land 2014, 2). The variety in terms of students' strategies for negotiating liminality also foregrounds the individual nature of the experience, which in turn results in changes for students. Because of the inextricable relationship between writing and thinking, the liminality students experience in writing is as much a confusion around the questions What do I think? and Who am I? as it is confusion around writing processes and outputs. As Barnett (2012) notes in his article "Learning for an Unknown Future" and with reference to his concept of supercomplexity,

> Under . . . conditions of uncertainty, the *educational task is, in principle, not an epistemological task.* . . . Amid supercomplexity, *the educational task is primarily an ontological task.* . . . Accordingly, this learning for uncertainty is here a matter of learning to live with uncertainty. It is a form of learning

that sets out not to dissolve anxiety—for it recognizes that that is not feasible—but that sets out to provide the human wherewithal to live with anxiety. (69)

Barnett talks about "being-for-uncertainty," and this notion has much purchase in the world of threshold concepts of writing studies, not least in the concepts *writing enacts and creates identities and ideologies* and *all writers have more to learn*. As writers are people, being-for-uncertainty calls for trying and failing and trying again to understand the world and how it might be expressed; building relationships and collaborating in learning; finding and articulating one's voice; and "encouraging forward a form of human being that is not paralysed into inaction but can act purposively and judiciously" (76).

REFLECTION AND ACTION

In keeping with our research methodology, we note the following potential action associated with supporting undergraduates as they negotiate liminality in their academic writing:

- to clarify with students what we understand as the nature of liminality in undergraduate writing and to continue to listen to their interpretations of liminality
- to do all we can to ensure our writing tasks and the more basic discipline-specific writing requirements are set out as clearly as possible as a means of scaffolding the writing process for our undergraduates
- to declare to our students that in writing "there is a tension between the expression of meaning and the sharing of it" and that "every expression shared contains risk and can evoke anxiety" (Bazerman 2015, 22)
- to share empathetically with them how bamboozling and tangled academic writing can seem and how we also face the challenges writing throws up as a social and rhetorical activity.

In this manner, and through the practice of providing dialogic feedback, and feed forward, we not only advocate for their questioning but we actively engage in coenquiry with them as learning partners.

As discipline specific and writing professors, the focus of our work must continue to be primarily an engagement with others—students and writers. In this manner we see ourselves as fellow travelers; "One goes forward not because one has either knowledge or skills but because one has a self that is adequate to such an uncertain world. One's being has a will to go on" (Barnett 2012, 72).

REFERENCES

Adler-Kassner, Linda, and Elizabeth Wardle, eds. 2015. *Naming What We Know: Threshold Concepts of Writing Studies*. Logan: Utah State University Press.

Adler-Kassner, Linda, and Elizabeth Wardle, eds. 2016. *Naming What We Know: Threshold Concepts of Writing Studies*. Classroom Ed. Logan: Utah State University Press.

Adler-Kassner, Linda, Irene Clark, Liane Robertson, Kara Taczak, and Kathleen Blake Yancey. 2016. "Assembling Knowledge: The Role of Threshold Concepts in Facilitating Transfer." In *Critical Transitions: Writing and the Question of Transfer*, edited by Chris M. Anson and Jessie L. Moore, 17–47. Perspectives on Writing Series. Fort Collins, CO: WAC Clearinghouse and University Press of Colorado. https://wac.colostate.edu/docs/books/ansonmoore/chapter1.pdf.

Allen, Belinda. 2014. "Creativity as Threshold—Learning and Teaching in a Liminal Space." In *Threshold Concepts: From Personal Practice to Communities of Practice. Proceedings of the National Academy's Sixth Annual Conference and the Fourth Biennial Threshold Concepts Conference*, edited by Catherine O'Mahony, Avril Buchanan, Mary O'Rourke, and Bettie Higgs, 31–37. http://www.tara.tcd.ie/bitstream/handle/2262/73147/EPub_2012Proceedings.pdf?sequenc.

Baillie, Caroline, John A. Bowden, and Jan H. F. Meyer. 2013. "Threshold Capabilities: Threshold Concepts and Knowledge Capability Linked Through Variation Theory." *Higher Education* 65 (2): 227–46.

Barnett, Ronald. 2012. "Learning for an Unknown Future." *Higher Education Research & Development* 31 (1): 65–77.

Bazerman, Charles. 2015. "Writing Speaks to Situations through Recognizable Forms." In *Naming What We Know: Threshold Concepts of Writing Studies*, edited by Linda Adler-Kassner and Elizabeth Wardle, 35–37. Logan: Utah State University Press.

Braun, Virginia, and Victoria Clarke. 2006. "Using Thematic Analysis in Psychology." *Qualitative Research in Psychology* 3 (2): 77–101.

Cohen, Louis, Lawrence Manion, and Keith Morrison. 2011. *Research Methods in Education*. 7th ed. London: Routledge.

Cousin, Glynis. 2006. "An Introduction to Threshold Concepts." *Planet* 17 (1): 4–5.

Das Bender, Gita. 2016. "Liminal Space as a Generative Site of Struggle: Writing Transfer and L2 Students." In *Critical Transitions: Writing and the Question of Transfer*, edited by Chris M. Anson and Jessie L. Moore, 273–98. Perspectives on Writing. Fort Collins, CO: WAC Clearinghouse and University Press of Colorado. https://wac.colostate.edu/books/ansonmoore/chapter10.pdf.

Estrem, Heidi. 2015. "Writing Is a Knowledge Making Activity." In *Naming What We Know: Threshold Concepts of Writing Studies*, edited by Linda Adler-Kassner and Elizabeth Wardle, 19–20. Logan: Utah State University Press.

Farrell, Alison, Sandra Kane, Cecilia Dube and Steve Salchak. 2017. "Rethinking the Role of Higher Education in College Preparedness and Success from the Perspective of Writing Transfer." In *Understanding Writing Transfer: Implications for Transformative Student Learning in Higher Education*, edited by Jessie L. Moore and Randall Bass, 81–92. Sterling, VA: Stylus.

Farrell, Alison, and Sharon Tighe-Mooney. 2015. "Recall, Recognise, Re-invent: The Value of Facilitating Writing Transfer in the Writing Centre Setting." *Journal of Academic Writing* 5 (2): 29–42.

Ferrance, Eileen. 2000. *Action Research*. Providence, RI: Northeast and Islands Regional Educational Laboratory at Brown University. https://www.brown.edu/academics/education-alliance/sites/brown.edu.academics.education-alliance/files/publications/act_research.pdf.

Gourlay, Lesley. 2009. "Threshold Practices: Becoming a Student Through Academic Literacies." *London Review of Education* 7 (2): 181–92.

Grundy, Shirley. 1987. *Curriculum: Product or Praxis.* Lewes: Falmer.

Hawkins Beverley, and Gareth Edwards 2015. "Managing the Monsters of Doubt: Liminality, Threshold Concepts and Leadership Learning." *Management Learning* 46 (1): 24–43.

Johnson, Patricia Claudette. 2010. "Writing Liminal Landscapes: The Cosmopolitan Gaze." *Tourism Geographies* 12 (4): 505–24. DOI:10.1080/14616688.2010.516397.

Kiley, Margaret. 2009. "Identifying Threshold Concepts and Proposing Strategies to Support Doctoral Candidates." *Innovations in Education and Teaching International* 46 (3): 293–304.

Kiley, Margaret, and Gina Wisker. 2009. "Threshold Concepts in Research Education and Evidence of Threshold Crossing." *Higher Education Research and Development* 28 (4): 431–41.

Kincheloe, Joe. L. 2003. *Teachers as Researchers: Qualitative Inquiry as a Path to Empowerment.* 2nd ed. London: Routledge Falmer.

Land, Ray, Julie Rattray, and Peter Vivian. 2014. "A Closer Look at Liminality: Incorrigibles and Threshold Capital." In *Threshold Concepts: From Personal Practice to Communities of Practice. Proceedings of the National Academy's Sixth Annual Conference and the Fourth Biennial Threshold Concepts Conference,* edited by Catherine O'Mahony, Avril Buchanan, Mary O'Rourke, and Bettie Higgs, 1–12. http://www.tara.tcd.ie/bitstream/handle/2262/731 47/EPub_2012Proceedings.pdf?sequenc.

Land, Ray. 2011. "There Could Be Trouble Ahead: Using Threshold Concepts as a Tool of Analysis." *International Journal for Academic Development* 16 (2): 175–78.

Land, Ray. 2014. "Liminality Close-Up." *HECU7 (Conference), Higher Education Close Up: Research Making a Difference.* Lancaster: Lancaster University. http://www.lancaster.ac.uk/fass/events/hecu7/docs/ThinkPieces/land.pdf.

Land, Ray, Julie Rattray, and Peter Vivian. 2014. "Learning in the Liminal Space: A Semiotic Approach to Threshold Concepts." *Higher Education* 67 (2): 199–217.

Lerner, Neal. 2015. "Writing Is a Way of Enacting Disciplinarity." In *Naming What We Know: Threshold Concepts of Writing Studies,* edited by Linda Adler-Kassner and Elizabeth Wardle, 40–41. Logan: Utah State University Press.

McNiff, J. 2002 *Action Research for Professional Development: Concise Advice for New Action Researchers.* jeanmcniff.com. http://www.jeanmcniff.com/ar-booklet.asp.

Meyer, Jan. H. F., and Ray Land. 2006. "Threshold Concepts and Troublesome Knowledge: An Introduction." In *Overcoming Barriers to Student Learning,* edited by Jan H. F. Meyer and Ray Land, 3–18. London: Routledge.

Meyer, Jan H. F., and Ray Land. 2006. *Overcoming Barriers to Student Understanding: Threshold Concepts and Troublesome Knowledge.* Oxon, England: Routledge.

Meyer, Jan. H. F., Ray Land, and Caroline Baillie. eds. 2010. *Threshold Concepts and Transformational Learning.* Rotterdam: Sense.

O'Brien, Sarah, Sharon Tighe-Mooney, and Alison Farrell. 2017. *University Writing Centre Tutoring Handbook.* Maynooth, Ireland: Maynooth University.

O'Mahony, Catherine, Avril Buchanan, Mary O'Rourke, and Bettie Higgs. 2014. *Threshold Concepts: From Personal Practice to Communities of Practice. Proceedings of the National Academy's Sixth Annual Conference and the Fourth Biennial Threshold Concepts Conference.* http://www.tara.tcd.ie/bitstream/handle/2262/73147/EPub_2012Proceedings.pdf?sequenc.

Open University, Centre for Outcomes Based Education. 2005. *Action Research: A Guide for Associate Lecturers.* Milton Keynes: Open University. http://repositorio.minedu.gob.pe/bitstream/handle/123456789/3590/Action%20Research%20A%20Guide%20for%20Associate%20Lecturers.pdf?sequence=1&isAllowed=y.

Opie, Clive. 2004. *Doing Educational Research: A Guide to First Time Researchers.* London: SAGE.

Peter, Mira, Ann Harlow, Jonathan B. Scott, David McKie, E. Marcia Johnson, Kirstine Moffat, and Anne M. McKim. 2014. *Threshold Concepts: Impacts on Teaching and Learning at Tertiary Level.* Waikato, NZ: University of Waikato Teaching and Learning Research Initiative.

Purdy, James P., and Joyce R. Walker. 2013. "Liminal Spaces and Research Identity: The Construction of Introductory Composition Students as Researchers." *Pedagogy* 13 (1): 9–41. Duke University Press. Retrieved August 30, 2019, from Project MUSE database.

Riedner, Rachel, Íde O'Sullivan, and Alison Farrell. 2015. *An Introduction to Writing in the Disciplines*. AISHE Academic Practice Guides, 5. Maynooth, Ireland: AISHE.

Roozen, Kevin. 2015. "Writing Is a Social and Rhetorical Activity." In *Naming What We Know: Threshold Concepts of Writing Studies*, edited by Linda Adler-Kassner and Elizabeth Wardle, 17–19. Logan: Utah State University Press.

Rose, Shirley. 2015. "All Writers Have More to Learn." In *Naming What We Know: Threshold Concepts of Writing Studies*, edited by Linda Adler-Kassner and Elizabeth Wardle, 59–61. Logan: Utah State University Press.

Ross, Jennifer. 2011. "Unmasking Online Reflective Practices in Higher Education." PhD diss., University of Edinburgh.

Ross, Pauline M., Shelly Burgin, Claire Aitchison, and Janice Catterall. 2011. "Research Writing in the Sciences: Liminal Territory and High Emotion." *Journal of Learning Design* 4 (3): 14–27.

Salmon, Paul M., Neville A. Stanton, Guy H. Walker, and Daniel P. Jenkins. 2009. *Distributed Situation Awareness: Advances in Theory, Measurement and Application to Teamwork*. Farnham: Ashgate.

Scott, Tony. 2015. "Writing Enacts and Creates Identities and Ideologies." In *Naming What We Know: Threshold Concepts of Writing Studies*, edited by Linda Adler-Kassner and Elizabeth Wardle, 48–50. Logan: Utah State University Press.

Stenhouse, Lawrence. 1975. *An Introduction to Curriculum Research and Development*. London: Heinemann.

Sunder, Jason. 2017. "Thinking Clearly About Confusion: Threshold Concepts, Bafflement, and Meaning as 'Contestation' in the English Classroom." *Teaching Innovation Projects* 7 (1): Article 7. https://ir.lib.uwo.ca/tips/vol7/iss1/7.

Turner, Victor. 1969. *The Ritual Process: Structure and Anti-Structure*. Chicago: Aldine.

Turner, Victor. 1979. "Betwixt and Between: The Liminal Period in Rites de Passage." In *Reader in Comparative Religion*, edited by William Less and Evan Vogt, 234–43. New York: Harper and Row.

Vivian, Peter. 2012. "A New Symbol Based Writing System for use in Illustrating Basic Dynamics." PhD diss., Coventry University.

Walker, Guy. 2013. "A Cognitive Approach to Threshold Concepts." *Higher Education* 65 (2): 247–63.

Whitehead, Jack. 1985. "An Analysis of an Individual's Educational Development: The Basis for Personally Oriented Action Research." In *Educational Research: Principles, Policies and Practices*, edited by Martin Shipman, 97–108. Lewes: Falmer.

Zuber-Skerritt, Ortun. 1996. *New Directions in Action Research*. London: Falmer.

PART 3

Threshold Concepts and Writing

Beyond the Discipline

15
RETHINKING EPISTEMOLOGICALLY INCLUSIVE TEACHING

Linda Adler-Kassner

Many institutions are paying particular attention to how they can make learning more accessible to students' diverse identities, experiences, and cultures. In this chapter, I draw on data from participants in a yearlong faculty-development seminar to describe a framework for epistemologically inclusive teaching that begins to stand at the intersection of two areas of research that attempt to address questions associated with this accessibility. One area focuses on identifying threshold concepts and aligned theories intended to make epistemological commitments of disciplines explicit and create learning activities for students to identify and participate in those commitments. The other focuses on questions associated with learner identities and the ways perceptions and treatments of those identities can foster or inhibit learning.

The framework I describe here emerged from both the design of the seminar (which itself builds on my experience as a researcher and teacher) and faculty members' insightful reflections in it. Initially, the seminar explored three broad themes:

- *understanding disciplines*: studying the boundaries of disciplines and identifying threshold concepts within them
- *fostering learning*: studying learning within disciplines/about the threshold concepts of those disciplines
- *understanding learners*: studying learners, identities, and emotions as each are associated with learning

These themes reflect a point ubiquitous in the threshold concepts literature: that systematically interrogating epistemologies, then making them more explicit for students through active learning, contributes to expanded access to learning within disciplines. To illustrate each of these themes, I draw on reflective writing and interview data from participants in the first year of the faculty-development seminar. Following this examination, I also describe a fourth theme I have added to a framework for epistemologically inclusive teaching that draws on the intersections of work in epistemologies (including variation theory) and the literature on diversity and inclusion. This theme explicitly addresses the ways faculty must consider how and whether to address the ways expertise and disciplinary values reinforce dominant cultural norms. This addition came after the first year of this research and has been informed by the analysis represented in this chapter. It also reflects the discussion of limitations of threshold concepts discussed in chapter 1 of this collection. In that chapter, we note that threshold concepts represent epistemic contexts that, by definition, include some ideas and exclude others. Working with faculty to create epistemologically inclusive classrooms, then, necessitates inviting faculty to explore these boundaries. However, the extent to which this invitation is taken up depends a great deal on the faculty members and the very boundaries of the disciplines they define as their "academic homes" (Poole 2009).

The data here were gathered as part of a study examining questions associated with epistemologies and access. Consent from faculty was sought after the seminar's conclusion; those who provided consent allowed me to draw on their writing from the year and interviews conducted following the end of the seminar. Drawing on these data, I describe the nascent framework. Following this extended illustration, I outline ways I am trying to more explicitly emphasize and connect the components of this framework in year two of the seminar.

THE ONDAS SEMINAR

The seminar I describe here represents a small component of a grant my institution, the University of California Santa Barbara, received from the US Department of Education in conjunction with its status as a Hispanic-serving institution (HSI). The grant is called Opening New Doors for Accelerating Success, or ONDAS. Its primary purpose is to narrow the achievement gap between underrepresented and first-generation students and non-first generation/underrepresented students in courses across the university where that gap is most pronounced, building capacities among faculty to enhance teaching. This chapter is based on data from faculty who participated in the first year of the ONDAS faculty seminar, which took place in the 2016–17 academic year. They came from a wide range of disciplines: economics, engineering, physics, biology, chemistry, history, communication, theater and dance, French/rhetoric, mathematics, and psychological and brain sciences.

The design of the first year of the seminar reflected my own research and activities, which focus in part on working from principles of writing studies to identify, understand, and incorporate threshold concepts in teaching and learning across a range of disciplines (Adler-Kassner and Majewski 2015; Adler-Kassner, Majewski, and Kosnick 2012). As a longtime director/chair of writing programs, I have talked with many of my colleagues outside writing about writing in their courses. Their questions and experiences have led to me to the perspective that writing is never just writing. Instead, writing facilitates, and, when it is perceived as accomplished, demonstrates *epistemological participation*—immersion in disciplinary perspectives of disciplines often reflected in threshold concepts and represented in construction of genres (writing) (Adler-Kassner 2017).

Opening discussions with faculty about threshold concepts and linking these to ideas about good writing (and pedagogies to foster this kind of writing) can be a productive way to work with colleagues about their questions because it is based in developing synergies between different areas of expertise. Faculty members bring expertise in their disciplines; those of us in writing studies bring experience studying composed knowledge in specific contexts, including disciplines (e.g., Wardle, this volume).

The material I developed to recruit faculty members to the first year of the seminar reflected this perspective. Drawing on research focused on novice-expert practices and threshold concepts (and aligned literatures), I explained the seminar would be organized around three principles synthesized from the literature on threshold concepts and novice-expert practices:

1. Faculty are experts in their disciplines.
2. Part of facilitating and supporting successful learning within disciplines and helping students become successful learners (an important distinction) involves making the constituent elements of this expertise accessible to learners.
3. Meaningful change involves rethinking teaching through research and theory. Faculty development, like all learning, is a recursive process involving articulation of ideas, development of interventions or new approaches, analysis of those, and reconsideration of them.

Extending from this analysis and beginning in the second year of the seminar, I recognized the need to add a fourth principle, described in the last section of this chapter. Additionally, since this writing, colleagues and I have developed a more elaborated model of epistemologically inclusive teaching that stemmed from the study that I describe in this chapter. (see Adler-Kassner, forthcoming). The four principles described in this chapter constitute the initial framework for that later model and stand at the intersection of research threshold concepts and the literature on identities and learning.

Framework Component 1: Understanding Disciplines

The first component of the framework for epistemologically inclusive teaching I outline here involves studying boundaries between disciplines and identifying threshold concepts of disciplines, especially threshold concepts faculty consider critical for success in gateway courses. Often, these courses have also constituted barriers for students, especially underrepresented students; for this reason, they are one of the areas targeted for change by the grant that provides funding for this seminar.

Using disciplinarity and threshold concepts as a starting point for faculty thinking in our seminar makes good sense at my institution, a research-intensive university that values cross- and interdisciplinary work. While faculty may not have extensive experience studying their disciplines per se, they certainly recognize the importance of disciplinarity. Starting with questions about what Gary Poole (2009) calls "academic homes," then, seemed logical.

For the first two meetings, faculty completed readings and writing activities that asked them to name what they identified as their disciplines and to reflect on how and when they felt as if they were members *of* that discipline. These activities are analogous to those outlined by Chris Anson, Chen Chen, and Ian Anson in this collection in that they ask faculty to closely analyze knowledge-making practices. To foster this way of thinking, I asked faculty to read the piece by Poole (2009), Jan Meyer and Ray Land's (2006) "Threshold Concepts and Troublesome Knowledge: An Introduction," and readings on novice-expert practices (Bransford, Pellegrino, and Donavan 2000). Readings, writing, and seminar activities asked faculty to perceive their discipline as a subject of study; reflect on the threshold concepts they had to encounter in entering those disciplines and, ideally, the troublesome knowledge they experienced in doing so; and articulate threshold concepts of the discipline, preferably in introductory or intermediate-level undergraduate courses. Success or failure in these courses correlates with students' successes in the discipline and even in the university more broadly.

Year-one faculty readily described moments when they recognized they were part of their disciplines, often associating those moments with participation in ways of thinking. Dolly, a faculty member in communication, described when she "instinctively" understood and began to speak "the language of the scientific approach" to studying communication. Biologist Rolf wrote about moving from "being a spectator of science . . . to designing experiments that answer questions with unknown outcomes." John, an economist, wrote about "finding useful perspectives on the world that would forever change the way [he] think[s]." Kate, who came to her field of history in graduate school, underwent a deliberate process of learning what the discipline was, describing "less a story of realizing that [she] was 'part of this discipline' and more a story of [her] making [her]self a part of the discipline"—though Kate also conceded "that's 'discipline' in a nutshell."

While not always adopting the language of threshold concepts, faculty members also astutely named important lenses for students' learning in specific undergraduate courses they would focus on in the seminar. This naming took place through reading and discussion with colleagues from disciplines quite different from their own. This grouping of faculty from unlike disciplines was helpful, as colleagues could question premises, ideas, or terms that (to someone in a like discipline) seemed commonsensical, or at least intuitively familiar. As part of this discussion, I also asked faculty to consider how they began to apply theoretical principles (e.g., ideas they found useful from Bransford, Pellegrino, and Donavan [2000] about novice-expert practices) to their thinking about threshold concepts in their discipline. I especially pressed them to identify what they needed to know, and how to use that knowledge, to do what they did: where to focus attention (in the reading, on terms) about their disciplines, and so on.

This attention to prior knowledge and action, too, proved important as faculty identified threshold concepts and learning bottlenecks (Middendorf and Pace 2004), moments when students get stuck in courses that are often closely associated (if not synonymous) with putting those concepts into action. For example, economist John opened his response by reflecting on the importance of "understand[ing]," which he contrasted with "memoriz[ing]." He then identified a threshold concept, "thinking on the margin," and returned to a description of "how many students rely too much on memorization" when working with this concept. Biologist Rolf's response also emphasized students' struggles with applying the concept he named, "deduc[ing] information about genes, alleles, and gene functions from analysis of genetic crosses and patterns of inheritance." In history, Kate also mentioned the challenge of "memorization of facts" and "the determination of what did and did not happen in the past" as bottlenecks, explaining that a commitment to memorization makes it difficult for students to engage the threshold concept that "historians . . . analyze why and how certain (historical, social, political . . .) narratives speak to particular audiences in particular times and places." These excerpts typify the extent to which faculty insightfully identified and thought through the first element of the framework of epistemological inclusivity, understanding disciplinarity.

Framework Component 2: Fostering Learning

As faculty participants articulated and began to consider new or different ways to address the threshold concepts they identified as part of their work with component 1, they also began to articulate a second element of the framework of epistemologically inclusive teaching as distinct (in their experience) from the first: helping students learn to learn within the discipline. Their articulation of this element emerged in considerations of threshold concepts in their disciplines and readings and activities in our seminar that focused attention on where and how participants were explicitly incorporating those concepts in the classes they had identified as foci for their seminar work (e.g., Bransford, Pellegrino, and Donavan 2000; Middendorf and Pace 2004). While the distinction between learning in disciplines and learning to learn is familiar within the pedagogical literature (e.g., Linkon 2011; Wineburg 2010), it is less familiar to faculty members who have not had extensive experience with this literature—in this sense, then, it is something of a threshold concept for some faculty.

The proximity of understanding disciplines and their threshold concepts and learning how to learn about and through these concepts is echoed in the literature on learning around and through threshold concepts and related research. The idea of "chunking," putting together "various elements of a configuration that are related by an underlying function or strategy" (Bransford, Pelligrino, and Donavan 2000, 32), resonated with many in the seminar, who saw it as both essential for and a signifier of meaningful learning. Ian Kinchin, Lyndon Cabot, and David Hay's work (2008) refines this idea, examining relationships between "chains," the ability to "select . . . essential information from that which is available," and "nets," the ability to contextualize this information within larger patterns of knowledge and practice appropriate to the context (319–20). Other literature has concentrated more closely on developing models for pedagogical practice focused on learning how to teach students to learn disciplinary content, especially the Decoding the

Disciplines framework (Middendorf and Pace 2004). To operationalize the fostering-learning element of the framework I am describing here, faculty members presented activities, interventions, experiments, or other applications of their thinking about threshold concepts in specific courses as part of the seminar.

Roger, a faculty member in physics who had thought extensively about the distinction between *learning* and *learning to learn* illustrates the proximity of learning threshold concepts and learning to learn in his course. Writing in response to a request to describe a "successful learner," Roger begins with content, noting that this learner "never gets bogged down by the details and is always on the lookout for the overarching, predictive themes." He then focuses on learning how to learn: "She's read all of the relevant textbook chapter and seriously challenged herself with the suggested homework questions (I always assign problems, but never grade them) before coming to class." He then describes the intersection of successful learning and disciplinary content: "She's done so actively, constantly trying to tease out what the pattern is, what the underlying idea is that unifies and that will allow her to predict the outcome of future, as yet un-performed experiments. Of course, just seeing the pattern is only part of the story; she also has to be ready to think hard about why the pattern exists. What is it telling us about the physics of the problem, and how can I apply what I have learned to unimaginable new systems?"

Kate's response, too, identifies behaviors and outcomes that demonstrate this learner knew how to learn through her threshold concept of "history and narrative." The student would

> leave the class with more questions than answers. More specifically, they leave the class with the knowledge that much of the work of history is formulating good historical questions. More specifically! They will know that history is narrative, and for that reason it is always told from a particular perspective. They will know to ask whose voice is not included here? How would including that voice change the story, interpretation, or argument? They will know *not* to ask "is this source biased?" and instead to ask, "how would or have historians approach(ed) the subjective nature of this primary or secondary source?"

In his final response for the year, Drew, a faculty member in statistics, was especially eloquent in describing the importance of formulating structures for students to create "chains and nets" by focusing on concepts and learning how to learn structures through making disciplinary practices accessible. The prompt for this reflection asked faculty to review two interviews with students conducted as part of the seminar, an activity I return to shortly, and to reflect on writing and thinking from the year. Drew wrote,

> In thinking about the interviews with students and the materials we looked at this year, there were two elements that stood out to me: how much students need to learn about how to navigate a college course and the degree to which this is translated into anxiety by the students. . . . My general takeaway . . . is the importance of considering that students are both learning statistics as well as figuring out how to "college." This issue is compounded when different disciplines have different ways of speaking and working. I enjoy talking about [my discipline and its content], and I do not like to spend a lot of time talking about how the students are supposed to go about learning. My approach is overly informed by my own experience of learning . . . , and I need to make room for students who have different levels of experience and preparation.

Drew's response illustrates another important point associated with engagement with threshold concepts and epistemologically inclusive teaching for faculty. As participants' responses here (and in other literature) demonstrate, exposing faculty to this literature or elements of it can provoke thinking. But in order to begin to address how to formulate teaching strategies to address both learning within disciplines and learning how to learn within them, faculty must experience and articulate this entanglement for themselves (just as students must experience and begin to articulate the concepts we want them to learn for themselves).

Just as learning through threshold concepts entails an identity transformation for students, then, learning through the elements of the framework of epistemologically inclusive teaching I am describing here meant faculty were rethinking their identities as teachers. For some faculty in the ONDAS seminar, this process was itself troublesome. But because faculty were experienced learners—and interested enough to participate in the seminar—they embraced this troublesomeness and addressed it, in part by starting to think deeply and carefully about learning to learn in their disciplines.

Framework Component 3: Understanding Learners

The third component of the framework for epistemologically inclusive teaching concerns understanding learners themselves. Although our focus was largely on students' experiences with threshold concepts, faculty often described how struck they were by students' emotional experiences, as well. The faculty's written and spoken reflections led me to realize this portion of the seminar (and the framework I am describing) needed additional development. In this section I describe how I framed this portion of the framework in year one and what I am doing differently in year two.

To help faculty think about understanding learners, the first year of the seminar included readings and activities focused on studying learners (e.g., Gutiérrez and Rogoff 2003); readings focusing on diversity, formations of racial identity, and student identities across institutions (e.g., Johnson 2016; Mallinson and Charity Hudley 2014; Milem, Chang, and Antonio 2005; Omi and Winant 1994; Smith 2016); and readings focused on the experiences of nonmajority learners and constructions of learning (e.g., Laird 2014; Stewart 2017; Roberts 2015). This portion of the seminar also included a workshop that asked faculty to consider issues of privilege in their own experience and in that of their students. Finally, as another part of our effort to understand learners, I asked faculty to conduct an interview with a student in one of their courses, preferably a student who hadn't done very well. Faculty recorded these interviews, which were then transcribed. The transcripts of these readings then constituted the majority of the reading for the latter part of the seminars (and proved to be profoundly important for faculty).

One of the most prevalent patterns among interview and written data related to this portion of the framework was faculty members' visceral expressions of the extent to which their experiences of learning differed from students' experiences. As biologist Rolf put it, "We are not our students." Faculty were surprised at how much more readily they were able to navigate learning as undergraduates, even if they didn't consider themselves especially successful students in retrospect. For instance, they remarked that they knew how to read a textbook (Hartman), how to use readings and lectures as the basis for asking questions (Plaxco), how to talk with faculty members (Christoffersen). To be sure, there is important research in writing studies attesting to the challenges of these issues for students, especially as they are associated with writing and questions of transfer. Beyond our discipline, too, there is extensive work on the barriers faced by students to these kinds of interactions, especially for underrepresented students. But seeing and hearing about students' experiences for themselves, especially in concert with their work around threshold concepts, was profoundly important for many of the faculty in the seminar (who often taught very large classes of three hundred or more on a regular basis) because it surfaced the important role of emotion—often, anxiety—in learning.

Drew's post, quoted earlier, referenced "how much students need to learn about how to navigate a college course and the degree to which this is translated into anxiety." Anxiety also stood out to biopsychologist Vanessa. She noted that "students in the interviews expressed a great deal of fear and anxiety about doing the wrong thing and expressed fear of not understanding the lecture/topics well." Vanessa also thought about "how to approach that effectively as the leader in the classroom. . . . This issue is prevalent in all students, but . . . more prevalent and/or more salient among URM students." Reading mathematician Xu's interview with one of his students, historian Kate commented, "The student had to learn to tell themselves, 'I'm not scared.' To me, this was a very powerful moment in the interview."

While all faculty reflected on what they would do differently in their courses as a result of the thinking they had done during our seminar, some faculty specifically addressed how they would address this issue of emotion—and specifically anxiety—in the future. Economist John reflected in the many actions his department had already taken to try to address anxiety associated with the gateway course he focused on in our seminar. He described pedagogical strategies for focusing on a "confusing and challenging topic," which he said would help students develop "the proper perspective of how to think and study while in an economics course." But he also focused on how to address students' concerns about learning by restructuring office hours.

Kate, the historian, said she planned to do more "signposting," "giv[ing] [students] a road map—for conceptual and applied knowledge—that will help them use the journey to become better historical thinkers." While this signposting was certainly connected to learning in disciplines, Kate also noted that it was associated with learning. "Each of us," she said, "thought of ways that we could try to lessen the anxiety that students feel in our courses so that [they] might be more demographically and epistemologically inclusive." But Kate also wrote that she wanted to "push back on this issue a little bit. . . . We can't signpost the anxiety out of a course, or signpost a given student's process from feeling over their heads to feeling like they have a handle on both school and life. Obviously, there are interventions that we can make [to] mitigate unnecessary anxiety. . . . But perhaps we are better off thinking about signposting in this context as a matter of signposting the anxiety. . . . [that] students *should* experience a learning arc, and that this learning arc should be both universal . . . and discipline specific." This kind of signposting, Kate suggested, "might help to create an environment in which failure/struggle/discomfort is seen as a norm. . . . This would create some space for students to work back and forth between everyday registers and scholarly registers."

YEAR TWO: EPISTEMOLOGICALLY INCLUSIVE DISCIPLINARITY

These insightful responses as well as others from faculty in the ONDAS seminar led me to begin to outline a fourth principle contributing to the framework of epistemologically inclusive teaching I am describing here, an element that stands at the intersection of the literature on cultures and identities and epistemological practice: in identifying and teaching constituent elements of expertise, faculty also must consider the extent to which that expertise reinforces ideas, norms, or practices that have historically included and excluded particular individuals and groups and reconsider whether or how to address these practices as a part of their teaching.

This principle draws on extensive research focusing on the experiences of students (and especially underrepresented students) across postsecondary education. Collectively, this body of work raises two critical issues. First, it asks faculty to consider whose cultures, values, and ideologies are reified through the content and linguistic practices identified as "appropriate" within disciplines? Of importance, whose are excluded (e.g., Chamany 2006; Charity Hudley et al. 2017; Johnson 2007; Prescod-Weinstein 2017a, 2017b)? These are especially important when working with faculty members to identify threshold concepts from their disciplines. Threshold concepts, after all, represent a consensus around disciplinary epistemologies, a point colleagues and I discuss more extensively in chapter 1 of this collection and that is also addressed by Deborah Mutnick in chapter 3. As communities of practice (Wenger 1998), disciplines enact and reinforce consensus in multiple ways, from peer review of other faculty to the development of curricula and course materials for students. Inevitably, then, threshold concepts reflect a dominant cultural perspective within disciplines.

Second, this work asks faculty to reflect on cultural identities, practices, and learning contexts, especially work focusing on how campuses have or have not addressed issues associated with multiple identities and diverse populations and the effects of that work (or lack thereof) on diverse learners. Through mixed-methods research and often drawing on large data sets, this research shows the importance of attending to diverse identities in students' development as learners and thinkers. It also attests to the multiple challenges to entry, access, and success underrepresented learners can face. It also provides overwhelming evidence of the importance of a supportive social and behavioral climate (Milem, Chang, and Antonio 2005) for diverse learners, the benefits that accrue to the entire campus from this climate, and the detrimental effects that occur in the absence of such a climate. For example, when this climate is not supportive and nonwhite learners are in the minority on a campus, they experience implicit bias, stereotype threat, and microaggressions more frequently and experience lower rates of persistence and retention than their majority culture peers (e.g., Hurtado et al. 2012; Steele 2011). Researchers also have suggested that "campus facilitated practices can help cultivate interpersonal and academic validation, social identity awareness, multicultural competencies, and habits of mind for lifelong learning," including "taking more courses as part of a curriculum of inclusion, an ethnic studies course, a women's studies course, studying abroad, and participation in co-curricular diversity activities, inclusive of racial/ethnic organizations" (Hurtado and Guillermo-Wan 2013, viii). Additionally, pedagogical processes that can foster "habits of mind for lifelong learning, . . . behaviors students employ to facilitate their own learning [like] asking questions, seeking academic feedback on their work, and seeking alternate solutions to a problem" are critical for success (6). These findings provide vital insight that can inform faculty members' understandings of student experiences across institutions, within broad disciplinary areas (i.e., STEM), and are crucial for informing both policy and practice. But they also often focus on students' experiences across the entirety of an institution (i.e., across courses in different disciplines; in experiences beyond courses) or, at the smallest levels, within broad disciplinary categories (e.g., STEM courses). The study of epistemologies within disciplines, especially by faculty, can thus complement this important work and situate it within specific instructional contexts.

A FRAMEWORK FOR EPISTEMOLOGICALLY INCLUSIVE TEACHING

In this last section, I describe the ways I am attempting to more explicitly emphasize this fourth principle, expanding the framework to build on the intersections among identities, diversity, and epistemologies. This more explicit focus has made clear another important consideration I am attempting to raise in the second year of the ONDAS seminar: the extent to which epistemologies (in this case, disciplinary epistemologies) and threshold concepts are permeable, such that the process of learning allows for students' cultural knowledge practices and identities.

At their core, *all* disciplines are "based on an organized body of facts and theories which are treated as true, . . . characteristic subject matter, [and] definite methods of control" (Winchester quoted in Kreber 2009, 23). Threshold concepts theory *is* so valuable in part because it provides a vocabulary and a heuristic for faculty to investigate the foundations underpinning their very constitution. But this constitution may, through its enactment, include and/or exclude particular values and ideologies aligned with particular identities. For this reason, Julie Timmermans (2010) argues that as faculty work to articulate threshold concepts, they must also take into consideration the context in which the concepts have emerged.

> We might begin by considering, at the macro level, the powerful historical, social, and cultural forces that converge and give rise to the relative prominence of certain disciplines. We may then consider how these forces shape, at the meso level, the epistemic context of the discipline itself; that is, the questions pursued (and funded) and the methodologies judged as appropriate for pursuing them. At the micro level, we may investigate how these forces manifest themselves in the selection by members of the disciplinary community of concepts deemed important, even thresholds, and around which curricula and programmes are designed. Finally, we must consider the ways of knowing and meaning-making of individual learners. (15)

Among researchers focusing on disciplinarity, there is a consensus that the very phenomenon *of* disciplinarity knowledge exists along a spectrum of permeability (e.g., Betcher and Trowler 2001; Donald 2002; also see Krishnan 2009). At either end of this spectrum, disciplinary knowledge is sometimes perceived to be more or less amenable to reflexive examination of the nature of knowledge (and values and ideologies) *of* the discipline and its threshold concepts and the extent to which this knowledge (and threshold concepts) permits expansion based on other values, ideologies, and knowledge practices. Within disciplines aligned with what Anthony Biglan calls "hard" paradigms or Tony Becher and Paul Trowler describe as "convergent" and "tightly knit," knowledge and threshold concepts may be understood as less permeable; within disciplines aligned with "soft" and "loosely knit" paradigms (Becher and Trowler 2001, 59, 64; Biglan 1973) there is a greater range of tolerance.

The STEM faculty in the first year of the ONDAS seminar, for instance, described a certain degree of stability associated with their discipline and its threshold concepts—but they also described the importance of making these concepts accessible. Biochemist Kevin wrote, "One of the things I love about science (just one of them) is that it is pretty close to being a meritocracy. Since we're all chasing after the same experimentally testable 'truth,' it really should not matter where you came from. It should only matter what you bring to the table in terms of being able to get the job done." Biologist Rolf, summarizing the consensus among his colleagues, said they believe "this is how the kidney works and is it different for the different audiences, how the kidney works? Most of us would say, 'No. What are you talking about? An atom's an atom.' . . . We just don't see that there's a big social wrapper around it." But, Rolf said, "Maybe there is." At the same time, some faculty, like Steven, the biological anthropologist, challenged this idea of disciplinary stability, reacting to a paraphrase of it in one of our readings. "I have to say that I think this is incorrect," he wrote. "I can see how one can come to this conclusion but the distinction . . . is simply a matter of what one might call the 'maturity' of the fields. The 'pure sciences' have more shared assumptions [than humanities] . . . because they've been in business longer. But for any field *to be* a science, those shared assumptions always have to be open to re-evaluation and rejection."

In this second year, then, I am more explicitly incorporating questions about the composition of threshold concepts (as dominant cultural practices) within disciplines. In part, this is prompted by responses like Steven's; in part it is prompted by my own ongoing process of education, especially wrestling with areas that are less familiar to me, like the literature on diversity and identities. In the midst of this effort to both articulate and situate our seminar within a framework of epistemologically inclusive teaching, I am also mindful of the liminal spaces my faculty colleagues in the seminar occupy. This idea of inclusivity itself is a threshold—and certainly more or less acceptable based on where disciplines position themselves along the spectrum I describe earlier.

Our colleagues, like our students, bring their own identities to their thinking about these issues. Also like students, these faculty are encountering, entering, and engaging multiple liminal thresholds; depending on their disciplinary affiliations and identities (within and beyond disciplines), these thresholds may entail participating in ontologies that are not part of the disciplines' identities or practices. An insight from threshold concepts researcher Glynis Cousin's (2006) study of the concept of Otherness in critical cultural media studies is salient here. "Learning can, of course, come through discomfort. . . . [but] there is a path to be navigated. . . . On the one hand, the right measure of discomfort requires a sensitivity to the defences of a defended learner. On the other hand, equal sensitivity is required for learners who are apparently rich in emotional capital" (142). My approach to coconstructing the "path" mentioned by Cousin has been to create conditions for faculty to develop a framework appropriate for them as people working *in* disciplines so they can, for themselves, define and enact more epistemologically inclusive teaching. My role is to extend invitations but to work with faculty within their identities and diverse ways of knowing and thinking with regard to our shared endeavors of facilitating epistemologically accessible teaching and learning.

REFERENCES

Adler-Kassner, Linda. 2017. "Because Writing Is Never Just Writing." *College Composition and Communication* 89 (2): 317–40.

Adler-Kassner, Linda. Forthcoming. "Designing for 'More': Writing's Knowledge and Faculty Professional Learning." *WAC Journal.*

Adler-Kassner, Linda, and John Majewski. 2015. "Extending the Invitation: Threshold Concepts, Professional Development, and Outreach." In *Naming What We Know: Threshold Concepts of Writing Studies,* edited by Linda Adler-Kassner and Elizabeth Wardle, 187–202. Logan: Utah State University Press.

Adler-Kassner, Linda, John Majewski, and Damian Koshnick. 2012. "The Value of Troublesome Knowledge: Threshold Concepts in Writing and History." *Composition Forum* 26. https://compositionforum.com/issue/26/troublesome-knowledge-threshold.php.

Bazerman, Charles. 2015. "Text Is an Object Outside of One's Self That Can Be Improved and Developed." In *Naming What We Know: Threshold Concepts of Writing Studies,* edited by Linda Adler-Kassner and Elizabeth Wardle, 61–62. Logan: Utah State University Press.

Becher, Tony, and Paul R. Trowler. 2001. *Academic Tribes and Territories.* 2nd ed. Buckingham: Society for Research into Higher Education and Open University Press.

Biglan, Anthony. 1973. "Relationships Between Subject Matter Characteristics and the Structure and Output of University Departments." *Journal of Applied Psychology* 57 (3): 204–13. doi: 10.1037/h0034699.

Bransford, John D., James W. Pellegrino, and M. Suzanne Donavan, eds. 2000. *How People Learn: Brain, Mind., Experience, and School: Expanded Edition.* Washington, DC: National Academies Press.

Chamany, Katayoun. 2006. "Science and Social Justice: Making the Case for Case Studies." *Journal of College Science Teaching* 36 (2): 54–59.

Charity Hudley, Anne, et al. 2017. *The Indispensable Guide to Undergraduate Research.* New York: Teachers' College Press

Cousin, Glynis. 2006. "Threshold Concepts, Troublesome Knowledge and Emotional Capital: An Exploration into Learning About Others." In *Overcoming Barriers to Student Understanding,* edited by Jan H. F. Meyer and Ray Land, 134–47. New York: Routledge.

Donald, Janet. 2002. *Learning to Think: Disciplinary Perspectives.* San Francisco: Jossey-Bass.

Gutiérrez, Chris, and Rogoff, Barbara. 2003. "Cultural Ways of Learning: Individual Traits or Repertoires of Practice." *Educational Researcher* 32 (5): 19–25.

Hurtado, Sylvia, and Guillermo-Wan, Chelsea. 2013. *Diverse Learning Environments: Assessing and Creating Conditions for Student Success.* Final Report to the Ford Foundation. Los Angeles: UCLA Higher Education Research Institute.

Hurtado, Sylvia, Cynthia L. Alvarez, Chelsea Guillermo-Wann, Marcela Cuellar, and Lucy Arellano. 2012. "A Model for Diverse Learning Environments." In Vol. 27, *Higher Education: Handbook of Theory and Research,* edited by John C. Smart and Michael B. Paulsen, 41–122. New York: Springer.

Johnson, Angela. 2007. "Unintended Consequences: How Science Professors Discourage Women of Color." *Science Education* 91 (5): 805–21. doi: 10.1002/sce.

Johnson, Eric. 2016. "Micro-Barriers Loom Large for First Generation Students." *Chronicle of Higher Education,* November 4.

Kinchin, Ian, Lyndon B. Cabot, and David B. Hay. 2008. "Visualising Expertise: Towards an Authentic Pedagogy for Higher Education." *Teaching in Higher Education* 13 (3): 315–26. doi: 10.1080/13562510802045345. http://dx.doi.org/10.1080/13562510802045345.

Kreber, Carolin. 2009. "Supporting Student Learning in the Context of Diversity, Complexity, and Uncertainty." In *The University and Its Disciplines: Teaching and Learning Beyond Disciplinary Boundaries*, edited by Carolin Kreber, 3–18. New York: Routledge.

Krishnan, Armin. 2009. "What Are Academic Disciplines?: Some Observations on the Disciplinarity vs. Interdisciplinarity Debate." Southampton: University of Southampton National Centre for Research Methods. http://eprints.ncrm.ac.uk/783/1/what_are_academic_disciplines.pdf.

Laird, Thomas. 2014. "Reconsidering the Inclusion of Diversity in the Curriculum." *Diversity and Democracy* 17 (4). https://www.aacu.org/diversitydemocracy/2014/fall/nelson-laird.

Linkon, Sherry Lee. 2014. *Literary Learning*. Bloomington: Indiana University Press.

Mallinson, Christine, and Anne H. Charity Hudley. 2014. "Partnering through Science: Developing Linguistic Insight to Address Educational Inequality for Culturally and Linguistically Diverse Students in U.S. STEM Education." *Language and Linguistics Compass* 8 (1): 11–23.

Meyer, Jan H. F., and Ray Land. 2006. "Threshold Concepts and Troublesome Knowledge: An Introduction." In *Overcoming Barriers to Student Understanding*, edited by Jan. H. F. Meyer and Ray Land, 3–18. London: Routledge.

Middendorf, Joan, and David Pace. 2004. "Decoding the Disciplines: A Model for Helping Students Learn Disciplinary Ways of Thinking." *New Directions for Teaching and Learning* 8 (98): 1–12. http://dx.doi.org/10.1002/tl.142.

Milem, Jeffrey F., Mitchell J. Chang, and Anthony Lising Antonio. 2005. "Making Diversity Work on Campus: A Research-Based Perspective." Washington, DC: Association of American Colleges and Universities.

Omi, Michael, and Howard Winant, eds. 1994. *Racial Formations in the United States*. 2nd ed. New York: Routledge.

Poole, Gary. 2009. "Academic Disciplines: Homes or Barricades?" In *The University and Its Disciplines: Teaching and Learning Beyond Disciplinary Boundaries*, edited by Carolin Kreber, 50–57. New York: Routledge.

Prescod-Weinstein, Chanda. 2017a. "Scientists Must Challenge What Makes Studies Scientific." *American Scientist*, August 15. https://www.americanscientist.org/blog/macroscope/scientists-must-challenge-what-makes-studies-scientific.

Prescod-Weinstein, Chanda. 2017b. "Stop Equating 'Science' With Truth." Slate, August 9. http://www.slate.com/articles/health_and_science/science/2017/08/evolutionary_psychology_is_the_most_obvious_example_of_how_science_is_flawed.html.

Roberts, Dorothy. 2015. "The Problem with Race Based Medicine." TED video, 14:28. https://www.ted.com/talks/dorothy_roberts_the_problem_with_race_based_medicine.

Smith, Edward. 2016. "Doing Science While Black." *Science* 353 (6307): 1586. doi: 10.1126/science.353.6307.1586. http://science.sciencemag.org/content/353/6307/1586.

Steele, Claude. 2010. *Whistling Vivaldi: How Stereotypes Affect Us and What We Can Do*. New York: W. W. Norton.

Stewart, Dafina-Lazarus. 2017. Language of Appeasement. *Inside Higher Ed*, March 30. https://www.insidehighered.com/views/2017/03/30/colleges-need-language-shift-not-one-you-think-essay.

Timmermans, Julie. 2010. "Changing Our Minds: The Developmental Potential of Threshold Concepts." In *Threshold Concepts and Transformational Learning*, edited by Jan H. F. Meyer, Ray Land, and Caroline Baillie, 3–20. Amsterdam: Sense.

Wenger, Etienne. 1998. *Communities of Practice*. Cambridge: Cambridge University Press.

Wineburg, Sam. 2010. *Historical Thinking and Other Unnatural Acts: Charting the Future of Teaching the Past*. Philadelphia: Temple University Press.

16
USING A THRESHOLD CONCEPTS FRAMEWORK TO FACILITATE AN EXPERTISE-BASED WAC MODEL FOR FACULTY DEVELOPMENT

Elizabeth Wardle

The writing-across-the-curriculum (WAC) movement in the United States began over thirty years ago, likely at Central College in Pella, Iowa, thanks to the efforts of Barbara Walvoord, who "gathered an interdisciplinary group of faculty to discuss student writing" (Walvoord et al. 2011, 1). Thousands of faculty from colleges and universities have since participated in "WAC workshops, discussion groups, 'fellows' programs, team-teaching programs, writing-intensive courses, linked courses, and other permutations" (1). Initially, WAC faculty-development programs typically taught "WAC strategies," defined as "deliberate action[s] of the teacher, intended to result in student learning" (1). Typical WAC strategies taught in these programs included "various kinds of informal writing ('journals,' 'prewriting,' 'informal writing,' 'ungraded writing'), explicit instructions and guidance for assignments, peer collaboration, teacher and peer feedback on drafts, and others" (91). Such programs have clearly had both impact and staying power as they have spread around the country. They have typically been designed around a model of sharing writing expertise with nonwriting faculty, with workshops on topics such as using writing-to-learn activities or helping students engage effectively in peer response.

Rolf Norgaard (1999) has noted that sometimes this model can make it difficult to reach faculty, particularly faculty in disciplines (such as engineering) with disciplinary cultures distinctly different from those of rhetoric and composition: there is a "distinctive culture of disciplinary expertise within the engineering professions and an equally distinct culture within composition, rhetoric, and writing across the curriculum, with its own professionally sanctioned notions of what constitutes rhetorical expertise" (44–45). While not specifically discussing faculty development so much as course design, he draws attention to the idea that writing faculty may struggle to reach across the varied disciplines engaged with WAC initiatives if we cannot find ways to value their expertise—including ways to help them name what they implicitly know and do as experts in a field. Norgaard argues for disciplinary contact zones that "serve as what Bazerman and Russell call 'interface discourse.' . . . This discourse occurs where experts meet each other without necessarily sharing the very same expertise" (49).

In a 2011 special issue of *Across the Disciplines* (*ATD*), faculty members from a number of different countries similarly argue for expanding the European notion of integrating content and language (ICL), or content and language integrated learning (CLIL), in order to foster "the exchange of knowledge and experience regarding collaboration between content (discipline based) and language (communication/academic literacies) lecturers in higher education contexts" (Gustafsson et al. 2011). They argue for "the creation of productive institutional discursive spaces transgressing disciplinary boundaries [with] the potential to bridge the distance between communication specialists and disciplinary specialists." In such spaces, "collaborating lecturers can reflect on what they are doing differently and theorise why they are doing it differently." The focus in such spaces, then, is not so much on having writing specialists teach others useful "WAC strategies" but "on disciplinary discourse as access to disciplinary content knowledge." In these interdisciplinary discursive spaces, participants name "a theoretical framework that shapes these collaborations" in order to "create an intellectually grounded space for describing and enacting this work" (Paretti 2011).

What can such a discursive space look like—one in which expertise of all parties is valued and the focus is "on disciplinary discourse as access to disciplinary content knowledge" (Gustafsson et al. 2011) in a forum where all parties, writing specialists included, think about why they do things differently from one another (and when and where their practices converge)? Marie Paretti (2011) warns that "larger macro structures—departmental, institutional, and cultural—impinge powerfully on ICL learning in ways that can either engage or destroy interdisciplinary possibilities." The options offered in the *ATD* special issue tend toward teaching sites, as does Norgaard's (1999) earlier discussion of ways to engage equitably in WAC collaborations with engineering faculty.

What would it look like to merge traditional WAC fellows programs and seminars with the notion of an expertise-based interdisciplinary discursive site where all parties are engaged in examining disciplinary discourse as access to content in order to innovate teaching practices? And what theoretical framework could inform such work? Since the early days of WAC, two widely recognized programs have taken shape that work from faculty expertise and program-wide versus individually-focused change: University of Minnesota's writing-enriched curriculum (WEC) and North Carolina State's communication-across-the-curriculum (CAC) program. Both follow a philosophy of department-based, bottom-up writing outcomes, and plans to achieve them.

The departmental profile used at North Carolina State University by Chris Anson and Deanna Dannels (2009) is described in this way:

> Each department generates communication outcomes specific to its discipline and to students' needs, then decides how it will assess those outcomes and what it will do internally to help to achieve them. This approach gives authority and control to those closest to the courses where instruction takes place, provides greater incentive for change based on the desire to prepare majors effectively, and avoids the imposition of generalized requirements that may have little meaning to those who must enact them. It also emphasizes the relationships among writing, knowing, and doing within the discipline, which helps faculty to recognize the importance of their own roles in students' writing development. (1)

During the follow-up phase, departments consult with the CAC administrators to create "a profile based on internal, consultative study of a program," which then "results in a report representing the department's current status: how writing and speaking are used, where, to what ends, and in what relationship to broader curricular, pedagogical, and career goals. Although designed eventually to map an institution's progress toward full implementation of CAC, these profiles play an interestingly heuristic role for specific departments and programs, moving them beyond the status quo" (Anson and Dannels 2009, 2). An important aspect of this project is that the "profiles [are] entirely for the benefit and use of the departments themselves"—and the writing specialists who run the CAC program and engage in campus-wide consultations use a "'ground up' philosophy and process" that empowers departments to opt in or out as they choose (4).

The UM WEC model operates in a similar way: departments develop writing plans "in a series of lively meetings with departmental faculty and specialists in writing pedagogy and assessment. These meetings allow faculty participants opportunities to think collaboratively about the roles played by writing in their fields, attributes they look for in student writing, and ways that writing instruction can be optimally situated in their curricula. Finally they strategize, making plans for locally-relevant instructional interventions and determining forms of needed support" (University of Minnesota 2018).

Both models emphasize the autonomy and expertise of faculty members and departments rather than the expertise and strategies to be imparted by the writing specialist, who here serves in a consultative role. Yet neither model includes an interdisciplinary discursive space or an explicitly theoretical frame.

In this chapter, I explore how a framework based in threshold concepts might assist in creating an interdisciplinary discursive frame that emphasizes faculty expertise around writing across and in the disciplines (an approach also taken up by Linda Adler-Kassner in this volume). I then outline a program we have implemented that utilizes this frame in a semester-long discursive space.

THRESHOLD CONCEPTS AND AN EXPERTISE-BASED MODEL OF FACULTY DEVELOPMENT

The literature reviewed above seems to be arguing—whether implicitly or explicitly—for an approach to professional development that values the expertise faculty members bring with them and for using a theoretical approach to examine expertise-based practices. This approach may be somewhat in contrast to the early WAC model of professional development as one expert imparting strategies to a roomful of learners. In other words, rather than sharing "WAC strategies" with established scholars and teachers from across fields, this approach (like the CAC and WEC models) argues for beginning with the expertise teachers and scholars bring with them.

Threshold concepts provide a possible framework for such an approach, as Chris Anson (2015) has suggested elsewhere. This theoretical approach emerged over fifteen years ago from a grant-funded international study of best pedagogical practices for helping students learn disciplinary material. Jan H. F. Meyer and Ray Land (2003), part of that grant team, noted that faculty in various disciplines identified what they came to call "threshold concepts"—learning thresholds students found troublesome but with which they must successfully grapple in order to continue to work in that area of study. Threshold concepts, as Meyer and Land came to define them, are transformational, integrative, illustrate the boundaries of disciplinary territory, and enact both ways of knowing and ways of practicing in a particular field.

A great deal of the research and theory that has emerged regarding threshold concepts is about students—how they learn threshold concepts and what their experiences are like in the liminal space that is often a hallmark of learning such concepts. Another good chunk of the research is specific to teachers and how they might more explicitly name threshold concepts of their disciplines and the pedagogies that will enable learning of them. Some threshold concepts theorists have suggested this framework is also useful for faculty development. Meyer and Land (2005) note that as faculty engage with the idea of threshold concepts, they first describe their disciplinary threshold concepts, then use them as an interpretive framework to help them consider their own teaching, then use them in their own teaching, and then often conduct research as a result. Linda Adler-Kassner and John Majewski (2015) at the University of California Santa Barbara have taken this suggestion a step further, interviewing disciplinary faculty about their threshold concepts and noting that "involving faculty in systematic discussions about threshold concepts in their discipline provides a welcome opportunity to reflexively consider the nature of their own expertise" (187).

Other threshold concept theorists such as Ian Kinchin, Lyndon Cabot, and David Hay (2010) have argued that the framework provides a way to move "away from the problematic binary of student/teacher centeredness" in discussions of pedagogy and professional development (81). Instead, they argue for an "expertise-based model" of teaching and thus, implicitly, of professional development. They argue that such a model of expertise places "subject specialists at the centre of pedagogic developments and provides a mechanism to initiate and monitor a more transactional curriculum" (81). Vimla Patel, José Arocha, and David Kaufman (1998) note that experts have extensive and tacit knowledge about their disciplines. Meyer, Land and Caroline Baillie (2010) point out that "this is coupled with the ability to perceive patterns in large amounts of information and to process their responses quickly and efficiently" (83). The expertise-based model "places teacher development within the disciplines, using familiar discourse. The tensions between educational developers and academics teaching within the disciplines can be eased if the complementary roles are made explicit . . . and the traditional battle grounds (e.g., student vs teacher centeredness [Cousin 2008, 261]) become obsolete, with the focus now on *expertise-centeredness*" (91). In other words, threshold concepts theorists argue that if we want university teaching to be successful, the people who study it can't only be "specialists in teaching and learning" (92). Teachers in every discipline must "consider the application of the [expertise] model to their own discipline and be granted time and resources to ensure that cycles of non-learning . . . can be avoided" (91).

Summarizing and extending, we might make an analogous argument: if we want the teaching of university-level *writing* to be successful, the people who study it can't only be writing specialists.

What this assertion means, in part, is that faculty in all disciplines can be helped to recognize explicitly what they already know and do (with both writing and with their disciplinary knowledge) and how to bring those things to conscious awareness in order to teach about and with writing more effectively. As Kinchin, Cabot, and Hay (2010) note, "Not all teaching has to change if the model is adopted. Rather than dictating to academics how they should act, part of the reason for visualizing the hidden processes of expertise is to make explicit how they already do act. The strength of the pedagogy of expertise therefore lies not in its prescriptive ability, but rather in its descriptive ability" (91–92).

Threshold concepts, then, provide a possible frame to help disciplinary experts examine what they themselves already know about and do with writing in their own personal and professional lives and how these uses of and conceptions about writing relate to their disciplinary knowledge and classroom practices. Anson (2015) has outlined several writing-related threshold concepts that might be central to any such endeavor: *writing in a discipline reflects the ways that knowledge is produced there; writing is a social and rhetorical activity; writing can be a tool for learning or communicating; improvement of writing is a shared responsibility; writing in all contexts involves situated learning, challenging the "transfer" of ability; and writing is highly developmental* (205–12).

In the remainder of this chapter, I outline a WAC program we developed at Miami University specifically to enact this expertise-centered approach to faculty development using threshold concepts as a framework within a space that promotes interdisciplinary dialogue.

THE HOWE FACULTY WRITING FELLOWS PROGRAM

I arrived at Miami University in 2016 to take over as the third director of the Howe Center for Writing Excellence. For nearly ten years, the center, supported by its $10 million endowment, had run a variety of faculty-development programs, as well as staffed a student writing center. Miami is widely recognized as having a strong commitment to undergraduate-student teaching (recently ranking first in the country among public institutions for its commitment to undergraduate teaching). In addition, the previous two HCWE directors had left a strong legacy of WAC development at Miami—many faculty had participated in the "May workshops" around assignment design, developed the now-ubiquitous

College of Arts and Sciences writing courses, and received grants to pursue writing-related scholarship. It became clear to me fairly quickly that Miami faculty were quite serious about teaching writing. In fact, at the many presentations I gave during my first semester on campus, I received only one complaint from an audience member, which was, "Teaching writing is my responsibility. Why should I send students to the Howe Writing Center when I should be giving them feedback myself?"

At the same time, the university was attempting to implement a new writing requirement, Advanced Writing, to take the place of the second-semester composition course, and to include writing and critical thinking in all general-education (known as "Miami Plan") courses. The Advanced Writing requirement as approved by the senate allowed any department to propose an existing or new course (or course sequence) that included extensive writing instruction, practice, and feedback. While the senate had approved this requirement several years prior, implementation had proven difficult, and the deadline for final implementation was looming.

These circumstances in their entirety led me to propose and then implement a new faculty-development program, which I named the Howe Faculty Writing Fellows Program, to replace the May workshop. The tenets of the writing fellows program as I initially envisioned them were as follows:

- Faculty would propose to participate in teams from their departments or programs because teams seemed more likely to be able to return to their departments to facilitate ongoing grassroots change in curriculum and pedagogy.
- Faculty would need to communicate their participation and goals to their department chair or program director in order to ensure there was departmental support for curricular work.
- Teams from three or four different departments/programs would participate at the same time (as a cohort), for a full semester, sharing ideas across disciplinary boundaries.
- Teams would spend the first three-quarters of the semester in discussions as a large cohort and then move to complete projects of their choosing near the end of the semester, returning to share their projects with the full cohort.

In the spring 2017 semester, we enrolled our first teams, from economics, anthropology, and interdisciplinary and communication studies. That summer, in a shortened but accelerated version, we enrolled teams from gerontology, history, and the new Business Integrated Core from our business school. Since then, we have worked with teams from social work and family science, political science, Project Dragonfly (a team of biology faculty who work with a large, online inquiry-based graduate program), teacher education, developmental psychology, TESOL composition, philosophy, international studies, biology, and modern languages and literature, among others. As this list of departments shows, the response to this new program has been strong, and teams have been enthusiastic—and have shared their enthusiasm with other faculty. Initial enthusiasm was likely because of the historical commitment to WAC, and to teaching, at Miami. But the enthusiasm after participating in the program seems to be for three reasons: the program provides a theoretical frame rather than a set of how-tos, the program enables disciplinary experts to engage with one another over an extended period of time, and the program enables disciplinary experts to see their work through the eyes of experts from other disciplines. In other words, the program provides a theoretical framework to guide expertise-based work in an interdisciplinary discursive space.

The Curriculum

The curriculum for the semester-long program is loosely divided into these parts:

- threshold concepts of participants' disciplines
- threshold concepts of writing
- disciplinary values and ideologies enacted in writing
- theories of learning, prior knowledge, and transfer
- ideas for teaching and responding to writing

Four of the thirteen weeks are devoted to threshold concepts. First, the teams are introduced to the framework, and then they spend time identifying their threshold concepts and explaining them to groups from other disciplines. Gerontology, for example, named concepts such as "aging is a social and cultural construction of a biological phenomenon" and "intersectionality." Theatre named "empathy" and "theatre as structured action." Anthropology named "ethnocentrism," "cultural relativism," "holism," and "biocultural change."

Next, teams are introduced to a variety of threshold concepts about writing, many of which align with the threshold concepts suggested by Anson (2015) (for example, *writing is a knowledge-making activity* and *texts get their meaning from other texts*). For each writing threshold concept, individuals are asked to identify how this plays out in/holds up to their own personal or disciplinary practices. For example, when discussing the

threshold concept *writing mediates activities through recognizable forms*, faculty are asked to name the activities and goals writing mediates in their own lives and then name forms writing takes in pursuit of those goals. They then compare these (very long) lists with the types of writing they introduce to students in the classroom. They are asked to explore all the ways they use writing to learn and then consider when (if ever) they make these writing-to-learn practices visible to their students. When they consider the threshold concept "good writing is dependent on context," they attempt to make a list of characteristics of good writing in their own context and explain these to other teams.

At this point, the teams turn to John Swales (1990) and Kenneth Hyland (2007) to begin to really dig into examples of discourse from their various disciplines and see if they can name their own conventions and the values they embody in more specific ways. They bring examples of good writing and exchange them with members of another disciplinary team. They then attempt to understand one another's conventions—what counts as evidence, how arguments are made, what values are suggested by particular conventions and citation styles. They share their perceptions of writing across disciplinary groups: What is strange? What is familiar? What values do they see embodied in these texts?

By this point, the teams have been generating ideas on large Post-it Notes that hang around the room and also taking notes in a shared Google drive. The intent is over time to compile a list of what they know about and do with writing they can then use to inform their projects at the end of the semester. Using all they have now compiled, each team attempts to write a statement for students that aims to make explicit, in operationalizable ways, their assumptions, values, and conventions as embodied in their disciplinary discourse. We call this fill-in-the blank activity the Mad Libs exercise.[1] Revisions of some of the statements the teams generate can be found on our Howe Center for Writing Excellence website: http://miamioh.edu/hcwe/hwac/teaching-support/disciplinary-writing-hwac/index.html.

For example, historians explained that their field values sensitivity to context and historical perspective:

> Writers are considered credible when they develop original, clear, succinct, well-supported arguments that engage in larger scholarly debate. History's citation practices embody these values, and you can see that in examples of how the field deeply engages and interrogates primary and secondary sources. Effective writing in History: Uses signposting, explicates relevance/ context, and balances larger argument with fine-grained analysis and pithiness. Concerning their writing, History majors should expect to: get

feedback, pay attention to writing, treat writing as a process and appreciate it, and recognize their own place in the larger conversation.

Gerontologists explained their conventions differently.

Being a Gerontologist means more than just studying later life and applying methods to solve problems. It means having a "Gerontological voice." That is, the field of Social Gerontology values applying knowledge and building theory using a social science lens. Writers are seen as credible when they present a conceptual context that draws from multiple disciplinary areas and demonstrate methodological sophistication and rigor. Papers should represent a "dialogue." The field's citations practices embody these values, and you can see that in the breadth of sources used, with specific citations from Gerontology sources. Citations should be purposeful, strategic, and support the writer's argument/claim and avoid overgeneralizations, oversimplifications, and unfounded opinions. Effective writing in Social Gerontology does the following:

presents logical, parsimonious argument with neutral language

uses standard signposts and structure

avoids absolutes

demonstrates respectful authority.

Teams generate these statements around week six, and by this point there has been little sharing of WAC strategies or tips. What has been provided is a framework for discussion and analysis. The insights regarding how writing works and can best be explained in each discipline come from the experts themselves; their implicit assumptions are more easily made explicit when they can see what other teams do with language.

Next, participants turn their attention to how learning works, using a book of that same name (Ambrose et al. 2010). We read chapters on how prior knowledge affects learning, how students develop mastery, the kinds of practice and feedback that enhance learning, and how students become self-directed learners. Faculty bring in their own writing assignments and syllabi and discuss changes they might want to make, given what they have read and generated thus far regarding threshold concepts of their disciplines and of writing, as well as theories of learning and mastery. Still, few tips or strategies are shared by me except in passing dialogue but are instead generated by the participants as they bring their own expertise and practices to conscious awareness, illumined by theoretical frameworks.

By this time, faculty are generally ready to begin working on team projects, so we spend only a little time (one or two weeks) highlighting the resources they can draw on from John Bean's (2011) *Engaging Ideas*. In an expertise-based workshop governed by a theoretical frame, it seems important to end with specific tips rather than start with them. By this point, faculty know what they want to say to and do with students and have a fairly clear idea of what might be impeding students from gaining the ground faculty hope they will gain. Thus, they use Bean selectively as they are brainstorming details of assignment scaffolding or daily activities. Although some participants like Bean a lot, others recognize at this point that the various and myriad WAC strategies he outlines sometimes aren't helpful outside a particular disciplinary context, but that faculty who have a theoretical understanding of both their discipline and how writing works can create their own. A faculty member from family science and social work noted she gives low-stakes assignments that ask students to write a few sentences about research circulating in popular culture—and then build on those sentences to start identifying essential elements of research project (methods, methodology, etc.)—and what is lost when research results are described to a lay audience. This low-stakes writing assignment makes sense in her class but relies on her disciplinary goals and values in conjunction with an understanding of how writing and research work more broadly. Bean also provides further language for some of what the participants have been attempting to name (for example, "writing to learn").

In the following weeks, teams begin work on projects of their choosing with help from me and the HCWE team as they request. These projects have varied widely. One team redesigned its entire graduate sequence and curriculum and mapped out where various kinds of writing and instruction would happen across courses and time. That team, from gerontology, also created new assignments around citation and interdisciplinary discussion (see Glotfelter 2018). The Project Dragonfly team, teaching a new and primarily online major, designed online modules that gave other faculty members in their program exposure to the kinds of framework and language they had been working with and created analytical activities and annotated examples of effective writing for their students. A third team created videos about writing, citation, threshold concepts, and disciplinary values for faculty in their programs to use and embed in their online courses (see Glotfelter et al. 2018).

The teams reconvene for one final cohort meeting in which each team presents its project to the other teams and asks for feedback.

The Follow Up

A primary goal of the program is to promote long-term change, driven by departments and programs themselves. Rather than beginning by naming what *I* hope these changes will be, the *teams themselves* name their desired changes at the end of the program. The history team, for example, led a full-day workshop for their own department and has revised the four courses each faculty team member is currently teaching. They are currently discussing how long-term change might be enacted.

In the HCWE, we are working to use materials, statements, and resources generated by the teams to help our writing center consultants and the students who visit the writing center. Our graduate assistants, Angela Glotfelter, Caitlin Martin, and Mandy Olejnik, have been working to follow up with departments to expand their drafts and notes into "Disciplinary Writing Guides" that are shared on our website (http://miamioh.edu/hcwe/hwac/teaching-support/disciplinary-writing-hwac/index.html) (Miami 2019).

We are now working on phase two follow ups to ensure continued collaboration and communication with each of the teams that has completed the program. We are piloting the WEC/CAC models as a way to offer department-wide discussions for teams who have completed our program. We have piloted student liaisons to some of these departments, and embedded consultants in courses redesigned in the program. We have begun offering lunches and week-long course redesign workshops limited only to Fellows alumni.

Faculty Response

We are working to understand not only response to the program but also what fellows have integrated into their practice and what changes they are enacting in the long term. We first give an anonymous survey at the end of each cohort's semester of participation, and now we are in the midst of an IRB-approved study to learn more about what is being taken up in practice. We have conducted focus groups with faculty from multiple teams and have conducted a number of interviews with individual teams.

There is value in having a lens for examining and naming expert practices, particularly in contrast to those of other disciplinary teams who are participating in the program. After the program, faculty note that now they understand why students are flummoxed by differing expectations across classrooms: "The main thing that I take with me is a deeper sensitivity to the fact that students are expected to write in different genres—each with its own conventions and accepted practices—every single day of the semester. No wonder they seem flummoxed by the differing expectations of professors. Among (many) other things, I will provide much more guidance regarding the practices and expectations of writing in History, as well as a much deeper understanding of the challenges that this poses."

Faculty also recognize they must explicitly teach the language of their discipline and how its values are enacted in conventions such as "polite disagreement." A faculty member in gerontology says,

> I now explicitly explain the writing goals of my discipline to students and even refer to these goals when discussing their writing. For example, I might say, "Remember that in our discipline we politely disagree by writing things like 'Although Smith gave an excellent overview of the topic, there is an important area that still needs more attention.'"

Additionally, faculty describe more robust conceptions of writing deeply linked to their disciplinary knowledge. For example, a history faculty member said in a follow-up interview, "This connection between threshold concepts and the goals that we're trying to reach and achieve through writing . . . [I am] just continually asking myself and prompting myself to think about and to articulate: 'Why am I assigning this piece of writing—what is this going to accomplish? What is the goal of this piece of writing? How is this not just getting them closer to the subject matter of the course, but how is this helping them to develop the skills that are important as an historian and as a scholar?'"

Faculty note how this higher-order understanding will influence their classroom practices. While we spoke little, if at all, about how to design assignments, faculty nonetheless reported this skill is what they took away from the program. For example, one faculty member said, "This program has taught me the importance of constructing your assignments carefully. Of course student writing is going to be not-so-great if you just give them a deadline at the end of the semester and offer them no opportunities to get feedback earlier."

Finally, faculty members describe the importance of dialogue within their department and learning from those dialogues across other disciplines: "I think the thing I value most is having a community of peers, both within my department and beyond, who now have a shared language with which we can communicate the challenges and opportunities associated with teaching our students how to be better writers."

There are challenges, of course. Faculty say the initial exposure to threshold concepts of their discipline did not immediately connect to writing or to their classrooms. As one faculty member put it in a follow-up interview, "It first felt so nebulous and big, like, 'think about the threshold concepts in your field'—there's value to do that. But I didn't see how it was going to be communicated to the students and that's what my mission was. . . . I can't emphasize enough [that at first] I really didn't think we were going to get to where we got [in the fellows program] . . . at the time I was like, what? I didn't think it was a good use of my time. I was grumpy about it, and it really blew my mind that we had the output that we did." Another faculty member described a similar feeling: "[At the beginning of fellows] I was like 'Whyyyyy, why? How is this going to help? Like, it's helping me but it's not gonna help the students.'" She noted it was not until they began to put everything they had learned together into the form of a Mad Libs statement that it all started coming together.

CONCLUSION: THRESHOLD CONCEPTS, WAC, AND AN EXPERTISE-BASED INTERDISCIPLINARY DISCURSIVE FRAMEWORK

Are threshold concepts a tool that can help us create this interdisciplinary discursive frame emphasizing faculty expertise around writing across and in the disciplines? Our experience at Miami suggests it is not only possible but productive to create a WAC professional-development framework that seeks to work from faculty expertise, make hidden practices visible, and help faculty make disciplinary values explicit. These goals are aided in productive ways by the threshold concepts framework and by working in groups that include teams from multiple disciplines so that similarities and differences can be noted more explicitly. Faculty are able to see their own conventions and values as one of many possible options when compared to those from other disciplines. With a theoretical framework that helps them understand how writing works and gives them a language for talking about it, they are able to create assignments and activities specific for their own disciplinary context rather than being urged to use the more generic practices such as journals or freewriting. Emphasizing theory over practice empowers faculty to name, examine, and even critique their practices and create assignments appropriate to their goals and contexts. Faculty are most engaged when they are acting from and examining their own expert practice. However, none of this is comfortable or easy, and it all takes a lot of time. And time, of course, is the institutional constraint most difficult to overcome.

NOTE

1. Heidi Estrem and Linda Adler-Kassner developed similar exercises at Boise State University and the University of California Santa Barbara, respectively, and their ideas influenced the activity we use at Miami.

REFERENCES

Adler-Kassner, Linda, and John Majewski. 2015. "Extending the Invitation: Threshold Concepts, Professional Development, and Outreach." In *Naming What We Know: Threshold Concepts of Writing Studies*, edited by Linda Adler-Kassner and Elizabeth Wardle, 186–202. Logan: Utah State University Press.

Ambrose, Susan A., Michael W. Bridges, Michele DiPietro, Marsha C. Lovett, and Marie K. Norman. 2010. *How Learning Works: 7 Research-Based Principles for Smart Teaching*. Hoboken, NJ: Wiley.

Anson, Chris. 2015. "Crossing Thresholds." In *Naming What We Know: Threshold Concepts of Writing Studies*, edited by Linda Adler-Kassner and Elizabeth Wardle, 203–19. Logan: Utah State University Press.

Anson, Chris, and Deanna Dannels. 2009. "Profiling Programs: Formative Uses of Departmental Consultations in the Assessment of Communication Across the Curriculum." *Across the Disciplines* 6: 1–15. https://wac.colostate.edu/atd/assessment/anson_dannels.cfm.

Bean, John. 2011. *Engaging Ideas: The Professor's Guide to Integrating Writing, Critical Thinking, and Active Learning in the Classroom*. 2nd ed. Hoboken, NJ: Jossey-Bass.

Glotfelter, Angela. 2018. "Discovering the Voice of Gerontology: Faculty Fellows Explore Disciplinarity to Make Pedagogical Innovations." http://miamioh.edu/hcwe/hwac/about/miami-writing-spotlight/gerontology/index.html.

Glotfelter, Angela, Jill Korach, Jamie Anzano, and Kevin Matteson. 2018. "Writing in Project Dragonfly." http://miamioh.edu/hcwe/disciplinary-writing/projectdragonfly/index.html.

Gustafsson, Magnus, Andreas Eriksson, Christine Räisänen, Ann-Charlotte Stenberg, Cecilia Jacobs, Jenny Wright, Bridget Wyrley-Birch, and Chris Winberg. 2011. "Collaborating for Content and Language Integrated Learning: The Situated Character of Faculty Collaboration and Student Learning." *Across the Disciplines* 8 (3). https://wac.colostate.edu/docs/atd/clil/gustafssonetal.pdf.

Hyland, Kenneth. 2007. *Disciplinary Discourses: Social Interaction in Academic Writing*. Ann Arbor: University of Michigan Press.

Kinchin, Ian M., Lyndon B. Cabot, and David B. Hay. 2010. "Visualizing Expertise: Revealing the Nature of a Threshold Concept in the Development of an Authentic Pedagogy for Clinical Education." In *Threshold Concepts and Transformational Learning*, edited by Jan H. F. Meyer, Ray Land, and Caroline Baillie, 81–96. Rotterdam: Sense.

Meyer, Jan H. F., and Ray Land. 2003. *Threshold Concepts and Troublesome Knowledge: Linkages to Ways of Thinking and Practising*. Rotterdam: Sense Publishers.

Meyer, Jan H. F., and Ray Land. 2005. "Threshold Concepts and Troublesome Knowledge (2): Epistemological Considerations and a Conceptual Framework for Teaching and Learning." *Higher Education* 49 (3): 373–88.

Meyer, Jan H. F., Ray Land, and Caroline Baillie. 2010. *Threshold Concepts and Transformational Learning*. Rotterdam: Sense.

Miami University, Howe Center for Writing Excellence. 2019. "Disciplinary Guides." http://miamioh.edu/hcwe/hwac/teaching-support/disciplinary-writing-hwac/index.html.

Norgaard, Rolf. 1999. "Negotiating Expertise in Disciplinary 'Contact Zones.'" *Language and Learning Across the Disciplines* 3 (2): 44–62.

Paretti, Marie. 2011. "Interdisciplinarity as a Lens for Theorizing Language/Content Partnerships." *Across the Disciplines* 8 (3). https://wac.colostate.edu/atd/clil/paretti.cfm.

Patel, Vimla, José F. Arocha, and David R. Kaufman. 1998. "Expertise and Tacit Knowledge in Medicine." In *Tacit Knowledge in Professional Practice*, edited by Robert J. Stemberg and Joseph A. Horvath, 75–100. Hillsdale, NJ: Erlbaum.

Swales, John. 1990. *Genre Analysis: English in Academic and Research Settings.* Cambridge: Cambridge University Press.

University of Minnesota. 2018. "Writing-Enriched Curriculum." https://wec.umn.edu/.

Walvoord, Barbara, Linda Lawrence Hunt, H. Fil Dowling Jr., Joan D. McMahon, with contributions by Virginia Slachman and Lisa Udel. 2011. *In the Long Run: A Study of Faculty in Three Writing-Across-the-Curriculum Programs.* Urbana, IL: NCTE. https://wac.colostate.edu/books/walvoord/.

17
TALKING ABOUT WRITING
A Study of Key Writing Terms Used Instructionally across the Curriculum

Chris M. Anson, Chen Chen, and Ian G. Anson

Faculty in the disciplines often expect students enrolling in their courses to have already acquired the writing skills and the rhetorical knowledge necessary to perform well. Yet previous studies document the struggles all writers encounter when they move across communities of practice and face new and unfamiliar genres, content, and ways of making knowledge (e.g., Anson 2016a, 2016b; Anson and Forsberg 1990; Beaufort 2007; Haswell 1991; Herrington and Curtis 2000; McCarthy 1987; Smart 2000; Sternglass 1997). To write successfully, students must be almost chameleonic in their adaptation to these differences as they move from course to course. This process is made more complicated and often confusing when different writing terms are used for the same or similar underlying concepts, or when students are unprepared to understand idiosyncratic uses of terms in their various courses.

As writers, faculty members have gained considerable knowledge about how writing works in their own disciplines, but this knowledge may be largely tacit, gained over years of slow enculturation and experience, a point highlighted in Wardle's chapter in this collection. When they assign, support, and evaluate writing, their classroom explanations and instruction may not reflect systematic, agreed-upon writing-related terminology (Anson 2015, 206) and the concepts that underlie it. Most writing-across-the-curriculum (WAC) or writing-in-the-disciplines (WID) leaders, therefore, face the challenge of helping to establish and promulgate common understandings of writing among highly diverse groups of faculty—challenges met in innovative ways in chapters by both Adler-Kassner and Wardle (this volume).

To explore the nature of these common understandings, we conducted a modest study of the writing-related concepts embodied in the

DOI: 10.7330/9781607329329.c017

key terms faculty use in courses across the disciplines as these relate to the terms commonly taught or used in a first-year writing program. As we explain below, key terms are not threshold concepts, although they may be related to them (in the same way *profit, scarcity,* and *choice* are related to the threshold concept *opportunity cost* in economics, or the way *unit length* is related to the threshold concept *temperature gradient* in the physics of heat transfer). Rather, they represent more general core concepts that play an important role in constructing conceptual schemas for writing that help students move across disciplinary boundaries and work productively on their texts (Meyer and Land 2006, 6). This chapter reports the results of the study, which surveyed faculty across a range of courses in STEM disciplines, the humanities, and the social sciences. The survey aimed to discover which key writing terms used by faculty across the disciplines intersect with the ones used by composition teachers and whether these terms carry different underlying meanings in those disciplines.

THRESHOLD CONCEPTS AND KEY TERMS

Acquiring threshold concepts leads to "transformative" and "irreversible" shifts in student learning, often "bounded" in disciplinary areas that may serve as gateways to new conceptual territories and new knowledge (Meyer and Land 2006, 7–8). Threshold concepts are transformative because they fundamentally change students' way of thinking in and practicing a subject. For example, *writing addresses, invokes, and/or creates audiences* is a threshold concept in writing studies because it complicates students' understanding of the relations, interactions, and boundaries between writers and audiences (see Lunsford 2015).

When students are on the verge of crossing a threshold, they may enter a state of liminality as they "oscillate" between old and new understandings (Heading and Loughlin 2017). Typically, such understandings develop within specific disciplinary boundaries; but threshold concepts for writing cross virtually all such boundaries and may not be acquired fully in one place. For example, students are routinely introduced to the concept of *audience* in first-year writing courses, but by the end of the course, they may not have developed a complex understanding of how writing addresses, invokes, or creates audiences. To continue moving beyond liminal spaces, students must be "explicitly assisted" (Davies 2006, 80); but if instructors neglect to use or invoke the concept of audience in other courses students take across the disciplines or in their majors, students may remain in a "suspended state in which understanding can approximate to a kind of mimicry or lack of authenticity" (Meyer and Land 2005, 380).

Learning threshold concepts also entails "the acquisition and use of new forms of written and spoken discourse and the internalising of these" (Land, Rattray, and Vivian 2014, 201), including the language and terminology that surrounds and reinforces new concepts. Specific terms can refer to what Jan Meyer and Ray Land (2006) call "core concepts," or "conceptual 'building block[s]' that progress understanding of the subject" (6). Although core concepts may be insufficient to transform student learning and behavior, they are a necessary part of the lexicon surrounding threshold concepts. The term *audience* does not fully convey the breadth of this threshold concept, but it instantiates the concept once learned and also helps teach the concept while it's being learned—along with other words such as *reader*, *response*, and *interpretation*. If a student is enjoined to focus on style, word choice, and syntax in a design engineering report in order to adapt it to an audience of marketers who know little about the report's technical specifications, the terms *style*, *word choice*, and *syntax* become part of a lexical network in which the concept of audience is instantiated. In this study, we refer to these lexical items as *key terms*—part of the working discourse of the writing process.

Key terms are assumed to be important for students' adaptation to new communities of practice and the genres and disciplinary conventions used there (Adler-Kassner and Wardle 2015) and "can foster cross-disciplinary work" (Wardle et al., this volume). Yet we know little about the extent to which teachers in other disciplines refer to the key terms that inform most foundational writing programs and are increasingly taught to students explicitly (see, for example, the initiatives described in the chapters in part 2 of this volume). For example, if certain key terms students learn in writing courses are absent or are different from those used by teachers in other disciplines, students lose an opportunity to experience explicit bridges between the contexts. Although a foundational course taught strongly in the spirit of "writing for transfer" might serve some students adequately (see Yancey, Robertson, and Taczak 2014), students are left to their own devices to use whatever metaconscious strategies they learned in the past to figure out how to perform effectively, adding to or transforming their previously gained knowledge. A more fortuitous situation is one in which subsequent courses in the disciplines refer explicitly to previously learned key terms and concepts (such as when a professor in a soil science course explicitly uses terms for concepts she knows are taught in foundational writing courses at the same institution). Such an approach requires intentional alignments between courses, programs, and curricula to facilitate students' adaptation to new communities.

Complicating such potential alignment and articulation is the possibility that different key terms may be used for similar underlying core concepts across the disciplines or that the same key term is used with different understandings. In this case, learners must be "taught new meaning for an existing signifier . . . discarding an existing understanding of a signifier in favour of a new one for the new concept. The learner may have to remember that the old understanding may still be appropriate in other contexts" (Land, Rattray, and Vivian 2014, 204). For example, the word *proofread* typically activates a canonical mental representation and subsumes core prototypical semantic features (see Anderson and Shifrin 1980; Davis 1991; Taylor 2003): a set of activities involving systematically scouring a text to ensure it contains no errors and conforms to a specific set of rules dictated by a style guide or an in-house manual of conventions. This process is different from reading the text to discover faulty logic or the misrepresentation of concepts, which is why a professional proofreader can usually perform the job without fully understanding what they are reading—unlike an *editor*.

At the same time, while *proofread* carries some degree of objective, agreed-upon meaning, it is also subject to both personal and localized variations, depending on a host of factors (see Lakoff and Johnson 1980). These contextual differences may account for disciplinary variations in the use of this key writing-related term in academic settings. For example, in the many WAC workshops one of us (C. Anson) has led at his institution and around the country, there have been times when faculty have used the key term *proofread* to mean both small repairs of error *and* larger-scale revisions (in content or structure) and other times when faculty have used the key term *revision* to refer to sentence-level minutiae (such as punctuation and spelling). However, it's unclear whether such differences come from the misuse or misunderstanding of key terms with relatively stable meanings or from contextually based variations of meanings shared within different communities. Regardless, the language used in teaching writing may carry different meanings when used by different instructors, especially those who are not from the discipline of writing studies and who may have had different experiences with academic writing than those who are trained to be writing teachers. When students travel from first-year writing courses to courses across the disciplines, if the language used to talk about writing is used inconsistently, it can be difficult for them to adapt to their new environments (see Lea and Street 2006).

A KEY-TERMS SURVEY

To better understand the landscape where students must cross disciplinary boundaries, we set out to explore the possible symmetry or lack thereof in the key terms faculty use to talk about writing. The context was one of our institutions (C. Anson's current and Chen's former institution), a large, research-extensive university where the vast majority of entering students enroll in a well-managed and well-staffed first-year composition course designed to introduce them to the discourse of three generalized disciplinary areas (the humanities, the social sciences, and STEM). Many courses across this university's nine undergraduate colleges involve some writing, especially within the major, in a longstanding writing-enriched curriculum (a departmentally focused communication-across-the-curriculum program; see Anson 2006; Anson et al. 2003; Anson and Dannels 2009). Undergraduates' writing experiences, therefore, are deliberately structured to help them move more easily between and among disciplinary contexts, adapting to the different genres and communicative conventions each requires. But at an institution as large and complex as this one, with 2,336 faculty and almost 34,000 students, the widespread articulation needed to support such adaptations is not easily achieved. Learning whether key writing terms are used consistently throughout a student's academic career provides programmatic information to better facilitate the process of transfer and instantiation of threshold concepts as students move from first-year writing to their other courses. At the same time, it raises interesting theoretical questions about the nature of the language used to talk about writing in widely different disciplines.

To derive a set of key terms reflecting common understandings among writing instructors, we consulted a popular textbook oriented toward writing across the curriculum (Anson 2016a). This text is designed in part to provide students with concepts they can use when they are asked to write in sometimes unfamiliar genres in courses across the curriculum. In its coverage, it also mirrors common faculty-development efforts in WAC and WID programs. Below is the final corpus of key terms we assembled for use in our faculty survey, each of which was followed by a common definition (for example, for the key term *revision*, we provided the following definition: "*Revision* means, literally, 're-seeing.' It requires attention to major elements of a piece of writing, such as its structure, voice, and presentation of ideas. It is not editing, and it is not proofreading, and it lies at the heart of improvement not only of a writer's own drafts but in his or her knowledge and abilities as a writer").[1] We provided the definitions so faculty respondents could gauge the extent to which they use a key term based on the meaning commonly assigned within the composition community. For example, in the field of computer science, the term *documentation* usually refers to information that describes a particular piece of software to its users or consumers. Similarly, *invention* in systems engineering typically refers to the creation of some novel idea or method and is distinct from *innovation*. If a teacher of computer science uses *documentation* instructionally in the computer science sense but not in the composition sense, their response to our Likert-scale survey would be quite different (and inaccurate) in the absence of our definitions.

In creating the list and definitions, we avoided specialized writing-related terms few faculty in the disciplines would know or use (such as *ad populum, encomium,* or *incubation*). We tried to include a blend of key terms representing different aspects of writing: process-related terms, rhetorical terms, form- or genre-related terms, and terms for the integration of information (such as *paraphrase* or *summary*). The list is by no means exhaustive, but for purposes of our modest campus project, we did not want to overly burden respondents with a long and detailed survey that would take more than ten to fifteen minutes to complete:

audience
documentation
editing
genre
invention
learning log or academic journal
low-stakes writing
peer review
paraphrase
proofreading
quotation
summary
primary research
secondary research
support
thesis
rubric

We sent the survey separately to faculty who teach in the first-year writing program and to faculty in other departments. Respondents totaled twenty-six composition instructors and fifty-one instructors from twenty-eight other departments that included art and design, systems engineering, management, plant and microbial sciences, chemistry, animal science, nutrition, electrical and computer engineering, history, and parks, recreation, and tourism management. Respondents were asked to indicate on a five-item Likert scale ("always," "often," "sometimes," "rarely," and "never") how often they explicitly refer to each of the writing concepts in their teaching. We enjoined respondents to think of any context in which they might use a term, such as their syllabus, a handout, an oral explanation of an assignment, or a one-to-one consultation with a student. An open-ended comment box asked them to explain whether they used different terms or phrases than those listed when referring to any of the concepts (as defined).

Table 17.1 presents two-sample t-test comparisons of means for the composition faculty and the disciplinary faculty. Each row presents the results of a statistical comparison of the two groups, with the greatest differences (as measured by the magnitude of t-values) at the top of the table. In the first column is a description of the term in question; in the next two columns are the means for each group as measured on a five-point scale, with 5 indicating the most frequent usage and 1 indicating no usage. An initial glance at the difference scores as reported in the table shows that almost every score is positive. This means teachers of first-year composition were more likely to utilize all but one term compared to teachers in other disciplines (the exception was the use of *primary research*). Composition faculty reported using the terms *revision, genre, paraphrase, quote, audience, invention,* and *peer review* more frequently than faculty in other disciplines to a highly statistically significant degree ($p < 0.001$). Results for the terms *documentation, summary, low-stakes writing, thesis,* and *proofread* also show statistically significant differences ($p < 0.05$). Terms without strong differences between the groups include *support, secondary research, editing, rubric,* and *primary research* ($p > 0.05$).

To some extent, these differences may be the predictable result of contrasting writing priorities in the two sets of contexts. The object of instruction for teachers of composition is intensive work with the rhetorical and linguistic principles behind text production—as a *primary* focus—rather than a body of content to be learned—so the language of writing is more often "in the air" than it is in a course in music history or soil science. The term *genre*, for example, which only 38 percent of the faculty across the disciplines reported using "always" or "often" (compared with over 88 percent of the composition faculty) may reflect an emphasis in composition on multiple contexts for and types of writing. Interestingly, the term *revision* yielded the strongest differences between the groups, while the term *editing* did not rise to a level of

Table 17.1. Statistical comparisons of survey results

Key Term	Composition faculty mean	Disciplinary faculty mean	Difference	t	p-value
Revision	4.765	3.525	1.24	5.674	$p < 0.001$
Genre	4.118	2.875	1.243	5.145	$p < 0.001$
Paraphrase	4.294	3.075	1.219	5.031	$p < 0.001$
Quotation	4.529	3.3	1.229	4.995	$p < 0.001$
Audience	4.794	3.75	1.044	4.502	$p < 0.001$
Invention	3.412	2.077	1.335	4.288	$p < 0.001$
Peer review	4.471	3.4	1.071	4.047	$p < 0.001$
Documentation	4.382	3.6	0.782	3.29	0.002
Summary	4.471	3.725	0.746	3.259	0.002
Low-stakes writing	3.471	2.487	0.984	3.088	0.003
Thesis	4.333	3.5	0.833	2.93	0.005
Proofread	4.118	3.6	0.518	2.097	0.04
Learning log/journal	2.618	1.973	0.645	1.918	0.059
Support	4.412	3.9	0.512	1.913	0.06
Secondary research	3.735	3.175	0.56	1.879	0.064
Editing	4.147	3.875	0.272	1.118	0.267
Rubric	4.118	4.1	0.018	0.064	0.949
Primary research	3.471	3.553	–0.082	–0.269	0.789

statistical significance. These results may reflect different understandings of the writing process or the possibility that teachers across the disciplines think of *editing* as making changes at any level of the text—that is, a more all-purpose, generic term. Or it could mean faculty across the disciplines tend to care more about the local concerns of writing (in the accurate definition of the term) and less about broader rhetorical, structural, and meaning-based transformations of a text, as *revision* implies. If students have learned to distinguish between these two key terms in composition classes, the more common use of *editing* later could confuse them as they work on drafts of their writing. If students are in a liminal space as they acquire the threshold concept *text is an object outside of oneself that can be improved and developed* (Bazerman and Tinberg 2015, 61), their full acquisition of this concept may be forestalled as they are asked to "revise" by tinkering with smaller surface matters in their writing.

The frequency of the key term *rubric* among the faculty across the disciplines (used to the same extent as the composition faculty) may reflect the uptake of certain evaluative methods across the curriculum. As an evaluative device, rubrics (whether holistic or analytic) represent only one kind of assessment method; other methods include impressionistic grading without reference to a set of criteria, various scoring systems, one-to-one meetings, or a mix of peer and instructor grading. Teachers across the curriculum may use *rubric* because they want to instill a set of standards for writing particular genres or objectify what they fear can be an arbitrary or subjective a process. This preference may also be tied to instructional conditions such as class size—with analytical rubrics perhaps offering faster, checklist-style evaluation in larger classes.

Some terms are not well represented in either group. Surprisingly, not many more than half (61.54 percent) of faculty in first-year composition use *invention* always or often, in spite of the historical importance of this term in the field of writing studies and its association with the threshold concept *writing is a knowledge-making activity* (Estrem 2015). However, two first-year composition teachers did explain in the comment box that they use the concept of invention by referring to it as "prewriting" activities or as "brainstorming," or use "freewriting" activities as a method of invention. The terms *learning log* and *academic journal* also share a low position of frequency by instructors of both first-year writing (30 percent) and courses across the curriculum (25 percent).

These results point to another possible phenomenon in the use of key writing terms to support students' work. First, terms are not stable but in a constant state of evolution, both in their underlying meanings or applications and in their currency in the field and in its pedagogical manifestations. The language used to talk about writing consists of key terms, but some may be on the trailing edge of the field's discourse while some are currently stable and some are on the leading edge (more recently entering the disciplinary and pedagogical parlance, such as *multimodal writing*). As a key term popular during the process movement in composition (Anson 2013) and fueled by the deliberate adoption of classical rhetoric into the composition curriculum (Lauer 2004; Young 1987), *invention* may be moving toward the trailing edge of key terms—that is, in its explicit use (it may well, as a term, have been collapsed, as our instructors suggested, into other related terms without losing its underlying meaning or operational utility). In this case, perhaps the underlying concept has been wrapped into other terms. Another phenomenon may be the gradual obsolescence not of underlying concepts (such as invention) but of certain processes or activities that enact such concepts. For example, highly used in the teaching of writing throughout the 1970s and 1980s (see Fulwiler 1987), journal writing could be fading from the first-year writing curriculum. But the key term *reflection* (not used in this study), which is encouraged in journal writing, could be practiced in other ways. Further study could discover whether there is a lag between the use of key terms in composition and in other disciplinary settings.

On the noncomposition side of the survey, over half the respondents indicated they use some of the key terms "always" or "often." The key term *audience*, used "always" or "often" by 66 percent of the faculty across the disciplines (a result dwarfed by almost 92 percent of the composition faculty), demonstrates that many instructors do value this concept and weave it into their instruction. The "always" and "often" results among noncomposition faculty for the key terms *documentation* (61.7 percent), *quotation* (55.3 percent), *summary* (63.8 percent), *primary research* (51.1 percent), and *support* (74.4 percent) point to the value placed on these aspects of academic writing. Also of note is the relatively strong percentage of faculty across the disciplines (57.4 percent) who use the term *peer review* always or often in their teaching (but still significantly fewer than teachers of first-year writing). Although it is impossible to know from the survey alone, NC State University's twenty-year-old campus writing and speaking program, which provides faculty development and departmental consulting across the university in support of a conscious effort to improve students' communication abilities, may partly account for these results. A more robust research project comparing the use of key terms at institutions with and without strong WAC/WID programs could determine the extent to which such programs influence the adoption and use of key terms and threshold concepts of writing.

WORKING WITH COMMON TERMS: POSSIBILITIES AND COMPLEXITIES

One implication of this study is that key terms are impermanent and varied, both in their use and their meaning, taking on different guises as they travel across instructional and disciplinary contexts. Participants in both groups, such as those commenting on *invention*, mentioned they have used other terms to convey similar concepts. Across the disciplines, faculty provided alternative terms or concept explanations for the key terms *documentation, genre, support, primary and secondary research, invention, rubric, low-stakes writing,* and *learning log/academic journal.* It is not difficult to recognize the resulting challenge for students who must try to "recover" these meanings from the variations. For example, in our survey, we define *documentation* as it relates to the use of sources in writing, but one noncomposition participant uses the term to mean "something a little different, usually as a type of deliverable supporting a professional goal; e.g., documentation on corporate policies, documentation on a certain procedure," which points toward genres of writing more than the use of sources. Other noncomposition faculty mentioned they use *citation* to mean *documentation* when they teach writing. If students are in a liminal space as they acquire the threshold concept *writing is a social and rhetorical activity* (Roozen 2015, 17)—in which, for example, source documentation serves multiple social and rhetorical purposes—then variations in the way the key term *documentation* is used across courses may not help them to fully acquire the threshold concept.

We also recognize that key terms in the world of discourse can't be highly coordinated across contexts. Students will always encounter new contexts in which the language of writing differs from what they have learned. Recognizing this problem, scholars have developed the concept of "threshold capabilities," which are "threshold to professional learning in a defined area of knowledge" (Baillie, Bowden, and Meyer 2013, 236). Emphasizing the "experience of variation" (233), threshold capability theory aims to help students develop their ability to deal with different situations they may encounter in their professional career. Consistent use of the same terms across a student's undergraduate career can potentially support the transfer of knowledge about writing, but it may also strip away the kinds of contextual diversity that help students develop strategies of adaptation. Therefore it is important to establish dialogues between faculty across the disciplines to fully develop a set of key terms with underlying threshold concepts that meet local institutional needs.

Although the findings of our study offer several interesting observations, it is not without its limitations. First, we constrained the key terms to those we thought represented a range of concerns related to the development of students' writing abilities from their first-year introductory course into the general-education program and their majors. A different but potentially illuminating study could ask instructors to provide a list of key terms they routinely use in their writing instruction or in support of their students' work on writing assignments. Such a study would reveal which key terms make up the instructional lexicon of different teachers in first-year composition and in courses across the curriculum and provide a litmus test of the extent to which there is symmetry both within the composition program and beyond. In addition, case studies could be conducted of teachers' instructional writing lexicons through more detailed analysis of texts (syllabi, handouts, or online materials), recordings of in-class explanations, and in-depth interviews with the instructors. Through such contextualized analysis, we can learn more about how key terms are used in writing instruction, arriving at a better theoretical understanding of the use of writing threshold concepts across the disciplines. Finally, our survey asked respondents to think in general ways about their use of key terms to support student writing. One theoretical problem with this approach concerns the highly contextualized nature of words; words in isolation often mean little. Research is needed to understand in more nuanced ways how instructors use particular key terms: in what contexts they use them, for what instructional purposes, and with what specific meanings. Such research might begin with programmatic approaches to faculty development around threshold concepts, with the goal of developing "expertise-based interdisciplinary discursive sites" as described by Wardle (this volume).

Our pilot study also raises some possibilities as well as some complexities for cross-campus work. A number of colleges and universities have created common-terms initiatives designed to establish a campus-wide lexicon to facilitate students' learning in different courses that involve writing. Appalachian State University's WAC program uses conversations with faculty to help them "build a common vocabulary for writing pedagogy that strengthens the unified writing curriculum and encourages transfer of skills and genre knowledge" (Bohr and Rhoades 2014). Terms are organized into six categories: WAC and WID terms, process-writing terms, terms for types of writing assignments, research terms, rhetorical terms, and terms for responding to writing (see https://wac.appstate.edu/writing-disciplines/wac-glossary-terms). Within the categories are terms such as "low-stakes writing," "synthesis," "rhetorical situation," "peer review," and "genre," along with brief definitions. The innovators of this program believe this initiative can mitigate challenges Mark Waldo (2004) describes concerning communication between writing instructors and teachers in other disciplines, recognizing the need for "community-based" assumptions (6).

At the same time, WAC/WID efforts must proceed cautiously. First, without extensive inquiry into the way writing works in different fields, both professionally and pedagogically, it is too easy to assume the terms generated and used within the field of writing studies represent universals. Such an assumption could lead to the unprincipled advocacy of language insensitive to disciplinary differences and could undervalue or subvert the expertise of faculty supporting writing (Doug Hesse and Peggy O'Neill's chapter in this volume, for instance, shows differences in threshold concepts between composition and the closely related sites of creative writing and journalism, suggesting even greater differences at farther reaches of the curriculum). For example, a high-school teacher explained on a listserv that a group of his colleagues wanted to create a school-wide list of writing terms every teacher would be mandated to use and teach. The list included terms such as *clincher, topic sentence,* and *transition.* The writer expressed skepticism about the effort, arguing that terms come from "a particular ideology, a particular enforcement of one notion of what good writing is." The strength of departments, he explained, "is in the differences in terms since that would allow our students to learn a variety of concepts of the essay, which will prepare them for the various interpretations they will find in college and beyond" (Reynolds 2002).

The solution to the tension between the need for common language and the need for the expression of context-specific processes and understandings of writing may be a less monolithic approach to cross-campus outreach (see Adler-Kassner's description in this volume of the use of threshold concepts as a framework to develop epistemologically inclusive teaching practices, especially through the kind of seminar she describes). Common-terms projects, for example, could provide more granularity in their presentation of the language used to talk about writing. Websites displaying such language could describe the results of consultations with faculty in different disciplines so both faculty and students could gain higher-level knowledge of lexical commonalities and differences. Perhaps more important, faculty-development efforts could focus on more overt ways to help students navigate terminological differences (see Wardle's description in this volume of her faculty-development initiative). Such pedagogies could include asking students to express their understandings of key terms and then discussing any differences in the use of those terms in their other courses. Or faculty could be encouraged to find out more about their students' learning experiences, including the way they are understanding key terms and threshold concepts, as described in Adler-Kassner (this volume).

Regardless of the methods adopted, much work remains to be done to help students and faculty not only think about the language they use when they talk about or practice writing but also work with threshold concepts that productively inform and guide writing in all settings.

NOTE

1. For purposes of economy, we include only the list of terms, without their definitions.

REFERENCES

Adler-Kassner, Linda, and Elizabeth Wardle, eds. 2015. *Naming What We Know: Threshold Concepts of Writing Studies*. Logan: Utah State University Press.

Anderson, Richard C., and Zohara Shifrin. 1980. "The Meaning of Words in Context." In *Theoretical Issues in Reading Comprehension*, edited by Rand J. Spiro, Bertram C. Bruce, and William F. Brewer, 33–448. New York: Erlbaum.

Anson, Chris M. 2006. "Assessing Writing in Cross-Curricular Programs: Determining the Locus of Activity." *Assessing Writing* 11 (2): 100–112.

Anson, Chris M. 2013. "Process Pedagogy and Its Legacy." In *A Guide to Composition Pedagogies*. 2nd ed. Edited by Amy Rupiper Taggart, Kurt Schick, and H. Brooke Hessler, 212–30. New York: Oxford University Press.

Anson, Chris M. 2015. "Crossing Thresholds: What's to Know about Writing across the Curriculum?" In *Naming What We Know: Threshold Concepts of Writing Studies*, edited by Linda Adler-Kassner and Elizabeth Wardle, 201–19. Logan: Utah State University Press.

Anson, Chris M. 2016a. *A Guide to College Writing*. New York: Pearson.

Anson, Chris M. 2016b. "The Pop Warner Chronicles: A Case Study in Contextual Adaptation and the Transfer of Writing Ability." *College Composition and Communication* 67 (4): 518–49.

Anson, Chris M., Michael Carter, Deanna P. Dannels, and Jon Rust. 2003. "Mutual Support: CAC Programs and Institutional Improvement in Undergraduate Education." *Language and Learning Across the Disciplines* 6 (3): 26–38. https://wac.colostate.edu/llad/v6n3/anson.pdf.

Anson, Chris M., and Deanna P. Dannels. 2009. "Profiling Programs: Formative Uses of Assisted Descriptions in the Assessment of Communication Across the Curriculum." In "Writing Across the Curriculum and Assessment," special issue, *Across the Disciplines* 6. http://wac.colostate.edu/atd/assessment/anson_dannels.cfm.

Anson, Chris M., and L. Lee Forsberg. 1990. "Moving Beyond the Academic Community: Transitional Stages in Professional Writing." *Written Communication* 7 (2): 200–231.

Baillie, Caroline, John A. Bowden, and Jan H. F. Meyer. 2013. "Threshold Capabilities: Threshold Concepts and Knowledge Capability Linked through Variation Theory." *Higher Education* 65 (2): 227–46.

Bazerman, Charles, and Howard Tinberg. 2015. "Text Is an Object Outside of Oneself That Can Be Improved and Developed." In *Naming What We Know: Threshold Concepts of Writing Studies*, edited by Linda Adler-Kassner and Elizabeth Wardle, 61–62. Logan: Utah State University Press.

Beaufort, Anne. 2007. *College Writing and Beyond: A New Framework for University Writing Instruction*. Logan: Utah State University Press.

Bohr, Dennis J., and Georgia Rhoades. 2014. "The WAC Glossary Project: Facilitating Conversations Between Composition and WID Faculty in a Unified Writing Curriculum." *Across the Disciplines* 11 (1). https://wac.colostate.edu/atd/articles/bohr_rhoades2014.cfm.

Davis, Patricia M. 1991. *Cognition and Learning: A Review of the Literature with Reference to Ethnolinguistic Minorities*. Dallas: Summer Institute of Linguistics.

Davies, Peter. 2006. "Threshold Concepts: How Can We Recognise Them?" In *Overcoming Barriers to Student Understanding: Threshold Concepts and Troublesome Knowledge*, edited by Jan H. F. Meyer and Ray Land, 70–84. New York: Routledge.

Estrem, Heidi. 2015. "Writing Is a Knowledge-Making Activity." In *Naming What We Know: Threshold Concepts of Writing Studies*, edited by Linda Adler-Kassner and Elizabeth Wardle, 19–20. Logan: Utah State University Press.

Fulwiler, Toby. 1987. *The Journal Book*. Portsmouth, NH: Boynton-Cook.

Haswell, Richard H. 1991. *Gaining Ground in College Writing: Tales of Development and Interpretation*. Dallas: Southern Methodist University Press.

Heading, David, and Eleanor Loughlin. 2017. "Lonergan's Insight and Threshold Concepts: Students in the Liminal Space." *Teaching in Higher Education* 23 (6). https://doi.org/10.1080/13562517.2017.1414792.

Herrington, Anne J., and Marcia Curtis. 2000. *Persons in Progress: Four Stories of Writing and Personal Development in College*. Urbana, IL: NCTE.

Lakoff, George, and Mark Johnson. 1980. *Metaphors We Live By*. Chicago: University of Chicago Press.

Land, Ray, Julie Rattray, and Peter Vivian. 2014. "Learning in the Liminal Space: A Semiotic Approach to Threshold Concepts." *Higher Education* 67 (2): 199–217.

Lauer, Janice M. 2004. *Invention in Rhetoric and Composition*. West Lafayette, IN: Parlor.

Lea, Mary R., and Brian V. Street. 2006. "The 'Academic Literacies' Model: Theory and Applications." *Theory Into Practice* 45 (4): 368–77.

Lunsford, Andrea A. 2015. "Writing Addresses, Invokes, or Creates Audience(s)." In *Naming What We Know: Threshold Concepts of Writing Studies*, edited by Linda Adler-Kassner and Elizabeth Wardle, 20–21. Logan: Utah State University Press.

McCarthy, Lucille. 1987. "A Stranger in Strange Lands: A College Student Writing Across the Curriculum." *Research in the Teaching of English* 21 (3): 233–65.

Meyer, Jan H. F., and Ray Land. 2005. "Threshold Concepts and Troublesome Knowledge: Epistemological Considerations and a Conceptual Framework for Teaching and Learning." *Higher Education* 49 (3): 373–88.

Meyer, Jan H. F., and Ray Land. 2006. *Overcoming Barriers to Human Understanding: Threshold Concepts and Troublesome Knowledge*. New York: Routledge.

Reynolds, Todd. 2002, September. "Common Terminology Among Professors/Teachers." WPA-L Archives. https://lists.asu.edu/cgi-bin/wa?A2=ind0209&L=WPA-L&F=&S=&P=85481.

Roozen, Kevin. 2015. "Writing Is a Social and Rhetorical Activity." In *Naming What We Know: Threshold Concepts of Writing Studies*, edited by Linda Adler-Kassner and Elizabeth Wardle, 17–18. Logan: Utah State University Press.

Smart, Graham. 2000. "Reinventing Expertise: Experienced Writers in the Workplace Encounter a New Genre." In *Transitions: Writing in Academic and Workplace Settings*, edited by Patrick Diaz and Anthony Pare, 223–52. Cresskill, NJ: Hampton.

Sternglass, Marilyn S. 1997. *Time to Know Them: A Longitudinal Study of Writing and Learning at the College Level*. Mahwah, NJ: Erlbaum.

Taylor, John R. 2003. *Linguistic Categorization: Prototypes in Linguistic Theory*. 3rd ed. Oxford: Oxford University Press.

Waldo, Mark L. 2004. *Demythologizing Language Difference in the Academy*. Mahwah, NJ: Erlbaum.

Yancey, Kathleen Blake, Liane Robertson, and Kara Taczak. 2014. *Writing across Contexts: Transfer, Composition, and Sites of Writing*. Logan: Utah State University Press.

Young, Richard. 1987. "Recent Developments in Rhetorical Invention." In *Teaching Composition: 12 Bibliographic Essays*, edited by Gary Tate, 1–38. Fort Worth: Texas Christian University Press.

Editors' Conclusion
EXPANDING AND EXAMINING WHAT WE (THINK WE) KNOW

Linda Adler-Kassner and Elizabeth Wardle

Since the publication of *Naming What We Know*, the two of us have had many opportunities to talk with faculty across a range of institutions and disciplines about threshold concepts. In the process, we have also built upon our collaborative work, as well as the work of many others, to create (and add to) a framework for thinking about teaching that draws on threshold concept theory. As we have led workshops for and discussions with faculty from disciplines as varied as philosophy, biology, engineering, and English studies broadly conceived, we frequently find ourselves repeating some version of the same point regarding this framework: It isn't the hammer that hits every nail, but it does seem to strike a chord with faculty who are interested in understanding their disciplines—including but not limited to where and how learners get stuck—and leads to some very productive discussions.

Part of the reason looking through and with the lens of threshold concepts seems to be productive is that scholars and teachers, just like everyone else, enjoy thinking about what they know and care about. The framework enables faculty to start from their own areas of expertise to consider what they already know about and know how to do with writing and disciplinary knowledge. Beginning with what all the participating interlocutors in a given conversation already know, rather than what the program director or workshop leader or department chairs knows, is one of the affordances the threshold concepts framework brings to faculty development around teaching and learning. Thinking through and with threshold concepts, as a strategy for focusing faculty members' attention on both disciplines and how people learn within disciplines, has also shown itself to be a productive and inclusive strategy. Again, not the hammer that hits every nail, but a tool faculty often find useful for challenges with which they have been grappling. Several chapters in

DOI: 10.7330/9781607329329.c018

this collection demonstrate these potentially pragmatic uses, including with faculty in our programs and departments (e.g., Blaauw-Hara et al.; Estrem, Shepherd, and Shadle; Mapes and Miller-Cochran; Phillips et al.; Tremain et al.) and beyond (as in our chapters and in Anson, Chen, and Anson's).

Conversations within our own discipline about what our field's threshold concepts might be have proven a more vexing task, for all the reasons we outline in chapter 1 with our coauthors. Doug Hesse and Peggy O'Neill's chapter raises other important issues associated with such efforts, as well. Other chapters here, like those by Kate Vieira, Lauren Heap, Sandra Descourtis, Jonathan Isaac, Samitha Senanayake, Brenna Swift, Chris Castillo, Ann Kim, Kassia Krzus-Shaw, Maggie Black, Ọlá Ọládipọ̀, Xiaopei Yang, Patricia Ratanapraphart, Nikhil Tiwari, Lisa Velarde, and Gordon West, and by Jennifer Maher, point to the importance of constructs and concepts critical to include in this thinking, while chapters by Matthew Fogarty, Páraic Kerrigan, Sarah O'Brien, and Alison Farrell, Deborah Mutnick, and Rebecca Nowacek, Aishah Mahmood, Katherine Stein, Madylan Yarc, Saul Lopez, and Matt Thul demonstrate some of the complexities around learning associated with threshold concepts and a threshold concepts framework. It is also true that most of the threshold concepts in our field that have thus far been named are the result of empirical research, which of course represents and prioritizes a particular set of values and ideologies, as Raúl Sánchez pointed out in a recent review essay (2018). Given the complexities of thinking about threshold concepts of our field, we think it is important to reaffirm that any discussion or list of threshold concepts doesn't—and can't—constitute anything close to a *comprehensive* list of those concepts. Any such list is always partial, and threshold concepts are always contingent and only ever stabilized-for-now. There is risk, then, in writing them down and trying to articulate the ways of thinking and practicing in which learners tend to get stuck around writing, rhetoric, and literacy.

From our perspectives, valuing articulation of concepts and research to illustrate them does not deny alternative perspectives or ideologies. We continue to see a risk in *not* naming ideas and *not* pointing to research that has been conducted about writing; the results of that particular risk are evident in the problematic practices enacted in schools every day around the United States and elsewhere: practices around writing that hurt all learners but typically most hurt those from nondominant groups. There are good reasons to try to help teachers, policy makers, lawmakers, and others understand how writing, language, literacy, and rhetoric work so their decisions can be informed by more accurate and equitable conceptions. What happens to those students if we fail to advocate for the best current conceptions and enactments of writing because we are waiting to understand them better? We take as a cautionary tale what Robert Watson-Watt said when developing early-warning radar in Britain during World War II. He argued for a "cult of the imperfect": "Give them the third best to go on with; the second best comes too late, the best never comes" (Brown 1999, 64).

The contributors to this collection have, we hope, pushed all of us to consider and reconsider what we know about writing, rhetoric, literacy, and composition. Their systematic applications of threshold concepts to specific contexts and practices, their reflections on those applications, and their rigorous examination of this framework open new questions and new avenues for investigation. We urge readers to view the chapters in this collection as jumping-off points for new research projects in which researchers continue to use this framework and investigate its usefulness and efficacy. We still have a lot to learn about writing, language, literacy, and rhetoric—and about how learners come to engage the threshold concepts, as well as aspirational and emerging concepts of our "dappled discipline" (Lauer 1984). From this perspective, a great deal of additional empirical work is needed if we are to understand how students learn, whether a framework that involves threshold concepts (of writing) supports that learning, and, if so, what curricular (and extracurricular) designs are most effective. The need for this kind of research does not negate the need for, nor the relevance of, other approaches to taking up questions about writing and learning.

In the end, we continue to argue that threshold concepts provide *a* (not *the* or *the only*) useful framework to help disciplinary insiders investigate, make visible, interrogate, and critique the epistemological foundations of their disciplines, the values and ideologies associated with those foundations, and what ideas are included and excluded in its discourse practices. Recognizing this as one useful area the threshold concepts framework can open up for us (rather than seeing threshold concepts as inflexible and static dogma, for example) is absolutely crucial if those of us in rhetoric and composition/writing studies are to continue our effort to make our disciplinary work as inclusive as possible, incorporating values and ideologies that have sometimes been excluded or at the margins.

In conclusion, then, we recognize the threshold concepts framework is one of many and has shortcomings. Nevertheless, its shortcomings do not seem to outweigh its usefulness for some purposes. Using this framework can have positive material consequences for faculty and students, and for that reason we remind ourselves and our colleagues not to let the perfect be the enemy of the good. Threshold concepts provide a way (and only *one* way) to ensure discussions about writing and what it should look like continue to persist and are taken up in engaged ways by faculty from many disciplines.

REFERENCES

Brown, Louis. 1999. *Technical and Military Imperatives: A Radar History of World War II*. Philadelphia: Institute of Physics.

Lauer, Janice M. 1984. "Composition Studies: Dappled Discipline." *Rhetoric Review* 3 (1): 20–29.

Sánchez, Raúl. 2018. "Review Essay: Moving Knowledge Forward." *College Composition and Communication* 70 (1): 111–25.

ABOUT THE AUTHORS

Linda Adler-Kassner is professor of writing, director of the Center for Innovative Teaching, Research, and Learning, and associate dean of undergraduate education at the University of California Santa Barbara. She is author, coauthor, or coeditor of ten books and many articles and book chapters. These include *Naming What We Know: Threshold Concepts of Writing Studies* (Utah State UP, 2015), which was recognized for Distinguished Contribution to the Discipline by the Council of Writing Program Administrators. A former chair of the Conference on College Composition and Communication and former president of the Council of Writing Program Administrators, her most recent research and teaching have focused on working with faculty across disciplines to design opportunities for epistemologically inclusive teaching and learning.

Marianne Ahokas is a lecturer in the English Department at Humboldt State University, where she teaches courses in both the major curriculum and the first-year composition program.

Jonathan Alexander is Chancellor's Professor of English and of Informatics at the University of California, Irvine, where he has also been founding director of the UCI Center for Excellence in Writing and Communication. He is the author, coauthor, or coeditor of fifteen books, including *Writing Youth: Young Adult Fiction as Literacy Sponsorship* (Rowman and Littlefield, 2017), *Unruly Rhetorics: Protest, Persuasion, and Publics* (Pittsburgh UP, 2018), *Literacy, Sexuality, Pedagogy: Theory and Practice for Composition Studies* (Utah State UP, 2008), and *On Multimodality: New Media in Composition Studies* (NCTE, 2014). He is the recipient of the 2011 Charles Moran Award for Distinguished Contributions to the Field of Computers and Writing Studies.

Chris M. Anson is distinguished university professor and director of the campus writing and speaking program at North Carolina State University, where he teaches graduate and undergraduate courses in language, composition, and literacy and works with faculty across the disciplines to enhance writing and speaking instruction. He has published nineteen books and over 130 articles and book chapters focusing on writing and has spoken widely across the United States and in thirty-one other countries. He has received numerous teaching awards and has been PI or co-PI on over $2 million in grants. He is past chair of the Conference on College Composition and Communication and past president of the Council of Writing Program Administrators, and currently serves on the steering committee of the International Society for the Advancement of Writing Research. His full CV is at www.ansonica.net.

Ian G. Anson is assistant professor of political science at the University of Maryland, Baltimore County (UMBC). Since earning his PhD in political science from Indiana University in 2015, Ian has published a variety of articles in the fields of public opinion, voting behavior, writing in the disciplines, media and politics, and quantitative research methodology. His first book, *Partisan Economies: Why Republicans and Democrats Disagree About Economic Reality*, is in preparation.

ABOUT THE AUTHORS

Sarah Ben-Zvi is a lecturer at Humboldt State University, where she teaches a variety of first-year writing courses, including STEM-focused courses designed for place-based learning communities.

Jami Blaauw-Hara is professor of English and Communication at North Central Michigan College, a two-year school in northern Michigan. She has published essays and articles in the popular press about teaching and writing.

Mark Blaauw-Hara is professor of English and writing program coordinator at North Central Michigan College. His writing has appeared in *Teaching English in the Two-Year College*, *Composition Forum*, the *Community College Journal of Research and Practice*, and several other journals. He has also coauthored chapters in several edited collections, including *WPAs in Transition* and *Teaching Composition at the Two-Year College*. Mark is currently the vice president of the Council of Writing Program Administrators.

Maggie Black is assistant professor of English and coordinator of the basic writing program at Southern Illinois University Edwardsville. She received her PhD in composition and rhetoric from the University of Wisconsin–Madison. Maggie teaches and studies at the intersections of basic writing, literacy studies, and composition pedagogy.

Dominic Borowiak is professor of English at North Central Michigan College, as well as adjunct professor of writing at Central Michigan University, teaching classes ranging from composition to screenwriting. He also serves as the writing center coordinator at North Central Michigan College.

Chris Castillo was born in Chicago, Illinois, and grew up on the border of Albany Park and Ravenswood Manor. He is the son of Mexican immigrants, a rapper, teacher, and performing artist. Some of his inspirations include Lupe Fiasco, Add-2, Noname, and Eve Ewing. Some of his main topics of exploration in written and audio form include the impoverishment of minorities, educational injustice, and models that ameliorate inequality rather than simply document it. He is currently pursuing a PhD in rhetoric and composition at the University of Wisconsin–Madison, where he studies the production of hip-hop music in Chicago as a multiliteracy.

Chen Chen is assistant professor of English at Winthrop University in Rock Hill, South Carolina, where she teaches first-year writing and professional and technical communication courses. She received her PhD in communication, rhetoric, and digital media from North Carolina State University. She studies how graduate students professionalize into the field of rhetoric and composition across different disciplinary spaces. She's also interested in how students write in the workplace and how they transfer their writing experiences beyond the university. Her other research interests are writing across the curriculum, digital rhetoric, and social media.

Sandra Descourtis is currently a PhD student in second language acquisition at the University of Wisconsin–Madison. She is interested in both child and adult second language acquisition, particularly how children socialize in multilingual households and their language awareness, and teaching French-language variation in the foreign-language classroom.

Norbert Elliot is professor emeritus at the New Jersey Institute of Technology and currently serves as research professor at the University of South Florida. With Mya Poe and Asao B. Inoue, he is editor, most recently, of *Writing Assessment, Social Justice, and the Advancement of Opportunity*. With Richard Haswell, he is coauthor of the forthcoming book *Early Holistic Scoring of Writing: A Theory, A History, A Reflection*.

About the Authors

Heidi Estrem is professor of English and director of the first-year writing program at Boise State University. Her research interests in first-year writing pedagogy, writing program administration, assessment, and instructor development and support have led to publications in *WPA: Writing Program Administration*, *Rhetoric Review*, *Composition Studies*, and several edited collections, including *Naming What We Know*. Her recent edited collection, *Retention and Persistence in Writing Programs* (coedited with Todd Ruecker, Dawn Shepherd, and Beth Brunk-Chavez), offers a variety of research-based perspectives on programs and initiatives designed to better support students in their initial college writing courses.

Alison Farrell, PhD, is teaching-development officer in the Centre for Teaching and Learning, School of Education, Maynooth University (Ireland), where she is also head of the university's writing center. She is a founding member and current cochair of the Irish Network for the Enhancement of Writing (INEW), and in 2014 she established the first national Summer Writing Institute for Teachers (SWIFT). Currently, she is principal investigator and chair of the European COST Action WeReLaTe, which is exploring frontier taxonomies and institutional synergies across writing, research, learning, and teaching. Her research interests include academic writing, collaboration, professional development, and institutional policy and power in higher education.

Matthew Fogarty is a PhD candidate in the School of English, Media and Theatre Studies at Maynooth University, where he holds a Government of Ireland Postgraduate Research Scholarship and a John and Pat Hume Research Scholarship. His dissertation, entitled "Friedrich Nietzsche and the Literary Works of William Butler Yeats, James Joyce and Samuel Beckett," examines the divergent ways these Irish modernists engage with Nietzsche's philosophical vision. His latest article, "'Most Foul, Strange and Unnatural:' Refractions of Modernity in Conor McPherson's *The Weir*," is available in the 2018 issue of the *Irish Journal of Gothic and Horror Studies*.

Joanne Baird Giordano is assistant professor of English at Salt Lake Community College. She previously coordinated the developmental English program for the University of Wisconsin System's two-year colleges. Her work has appeared in *College Composition and Communication*, *College English*, *Teaching English in the Two Year College*, other journals, and edited collections. With Holly Hassel, she is a corecipient of the Council of Writing Program Administrators Outstanding Scholarship Award.

J. W. Hammond is a postdoctoral researcher in the School of Education in the joint program in English and education at the University of Michigan, where he researches writing assessment history, theory, and technology. His scholarship has appeared in the *Journal of Writing Assessment*, the *Encyclopedia of Educational Philosophy and Theory*, and the edited collections *Teaching and Learning on Screen: Mediated Pedagogies* and *Writing Assessment, Social Justice, and the Advancement of Opportunity*.

Holly Hassel is professor of English at North Dakota State University in Fargo. She taught for sixteen years at the University of Wisconsin–Marathon County, a two-year campus in Wisconsin. Her research and scholarship have appeared in *College Composition and Communication*, *College English*, and *Feminist Teacher*, among other journals. She is currently the editor of the journal *Teaching English in the Two-Year College* and coauthor of the textbook *Threshold Concepts in Women's and Gender Studies: Ways of Seeing, Thinking, and Knowing* (Routledge, 2nd ed., 2018).

Lauren Heap previously taught high-school English in central Illinois and is currently a PhD candidate in the Department of Curriculum and Instruction at the University of Wisconsin–Madison with a minor in composition and rhetoric. Her dissertation research centers on writing in the secondary English classroom with a focus on feedback and revision. She is also interested in teacher education and the relationship between student, cooperating teacher, and supervisor.

Jennifer Heinert is professor of English at the University of Wisconsin–Milwaukee at Waukesha. A former department chair and faculty developer, she has spent thirteen years teaching and studying the teaching of writing. Her work has appeared in *Pedagogy, WPA: Writing Program Administration,* and *Arts and Humanities in Higher Education*.

Doug Hesse is founding executive director of writing and professor of English at the University of Denver, where he's been named university distinguished scholar. He is past president of the National Council of Teachers of English, past chair of the Conference on College Composition and Communication, past president of the Council of Writing Program Administrators, and past editor of *WPA: Writing Program Administration.* He's published several dozen articles and chapters, mostly about creative nonfiction, narrative and rhetoric, and professional issues in writing and English studies. He's won the Donald Murray Prize for creative nonfiction and coauthored, with Becky Bradway, *Creating Nonfiction.* He sings professionally.

Jonathan Isaac is a PhD student in composition and rhetoric at the University of Wisconsin–Madison. His interests are in community engagement, education policy, and composition studies interventions in the neoliberal university.

Katie Kalish is associate professor of English at the University of Wisconsin–Platteville, Baraboo/Sauk County. She has spent the last thirteen years working for various UW campuses, where she has taught a wide range of learners in composition and literature courses. In addition to teaching, her most recent research focuses on student learning and has been published in *Pedagogy* and edited collections.

Páraic Kerrigan is a teaching fellow within the School of Information and Communication Studies at University College Dublin. He was previously an Irish Research Council Scholar and John and Pat Hume Scholar in the Department of Media Studies at Maynooth University, where he will complete his PhD in October 2018. His dissertation is titled "Queering in the Years: Gay Visibility in Irish Media, 1974–2014." He has published work in *Media History,* the *Journal of Radio and Popular Media,* and *LGBTQS, Media and Culture in Europe: Situated Case Studies,* along with various popular outlets such as the *Irish Examiner.* He has been a regular contributor in Ireland's national media on gay culture and politics and has been a researcher on a number of documentaries.

Ann Meejung Kim is a PhD student in composition and rhetoric at the University of Wisconsin–Madison. Her research interests are rhetorics of space and place, transnational rhetoric, and the teaching of composition in international contexts. She occasionally moonlights as a translator, focusing on translating Korean literature into English.

Kassia Krzus-Shaw is a PhD student in composition and rhetoric at the University of Wisconsin–Madison. Her research focuses the intersection of embodiment, writing, and environment, especially the way these themes shape individual citizenship and community identity narratives.

Saul Lopez is a senior at Marquette University, where he is double majoring in writing-intensive English and Spanish. Along with his undergraduate studies, he is also pursuing a Spanish MA through Marquette and its accelerated degree program. He currently serves as High School Connections coordinator and a peer tutor at the Ott Memorial Writing

Center. He is also one of the tutors involved in Marquette's WRITE (writing and research integrative tutor experience) fellows program.

Jennifer Helene Maher is associate professor of English at the University of Maryland, Baltimore County where she teaches in the department's Communication and Technology Track and is affiliate faculty in the interdisciplinary Language, Literacy, and Culture PhD Program. Her work in rhetoric includes such topics as software evangelism, feminist hacking practices, the city of Baltimore, and the discipline of rhetoric and composition.

Aishah Mahmood is an undergraduate in her third year at Marquette University, where she is earning her degree in writing-intensive English and literature. She currently holds the position of undergraduate assistant director and peer tutor at the Ott Memorial Writing Center. She is also one of the tutors involved in Marquette's WRITE (writing and research integrative tutor experience) fellows program.

Aimee C. Mapes is associate professor of English and associate director of the writing program at the University of Arizona. Her research focuses on literacy studies, composition studies, teacher training, and situated learning theory, with work appearing in the *Journal of Adolescent & Adult Literacy*, *College Composition and Communication*, and *Reflections*. She currently serves as associate editor of *Prompt: A Journal of Academic Writing Assignments*.

Kerry Marsden is a lecturer in the English and Critical Race, Gender, and Sexuality Departments at Humboldt State University.

Susan Miller-Cochran is professor of English and director of the writing program at the University of Arizona, where her research focuses on instructional technology, writing program administration, labor in writing programs, and multilingual writing. Her publications include coediting *Composition, Rhetoric, and Disciplinarity* (Utah State UP, 2018) and *Rhetorically Rethinking Usability* (2009) and coauthoring *An Insider's Guide to Academic Writing* (2019), *The Cengage Guide to Research* (2017), and *Keys for Writers* (2016). She currently serves as immediate past president of the Council of Writing Program Administrators.

Deborah Mutnick is professor of English at Long Island University Brooklyn. She is author of *Writing in an Alien World: Basic Writing and the Struggle for Equality in Higher Education* (1996), which received a Ross Winterowd Award for the most outstanding book in composition theory in 1997. Her work has appeared in *College Composition and Communication*, *College English*, *Rhetoric Review*, *WPA: Writing Program Administration*, the *Journal of Basic Writing*, and the *Community Literacy Journal*. The Pathways to Freedom project referenced in her chapter was supported by an NEH Digital Humanities Startup Grant in 2012.

Rebecca Nowacek is associate professor of English at Marquette University, where she directs the Ott Memorial Writing Center. She is the author of *Agents of Integration: Understanding Transfer as a Rhetorical Act*, and her work has also appeared in *College Composition and Communication*, *College English*, and *Research in the Teaching of English*. Her chapter in *Naming What We Know*, coauthored with Brad Hughes, received the IWCA Outstanding Article award. Rebecca was a Carnegie Scholar with the Carnegie Academy for the Scholarship of Teaching and Learning and the 2012 recipient of Marquette's Gettel Faculty Award for Teaching Excellence. She is particularly delighted to have coauthored this chapter with the terrific undergraduate tutors participating in Marquette's WRITE (writing and research integrative tutor experience) fellows program.

Sarah O'Brien is a PhD candidate in the Department of English at Maynooth University, Ireland. Sarah works primarily within the field of world literature, with a particular focus on post-9/11 fiction, and has published work in *Transnational Literature* and the *Journal of Postcolonial Writing*. Sarah's work involves engagement with fields of theoretical enquiry such as memory studies, trauma theory, and media studies. As a tutor in the English department and university writing center, she has developed an interested in pedagogy, winning a Postgraduate Teaching Award in 2018.

Peggy O'Neill is associate dean for humanities and professor of writing at Loyola University Maryland, where she also served as the composition director and department chair. Her scholarship focuses on writing pedagogy, assessment, program administration, and disciplinarity and has appeared in many different journals and edited collections. She has also edited or authored six books.

Ọlá Ọládipọ̀ is a doctoral student in English at the University of Wisconsin–Madison. In the past, he was a Fulbright Scholar, also at the University of Wisconsin–Madison.

Cassandra Phillips is professor of English at the University of Wisconsin–Milwaukee at Waukesha. She has been teaching on a two-year campus for eighteen years and previously served as the writing program administrator for the University of Wisconsin System's two-year colleges. Her work has appeared in *Teaching English in the Two-Year College*, *WPA: Writing Program Administration*, *Pedagogy*, and edited collections.

Mya Poe is associate professor of English and director of the writing program at Northeastern University. She is the coauthor of *Learning to Communicate in Science and Engineering* (CCCC Advancement of Knowledge Award 2012), coeditor of *Race and Writing Assessment* (CCCC Outstanding Book of the Year 2014), and coeditor of *Writing Assessment, Social Justice, and Opportunity to Learn*. Her scholarship has appeared in *College Composition and Communication*, the *Journal of Business and Technical Communication*, and the *Journal of Writing Assessment*. She has also guest edited special issues of *Research in the Teaching of English* and *College English* and is series coeditor of *Oxford Brief Guides to Writing in the Disciplines*. In 2015–2016, she won the Outstanding Teaching Award and the Teaching Excellence Award at Northeastern University.

Patricia Ratanapraphart is a PhD student in the department of curriculum and instruction at the University of Wisconsin–Madison. Prior to moving to Wisconsin, Patricia worked as an early-childhood educator and adult ESL instructor in central Florida. Her research is focused on studying the affordances of classroom-based play for bridging home and school experiences and supporting young English-language learners' linguistic, academic, and social development.

Jacqueline Rhodes is professor of Writing, Rhetoric, and American Cultures at Michigan State University. She is the author, coauthor, or coeditor of a number of works that explore the intersections of materiality and technology, including *Radical Feminism, Writing, and Critical Agency* (SUNY, 2005); *On Multimodality: New Media in Composition Studies* (NCTE, 2014); the born-digital *Techne: Queer Meditations on Writing the Self* (CCDP, 2015), available online at https://ccdigitalpress.org/techne; *Sexual Rhetorics: Methods, Identities, Publics* (Routledge, 2015); and *The Routledge Handbook of Digital Writing and Rhetoric* (2018). She is currently completing production of *Once a Fury*, a documentary on a lesbian separatist collectives from the 1970s.

Samitha Senanayake is a graduate student in literary studies at the University of Wisconsin–Madison. Her research focuses on modern South Asian fiction and Buddhist culture. She has studied and taught at the University of Peradeniya, Sri Lanka, and has a continuing interest in thinking about composition in second language acquisition contexts.

About the Authors

Susan E. Shadle, PhD, is director of the Center for Teaching and Learning and distinguished professor of chemistry and biochemistry at Boise State University. Her work is focused on supporting faculty development, with a particular focus on effective course design, assessment of student learning, and the development of rich pedagogical toolboxes. She contributes time, energy, and leadership to both the national POGIL Project (process oriented guided inquiry learning) and the POD Network (Professional and Organizational Development Network in Higher Education). Her scholarly interests are focused on factors that impact faculty and institutional change.

Dawn Shepherd is associate professor of English and associate director of the first-year writing program at Boise State University. She is the author of *Building Relationships: Online Dating and the New Logics of Algorithmic Culture* and coeditor of *Retention, Persistence, and Writing Programs*. Her work has been published in edited collections as well as *Computers and Composition* and *WPA: Writing Program Administration*, and two chapters on genre and weblogs, coauthored with Carolyn R. Miller, have been translated into Portuguese. She teaches undergraduate courses in rhetoric, writing, and media and graduate seminars on research methods and digital rhetoric.

Katherine Stein is an undergraduate honors student at Marquette University graduating in 2019 with degrees in English literature and history. She has been a writing tutor at Marquette University's Ott Memorial Writing Center for five semesters. Katherine has been thrilled to work as part of Marquette's WRITE (writing and research integrative tutor experience) fellows program to produce this chapter.

Patrick Sullivan teaches English at Manchester Community College in Manchester, Connecticut. He believes deeply in the mission of the community college, and he is very grateful to have had the opportunity to work with so many amazing community college students over the years. He is the editor, with Howard Tinberg, of *What Is "College-Level" Writing?* (NCTE, 2006) and, with Howard Tinberg and Sheridan Blau, of *What Is "College-Level" Writing? Volume 2: Assignments, Readings, and Student Writing Samples* (NCTE, 2010) and *Deep Reading: Teaching Reading in the Writing Classroom* (NCTE, 2017). He is also the author of *A New Writing Classroom. Listening, Motivation, and Habits of Mind* (Utah State UP, 2014) and *Economic Inequality, Neoliberalism, and the American Community College* (Palgrave Macmillan, 2017). Patrick has also edited, with Christie Toth, *Teaching Composition at the Two-Year College: Background Readings* (Bedford/St. Martin's, 2016). His new book, *Sixteen Teachers Teaching: Two-Year College Perspectives*, is forthcoming from Utah State University Press.

Carrie Strand Tebeau is part-time professor of English at North Central Michigan College. She won the 2017 Donald Murray Prize for an essay on the intersection of threshold concepts and creativity.

Brenna Swift is a PhD student in composition and rhetoric at the University of Wisconsin–Madison. Her primary interests are writing center studies, community writing centers and community engagement, disability studies, critical pedagogy, and college equity and access. She is interested in how writing instructors and students can use writing to challenge systemic inequality. Her other interests include student engagement, writing program administration, and writing center tutor education. She grew up in Woodland Park, Colorado and previously worked as a journalist covering education policy.

Matt Thul, an English major at Marquette University, began working as a tutor in the Ott Memorial Writing Center in fall 2016 and worked as a WRITE fellow during the fall 2017 semester.

ABOUT THE AUTHORS

Nikhil Tiwari is a former high-school English teacher and consultant for nongovernmental organizations and education technology enterprises in South Asia. He is currently a PhD student in the department of curriculum and instruction at the University of Wisconsin–Madison with research interests in English as a second language and global studies, particularly as they relate to the transnational movements of people and ideas.

Lisa Tremain is assistant professor of English and director of the first-year composition program at Humboldt State University. Her research investigates the ecologies of writing-knowledge transfer, with a specific focus on instructor development and uptake, writing program design and assessment, and writing across the curriculum. She has a forthcoming chapter in *Next Steps: New Directions for/in Writing about Writing*. She currently leads the Writing-Enriched Curriculum pilot at Humboldt State.

Lisa Velarde is a PhD student at the University of Wisconsin–Madison in the Department of Curriculum and Instruction. Prior to pursuing her doctoral studies, she was a middle-school language-arts teacher and also worked as an English-as-a-foreign-language teacher in Sonora, Mexico, with youth and adults. Her research interests focus on the effects of space and mobility on digitally mediated literacy practices of youth in transglobal contexts.

A former elementary- and high-school teacher, **Kate Vieira** is associate professor and the Susan J. Cellmer Distinguished Chair in Literacy in the School of Education at the University of Wisconsin–Madison. She is the author of *American by Paper: How Documents Matter in Immigrant Literacy* (U of Minnesota Press, 2016; honorable mention CCCC Outstanding Book Award); *Writing for Love and Money: How Migration Drives Literacy Learning in Transnational Families* (Oxford UP 2019); and numerous essays and articles on literacy. She is a 2018–2019 Fulbright Scholar in Colombia researching writing for peace.

Elizabeth Wardle is Roger and Joyce Howe Professor of Written Communication and director of the Roger and Joyce Howe Center for Writing Excellence at Miami University (Ohio). She was formerly director of writing programs at two universities and served as chair of a writing and rhetoric department. Her books include *Naming What We Know*; *Composition, Rhetoric, and Disciplinarity*; and the forthcoming fourth edition of *Writing about Writing* (now in its fourth edition). In her current role, she facilities frequent faculty-development workshops and is conducting research on their efficacy and impact. She speaks and give workshops around the country on transfer, threshold concepts, and writing program design.

Gordon Blaine West is a PhD student in second language acquisition at the University of Wisconsin–Madison. He previously worked as a teacher and teacher educator in South Korea, Japan, and Hawaii.

Anne-Marie Womack, PhD, is professor of practice and former director of writing at Tulane University. Her research focuses on disability studies, writing pedagogy, and evidence practices. Her work has appeared in *College Composition and Communication, Composition Forum, Pedagogy*, and the *Chronicle of Higher Education*, and she recently coauthored the forthcoming edition of *Reading and Writing for Civic Literacy: The Critical Citizen's Guide to Argumentative Rhetoric* with Donald Lazere. She has won several teaching awards at Tulane and Texas A&M University and is the creator of AccessibleSyllabus.com, a universal design guide for educators.

Kathleen Blake Yancey, Kellogg Hunt Professor of English and distinguished research professor at Florida State University, has served in several national leadership roles, including as president of the Council of Writing Program Administrators (CWPA), chair of the

Conference on College Composition and Communication (CCCC), and president of the National Council of Teachers of English. Currently, she is the lead PI for an eight-site research project on the teaching-for-transfer writing curriculum documented in her coauthored *Writing across Contexts*, winner of the CCCC Research Impact Award and the CWPA Best Book Award. She has edited/coedited two journals; authored/coauthored over one hundred articles and book chapters; and authored or edited/coedited fifteen books. She has received several awards, among them the FSU Graduate Mentor Award and the CCCC Exemplar Award.

Xiaopei Yang is a doctoral student in the department of curriculum and instruction at the University of Wisconsin–Madison studying early childhood education. She has previously worked as an early-childhood educator in various school settings.

Madylan Yarc is a juris doctorate candidate at the John Marshall Law School in Chicago, Illinois, graduating in 2021. Madylan graduated magna cum laude from Marquette University in 2018 with a bachelor of arts degree in English literature and history. She worked as a student writing tutor and mentor at Marquette University's Ott Memorial Writing Center from August 2017–May 2018. Madylan also worked as part of Marquette University's WRITE (writing and research integrative tutor experience) fellows program.

www.ingramcontent.com/pod-product-compliance
Lightning Source LLC
Chambersburg PA
CBHW060513080526
44586CB00012B/466